Durkheim's Ghosts

Durkheim's Ghosts is a fascinating presentation of the tradition of social theory influenced by Emile Durkheim's thinking on the social foundations of knowledge. From Saussure and Lévi-Strauss to Foucault, Bourdieu, and Derrida, today's criticisms of modern politics and culture owe an important, if unacknowledged, debt to Durkheim. These engaging and innovative essays by leading sociologist Charles Lemert bring together his writings on the contributions of French social theory past and present. Rather than merely interpret the theories, Lemert uses them to explore the futures of sociology, social theory, and culture studies. *Durkheim's Ghosts* offers the reader original insights into Durkheim's legacy and the wider French traditions in the cultural and social sciences. Of special note is the book's new and exciting theory of culture and semiotics. Provocative, scholarly, imaginative, and ambitious this book will be invaluable to anyone interested in social theory, culture, and the intellectual history of modern times.

CHARLES LEMERT is Andrus Professor of Sociology at Wesleyan University, Connecticut. His many books in cultural and social theory include *Muhammad Ali: Trickster in the Culture of Irony*, *French Sociology: Rupture and Renewal since 1968*, *Michel Foucault: Social Theory and Transgression*, and *Social Things: An Introduction to the Sociological Life*. His book *Social Theory* is a best-selling text in the field.

Durkheim's Ghosts

Cultural Logics and Social Things

Charles Lemert

CAMBRIDGE
UNIVERSITY PRESS

CAMBRIDGE UNIVERSITY PRESS
Cambridge, New York, Melbourne, Madrid, Cape Town, Singapore, São Paulo

Cambridge University Press
The Edinburgh Building, Cambridge CB2 2RU, UK

Published in the United States of America by Cambridge University Press, New York

www.cambridge.org
Information on this title: www.cambridge.org/9780521603638

First published 2006

Printed in the United Kingdom at the University Press, Cambridge

A catalogue record for this book is available from the British Library

ISBN-13 978-0-521-84266-2 hardback
ISBN-10 0-521-84266-2 hardback

ISBN-13 978-0-521-60363-8 paperback
ISBN-10 0-521-60363-3 paperback

In memory of Philippe Besnard,
with thanksgiving for a life-time of contributions
to the scholarly study of Durkheim.

Contents

viii   Contents

Preface

What follows is a book both original and composed out of the past. *Durkheim's Ghosts* had started in the mind's eye as a collection of previously published writings on and about French social theory. Then, in an attempt to introduce, ultimately to frame the essays and selections, another book emerged, superimposed on the original idea – which of course had the effect of making it something other than I thought it would be.

All but one of the shorter essays set before the main chapters are new to *Durkheim's Ghosts*. So too are the first two chapters – the one is meant to present the ghost-theme as a serious idea, while also taking on several of the more foolish dismissals of French social theory; the other new chapter, the second, means to establish a stake in the controversies surrounding the social study of culture. Together, they and the other new essays serve, not just to set up the previously published writing, but to form an argument to the effect that, if culture is a semiotic (and the study of culture is a semiology), then one has little choice but to take seriously the French who, more than any other enduring tradition of social studies, have invented, criticized, revised, and reinvented the idea of culture studies (by whatever name) as a study of meaningful signs.

I use the terms *semiotics* and *semiology* interchangeably for the most part. Umberto Eco reminds that while *semiology* was the term used by Saussure and those (including Lévi-Strauss and Barthes) who followed him, *semiotics* was the term used by Charles Sanders Peirce. I treat them as roughly equivalent less to ignore the more mathematical and formal contributions of Peirce (who in fact, stands behind the discussions of Eco) than to lessen the impression of a difference. If one must be made, I think it best to reserve *semiotics* for the social facts of which culture itself is composed, and *semiology* for the study of the culture (though I admit that this distinction is not held to consistently between the new and older texts). Also as to format, whenever I give the French title to a text, the English version is offered somewhere close by. The dates of publication for books are generally of the original French text unless otherwise indicated. Also, I should add that, for various reasons (some of them slightly transgressive), I do not offer citations to the texts quoted or referred to in the shorter essays before each chapter. These are meant to be, in effect, somewhat more in the vein of personal conversations with readers whom I trust to know the references or be able easily to look them up. By contrast, the citations in the previously published work are a bit overdone as befits the young man I was when many of them were published in professional journals.

I owe the inspiration for the idea of sociology as a ghostly matter to Avery Gordon. The idea had been around for a very long time since Marx, but notably in Heidegger, Levinas, and Derrida, before Gordon in *Ghostly Matters* gave haunting the central place it must have in social studies. Anthony Elliott has been a haunting presence behind the writing. At every turn, whenever I returned to many of the writers I discuss, I felt the constraint of his considerable body of work in the same field. Immanuel Wallerstein personally helped me with the facts of his relation with Fanon and, through his writings, with unthinking social science. I am far from confident that any of the three would be satisfied with what I say here – from which, in either case, they are excused from responsibility with thanks for their generosity.

Very special thanks go to Willard A. Nielson, Jr. and Garth Gillan who were co-authors of two of the selections, both written during earlier days in Illinois. Quite apart from the pleasure of having this latter day occasion to renew contact with both of them, the renewal brings back all the better memories of a time in life when I started on this line of work and when, even then, there was a growing interest in what the French were doing, thus a kind of underground culture wherein one could discuss such strange things. I give more personal tributes to both Willard and Garth in the front notes to the selections they wrote with (actually much more than simply *with*) me.

In the work of preparation Victoria Stahl caused the previously published texts to be transformed back into Word; she then set up the notes into a consistent form. She also wrote for the permissions from previous publishers who are acknowledged in notes at the foot of the chapter selections they originally printed. Thanks to her and to Sarah Caro for her patience and confidence in the work.

Part I

Cultural logics

1

Frantz Fanon and the living ghosts of capitalism's world-system

Frantz Fanon died of cancer December 7, 1961 in Washington, D.C. He had gone to the United States seeking treatment unavailable elsewhere. Given all that he stood for, he died in the most alien of lands – far from Algeria, the home of his medical practice and literary fame; just as far in social distance from Martinique, where he was born, thirty-six years before, on July 20, 1925. In a short life Fanon had traveled light years across the colonizing belt that for half a millennium had held up the pants of the capitalist world-system.

His death in Washington, at the core of the world system against which he fumed, was a final exclamation on the cruelty of Atlantic colonialism. Fanon had been trained at the medical faculty in Lyon and practiced medicine in France's North African colonies. Still, the fabled French paternalism that each day airlifts bread from Paris to the overseas departments would not deliver adequate medical care to its colonial subjects. The violence of the world system cuts even the decomposing bodies of those off whom it feeds.

And, those who die young never quite go away. They are lost but never far off. If we knew them in this life, we remember them as they were before they fell. If we knew them only by what they left behind, we imagine them in their prime. None was more ordinal to the crisis of his times than Fanon.

Black Skin, White Masks appeared in Paris in 1952 as *Peau Noire, Masques Blancs*. Fanon was twenty-seven, not long out of medical school; still young to his work as a psychiatrist; still a year before taking up his post at Blida, the notorious asylum outside Algiers. The book was, among other of its rebellions, a first strike against the received wisdom of the white world whose insufferable culture was his ticket to cultural and political power.

The title, *Black Skin, White Masks*, suggests a play on the double-consciousness theme of which W. E. B. Du Bois had written fifty years before in *Souls of Black Folk*. On the contrary, *Black Skin, White Masks* was radical even by the pointed standards Du Bois had set. Fanon's

Negro is the Negro subject of the colonial system. His experience is Black through and through, but governed by a remote class of white officials administering the policies of a distant metropolis. The American Negro of whom Du Bois wrote was in daily contact with a greater number of latently aggressive whites who could be counted upon to leave the bodies burned and hung for all to see. This sort of neighborhood violence is done in and for the middle ground – a ground onto which the American Negro stepped to serve, from which otherwise he was meant to keep himself.

It is not that the colonized do not suffer racial violence. They do. But the violence upon which the capitalist world system is built gets deeper under the skin. For Fanon there was very little doubling of the Negro consciousness. The white mask has the upper hand – so much so that, against every ounce of conviction, one may be forced to turn over his body for last medical rites.

"The Black man is not a man." Thus began *Black Skin, White Masks*. For Fanon there is no middle ground for the Negro because he is formed by the white colonizers. "The Black is a Black man; that is, as a result of a series of aberrations of affect, he is rooted at the core of a universe from which he must be extricated." Negritude thus became the zero-signifier of the silences upon which the modern world was founded – exclusions so close to the quick of its being that its culture cannot speak of it. Any system that thrives on mute exclusion is one so morbid that only violence can overcome it.

Black Skin, White Masks is an unruly book, ranging rowdily over literary, medical, political, and psychiatric themes – always literate, unnerving, and eerily remote in its condemnations. One of its more acerbic lines is Fanon's clinical savaging of the oedipal legend so dear to his profession. Referring to his native Martinique, he says: "The Martinican does not compare himself with the white man *qua* father, leader, God." The colonial subject's primary desires are not sexual ones for the parental-Other. The Other of colonized desire is the racial Other he can never hold. No middle ground. The Black man is already white. His longing for the white-Other is the ever open wound. In wishing to be other than he is, he confirms that he is not a man. He partakes of his own devastation. "The Negro is a slave who has been allowed to assume the attitude of a master" – Black skin, white mask. Therein, the first inkling of Fanon's scorching idea that the colonial system must die by the violence it has wrought. The corollary is that to kill the master, the slave must kill himself. No middle ground. This is the unspeakable violence of the capitalist world system.

Fanon saw the pages of *Les Damnés de la terre* just before dying. They gave him little comfort. But, this is the book, translated after his death as *The Wretched of the Earth*, that would become the spiritual manual of the revolutionary decade. In it Fanon slashed back at the heart of white power. "The naked truth of decolonization evokes for us the searing bullets and bloodstained knives which emanate from it." The violence of the modern world comes back to haunt. "The colonial world is a world cut in two."

In Fanon's last months, liberation struggles were severing the already cut parts of the Francophone colonies. The French lost Tunisia and Morocco in 1956 and Vietnam in 1954 at Dien Bien Phu. They would lose Algeria in July, 1962, months after Fanon's death at the end of 1961, the year that Patrice Lumumba, having liberated the Congo from Belgium, was assassinated by the CIA. Those were the years when the colonial egg began to totter slowly toward its shattering fall.

Immanuel Wallerstein, but five years his junior, met Fanon in 1960 in Accra, Ghana at the World Assembly of Youth. Wallerstein recalls that "since neither of us had any obligations at this meeting (apart from my talk), and we hit it off, we spent a lot of time together." Many years later, he would claim Fanon as a "substantial influence" on his work. There is poetic symmetry in the off-chance of their few days together in decolonizing Africa. Though neither Fanon's *Wretched of the Earth* in 1961 nor Wallerstein's *Modern World System* in 1974 would normally be considered works of poetry, there is a literary justice in their having framed the decade that cracked the blithe innocence with which modernity mistook its global colonial empire for providence.

Frantz Fanon was the first of the great French social theorists of the dismantling of the colonial world from which capitalism extracted its wealth. More even than his fellow Martinican, Aimé Césaire, or his fellow North African, Albert Memmi, Fanon set down the terms of colonization as a global system of racial terror. He was not the first to define racism as the foundation of the capitalist world system. In his later years, W. E. B. Du Bois did much the same. Nor was Fanon a world systems analyst before the fact. But he did unravel the inscrutable knot in which modern culture had tied itself. Modernity's enlightened reasonableness so dazzles the gullible eye as to blind it to the brutality that subsidizes its cultural finery. And no more so than in its sweet inducements to see the world as one, when in fact it is inherently and necessarily divided in two.

Therein may lie the appreciation that led Wallerstein to read Fanon in French even before they hit it off in 1960 in Accra. Wallerstein, in turn, began his work as a specialist in African studies. This may be why the younger of the two men understood before others what Fanon, by experience, understood before him. The global system of capital greed was first and foremost based on the Atlantic violence of the slave trade triangle since the painfully long sixteenth century. Fanon and Wallerstein mark off, in effect, the beginning and the end of the time of the French social thought that arose in the decolonizing movements of the 1960s to grow into an acute heaviness in the world revolutions of 1968, after which, all the king's men of the modernist dream could not put their humpty back together again.

Though worlds apart, in work and experience, Fanon and Wallerstein were, in their youths, both students of France and her colonies; from which, by different lessons, they learned that, dreams aside, the modern world is a system united in the illusion that capitalism's violence is benign. Now, in the face of realities hard to deny, that world is more evidently one always divided in two – a prosperous powerful core; a bleak, eroded periphery. Being colonial to the core, it is a world of incommensurable parts, joined by a pervasive violence from which there is no escape. The truth of this fact is hard to swallow, especially in the early years of the twenty-first century when the global viscera are regurgitating modern violence back up through its over-stuffed gullet.

Ghosts are beings without bodies. When they appear, they are more real than the living. They visit with impunity, by their own pleasure. The living cannot easily shake them off because even the courageous would rather not hear what they have to say.

During his last months in hospital in Washington D.C., Wallerstein was reunited with Fanon. "I don't know," he recalls many years later, "if I was the only white American to have that kind of relationship with him. Maybe. In any case, there couldn't have been very many. There were hardly any Americans, white or Black, who had even heard of Fanon in 1961. For one thing, he wasn't translated yet into English." Fanon died young, before his time had come. This sad fact of Fanon's death may be among the reasons he continues to haunt the colonial world system. He died before the core of the system could know him.

Whoever conjures up the ghosts – whether it is the living searching for what they lost or the dead refusing to go away until their stories register – ghosts haunt the living for some good reason. Whatever it may be, Fanon is the apparition that appears in the bad dreams of the capitalist overlords who, having drunk too much and stuffed their guts too full, awake restive in the stupor. They will not very often know Fanon's name, but they recognize him in the faces of those they skip over as they surf the channels of their late night insomnia.

Durkheim's ghosts in the culture of sociologies

There are risks ahead at the turn of a phrase like *Durkheim's Ghosts*. None is more fraught than the dread that a sacred corpse is about to be defiled. Still, the risk is worth taking. Like most of his age, Durkheim is dead. Like few others, his body of work lives on to haunt the present.

Durkheim's claim on the minds of generations of social thinkers owes, as these things often do, to an ever heightening sensibility to the concerns he addressed in his time. The industrial and social conflicts that shocked his generation in the waning years of the nineteenth century have, in the early twenty-first century, passed on, but not away. Perturbations interior to a national-community have not so much disappeared as been caught up in a jumble of global conflicts. As a result, it is no longer possible to look for the cause of social disorders where Durkheim did – in the entrails of an encompassing Society defined implicitly by a territorial polity covering a purportedly distinct national culture.

Whether global conflicts are more or less severe than those of early industrial nation-states is an open question. But they are more pervasive – normal enough to require ever more explosive outbursts of violence to keep media attention focused; or, if not more pervasive, then more visible. Durkheim's generation saw what it saw of the wider world through glasses dimmed by the blush of European colonial domination. In the comparison, the unsettlements in Europe in Durkheim's day – even those leading up to the Great War which ended the innocence of his generation – seem local and passing. Today's troubles may be different in degree, perhaps modified in kind, but they are similar enough to render Durkheim's definition of the crisis, if not his solutions, disconcertingly apt to a much different time.

It may be that the dead stir up dread because they are not dead-enough. Legion are they who prefer their dead to stay put as are, say, Comte and Spencer who haven't budged in years. We visit them, if at all, as curiosities. Then there are ones like Durkheim and Marx, who are far from ready for the wax museum. The living dead, when they are not a comfort (as, remarkably, they can be), disturb the hold people like to have over their own times and places. Yet, they haunt variously according to their several natures.

Durkheim disturbs for reasons different from the others. Marx and Freud are two contrary examples of theorists from another time, who, while living, wrote convincingly of ghosts haunting Europe and of uncanny visitations from the Unconscious, which may be why, while dead, they will not quit the scene even when hunted down by detractors. They exposed themselves to attack on the critical flank of their daring theories of modernity's dishonest social veneer. Though differently, to be sure, Marx and Freud believed as Weber and Durkheim could not: that to understand modern societies of the industrial age it was necessary to begin from the assumption that the appearances of the new technological wonders were false representations of the underlying realities. For them, the facts of modern matters are haunted by hidden and contrary forces – the mode of production in Marx's case; the Unconscious in Freud's.

Durkheim, in this one respect, was more like Weber. Each struggled, in his way, to explain the new world as it presented itself. Neither could quite believe that what met the eye was as far as it was from the whole truth. Weber, however, and unlike Durkheim, had the stronger inkling that something inscrutably perverse was wrong on the surface of social things. Still, unlike Marx and Freud, the best Weber could do was to describe the enigma where the others insisted that the perversities of modern life were, in truth, interpretative guides to the underlying and contrary realities. In the end, Weber could do little more than bemoan the facts that cut both ways at once – modern rationality enhanced human freedom, while at the same time trapping the modern in the iron cage of rational efficiency.

Durkheim, at least in the early empirical studies, notably *Suicide*, was barely skeptical at all – a character trait lacking in Durkheim to the extent that it was prominent among the other three. For Durkheim, the social facts he took as social things in and of themselves were drawn up in numerical rates he had culled from Europe's dusty archives. This – the naïve move of an ambitious younger man – led him down the slope of scientific trouble greased by the all-too-comfortable slippage from reality to gathered data to fact to analytical stabs at the truth. The others held fast to a higher, if equally vulnerable, ground.

Marx and Freud, by developing their reconstructive sciences of material and emotional netherworlds, complicated the logic of daily life at some embarrassment to their methodological boasts in the triumph of the aggravated revolution and the patient therapy of the talking cure. Weber, by setting forth the grand interpretative method of understanding, was in his way the more daring of the lot, though at the cost that accompanies even so astute an appeal to the intersubjective: that of freezing modern man in his tracks, the lost soul cut off from the traditions, looking foolishly for the charismatic prophet. By contrast, one could make the case that Durkheim's caution, though it cost him dearly on the political side, left him the option he chose, however unwittingly, of revisiting the scientific side to supply the traction his early theories lacked.

Still, none of them would come to life today were it not for one or another nod to the finitude of social life – its politics and sciences included most especially. With or without a theory of ghosts, all were consumed by the past. They were at the head of the short list of survivors from a generation preoccupied with the lost past – a preoccupation without which what today we call the social sciences might not have come into being in their present form. Sociology, in its earliest days, was nothing if not a running commentary on the fate of traditional values in the caldron of modern times. It was precisely the question of human values that united all the European men, if not others. The quest for values in a value-less world led to the classic European experiments with four of the essential methods still at work in social theory and sociology. Marx's foundational value of the elementary labor process as a transcending critical tool, Weber's intersubjective value as the probative method of the ideal typical, Freud's imputation of scientific and therapeutic value to the chaos of dream talk, Durkheim's imbrication of social values upon the isolated individual – these were the subtly hidden, but evident, concerns that moved the European men of classic social theory. Each was an attempt to measure the continuity of the new modes of social order against what was to them a dead or dying past.

Durkheim led both academic and social movements promoting the reform of science and of the educational system in France. He believed, and many agreed, that the science he conveyed could heal the discord in and among over-individualized moderns. While controversial in his day, this aspect of Durkheim's life work seems a bit pathetic today – and no more so than when imagined as a solution to the divisions in the wider global spheres. Still, in surprising ways, Durkheim's ideas stand among the living-dead – even when, in some aspects, their enduring viability courses along a thin vein oblique to the heart of much social theory.

The surprise is palpable because Durkheim, more than the others, was the one forced by his times as by the mistakes of his early method to change course later in his work. Without getting onto the line Louis Althusser made famous in regard to Marx – whether there were two of him, the one young and the other mature, from which we get the question of whether there *can* be two anyones other than Jesus and Wittgenstein – it is fair to say that, though all purportedly great thinkers change their minds to some degree, few changed theirs as much as Durkheim did his.

Though it could hardly be said that Durkheim was the most intellectually courageous of the four, when compared to standard fare in that or this day, he was in his own fine way. And no more so than in the notable change of emphasis he came to in the last years of his life and work – a change all the more difficult to make because those were the years of his public life when his ideas were most exposed to scrutiny for his work as the leader of a school of social thought but even more as the leader of a movement to reform the foundations and practices of public education in France.

It is too easy to complain, as some do, that Durkheim was the conservative among the founding fathers. The merit of the plaint is barely sufficient to the lie it covers. By contrast to, say, Marx or even contemporaries in the European Diaspora – writers like W. E. B. Du Bois and Charlotte Perkins Gilman in the United States – Durkheim was among those more comfortable against the odds of social facts. But when measured against garden variety social thinkers, he was far from hide bound. Otherwise, he would not haunt. The method of the early years, which may have required the change of heart and mind in the later years, turned on a concept that has enjoyed a robust staying power – a power that outruns, in many ways, its generator.

The concept, of course, is his most famous: *anomie* – the state of mental confusion caused by the absence of workable norms for the conduct of daily life. A century later, the exact conditions for which Durkheim invented the concept have passed. Still, *anomie* reminds that, whatever else might be among the necessary functions of the larger social things, the group, however massive (even global), must provide some effective grade of social regulation. When individuals are left without guidance by the group, the anomic state of mind undermines the benefits of individual liberty, leading to confusion of which suicides, as horrifying as they are, are not the most terrible of social tragedies, as survivors of ethnic wars and terrorist attacks in our time will testify.

In a century well after Durkheim's, the inability of the larger social wholes to guide the lonely individual is all the more salient in proportion to the individual's inability to know what exactly a social whole might be. At the end of the nineteenth century, even when one was, as Durkheim, a member of a stigmatized minority, a Frenchman had little trouble imagining France as somehow the name for a society capable of ministering to his need for protections of various kinds. Durkheim, with Zola, was on the winning side of the Dreyfus Affair. But, at the beginning of the twenty-first century, not even the wine merchants of Burgundy can locate the definitive border where France ends and, say, northern California begins; nor, accordingly, from whence they might draw what moral aid they require.

Just the same, the writings that gave rise to the concept *anomie* resist easy reading today because they come to us through time's digressions. Durkheim's key word was dated already at the very moment it was revived for future use. In the case of *anomie*, it was not Durkheim's writings of the 1890s that lend it value today, but that of a single essay written in the late 1930s. Robert K. Merton's "Social Structure and Anomie" (1938) fortified the concept by embodying it with a more robust theory of social structures – notably, a theory of structures that turned on the failure of societies to provide the means by which social protections could be gotten: jobs. Merton had the advantage, not just of time, but of the perspective of the Great Depression of the 1930s.

By introducing the income-producing job as the institutionally normal means by which the individual achieves the cultural goal of social recognition, Merton killed with one stone the two birds that eluded Durkheim. The one was Durkheim's unrequited confidence in the norms of a national culture as glue sufficiently fast to hold unsettled social structures in place. Merton bolstered this flimsy idea with the material bond of economic structures. In the same shot, Merton set to rest Durkheim's over-wrought theory of the social as the near-exclusive dominating force in the lives of individuals. He shored up the social by buttressing the individual with a moral power of its own – that of adapting to the anomic bewilderments structural failure produces. The repair was passive, to be sure, but fungible enough to purchase a theory stronger than Durkheim's original.

By diverting the blame for social deviation toward the social, Merton thus relieved the individual of responsibility for a failure of moral nerve. If the moral whole is to demand cultural achievement of a certain kind, it must provide the means. In the case of the market-driven, capitalist democracies the means were those generated in the labor market. Whether in the 1890s, or the 1930s, not to mention the 2000s, even in the more advanced societies, such as they are, there never were, nor ever will be, income-producing jobs for all sufficient unto the goal of the decent life, much less the successful one. With this recognition, Merton allowed for meaningful responses to anomic confusion less severe than self-slaughter – in particular the time-honored one of innovation: walking the straight and narrow by crooked means. Merton's *anomie* of the 1930s stands up to the global miseries of the 2000s better than Durkheim's original in the 1890s, making him, incongruously, the latter-day giant upon whose shoulders the original stands.

In more ways than this celebrated one, Durkheim's ideas continue to haunt social thought today. Even those who harbor a prejudice against the very idea of reading the classics can be found among the great number of those who appreciate that ideas, as such, survive for the good when they are passed down as exemplars of good practical work. Such was the endowment of Durkheim's unquestionably prudent definition of scientific sociology. Still today, all the objections notwithstanding, it would be hard to come up with a definition of sociology that improves on Durkheim's; or one alluded to more often even by those whose sympathies for its author are as tepid as their acquaintance with its source.

The genius of Durkheim's approach was that he defined sociology not as a philosophy but according to its method. In the memorably succinct words of his preface to *Suicide:* "Sociological method as we practice it rests wholly on the basic principle that social facts must be studied as things, that is, as realities external to the individual." To whatever extent the definition may have been a rhetorical move to separate sociology from the prevailing individualisms and psychologies of his day, it remains a monument to what is easily forgotten: There are things in these worlds that are social through-and-through; and not, thereby, susceptible to distillation or reduction into any other sort of reality. By stipulating sociology as a method of the social as a thing unto itself, he avoided the philosophical burden of having to elaborate an ontology of social things. Had he done otherwise – as by training he was more than well equipped to do – Durkheim would have surely lost in open debate with the psychologizing philosophers of that day, a lesson no doubt learned from the fabulous success of his *normalien* schoolmate, Henri Bergson. Thus, after a clumsy attempt to stipulate the protocols of his method in *Rules of Sociological Method* (1894), Durkheim made his point in *Suicide* (1897), a masterpiece that bore a conspicuous subtitle: *A study in sociology.*

Suicide was Durkheim's own occasion to kill two birds with a single shot. The one was defense of his definition of a field so new in 1897 as to require the precise language of the sub-title to distinguish it as a study from the pre-existing sociologies of Auguste Comte, among others, which were not studies of any real thing in particular. In *Suicide*, Durkheim was establishing an empirical social science. Such a task was not original to him, but, notwithstanding the institutional barriers he could not overcome in his day, sociology today is a university discipline in part because Durkheim was one of those who put it to a definition serviceable enough to justify the enterprise in the research university. At the same time, Durkheim's method of sociological study was and is consistently much more majestic than many of the enterprises that, in subsequent years, would make ill-informed appeals to *Suicide*, in particular, as a classic textbook for what all-too-sadly is misidentified as quantitative sociology.

One of the pities of professional sociology is the way so many of its adherents divide themselves and each other into rival camps – one quantitative; the other qualitative – as if any serious empirical research into social things could ever forswear one or the other. At the very least, Durkheim did not. When he engaged himself in the quantitative study of suicide rates, for example, he did so because of his prior concern with the quality of modern life, which concern required the interpretative tools necessary to tenderize his very hard data. By the standards of subsequent generations, Durkheim's technical method is a model of intellectual style. By defining the field as one of empirical study he allowed himself room to engage the philosophical controversies of the day, while simultaneously advertising the new discipline as science, yes, but also much more – ultimately, as an informed palliative for modern society's then most acutely painful crisis: How, in practical terms, can the social whole – whether tribal, national, or global – maintain even the minimally necessary degree of integrity so as to hold the straining members at peace, if not exactly in harmony?

Durkheim surely understood the difference between peace and harmony. He was born and bred Jewish in one of Europe's more severely anti-Semitic Catholic nations; the son of generations of rabbis who left the religious profession of his fathers for a secular career; the child of village life who quit his home in search of urban trouble; a public renown in a nation of vanities who, nonetheless, chose burial not in the urban pantheon but in the village plot of his ancestors. That Durkheim ran his life course with a sober respect for what he had left behind is one of his more remarkable personal achievements. Few others of his station in that day came anywhere close to Durkheim's ability to make present peace, if not harmony, with his past. Weber could not come to terms with his father. Freud never got over his mother. Marx was expelled from the fatherland.

That Durkheim seems to have worked through his personal past may have conditioned his scientific honesty before the fading past of Europe's urbanizing adolescence.

This is the trajectory of one who might recognize the difference between peace and harmony – the former being a state of acceptance that depends on the parties knowing who they are in relation to the others; the latter being an idealized state of social intimacy the embrace of which is tender but fleeting. It is possible, if not certain, that the exile who is able to make peace with home, as Durkheim did, is the one better prepared to face the dislocations of the urbanizing world. Marx, another exile, his more bracing revolutionary ideas notwithstanding, retained a bit of the nostalgia for the simpler past which he tried to project onto a socially classless future. Durkheim, at least, had fewer illusions about the past, including its religious culture which he obviously regarded as, if not a paradise, at least the standard for social health. While he limited himself, perhaps, by clinging to the principles of the traditional social bond religion provided, he faced his present for what he thought it was: a present that would not revert to better times. If he was optimistic as to the social whole's ability to reknit a secular version of the moral order religion once provided, he was at least clear-headed enough to name the problem soberly, thus to point in the directions where solutions might be found.

A temperament that values peace over harmony, while loathing conflict, is one balanced enough to allow acceptance of one's limits, which in turn promotes the ability to rethink the errors made. On this, one speculates. Still, apart from whatever may have been the interior reserves from which Durkheim's wisdom grew, he was a social thinker able to change his mind sufficiently much as to correct course. The work of his later life, after settlement in Paris in 1902, produced a book that is certainly as great as it is different from *Suicide*. *Elementary Forms of the Religious Life* (1912) did not abandon the principles of his earlier studies, but it did reconsider them in strikingly original ways – original enough to have given life to a second ghost.

In 1903, the year after satisfying the traditional French sacred pilgrimage from provincial birth to a spot in the Parisian lights, Durkheim published, with his nephew Marcel Mauss, the long and famous essay on knowledge and science, *Primitive Classifications*. For the decade that led from there to *Elementary Forms* in 1912, he worked on many fronts, but none more consistently than the interwoven themes: knowledge, education, and religious culture. Taken as a whole, the subjects led to a book not so much about religion as about what we today so innocently call "culture." These writings of the decade from *Primitive Classifications* in 1903 to *Elementary Forms* in 1912 were, in effect, the first thoroughly systematic *and* enduring study of the cultural logics by which socially bound people represent themselves to themselves – the logic of *collective representations*.

No other term in the Durkheimian vocabulary, not even the more famous *anomie*, gathers together so many of the strands of the intellectual patrimony he left the generations to come. In these latter days, when culture is widely taken as applicable to everything under the sun – from the newest turn in social theory to the necessary conclusion to which material realities are forced when the worlds are bound so tightly (or is it loosely?) by the thread of telecommunications – Durkheim's elegantly precise *collective representations* does the work of a thousand variations on its weaker cognates.

What more exact way could there be to describe the intended effect of the over-conceptualized sociology of culture than Durkheim's original? The collective representation is precisely the form by which a culture, as the concept has come to be plied in social science, does the work of expressing the collective self-identity of those who gather in the name of a local culture – of, that is, as Durkheim himself put it at the very end of *Elementary Forms*: "the consciousness of consciousness." Here, of course, he was redefining the foundational Cartesian principle in sociological terms. By replacing the individual *cogito ergo sum* with consciousness of the collective whole, he sought to buttress the foundations of knowing with the mortar of social life.

At the end of Durkheim's last major work, he summarizes the high purpose of the sociology he began to define in the 1890s as very much more than an academic field – as, in fact, the proper subject of knowledge reflecting upon itself:

> In summing up, then, we must say that society is not at all the illogical or a-logical, incoherent and fantastic being which it has too often been considered. Quite on the contrary, the collective consciousness is the highest form of the psychic life, since it is the consciousness of the consciousness. Being placed outside of and above individual and local contingencies, it sees things only in their permanent and essential aspects, which it crystallizes into communicable ideas. At the same time, it sees farther; at every moment of time, it embraces all known reality; that is why it alone can furnish the mind with the moulds which are applicable to the totality of all things and which make it possible to think of them.

The logic of collective representation is the logic of logic – the foundation of all thought in social as distinct from mental life.

Durkheim's idea, with all of its talk of essences and permanencies, would appear to be old-fashioned epistemological foundationalism. To be sure, the categories of modern philosophy, most of all those of Kant, were very much on Durkheim's mind. Yet, his sociological solution to the neo-classical question of how the mind knows was one that got around problems philosophy did not begin to get to until Nietzschean ideas blossomed late in the century of Durkheim's death when Richard Rorty among others shattered the philosophical mirror by thrusting a stake to the heart of metaphysical realism. Not even the traditions of Kantian idealism of practical knowledge nor the American pragmatism issuing from William James and the Metaphysical Club – both working in full force at the time Durkheim was rethinking his theory of knowledge – dared to slay the vampire of Being as such that sucked the life out of any possible empirical sociology of historical forms.

What even pragmatism in America and neo-Kantian idealism in Europe lacked was an ironic sense of practical knowledge – of, that is, the principle that truth claims made in reference to purportedly real worlds do not require the *a priori* of Truth as a naturally occurring entailment of the real things in and of themselves. Kant invented the robust modern notion of practical knowledge apart from knowledge-certain of the things themselves as an idealized state of Being outside of, but corresponding to, the categories of mind. Pragmatism, though an independent philosophical tradition, had the effect of supplying the moral nerve Kant shrank from – that the final test of the truth of real things was in the practical pudding. Durkheim was far from a pragmatist as pragmatism came to be after his American contemporary William James. Yet, the effect of his achievement in these later works was comparable while serving the different purposes he intended from the beginning – those of establishing a sociology not of knowledge but of knowing – one that would stand the test all sociologies must pass: of being a workable ethic of knowing in which the practical consequence of knowledge of social things issues from the same social things to which it applies. Though little remarked upon, this was a bold, if half-witting, move on Durkheim's part and one that exceeded even the subtleties of any and all theories of the double hermeneutic.

Durkheim meant to define and develop a sociology that would serve two gods – the modern science of social things; the modern social ethic of the good society. He knew very well that sociology, the science, could not retreat into the culture of academic categories. He knew just as well that there would be no sociology worthy of its moral purposes without a theory of knowledge of its own kind that could, at the very least, come to terms with the categories of social knowing – by being, that is, a recognizable source of plausible truth claims in regard to social categories or classes as distinct from metaphysical Being or beings.

Durkheim had begun in the 1890s defining sociology as a method, thus to avoid the trap of philosophical dead ends. Yet, his first ventures in *Rules* and *Suicide* veered too far in the direction of a technology of facts and was, thereby, insufficient to a theory of social facts for which is required a technique that accounts equally for the constitution as for the collection of facts. Did he know this? Did he recant the early and innocent elementary form of his science? Not exactly; at least not in so many words. What he did, however, was to instigate a series of individual and collective works that consumed the years of his fully adult life in Paris, where his prominence allowed him to form the group of brilliant scholars who adumbrated the details of Durkheimian sociology; while also teaching teachers who would reform the French educational system in terms that would, in principle, remake the secular French national consciousness by means of the cultural tool of transmitting the high culture that would serve as the collective representation of a moral France able to ameliorate the pain of uneven social divisions of labor. It was a collective labor that required, all at once, an adequate representation of social things, but also of science, hence also of the social foundations of knowledge. The plan bore all the traces of the Enlightenment project, as of the philosophical traditions of the nineteenth century. But, in being a moral sociology – being, in pragmatic effect, a sociology as social ethics – Durkheim's sociology as it came to be in the latter works was, in the words he used to describe the representations of the *conscience collective*: a "communicable idea" able "to embrace all known reality" thus to "furnish the mind with the moulds which are applicable to the totality of all things" thus to "make it possible to think of them."

Had these later works not been offered to a reading public familiar with Durkheim's early empirical writings, they might have been taken as little more than a backhanded entry into the classically nineteenth-century debates over idealism and realism. *Elementary Forms* would have seemed to be a mere social epistemology founded in an ontology of social spheres – somewhat the problem Weber's hermeneutic method suffered. Here, the key intervening text is, again, *Primitive Classifications* where, with Mauss, Durkheim gives good, if insufficient, evidence that, when thinking is thought as a social thing, Class replaces Being as the point of departure.

The difference is an important one – for Durkheim; and for the social thought that would creep up under the shadow of the second of his ghosts. The one fatal flaw in Durkheim's *Suicide* was a classic one – that of assuming a direct and uncomplicated correspondence between facts and the social things they were assumed to represent. In his effort to lay sociology out upon a methodological bed unadorned by philosophical controversy, Durkheim began with an assumption that he believed was methodological when in fact it had to be philosophical: "Sociological method as we practice it rests wholly on the basic principle that social facts must be studied as things, that is, as realities external to the individual." He would have kept within the limits he imposed on himself had he been more disciplined in studying social facts as if they were things external to the individual. In fact he studied his facts as things in themselves, thus slipping unawares under the cover of Kant's partial solution to the dilemma of a post-metaphysical practical knowledge; hence, the striking rhetorical structure of *Suicide*.

Suicide begins with the peculiar Book One wherein the author devotes himself to the dismissal of "extra-social factors" as causes of suicide: psychopathic states, normal psychological factors, climate, and imitation.

Today's reader, were he unbothered by the history of debates in Durkheim's day, would be forgiven for wondering why these alternatives? Yet, they have one element in common – each is a factor that could be said to turn on the principle that the psychological state of the individual is the point of vulnerability to forces that might cause self-murder. The rhetoric here is that of addressing the most popular theory of that day, or any other – that individuals kill themselves because of mental stress or influences depressing the individual's state of mind (which would, thus, include even the climatic factor). He is, in short, taking up one of the more apparently obvious effects of the psychological factor in order to show that *even suicide* is a social thing. Then Durkheim turns abruptly to the book itself – to, that is, Book Two on "Social Causes and Social Types." Here is where he makes the case for what on the surface would appear to be a scientific study of the facts of a particular social thing, which in the end turns out to be, in effect if not intention, a philosophical meditation on the nature of social facts.

Nowhere is the unintended philosophical nature of the book more apparent than in the riddle Durkheim himself comes just shy of addressing directly. In a manner vaguely consistent with the protocols he announced in *Rules* in 1894, the frame of Book Two of *Suicide* is the question: What are the types of suicide and what are their separate causes? Later in *Durkheim's Ghosts*, I discuss this riddle in detail. For the present, let it suffice to explain by allusion to two of *Suicide*'s most striking anomalies.

One is the famous footnote at the very end of chapter 6 of Book Two, where Durkheim, having just discussed with impeccable care three of the four allegedly distinct types of suicide – egoistic, anomic, and altruistic – concludes that there must be a fourth type: "The above considerations show that there is a type of suicide the opposite of anomic suicide, just as egoistic and altruistic are opposites." This type is that, the cause of which is excessive regulation: fatalistic suicide, which he admits is "of little historic interest" because not only is it difficult to find clear examples of the type but even the ones he made up are so like altruistic as to be virtually indistinguishable on empirical grounds.

Hence, a second anomaly: If the fourth type of suicide, fatalism, is a logical, not empirical, necessity, then all four types might be as well. On close reading, the fatalism footnote sticks out like a sore thumb, calling attention to the difficulty Durkheim has in distinguishing on empirical grounds the two most important types: egoistic and anomic. If the former is the type caused by too much individualism, and the latter by too little social regulation, then the distinction collapses on Durkheim's conviction that the suicide-prone individual is precisely the man who, left to his own moral devices, lacks a sufficient individual autonomy. If such a man is inherently social, how else could he fall into a state of excessive individualism but by the lack of social regulation? It would seem, therefore, that *Suicide*, the proudest accomplishment of Durkheim's sociological method, derives what explanatory authority it has not from social facts but from the theory of social facts upon which his ideal of sociology is founded. But the reader will have already begun to sense the dilemma at that point, near the beginning of Book Two of *Suicide*, where Durkheim, in the midst of outlining his method of types and causes, lets slip the logical necessary of his pseudo-empirical philosophy of sociological knowing. "We must not forget that what we are studying is social suicide-rates." This is true of course, but the remark fails to nod in the direction of the methodological dilemma the all-too-easy statement does not make: What then becomes of the connection between rates – an analytic expression of alleged social facts – and social things, the practical knowledge of which is the purpose of the sociological method?

Given Durkheim's aspiration to found sociology on the method of social facts as things in themselves, it is evident that the outcome of *Suicide* would not do. This may be why, over the fifteen years following 1897, his thinking underwent a change slight in appearance only. The difference is not in the axial theme of the primacy of the social over the psychological – but in the method itself. By 1912, in *Elementary Forms*, he drops all pretense of inventing a new method designed to tease out the social from a field of empirical things. In its stead is the classically French ethnological method of secondary analysis of field reports of the more elementary forms of social order. Since Montesquieu, at least, the French paved the way for what became modern ethnography, which was originally and literally the writing of a people's social forms – where the facts derive less from their numerical freshness than from their comparative logic; and where the data are precisely the collective representations of social forms. In other words, the purposes of the study cannot be achieved without a theory of the consciousness of consciousness, of knowledge as knowing from the social inside of such things.

Durkheim may have had little choice but to give up the methodological convictions in *Suicide*. At least this is what he did, presumably because he wished to complete the sociological project in *Suicide*. If we may engage our own method of sympathetic speculation, it seems that he could not possibly have been entirely satisfied with the early results which left his new science so exposed to the criticism of being little more than just what he intended it not to be – a thin science that pursued the empirical status of social things on the grounds of a *synthetic a priori* of types stipulated not by the evidence but by the mental categories of social logic. Whether or not some archivist will ever determine (if one has not already) what

Durkheim may have privately thought of his dilemma, we can rest assured that a departure so striking as that of *Elementary Forms* from *Suicide* was taken only in the complete expectation that it would be noticed – indeed in the wish that it would be.

Modern social theory can only be grateful that Durkheim took the step, whether or not he knew what he was doing. It became the move that led to what some call cultural studies, others call cultural sociology, and still others call post-structuralism – none meaning quite the same thing. As indefinite as the labels may be, what all the early twenty-first-century variants of the social study of cultures have in common is a genetic filiation from and against the structuralism of Claude Lévi-Strauss whose cultural method stands at the crossroads of two of Durkheim's contemporaries, neither of whose relation with Durkheim was as direct as one would suppose, given the obvious similarities of thought.

The one was Lucien Lévy-Bruhl, Durkheim's younger colleague at the Sorbonne, whose *How Natives Think* in 1910 posed one of the questions Durkheim was dealing with in *Elementary Forms*. In the search for an account of the social origins of knowledge in the elementary forms of religion, Durkheim was necessarily asking one of the pivotal questions of modern social science: If there can be a science of social moderns must we conclude that the social traditionals, being without a science, were thereby unable to think as moderns do, thus unable to progress toward fully enlightened humanity? Durkheim's answer, like Lévy-Bruhl's, anticipated Lévi-Strauss's: No, on the contrary, it is their sciences that are different, not their humanities. Thinking, hence science, derives from a common aspect of all forms of social life: the social order itself.

The other largely unmediated line from Durkheim's time to ours is that from the notoriously anonymous Swiss linguist, Ferdinand de Saussure, whose theory of language as a social arbitrary is so acutely Durkheimian as to be painful to the absence of evidence of a direct relation. The Saussurian principle that would surface in the structural anthropology of Lévi-Strauss had at its heart the primacy of the arbitrary social contract. If, as Saussure claimed, the linguistic sign bore no evident relation to the thing it signified, then, as Lévi-Strauss would say, the cultural myth was similarly not an expression of social things themselves but of the mental state that only the collective life can nurture, then it stands to reason that the collective representation is at the foundation of social thinking itself. Or linking the two aspects, as Durkheim did with the idea of collective representations: *Social things can be thought only by social things because thought itself is social in nature.*

This is the remarkable difference between Durkheim's idealism of the social subject and Weber's of the hermeneutic circle. In the German line the knowing subject uses subjecthood as the instrument of interpretation of social things. In Durkheim's line, the subject knows because, and only because, he is a social thing. In other words, what Durkheim achieved – innocently in relation to the Germans; and knowingly in relation to his earlier experiment at, in effect, a sociological transcendence of Descartes by way of Rousseau – was not so much to eradicate the subject, as is sometimes thought, but to locate the subject amid social things. This could only happen with an implicit theory of culture as collective representations – as, in effect, a theory of discourse as not the expression of intersubjective truth but as the primary surface of intelligible social encounter with the collective – an encounter that can only be thought by way of consciousness of collective consciousness, which is to say: by life within the representations of bounded social life. This is the move Durkheim stumbled upon early when he slipped a particular social thing, suicide, under the discursive form of its representation, suicide *rates*. But the statistical rate would not do the work he intended of inserting the action of individuals, even the extreme action of self-slaughter, into the realm of social things. In short, the final solution was to replace beings with classes, where classifications are mental categories that enjoy a necessarily duplicitous and doubled relation to social reality: *social classes*, in all the usual, including formal sociological, senses of the word *class*. Classes – high, low, or middle, and all their finer distinctions – constitute the scale of social differences where science and injustice meet. They are the practical means of classification of all things, including social ones, into some scheme whereby the time, place, and totality of their relations to each allow for the very possibility of their causal relations.

Durkheim was, thereby, the first sociological constructionist – which accomplishment relied upon an implicit semiotics of the systems of social meanings classified according to the syntax of their logical possibilities. This, in turn, opened the door to Lévi-Strauss's full-blown semiotics of cultural meanings in the 1940s, which required, even as it anticipated, the so-called post-structuralism of the 1960s, which in its turn entailed a series of cultural and social studies of the 1970s and 1980s, which led to some of the more conspicuous features of the current situation.

Looking back from a century's long retrospect, it is shocking to see how Durkheim's thinking in his later years so thoroughly defined the terms of debates that rage in our time. What boggles is the list of issues at stake in another millennium that can be traced back to the ghosts of the other Durkheim, including but not limited to: the troubling idea that knowledge is socially constructed; the crisis unsettling the principles of representation (political as well as scientific); the not entirely false turn to language; the disturbing instability of analytic categories; the unavoidable uncertainty of foundations to modern knowledge; the ruthless arbitrariness of social as well as cultural categories, the moral liquidity associated with relativity of forms of truth; the evident indefiniteness of the Subject in moral action as well as scientific knowledge; the clever idea of a new science of literary tropes; among others.

It is not that Durkheim himself is responsible for all this. Indeed, a man so thoroughly and righteously cautious as he was could not have been expected even to dream of such things. Yet, it may well be that his scientific caution is what led him to correct the slippages of his early method of social facts as statistical representations by substituting a comparative method of collective representations of social forms. Which correction may be interpreted less as a maturation of his thinking, more as a resolution of an internal contradiction that has always been at the heart of empirical social research – one that Durkheim, more than any of his contemporaries (with the possible exception of Freud) realized had to be gotten around. His getting around it appears only superficially as a change of heart and method. Under it all, it was – to use the figure of speech – his own coming to terms with the haunting suspicion that he had not gotten the social fact thing right the first time. It is therefore Durkheim's own cautious restlessness that conjured up the two ghosts of subsequent sociology – that of the heroic dream of social things as a quantifiable utopia of facts; and that of the ironic joke that social things are facts insusceptible to representation by any foreign language, not even the pure discourse of formal arithmetic.

Far from being merely the first serious formalizer of an expressly sociological method, and thus the one to expose earlier sociological positivisms as little more than regurgitations of Comte's half-baked cult of science, Durkheim was in the end as much a skeptic as a believer in progressive science. For it was he alone – and he more than the outspoken skeptics of his time, Weber and Freud – who doubted in the end that facts are positive occurrences waiting only to be captured, or alternatively to be caught unawares by a hermeneutic trick. In the turn from the positive facts of self-slaughter to the inscrutability of collective representations Durkheim fulfilled the foundational principle of sociology as a method for the study of social things in the only way it can be fulfilled. That is: by granting the social thing its due as truly a member of its own class of things which class is not ultimately reducible to any other, nor plastic to representation by direct or formal languages.

To put it otherwise, Durkheim knew, without ever saying so, that social things are never fully present or visibly positive to the naked eye. Social facts are like none others more than astronomical ones. As the light by which stellar space-time is measured represents a long-dead body of mass and density long since gone from the measurable surface of universal things, so too the light of collectively represented social forms is the attenuated reflection of long-dead structures whose form can never, ever, be measured in their own space-time. There is always a death behind facts of these kinds.

The younger, if not young, Emile Durkheim of the 1890s seemed to believe, as young men do, that deaths are real only insofar as they are transposed into facts. He could thus write of the suicide as if death were a cold, hard fact. But, as everyone who has faced the dead knows, death is never merely a fact of this kind. For the living, the beloved dead, however and whenever they died, continue to live on. One wants never to believe the fact of their absence. Their deaths are (in the famous word) always *deferred*. Or, one might say: the fact of death is always unclosed for the living. If so, then it must follow that social facts are those facts so preoccupied with how the living sustain their relations with others that they, too, are ghosts ever open to revision. And this was what Durkheim unwittingly was trying to avoid saying in his social theory of knowledge in *Elementary Forms*. If, in the end, facts are known by the social categories of life with others; then, since others do in fact change their collective mind, knowledge itself is always a struggle to hold on to the elusive dead. If so, if even possible, then is not sociology a study not of social facts as such but of their loss to present time? Did not Durkheim measure the facts of anomic sufferers in his data against their loss of the moral body religion once provided? And did he not, later in his days, push the envelope of sociological measurement not forward to the purified technology of statistical significance but backward into the infinite regress of the elementary social form of social knowledge itself? What members of social groups cherish, whether or not they have the collective language to say it, are the dead structures of their possibilities.

All social science is gnostic – a secret code to wisdom passed down by the apparitions of realities that present themselves under the guise of fact. They are made to appear as if they were, if not quite hard, at least erect members of a representative body of truths, when in truth they are limp digits that depend for their potency on the fast hands that shake them to life.

Hence, the upsetting, and to some appalling, turn of events at a certain moment in the history of the twentieth century – a moment conspicuously different from its surface appearance, one in which the affluence of a postwar recovery covered the decrepitude of the European Diasporic culture of confidence.

That moment was just after World War Two. The place was, for the most part, Paris. And the reason was, in a word, the exhaustion of the Western powers after a good half-century of political turmoil, war, depression, and loss of faith in their own promises. As John Maynard Keynes, Georg Lukács, and Reinhold Niebuhr, among many others, said early in the decades after World War One had devastated the political dogmas of classical, nineteenth-century liberalism, we can no longer take the moral individual at face value. He (so to speak) is not, as history had then already proven, the motor force of human Progress. Hence, the interregnum of new deals and state-directed monetary policies that prepared the historical ground for another war. As Immanuel Wallerstein describes it, the interregnum was actually a truce amid one continuous war of the first half of the twentieth century between the United States and Germany for control of the world order. Still, the despair of the wars, and much else, and the failure of the classic version of the liberal ethic of free markets and enlightened individuals, helped prepare for the appeal of structuralism in France and elsewhere in Europe (not to mention in American academic sociology, with Talcott Parsons and Merton) after World War Two. The French, in particular, among others on the European Continent (and in contrast to the British and the Americans) could resist German occupation only as courageous individuals in small clandestine groups, underground. To rid the surface of the earth of Nazi evil quite naturally was to open the intellectual skies to the idea that the truth of human things is in the visible structures, waiting to be seen, or (better) interpreted. Hence, too, the hermeneutic impulse that in France took the surprising quasi-scientific version of a structural semiotics of cultural forms.

This is the time and place where something began. Structuralism, henceforth, developed for a while, then prompted a reaction that came to be known as post-structuralism. Though at considerable odds in certain ways, the one could not have held forth without the other and in many instances the relations between structuralism and its alter were incestuous. Roland Barthes, a founder of structural semiotics, was also, later in his all-too-short life, a figure in the post-structural movement in *Mai '68*. Louis Althusser, than whom few were more the scientizing Marxist, was among Michel Foucault's teachers, as he was a colleague of Jacques Derrida. And Derrida cut his eye-teeth, first, on the interpretation of Husserl, an oblique source of the post-structural, who led, in some small way, to his famous 1966 essay on the decentering of human sciences which turn on a most appreciative criticism of Lévi-Strauss's structural logo-centrism. To the extent that structuralism was, as has been said over and over again, a reaction to the subjectivism of post-war existentialism – the philosophical thread of the Resistance experience; then, to the same extent, post-structuralism was only superficially a reaction to structuralist objectivism. Both movements were, in some very fundamental way, a coming to terms with the impossibility of liberal-modern culture, which had not very well endured the wars of the twentieth century (save in a bastardized form in the United States where the ideology of liberal consensus had its very short day before the Red Scare took away its breath).

The impossibility of liberal culture is a hard notion. One that is far from being widely accepted. One against which the resistance is scrupulous, if unevenly informed. But it is also a notion that had been a long time coming. It was in fact a concern that occupied Durkheim and his generation in Europe – and concerned him to such an extent that one of the reasons for his turn to culture was a proper and abiding concern over the liberal culture he believed so strongly could save the modern social order. In the end, sadly, it is possible that the impossibility of the liberal moral bond killed Durkheim.

Emile Durkheim died in Paris in 1917, at the height of his adult powers, just when, it happens, the Great War was breaking the heart of the European Diaspora. Ghosts arise from unsettled graves – from deaths that trouble the living because they come too inexplicably soon. Those who die young may not always be good, but whatever they are, they leave behind an untold story. Ghosts are the apparitions of the Unclosed because they remind the living that they really don't know all the answers. The better part of a century after Durkheim's death amid war in Europe, many well settled in the better positions of the house Europe built are spooked by reveries of their nineteenth-century ancestors who promised so much and delivered so little.

Durkheim died of a heart broken by the death of his son who was lost in the war and who, like all sons who die in such a service, are for their survivors the nightmares of what could have been. In his youth, Durkheim trusted, as could only a man raised on faith, that the Good Society would repair itself, even on the wounds of industrial conflict. This he believed so very well that he invented his version of scientific sociology that was to be both the true and the good of the Good Society. Yet, as could only a man of faith, nurtured in a Jewish village in the provinces of an anti-Semitic nation, Durkheim's faith was always cut with vinegar. He knew that faith in the social was as much a risk as was the modern idea that a good enough science could both tell *and* establish the truth of social things. Hence, from this young Durkheim came the ghost of a scientific positivism so foolish that not even Comte, himself no minor fool, could have conjured up such a one.

To the extent that ghosts are the spirits of the Unclosed, they always come in twos. We, who have actually seen ghosts, first think the apparitions are a case of double vision. We reach in the dark for our glasses only to find that the doubling remains. This is as it must be if we are being spooked by whatever came to an unnatural end. The end that fell upon the one lost is very, very real. In fact, it takes on a life of its own. In the case of Durkhiem's empirical sociology the presence was, as it must be in these matters, the presence of an absence. Durkheim, thus, had to see (so to speak) that social facts could not produce a moral order sufficient to ward off the *anomie* that led to self-destruction. By 1914, France and the rest of Europe, soon to be joined by its North American Diaspora, had already embarked on the path of self-destruction.

The ghosts of Emile Durkheim are so much more upsetting than their author would have ever dreamt or wished them to be. That is very often the way with ghosts, especially those that rise from the bodies of writing. Durkheim, the man, was a serious and sober man of science. As such he left behind the written record of his own attempt to come to terms with the ghosts that required sociology be what it has become – a science of sorts; a social ethic no less; a politics of social change; a monument to the lost past of human values. In so many remarkable ways Durkheim's ghosts were more honest than those more often thought to have been the radical thinkers. Marx, who was certainly the better writer and the more brilliant thinker, was a bit too old hat. He held too strongly to the axiom that, though perverse, the world could be made to revert to its better being. Weber, who was certainly the more subtle scholar, was too troubled by his own ghosts ever to face as thoroughly as Durkheim did the ones in his own method. Freud, who was the more successful in advancing his program for the treatment of social and psychological ills, was unable, or unwilling, to offer up very much more of a social criticism than that the civilization was discontented due to its own interior instincts for violence.

Durkheim was, almost certainly, the lesser of these founding fathers of classical Europe in one or more aspects. But when it comes to haunting, he stands up very well, perhaps in the long run even better. In the long run, Durkheim's struggle to get from the study of suicide to a full theory of social knowledge yielded up a disposition to rework the social form by the only method available – that of taking the cultural as the more or less only but still good enough representation of the structures of social things. To say, thus, that the truth, such as it is, is a social thing unsettles the hope that the social order is both real and good, even if not entirely good enough to be true. Still, the thought was the bracing inspiration of the other ghost of social theory.

Because sociology, at least, and very likely all cultural forms, cannot avoid the haunts it would be rid of, it fell unto hard times well before it realized. The slippage, however, was not so much a tragedy as an ironic comedy of errors whereby the field fell, oddly, back onto the historical conditions of its emergence in Durkheim's time, thus back into the practical soup from which its science draws the breath of what human value it has. Academic sociology's first generation in the 1890s at Chicago was a motley crew of schoolteachers, philosophers, newspapermen, clubwomen, clergy, political troublemakers, and the like. Before there was a professionalized academic sociology, there was not much that was more organized than Marx's writings. Still the generation of the 1890s, with the possible exception of Weber, and the partial exception of Durkheim, had no other pool from which to draw the students who would become academic sociologists. They drew what they could, especially in Chicago, from the streets and poorhouses, and the schuls and churches, where reformers were at work.

When asked why sociology is always different from other of the social sciences – always in spite of itself more unruly and uneven – the answer is because of our ghosts. They are the ghosts of the practical sociologies that come before sociology proper – the spirits of those who came to the field from the streets and back alleys. Durkheim differed only by having experienced a childhood in the rural past already fading as the urban centers overtook the villages that, for more than a few millennia, were the true glue of moral societies surrounded by agricultural fields.

The word *culture* derives, over those same millennia, through many languages as, first, "the place wherein a local god is worshipped" to "the more literal field of horti- and agri-culture enterprise," to the scientific field wherein cultures are the intended breeding grounds of microbes, to the capital-C Culture of the early ethnologists and ethnographers to whom Durkheim turned, late in life, to plant the truth of his sociological method in a well-cultured field, which, in this day, many (Bourdieu most poetically) take as the *champ* in which the practice of sociological habits takes place.

Culture is not a subfield. It is the field itself, without which there is nothing we can know. Durkheim was the first to recognize this fact of our life, which is why he haunts us in so many ways.

2

Lévi-Strauss and the sad tropics of modern cultures

Claude Lévi-Strauss was born in Belgium in 1908 in the early days of the twentieth century. Nearly a century later, in the first years of the twenty-first, he was still alive. He thereby outlived, in both absolute and relative years, the most deservedly famous of the post-World War Two social theorists in France. His ideas endure today, long after the rejection of his structuralism. In this respect, Lévi-Strauss's ideas share a similar fate to those of Marx which outlive the collapse of state socialism and those of Freud which outlive the eclipse of the literal interpretative methods of classical psychoanalysis.

Ideas transcend their original embodiments only when they keep faith with some unresolved – perhaps even irresolvable – practical concern of human community. In the cases of Marx and Freud, the longevity of their key ideas is easy enough to explain. The industrial capitalism Marx embarrassed in 1867 in *Capital* is nearly as dead as the socialism he proposed in 1848. Yet, the elemental logic of Marx's original riddle in the *Economic and Philosophical Manuscripts of 1844* is more, not less, an issue in the twenty-first century. "With the *increasing* value of the world of things proceeds in direct proportion the *devaluation* of the world of men." Likewise, the puzzle with which Freud began *Interpretation of Dreams* in 1899: "The unsophisticated waking judgment of someone who has just woken from sleep assumes that his dreams, even if they did not themselves come from another world, had at all events carried him off into another world." In both cases, the enigmas upon which they mounted a lifetime's ride appeared in their writings of relative youth. Though both Marx and Freud moved, thereafter, to develop more programmatic positions, nothing in the later work made their early ideas obsolete. This was, in part, a consequence of their having seized the moment to set their theories to the work of resolving social troubles then particularly acute.

For Marx, as early as 1844, it was evident that the coming capitalist revolution would betray its own inflated principles. Far from improving the human condition, capitalism worsens the circumstances of the most poor. One had only to look at the economic realities to see that. For Freud, as early as 1899, the breach between the dream and the reality was as wide as that between the worlds. Far from providing reasonable social order, the liberal democratic societies were headed toward a nightmare of their own making. The Great War of 1914 was already in the offing. As early as 1899, one had only to look to the extent of civil and interstate strife to see it coming.

As today, one need only look at the worlds of the twenty-first century to see how far the best minds fall short of resolving the contradictions of modernity. So long as economic progress bends away from justice, so long as people awake in this world, out of dreams of a better one, Marx and Freud – whatever the fate of parties and schools founded in their names – will remain of interest to anyone willing to consider social things as they are, as distinct from how we are told they ought to be.

What then of Lévi-Strauss who has claimed both Freud and Marx as among his spiritual guides? Lévi-Strauss obviously was not by any means the only social thinker who identified a morally urgent conundrum that outran aspects of the formal system that grew up around it. Yet, he did put himself in the lineage of both Freud and Marx in one of his earlier works, *Tristes tropiques* in 1955.

Marxism seemed to me to proceed in the same manner as geology and psychoanalysis (taking the latter in the sense given it by its founder). All three demonstrate that understanding consists in reducing one type of reality to another; that the true reality is never the most obvious; and that the nature of truth is already indicated by the care it takes to remain elusive.

The oft-quoted reference to geology is not often well understood, an understanding that can only be arrived at by the comparison to Marx and Freud. The structural method Lévi-Strauss was already practicing by 1955 in his more formal scientific writings would seem to betray the methodological point he makes in the comparison. In fact, behind the formal structural analyses of myth in his professional work, lies an elegantly subtle methodological principle of considerable practical significance.

To concede that social and cultural realities are not simply non-obvious but elusive is to require for their understanding an extraordinary method and certainly one that moves outside the protocols of modern science. The method, as Lévi-Strauss described it in *Tristes tropiques*, is in effect a trickster method – a manner of sneaking up on the elusive meanings, catching them off-guard. Here Lévi-Strauss describes this as a method of reduction – one level for another; but, a few paragraphs on, he uses the word that would eventually be absorbed into his formal method: *transformation*. The trickster method is one of discovering the rules of transformation between the worlds.

Far from being a hero, as Susan Sontag said of him, Lévi-Strauss was more the trickster and nowhere more so than in his memoir of relative youth. Lévi-Strauss was still in his twenties in 1935 when he first went to Brazil to teach sociology in São Paolo. There began a number of expeditions, over many years, to visit the cultures of the Americas and Asia. *Tristes tropiques* is the memoir of how he was made an anthropologist (an intentional passive construction reflecting his view that cultures think individuals). *Tristes tropiques* appeared twenty years after his first visit to the Americas. He was forty-seven. A long life lay ahead, but the lessons that made him an anthropologist were those of the very travels for which he is criticized. Lévi-Strauss, the anthropologist, never did what field ethnographers are supposed to do – settle down for a long stay with a society of savages. More than once he had planned to pass such a time among Brazil's Amazon peoples. Always he moved on. As a result, *Tristes tropiques* is more a literary travelogue than anthropology in the usual sense of the vocation.

Still, *Tristes tropiques* is anthropology in that it ranges wildly over cultures dispersed around the world – their art, their hotels, their tools, their families. What struck him most were the similarities. A hotel near Curituba is like one in Karachi. The art of the Chavin of northern Peru and of Monte Alban in Oaxaco is like that the Hopewell of the Upper Mississippi. The customs of Toba in Paraguay and the Caduveo of Brazil remind him of Lewis Carroll's wonderland. These parallel realities are, of course, the stock in trade of ethnology. But Lévi-Strauss makes of them something unusual. Though he accounts for the Aleutian migrations from Asia to the Americas, his final reckoning of the similarities lies with the then yet-to-be fully developed idea of anthropology as the trickster method of the transformational logic of human being. Hence, in *Tristes tropiques*, Lévi-Strauss extends the allusions to Marx, Freud, and geology (for which I supply the emphasis):

Between Marxism and psychoanalysis, which are social sciences – one orientated towards society; the other toward the individual – and geology, which is a physical science – but which has also fostered and nurtured history both by its method and its aim – *anthropology spontaneously establishes its domain: for mankind, which anthropology looks upon as having no limits other than those of space, gives a new meaning to the **transformations** of the terrestrial globe, as defined by labour which goes on all through the ages in the activities of societies as anonymous as telluric forces*, and in the minds of individuals whom the psychologist sees as particular case histories. Anthropology affords me intellectual satisfaction: as a form of history, linking up at opposite ends with world history and my own history, it thus reveals the rationale common to both.

What a curiosity, this claim as to the unique value of anthropology among the sciences of man – that of giving meaning to the transformations between and among the levels of reality – histories of the earth, the world, the individual.

Herein may lay the mystery that Lévi-Strauss, more than anyone of his time, has named, described, and embedded in the consciousness of modernity. This, it happens, is the mystery of human knowledge of the human. In what sense can there be a human science of human meanings? Or, differently put, how can cultured beings understand the most elusive of all the realities they must understand – culture itself?

In 1962, Lévi-Strauss published the most important of his theoretical works, *La Pensée sauvage*. For the general reader the book is famous for its concluding essay, "History and Dialectic" – his critique of Jean-Paul Sartre's then just published masterwork, *Critique de la raison dialectique*. They had known each other since school days in Paris, joined in a network of France's most brilliant young intellectuals in the years before and during the Nazi occupation. His criticism was that Sartre did not escape the analytic rationality of those he attacked. It was, all too briefly put, a question of how one knows human history. For Lévi-Strauss, Sartre's work was, in effect, too much the fourth critique that Kant could never have written.

But to the social scientist, the more important essay in *La Pensée sauvage* is the first, "The Science of the Concrete," which turns on the question of the social foundations of knowing – a central issue of French social thought since the days of Durkheim's *Les Formes élémentaires de la vie religeuse* (1912) and Lévy-Bruhl's *Les Fonctions mentales dans les sociétés inférieures* in 1910 (translated as *How Natives Think*). Here is where Lévi-Strauss introduces his now well-known, and sadly abused, idea of mythic thought as *bricolage* – as, that is, a kind of handy-man's borrowing from materials and tools at hand to craft a product of some value to others. "We have already distinguished the scientist and the 'bricoleur' by the inverse functions which they assign to events and structures as ends and means, the scientist creating events (changing the world) by means of structures and the 'bricoleur' creating structures by means of events." A transformational logic of human culture can only be achieved by the latter course. Culture comes to pass as events, out of which the student and the practitioner of them compose meaningful structures.

Why, then, this conundrum? It was 1962. Fanon had died the year before. Algeria won its independence the same year. *Mai '68* was still to come. Charles de Gaulle governed. But for Sartre, who had been a partisan against the Nazis, and Lévi-Strauss, who was effectively an exile at the New School for Social Research in New York during the Nazi occupation, that war remained a defining experience. For the sciences of the human the abiding question could not be walled off in a garden of philosophical meditation. The meaning of human history was the question of the generation that came of age in France in the 1940s. Lévi-Strauss's science of the concrete was the basis for his criticism of Sartre. Much as Michel Foucault would later set himself as the specific intellectual against Sartre, the grand intellectual of universal truths, Lévi-Strauss made a similar claim from the point of view of the *bricoleur* – the one who takes the concrete givens for what they are, makes of them what structures can be made. He opposed the incomplete criticism of analytic science he saw in Sartre. "Science is based on a distinction between levels." The science of the concrete – that is, the method of mythic thought, and the discourse of the savage mind – makes no distinctions and accepts no analytic cuts among the parts of its material and cultural realities. "The characteristic feature of mythical thought is that it expresses itself by means of a heterogeneous repertoire which, even if extensive, is nevertheless limited."

When the cut-realities upon which the modern world was built start to come apart, as they were already beginning to do when Lévi-Strauss left for Brazil in 1935, as they did when the Nazis overran Paris in 1940, as they did when Algeria severed the final official cord linking France to North Africa and its colonial empire in 1962 – when cuts like these cut close to home, then the question of how we know what we know is particularly acute. It is no longer an academic question, but one rooted in the practicalities of daily life. During the occupation those who remained in Paris ate rats. Even in New York food and petrol were rationed. In such cases, what could be known was very concrete; what structures could be made were made of whatever was at hand.

In 1960, just before *La Pensée sauvage*, Lévi-Strauss was inducted into the newly created chair of social anthropology at the Collège de France. His *Leçon Inaugurale* (later translated as *The Scope of Anthropology*) was a homage to the founder of French sociology. "Durkheim was probably the first to introduce the requirement of specificity into the sciences of man, thereby opening the way for a renovation from which most of these sciences, and especially linguistics benefited at the beginning of the twentieth century."

The appreciative nod toward Durkheim was to the past of his intellectual history. The other whom he acknowledges is Ferdinand de Saussure, a Durkheimian by coincidence, who lent to the structuralist age the science of signs, semiology. This was Lévi-Strauss's nod to his then still developing future. Again, the logic of transformation is prominent. "Signs and symbols can only function in so far as they belong to systems, regulated by internal laws of implication and exclusion, and the property of a system of signs is to be transformable, in other words, *translatable*, in the language of another system with the aid of permutations." He meant nothing more than what he had previously said about anthropology in *Tristes tropiques*, and would say in different ways in *La Pensée sauvage*. The analytic levels of reality upon which science proper depends for its variables and controls disallows the sciences of culture, wherein the number of worlds (of levels, if you must) is many but finite – thus allowing a logic of transformations, a cultural science as translation, a cultural scientist as a *bricoleur*, and a practical method for understanding meaning as myth-making.

Meaning is one of the more over-used and poorly defined terms in the popular and professional vocabularies. Strictly speaking, *to mean* is *to signify* – to create significance – which is to say that to create meaning is to use and produce signs that transform concrete experience into some other more general language. One might even say, formulaically, that *meaning* is to *culture* as *significance* is to *language*; hence, the emergence of language in the human and social sciences. More than anyone at the time, Lévi-Strauss explained in empirical language the general value of semiotics to culture studies as a science of meanings.

Tristes tropiques is, by the author's insistence, the untranslated title used for the English edition. Some things are not to be translated, and especially not when several meanings must be held to their concrete relations. *Tristes tropiques* is, as its English translator observes, "at once ironic and poetic" – among other options, either "sad tropics" or "tragic tropics." Between the notes of delight and discovery, the book seems always to leave the peoples it visits in the manner of 1950s travel films, with the sun setting on a place unlikely to be visited again. The literary tensions of *Tristes tropiques* generally resolve, and especially in its unforgettable final pages. "The world began without man and it will end without him." These people of grand cultures eroded by misery are the vision of what is to come in the final long run.

Just as the individual is not alone in the group, nor any one society alone among the others, so man is not alone in the universe. When the spectrum or rainbow of human cultures has finally sunk into the void created by our frenzy; as long as we continue to exist and there is a world, that tenuous arch linking us to the inaccessible will still remain, to show us the opposite course to that leading to enslavement; man may be unable to follow it, but its contemplation allows him the only privilege of which he can make himself worthy; that of arresting the process, of controlling the impulse which forces him to block up the cracks in the wall of necessity one by one and to complete his work at the same time as he shuts himself up within his prison; this is the privilege coveted by every society, whatever its beliefs, its political system or its level of civilization; a privilege to which it attaches its desire, its pleasure, its peace of mind and its freedom; the possibility, vital for life, of *unhitching*, which consists – Oh! fond farewell to savages and explorations! – in grasping, during the brief intervals in which our species can bring itself to irrupt its hive-like activity, the essence of what it was and continues to be, below the threshold of thought and over and above society. . . .

Tristes tropiques is, you can see, also a book of irony in that the tragedy of the wild (*sauvage*) people Lévi-Strauss visited is no more and no less than the fate of the human. They were, when he visited them, already fading into their pasts by the aggressions of a present over-confident in its future. Their futures are the futures of the modern world, which is founded on a culture that believes in unending progress toward some vanishing point beyond the present. The culture of modernity blinds the people it makes to the reality beyond what can be seen – that of a world, having begun without man, ending without him.

Sad tropics! Tragic tropics! – the irony is in the double meaning. The sadness Lévi-Strauss saw on the disappearing cultures is none other than the tragic vision behind the blindness of modern cultures. They, the modern ones, are, in the end, no different from any other. All cultures are but a short-term organization of information against the second thermal law of cultural dynamics. In the end there is entropy where cultures once again meet nature, which of course would never have been called *nature* had it not been for the modern word *culture*. When the worlds end in this way, both sadness and tragedy will have already passed away into the steaming rainforests where the cockroaches, indifferent to the absence of classical philosophy, may or may not hear the trees crashing.

In the meantime, all we can do is to signify – to use the universally various languages of our cultures to make what meanings we can out of the events that crash in upon us. The final future will take care of itself.

What is culture? Amid the flowers, seeds or weeds?

What is culture? Not exactly what one supposes, if only because the use of the term, whether high brow or low, demands closer inspection than most are willing to muster. Practitioners of the social sciences, for example, use the term *culture* with abandon. For years they have sought common definitional ground that was nowhere to be found. Thus, in the absence of accord many will yield to an implicit understanding that *culture* is a name for the beliefs and activities of human communities that lend powerful, if hard to define, meaning to the routines of daily life. Then again, in fields like sociology, neither this thin definition, nor any other, can be expected to quench a throat parched by all the talking in circles.

To those not certifiably implicated by association with so hard bitten an enterprise as social science the word *culture* refers to a laundry list of subjects so mixed that, when washed together, the colors bleach and fade. Still, every now and again, one comes across an ingenious compilation of usages to which the notorious word has been put. One such list, reproduced just below, is of particular intrigue because, apart from the amusement-value of the juxtapositions, it was composed for a virtual college course in literature.[1] One would think, thereby, that the application is, if not low-brow, at least mid-brow, but in fact the list here following is subtly researched and begins with the highest brow of all culture theorists:

Culture is properly described as the love of perfection; it is a study of perfection. (Matthew Arnold, *Culture and Anarchy* (1869))

Culture looks beyond machinery, culture hates hatred; culture has one great passion, – the passion for sweetness and light. (Matthew Arnold, *Literature and Dogma* (1873))

---

[1] This list is composed by Eric Miraglia, Richard Law, and Peg Collins of Washington State University. The authors are associated, respectively, with the University's English Department, the Student Learning Center, the General Education program, and the Information Technology Learning Systems Group. The address is http://www.wsu.edu:8001/vcwsu/commons/topics/culture/culture-index.html.

Culture is to "know the best that has been said and thought in the world." (Matthew Arnold, *Literature and Dogma* (1873))

That is true culture which helps us to work for the social betterment of all. (Henry Ward Beecher)

A man should be just cultured enough to be able to look with suspicion upon culture. (Samuel Butler)

Culture is everything. Culture is the way we dress, the way we carry our heads, the way we walk, the way we tie our ties – it is not only the fact of writing books or building houses. (Aimé Césaire)

Culture, with us, ends in headache. (Ralph Waldo Emerson, *Experience* (1841))

No culture can live, if it attempts to be exclusive. (Mahatma Gandhi)

Men are so inclined to content themselves with what is commonest; the spirit and the senses so easily grow dead to the impressions of the beautiful and perfect, that every one should study, by all methods, to nourish in his mind the faculty of feeling these things. . . . For this reason, one ought every day at least, to hear a little song, read a good poem, see a fine picture, and, if it were possible, to speak a few reasonable words. (Goethe, *Wilhelm Meister's Apprenticeship*. Bk. v, ch. 1 (Carlyle, tr.))

Culture is but the fine flowering of real education, and it is the training of the feeling, the tastes and the manners that makes it so. (Minnie Kellogg, Iroquois leader)

The poor have no business with culture and should beware of it. They cannot eat it; they cannot sell it; they can only pass it on to others and that is why the world is full of hungry people ready to teach us anything under the sun. (Aubrey Menen)

A cultivated mind is one to which the fountains of knowledge have been opened, and which has been taught, in any tolerable degree, to exercise its faculties. (John Stuart Mill, *Utilitarianism*, II (1863))

Culture is what your butcher would have if he were a surgeon. (Mary Pettibone Poole, *A Glass Eye at a Keyhole* (1938))

The primary indication, to my thinking, of a well-ordered mind is a man's ability to remain in one place and linger in his own company. (Seneca, *Epistulae ad Lucilium*. Epis. ii, sec. 1)

Culture is an instrument wielded by professors to manufacture professors, who when their turn comes will manufacture professors. (Simone Weil, *The Need for Roots* (1949))

Are not the processes of culture rapidly creating a class of supercilious infidels, who believe in nothing? Shall a man lose himself in countless masses of adjustments, and be so shaped with reference to this, that, and the other, that the simply good and healthy and brave parts of him are reduced and clipp'd away, like the bordering of a box in a garden? (Walt Whitman, *Democratic Vistas* (1870))

To these, the social scientist would add the classic definition as it came into play early in the days of scientific anthropology:

Culture is that complex whole which includes knowledge, belief, art, morals, law, custom, and any other capabilities and habits acquired by man as a member of society. (Edward Tylor, *Primitive Culture* (1871))

One might be more seriously tempted to explore the history of the term's use in the social sciences were it not for the discouraging fact that Tylor's famous definition led more to dispute than to accord.

It hardly need be said that none of these, amusing though they are when set side-by-side, relieves the definitional confusion. Not even the average social scientist, notwithstanding a professional duty to think about things others take for granted, would be persuaded even by Tylor's foundational definition, much less the others. In fact, for years now, social and cultural anthropologists have spent a good bit of their energies arguing over the meaning of culture; just as, in the last decade-plus, sociologists, having at long last caught up with literary theorists, have devoted themselves to a series of floor fights as to who will have the last word as to the meaning of *culture*.

However ill-advised it may be, one further venture into the semantic thickets that have grown up around this word of many meanings is justified, if only, as is my intent, to demonstrate that whatever one thinks of *culture*, it is not something that lends itself to operational definitions. Though social scientists are loathe to do so, when the dictionary is to be trusted, resort to one is sometimes a good place to start. In this case, the *Oxford English Dictionary*, by giving a better history of English words than any other, begins to justify the aversion to attempts to define it. Some words may well have a rather straightforward history, but *culture* does not. Quite the contrary, it is a marker that has traversed so many semantic fields that the inspectors can hardly discern that its passport was original stamped as Latin by way of Old French:

Culture (in OF. *couture*), ad. L. *cultura*, cultivation, tending, in Christian authors, worship, f. ppl. stem of *colere:* see CULT (*Oxford English Dictionary*)

Thus we see that the modern word *culture* in English enjoys a simultaneous affinity with French fashion (*couture*) and to religious worship, especially as practiced in cults. This discovery clarifies somewhat the recent complaints about French theories of culture as being little more than a fad. Being a fashion of sorts, cultural studies may not be a fad, though of course those who engage in the practice are exposed to the charge that they are cult.

The *OED* gives further historical account of the word. From the fifteenth through the sixteenth centuries, *culture* was associated almost exclusively with "the action or practice of cultivating soil; tillage; husbandry" – from which we get "cultivation." Significantly, beginning in the seventeenth century, *cultivation* came to be attached more to the cultivation of a particular crop or plant. This no doubt owes to the then new division of agrarian labor that was necessary for the development of capital surpluses sufficient to bankroll early mercantile capitalism. This was, apparently, just one of many elaborations of the meaning of *culture* as *cultivation*, the gerund of the verb: *to cultivate* – as in the cultivation of body, mind, or manners. Thus Hobbes, in *Leviathan* (1651) writes of the education of the young as a "culture of their minds." There is no good reason to infer that Hobbes, skeptical though he was in other matters, had in mind the bureaucratic development of schooling which today is very much a hothouse of pedagogical misinformation.

Just the same, the gerund *cultivation*, in its verb aspect, allows for the expression *to culture*, which came into usage in school-based academic science as late as the 1880s after the science of microbes had been weaned from the classical epidemiological theories of disease. Hence, culture became the medium in which is grown microbes for clinical or scientific diagnoses. This usage is, of course, behind the hard to adjudicate distinction, often today associated with Johann Gottfried von Herder in the eighteenth century, between *Kultur* and *Zivilization* – in respect to the line drawn through the word *Bildung (formation)* which came, especially after Herder, to be applied more to culture as the means by which human beings are cultivated by the higher ideas that may or may not be firmly held by a civilization. Though "cultivation" as applied to animal husbandry (and, if Herder is to be trusted, to the husbandry of the human spirit) had been in play for a good century, the application of it to microbiology did not come into play until a scant decade after Tylor's anthropological definition of culture as, again, "that complex whole which includes knowledge, belief, art, morals, law, custom, and any other capabilities and habits acquired by man as a member of society."

Thus we see one of the reasons why the term *culture* permits comparison of the informal kind. Even the formal derivation is, if not funny, at least serious in surprising ways: Culture owes first to religion, then to animal husbandry, then to cultivation of crops and minds, finally to Petri dishes for germs of various kinds including the germs of knowledge, belief, morality, custom, and the like. Culture studies owe, thereby, a debt of kinship to microbiology no less than anthropology, which Lévi-Strauss compared to geology. One might forgive the microbiologists for borrowing so rudely, but the early anthropologists have less excuse for inventing definitions of uncertain meaning and meager charm.

The awkwardness of Tylor's definition need not bear the brunt for these failures of the poetic imagination. Indeed he did as well as any and better than most of those who came after. This is well illustrated by the single most famous social scientific text on the history of the word. Alfred Kroeber's and Clyde Kluckhohn's 1952 essay "Culture: a Critical Review of Concepts and Definitions"[2] unsettles the reader with its bewildering list of some 160 definitions, from which the authors deduce the following:

Culture consists of patterns, explicit and implicit, of and for behavior acquired and transmitted by symbols, constituting the distinctive achievement of human groups, including their embodiment in artifacts; the essential core of culture consists of traditional (i.e. historically derived and selected) ideas and especially their attached values. (Kroeber and Kluckhohn, *Culture* (1952), 66)

In the reach of eight decades from Tylor in 1871 to Kroeber and Kluckhohn in 1952 there were of course important definitional discriminations, yet none so persuasive as to prevent this latter version from distinguishing itself scantily by the heady abstractions it introduces upon Tylor's vastly less wordy original.

Here following are some of the more striking examples selected to illustrate the several types of definitions from which Kroeber and Kluckhohn deduced theirs[3]:

Descriptive definitions of culture

That complex whole which includes all the habits acquired by man as a member of society. (Ruth Benedict, *Making of Man* (1931))

Embraces all the manifestations of a community, the reactions of the individual as affected by the habits of the group in which he lives, and the human activities as determined by these habits. (Franz Boas, *Anthropology* (1930))

Historical (as social heritage)

The sum total and organization of the social heritages which have acquired a social meaning because of racial temperament and of the historical life of the group. (Robert Park and E. W. Burgess, *Science of Sociology* (1921))

This social heritage is the key concept . . . it comprises inherited artifacts, goods, technical processes, ideas, habits and values. (Bronislaw Malinowski, *Culture* (1931))

---

[2] "Culture: a Critical Review of Concepts and Definitions," *Peabody Museum Papers*, 47, Harvard University Press, 1952 (reprinted: New York: Random House, 1952).

[3] *Ibid.*, part II. So obsessed were they with analytic thoroughness that Kroeber and Kluckhohn provided a residual category for incomplete definitions, omitted here because it is as unenlightening as is their sixth analytic group, "Genetic" (also omitted), which defines culture generally as, for one instance, "a product of human association."

Normative (as a way of life)

All the things that a group of people inhabiting a common geographical area do, the ways they do things, the ways they think and feel about things, their material tools and their values and symbols . . . (Robert Lynd, *Knowledge for What?* (1940))

The way of life of a people; while a society is the organized aggregate of individuals who follow a give way of life. In still simpler terms a society is composed of people; the way they behave is their culture. (M. J. Herskovits, *Man and his Works* (1948))

Psychological (as adjustment to social problems)

The total equipment of technique, mechanical, mental, and moral, by use of which the people of a given period try to attain their ends. (Albion Small, *General Sociology* (1905))

The sum of men's adjustments to their life-conditions is their culture or their civilization. (W. G. Sumner and A. G. Keller, *The Science of Society* (1927))

Structural (as organized patterns)

An organization of conventional understandings manifest in act and artifact, which, persisting through tradition, characterizes a human group. (Robert Redfield (1940, unpublished))

In the last analysis, nothing more than the organized repetitive responses of a society's members. (Robert Linton, *The Cultural Background of Personality* (1945))

This list is nowhere near as risible as the earlier one composed primarily for students of literature who tend to tolerate nonsense better than the rest of us. But it has its moments. In collecting the definitions at work in the social sciences up until 1952, Kroeber and Kluckhohn marvelously illustrate the extent to which definitional labor is the sweating of small differences.

The ingenuity of Kroeber and Kluckhohn's analytic list relents in time to the fatal flaw of all such definitional strategies. Their list, embedded in more than 400 pages of commentary, is decidedly less high-minded than the previous one but nearly as hilarious for its variations of uncertain congruence. The absurdity of it all must have dawned on Kroeber and Kluckhohn during the hard labor of making analytic sense of the inchoate array.[4] Yet, in the rosy blush of American social science in the 1950s,

---

[4] This I conclude less out of prejudice against the effort, than from the fact observed by Clifford Geertz that Kluckhohn, for one, had associated himself with no fewer than eleven different definitions that could easily cover the several analytic categories in the work with Kroeber. See Clifford Geertz, *The Interpretation of Cultures* (New York: Basic Books, 1973), 4–5.

imposing order against the odds seemed the obvious thing to do. As a result, the Kroeber–Kluckhohn groupings of the straining mix of earlier definitions offers slight, but not negligible analytic value.

The value of listings of this kind is in their survey of the variations at play in the culture of those preoccupied with the study of culture. The one list celebrates the differences. The other, that of the social scientists, searches for a harmony not to be found. This resistance, in the latter case, is, however, of second-order cultural interest because, behind the strain toward difference, there are two quite evident themes that run across the multitudes. For one, many if not all of the definitions recognize that, however normal it might seem to think of culture as spiritual or otherwise among the ideal elements, it must also be recognized for its relation to material products and means: artifacts, goods, techniques, mechanical equipment, material tools. For the other, however much culture might be viewed as from on high, its social pertinence is judged by its value in the practical details of daily life, including: habits (a particular favorite), historical life, ways of thinking and feeling, adjustments to life-conditions, repetitive responses, and so forth. These two generic qualities, apart from rendering the Kroeber–Kluckhohn analytic groupings trivial, reflect the concerns of Tylor's time in that both are questions around which nineteenth-century social thought turned.

To a striking degree, these two themes remain among those prevailing in culture studies early in the twenty-first century. *What is the relation of culture to the more material social and economic orders?* And: *What is the relation between culture as an analytical feature of social science and culture in the more ordinary sense of the word, as a feature of social practices, including aesthetic ones?* Quite apart from how one might, if at all, define the word, *culture* remains an open question in large part because these reasonably old-fashioned riddles are still unresolved. This fact glitters even in the strobe of globalizing effects that, one would think, might put culture in a different light as it has nearly every other social thing under the sun. Thus, to a remarkable degree, as silly as the Kroeber–Kluckhohn essay may seem in this post-analytic era of the twenty-first century, the definitional exercise fortifies conviction that, for whatever reasons, culture is as important today as it was late in the 1860s when Karl Marx and Matthew Arnold first posed the two questions as they recur between the lines of the Kroeber–Kluckhohn list which, against its better intentions, carried them forward to our time.

Though in the 1860s Marx and Arnold in London and Oxford were only a half day's float distant on the Thames, it is not evident that they had each other specifically in mind in *Capital I* and *Culture and Anarchy*. Yet, Marx's first volume of *Capital* in 1867 was his most unambiguous assertion of the material conditions of life in respect to those ideal elements that, a few years later in 1871, Tylor would gather together in his definition of *culture*. By contrast, just two years after Marx and two before Tylor, Arnold's *Culture and Anarchy* in 1869 would present his famously spirited defense of the practical value of culture, understood not as an analytic category but as the uttermost embodiment of high society's moral perfection.

Even if the juxtaposition of Marx to Arnold is figurative, the queries for which they stand are central to any attempt to account for culture – of which no account endures longer than the debate over culture's causal force in the wider array of social variations. Jeffrey Alexander, with the succinctness for which he is famous, has put the causal issue as a question of whether culture is the gearbox or the engine of social meanings.[5] It might be better, in respect to culture, to substitute a more organic figure of speech, in particular: whether culture is a weed (as Marx thought it was) or a seed (as Arnold thought). Even today, when it is common to celebrate popular culture (thought by many to be at best a weed) against high culture (thought by others to be the flower of human perfection), the question remains whether culture, in either the academic or practical application, is a seed of new life or a weed obscuring the realities. Both Marx and Arnold were poets after a fashion – at least in the sense that both appreciated the blossom of fine language. Whether culture is, thereby, a flower amid weeds or the seed of social hope is the crucial difference.

As to Marx's side of the contrast: *What, then, is the relation of culture to the more material social and economic orders?* One of the more influential of the social scientific definers listed by Kroeber and Kluckhohn was Bronislaw Malinowski, who more than the others stipulated culture as necessarily bound up with the material needs of human beings:

[Culture] obviously is the integral whole consisting of implements and consumers' goods, of constitutional charters for the various social groups, of human ideas and crafts, beliefs and customs. Whether we consider a very simple or primitive culture or an extremely complex and developed one, we are confronted by a vast apparatus, partly material, partly human and partly spiritual, by which man is able to cope with the concrete specific problems that face him. These problems arise out of the fact that man has a body subject to various organic needs, and that he lives in an environment which is his best friend, in that it provides the raw materials of man's handiwork, and also his dangerous enemy, in that it harbors many hostile forces. (Malinowski, *A Scientific Theory of Culture* (1944: 36))

---

[5] Jeffrey Alexander, *The Meanings of Social Life* (New York: Oxford University Press, 2003), 18.

Malinowski's definition enjoyed a considerable influence for its contributions to the functional theory that had such a currency in the 1950s. Then, especially in the United States, functionalism served as a kind of black hole in which the density of materialist theories could be protected from the ravages of an insane anti-communism – shielded thereby in order to secure the necessary place of material things in any plausible post-war sociology. Though the 1950s in the West were a season of unrealistic idealism, even the most brazen of liberal ideologues had to account for material progress. Material realities were an essential consideration, even then, because post-war reconstruction efforts in Europe and Asia were joined with, and by, the economic exuberance in the United States to set the economic environment square before the promises of social progress.

Functionalism throve in those times. In the hands of writers like Talcott Parsons, the then dominant academic sociologist in the West, the apparent triumph of the economic function in the capitalist world system had all the appearances of a liberal affirmation of the productive forces of Western culture. Culture, in Parsons's authoritatively brilliant scheme, was the source of normative information that guided the social system from above while economic adaptation to environmental necessities was the motive force from below.[6] Once the back of the anti-communist movement was broken in the 1960s, it became a badge of honor (if a bit too sharp to the point) to accuse functionalism of a certain innocence, if not downright conservativism. Yet, this notwithstanding, the fact remains that sociological functionalisms like Parsons's sociology served, as did Malinowski's in anthropology, to steady the focus on the material foundations of human society.

If not a material*ism*, functional theory was at least a serious effort to remind students of culture that culture's contributions to meaningful human order cannot be made apart from satisfaction of society's material needs and means. This conviction Malinowski summarized more insistently than others as "a vast apparatus, partly material, partly human and partly spiritual, by which man is able to cope with the concrete, specific problems that face him." And no problem is more pervasively before the human face than that of biological survival in a sometimes friendly, sometimes hostile environment.

---

[6] Parsons's scheme (known as the AGIL paradigm) underwent a number of transformations, including the addition of both Freudian and cybernetic themes that sharpened the interplay of culture (that is: L or latent pattern maintenance, the informational function) and the economic (that is: A or adaptation, the motive energy of the system). The clearest, most readable, of his mature statements is, I think, *The System of Modern Societies* (Englewood Cliffs, NJ: Prentice-Hall, 1971).

Functionalism may rightly be accused of having begged the question of culture's relation to material forces by seeking to generate a theoretical scheme that distributes the functioning elements each to its proper, necessary, and separate place in the division of social labor. At the same time, Marxism – no inconsequential functionalism itself – can be accused of the opposite failure: that of having eliminated ambiguity at the cost of emasculating the force of culture as a power (if not a variable) in the play of social life.

Either way, social sciences willing to account for social realties have a hard row to hoe if they are to do much better than either Marx's or Malinowksi's, even Parsons's, functionalist theories of the perverse or effective necessities of culture in material life. This revival of a faded controversy is worth the while now, long after the fact, because it suggests a way of accounting for the persistence of the question of culture's material value during a time of globalization. In the 1860s, when Marx and Arnold joined the debate as the remove of their different attitudes, material realities in the form of early industrial capitalism were unambiguously the salient structural realities of modern societies. Hence Matthew Arnold's often-quoted line which stood behind his fear of social anarchy:

> Wandering between two worlds, one dead,
> The other powerless to be born[7]

The same could just as well be said of the new millennium of globalized social experience.[8] The difference would lie, simply, in the reversal of fortunes between the material and cultural forces.

Under the reign of global capital economies it could well be said that culture tends to trump material realities. As the salience of the factory fades before the looming electronic machine, machinery itself is transformed. One wonders what Marx might have said about the mode of production typical to such a time when the working day and the machine still generate surplus value, but do so at a distance. Those reduced to the subsistence wage are hidden away in the dark corners of the third and fourth worlds, while the machines that work the global magic sit prominently in the salons and studies of the first. Today, the machinery of global technology is itself cultural, hence the expression "information technology" in which the technical tool slips to second place after the primacy of information. The machine is itself transposed into a cultural thing. Not, to be sure, the sweet perfection Arnold imagined, but culture

---

[7] From Arnold's "Stanzas from the Grand Chartreuse" (1855).

[8] In point of ironic fact, Arnold's line is used today by, among others, NEURO – Networking Europe, a Porto Alegre movement of the cultural left against economic globalization. See http://www.makeworlds.org/.

nonetheless. The machinery that moves and makes money – whether a market trading board or a weapon of remote destruction – depends on the language of electronic communications. Today's *lingua franca* is not so much English as Windows, by which all things real are readily translated one into the other.

As a result, much after the fashion of Malinowski's definition of culture, material and cultural things are returned to their ambiguous, hence problematic, relation. In his day, in 1944, it was felt necessary (in the West at least) to remind social science that the spiritual elements in culture are part and parcel of the material. In this day, in 2004 as I write, it is rather more necessary to remind that the material realities are, if not spiritual, at least uncertainly flawed cultural things. Either way, culture has yet to outrun the material so long as such a vast number of human beings suffer the dangers of a hostile environment. When people live, as most do, on the margins of subsistence, the human interest in material things squats full face as the problem that must be solved. In this day, the solution ultimately is by access to a strange cultural competence that is the key to the kingdom of what earned income there may be. Whether the world is McDonaldized is hard to say. But it is perfectly evident that even the poor who sell the hamburgers must know how to punch the right keys. The keyboard is the tie that binds the economically marginal to the high-flying stock trader. Does either understand how the machines work? All that matters is that they perform magic, broadcasting local action into global space from which returns the small coin of transaction.

If, then, Marx on the heels of Hegel set a materialist head atop of idealist philosophies of history, today the reversal is itself reversed – not, however, back to the original relations but into a wholly new configuration. What differs is the path by which culture and economy are joined. In Marx's day the bloom of modern bourgeois sentimentality puffed hot air into the clotted lungs of early industrial society. Who, then, among the settled classes would have found it hard to believe that the capital bustle of industrial wealth was the natural issue of the new culture of human freedom? Marx was chief among the relatively few who, from the first, diagnosed the mode in which human degradations were produced below and behind the face of political and cultural idealism. Marx was not wrong in his time, when the contrast to Arnold appeared, for good reason, so stark. In our time, had he been among us, Marx almost certainly would have appreciated – if neither a new post-capitalism mode of production, nor an updated version of Arnold's ethic of high culture – the new modes of cultural production affecting the common, and material, life.

Matthew Arnold, the poet of bucolic Oxford, was anything but the greedy Mr. Moneybags Marx ridiculed in *Capital*. Arnold was a man of the highest cultural tastes who thus believed that culture alone could save the world from wandering aimlessly between its past and a new world, powerless to be born. To speak of culture as sweetness and light, as Arnold did, might well turn the stomachs of the masses who hunger for meat and potatoes. Yet, this does not mean that Arnold lacked a social feeling, as is plain from the fuller statement of his idea of culture:

> But there is of culture another view, in which not solely the scientific passion, the sheer desire to see things as they are, natural and proper in an intelligent being, appears as the ground of it. There is a view in which all the love of our neighbour, the impulses towards action, help, and beneficence, the desire for removing human error, clearing human confusion, and diminishing human misery, the noble aspiration to leave the world better and happier than we found it, – motives eminently such as are called social, – come in as part of the grounds of culture, and the main and pre-eminent part. (Arnold, *Culture and Anarchy* (1869, 1: 3))

Whether Arnold's social feeling for human misery extended to the miseries of those for whom Marx wrote is less than clear. Still, the liberal sentiment is there behind it all. We can see in the words of someone like Arnold, whose attitude toward culture would today be called elitist, the degree to which culture, including high culture, must stand the test of its application to the practical necessities of social life.

Thus, from Arnold we can take the second of two major, still unresolved, puzzles: *What is the relation between culture as an analytical feature of social science and culture in the more ordinary sense of the word as a feature of social practices, including aesthetic ones?* The invocation of Matthew Arnold implies, more or less accurately, that one is nearing the vicinity of high culture which, in its way, epitomized the extremes of bourgeois culture against which Marx set his own implicit, if uncertainly invoked, revolutionary culture of the masses. One of the ironies of intellectual history is that the Marx of the 1860s would, amid the crises of the 1930s and 1940s, come to be viewed as vulgar against the apparently more humanistic Marx of a century before in the 1840s – the fabled early Marx still tugged along by the sway of Hegel's extremes with respect to ideas.

One would not want to propose a union of interests between the lines established by Marx and Arnold; nor, however, ought one suppose they wandered in two entirely different worlds. In fact the world once powerless to be born was born in fact in the violence of the twentieth century – stillborn perhaps. And culture, whether weed or seed, had lost its bloom. The single most severe attack on mass culture was authored in the spirit of Marx by Max Horkheimer and Theodor Adorno in "The Culture Industry: Enlightenment as Mass Deception" (1942). In this famous essay one encounters statements that, though phrased after Marx, would not have displeased Arnold, notably[9]:

Culture today is infecting everything with sameness. Film, radio, and magazines form a system. Each branch of culture is unanimous within itself and all are unanimous together. . . . All mass culture under monopoly is identical, and the contours of its skeleton, the conceptual armature fabricated by monopoly, are beginning to stand out. Those in charge no longer take much trouble to conceal the structure, the power of which increases the more bluntly its existence is admitted. Films and radio no longer need to present themselves as art. The truth that they are nothing but business is used as an ideology to legitimize the trash they intentionally produce. They call themselves industries, and the published figures for their directors' incomes quell any doubts about the social necessity of their finished products. (Horkheimer and Adorno, "The Culture Industry" (1942–44))

The critical idea here came to be more strongly associated with Adorno's devastating criticism of mass culture was, nonetheless, a joint, if unreconciled, issue of the two founders of the German school of critical theory.

At first it would seem absurd to associate the twentieth-century school of exiles from fascist Germany with the sublime idealism of Matthew Arnold's idea of culture. Yet, on second thought, if not in point of actual intellectual influence, the radical German exiles and the liberal English poet share at least one thing in common, and such a thing it is. Both were repulsed by the degradations of popular life because both viewed culture as, if not exactly perfection, at least the normal bearer of the sublime into the warp and woof of practical human life.

Though it could hardly be said that Arnold owed the same debt to the idealism of the German Enlightenment, his somewhat crotchety view of culture could hardly help but come back to the references from which critical theory, after a fashion, began. Thus Arnold, at the conclusion of his first, and best known, essay on culture's ideal value to humankind, concludes:

This is the *social ideal*; and the men of culture are the true apostles of equality. The great men of culture are those who have had a passion for diffusing, for making prevail, for carrying from one end of society to the other, the best knowledge, the best ideas of their time; who have laboured to divest knowledge of all that was harsh, uncouth, difficult, abstract, professional, exclusive; to humanize it, to make it efficient outside the clique of the cultivated and learned, yet still remaining the *best* knowledge and thought of the time, and a true source, therefore, of

---

[9] Max Horkheimer and Theodor Adorno, "The Culture Industry: Enlightenment as Mass Deception," *Dialectic of Enlightenment: Philosophical Fragments* (Stanford, CA: Stanford University Press, 2002), 94–95. The editor, Gunzelin Schmid Noerr, identifies the text translated by Edmund Jephcott as one found posthumously among Horkheimer's papers, signed by him, and dating to 1942.

sweetness and light. . . . Such were Lessing and Herder in Germany, at the end of the last [that is: the eighteenth] century; and their services to Germany were in this way inestimably precious. Generations will pass, and literary monuments will accumulate, and works far more perfect than the works of Lessing and Herder will be produced in German; and yet the names of these two men will fill a German with a reverence and enthusiasm such as the names of the most gifted master will hardly awaken. And why? Because they *humanized* knowledge. . . . (Matthew Arnold, *Culture and Anarchy*, 1: 62)

No discussion of the meaning of culture is possible without reference to Herder and thus to the romantic elements unique to German thought, which, for Herder, was a world apart from the Enlightenment of the eighteenth-century *philosophes*. In time – and most especially in the time of Adorno and Horkheimer – German idealism, quite necessarily, distinguished itself from the evil of National Socialism in the 1930s which drew its justification from the romance of mass culture behind fascist nationalism. As Fred Inglis explains, the romantic ideal that stood behind German nationalism was quite a different matter in the eighteenth century when Germany was a best a federation of lesser states than in the twentieth when a unified German nation was under the fascist heel of the Nazis.[10]

On the surface, it would appear to be more a contradiction than a dialectic to suggest a latter-day association of Arnold late in the nineteenth century and the German school of critical theory in the twentieth drawn down from roots in the eighteenth century in such apparently adversarial movements as Kant's idealism and Herder's romanticism. But, as Isaiah Berlin has shown in many writings, Herder's differences with Kant over the general values of enlightenment are too often over-stated. In this respect, even more important than his role in differentiating *Kultur* and *Zivilization*, was Herder's theory of cultures as the spirit of their times. Hence the fabulous complications of social thought in Germany in the Enlightenment era.

Though Herder was, apparently, influenced by Kant's earliest teachings, he soon parted ways, most especially over Kant's commitments, even and especially after the first critique in 1884, to a universal idea of human nature. Herder's opposition to the Enlightenment was most strongly directed at the unyielding rationalism of the French encyclopedists. In Germany in the eighteenth century, romanticism and idealism

[10] Fred Inglis, *Culture* (Cambridge, UK: Polity Press, 2004), 10–12. Inglis's first chapter, "Birth of a Concept," is in my view the single best account of the history of culture (the concept), trumping even Raymond Williams's *The Sociology of Culture* (Chicago: University of Chicago Press, 1981; reprint, 1995). See also Chris Jenks, *Culture* (London: Routledge, 1993), which does an excellent job of unraveling the literary and philosophical traditions behind the use of the term in social and cultural studies.

enjoyed a very much more complicated relationship than might seem likely from too far an historical remove. To be sure Herder and the romantics objected sternly to Kant's analytic sensibility, as Berlin puts it with such easy grace[11]:

The hard and fast distinctions between orders of experience, mental and corporeal faculties, reason and imagination, the world of sense and the worlds of understanding or of the ethic will or an *a priori* knowledge seemed to him so many artificial partitions, 'wooden walls' built by philosophers to which nothing corresponded in reality. His world is organic, dynamic, and unitary; every ingredient of it is at once unique, and interwoven with every other by an infinite variety of relationships which, in the end, cannot be analysed or even fully described. (Isaiah Berlin, *Vico and Herder*)

It may be stretching the differences (but not by much) to say that, in Herder's hands, the search for a practical ethic of universal consequence in the absence of pure reason was at best a clearing of the ground rather than an ordering of the world according to a synthetic *a priori*.

Herder, his objections to the French Enlightenment notwithstanding, was actually close in important ways to a contrarian amid the more rationalizing and universalizing French thinkers of the eighteenth century – to, that is, the idea Montesquieu developed separately in *The Spirit of Laws* (1752) that enlightenment (hence, cultures) varied according to their social conditions.[12]

One can see why in reality no nation after another, even with all the accoutrements of the latter, even became what the other was. Even if all the means of their cultures were the same, their culture was never the same because always all the influences of the old, now-changed nature needed for that were already missing. Greek sciences which the Romans drew to themselves became Roman; Aristotle became an Arab and a scholastic; and in the case of the Greeks and Romans of modern times – what a miserable affair! Marsilius, thou art Plato? Lipsius, thou Zeno? Where art thou Stoics? Thy heroes who formerly did so much? All you all modern Homers, orators, and artists – where is your world of miracles? . . . Also, into no land has civilization [*Bildung*] been able to take a step back so as to become a second time what it was – the path of fate is iron and strict. (Herder, *This Too a Philosophy of History for the Formation of Humanity* (1774))

From Herder thus came the disambiguation of civilization as a universalizing form into cultures – plural. This distinction, in turn, stood behind Norbert Elias's massive historical study of the specific civilizing process that arose from courtly manners to become the cultural process behind

---

[11] Isaiah Berlin, *Vico and Herder* (London: Hogarth Press, 1976).
[12] The extract following is from Herder, *Philosophical Writings* (Cambridge, UK: Cambridge University Press, 2002), 339–340. Marsilio Ficino was a fifteenth-century Florentine Platonist, while Lipsius was a sixteenth-century Dutch neo-Stoic.

monarchical absolutism which – after the symbolic (if no longer agreed-upon) date of the peace of Westphalia in 1648 – was transposed into the differentiation cultures of the several nation-states constrained within the plural interstate system.[13]

Even more to the point of the history of social scientific theories of culture is the rhizomatic homology linking Kant's idealism rooted in practical as distinct from pure reason, and Herder's idea of cultures as historically various. By many and different cultural tendrils, the unsettled correspondence between Kant and Herder came together in the single most important founding principle of culture studies: *Geisteswissenschaft* – cultural science as inherently different from natural science, in method as in substance. Though usually (but not wrongly) understood as a method founded in idealist principles, *Geisteswissenschaft* embraces the same dialectic of enlightenment found in the unstable relation of Herder to Kant, and elegantly described, two centuries later, by Horkheimer and Adorno. Dilthey, for unavoidable example, just after referring favorably to Herder, says:

We deduce the general principle that, in the system of interactions of the great events of the world, the conditions of pressure and tension and the feeling of insufficiency of the existing state of affairs – that is negative emotions of rejection – form the basis for the action which is sustained by positive valuations, desirable goals and ends. The great changes of the world originate in the cooperation of these two. The real agents of the system of interactions are the mental states which can be formulated in terms of value, good and purpose; among these states are not only the tendencies towards cultural goods but also the will to power, culminating in the inclination to subjugate others, must be considered as active forces. (Wilhelm Dilthey, *Patterns and Meaning in History* (1910)[14])

Though the text clearly comes down on the side of universals, as much in the fashion of Hegel as of Kant, one can plainly see the other side of the methodological dialectic, most especially in the allusion to Nietzsche, whose distinction between the romantic Dionysian and the rational Apollonarian remains, as for Weber, the classic literary expression of the tensions internal to the ideal of culture and its sciences. Herder's organic theory of cultural meaning, in turn, stood behind Nietzsche, whom Dilthey and Weber tamed, after Kant. Hence, Weber's methodology of subjective meanings is the first more or less explicit program for

---

[13] Norbert Elias, *State Formation and Civilization* (Oxford, UK: Blackwell, 1935; translated by Edmund Jephcott, 1982). See especially, Part Two (Vol. II), "Toward a Theory of Civilizing Processes."

[14] Wilhelm Dilthey, *Patterns and Meaning in History* (New York: Harper Torchbooks, 1962), 145.

a social science as a science of cultural meanings.[15] Thus it happened that the methodological line drawn between natural and cultural science, while based on a search for objectivity of a different kind, was made possible, if not necessary, by Herder's organic theory of meanings as multiple according to the varieties of cultures.

Returning now to the original riddle associated with Marx by way of Horkheimer and Adorno, one can see, behind all the historical digressions and abstractions, the critique of mass culture required three conditions – each acute to an attack on the crass materialism of radio and cinema in the 1940s. The twentieth-century critiques of mass culture derived, thus, from three elements already uniquely evident in eighteenth-century German cultural science, namely: (1) that culture is the highest embodiment of human values, (2) that human values may vary according to time and place, (3) that their political expression in unbridled nationalism destroys the dialectic on which enlightenment depends. Hence, in *Dialectic of Enlightenment* the famous "Culture Industry" essay is preceded by three essays on enlightenment all of which turn precisely on the figure of Homer, whose passing Herder so lamented.[16]

The *Odyssey* as a whole bears witness to the dialectic of enlightenment. In its oldest stratum, especially, the epic shows clear links to myth: the adventures are drawn from popular tradition. But as the Homeric spirit takes over and "organizes" the myths, it comes into contradiction with them. The familiar equation of epic and myth, which in any cases has been undermined by recent classical philology, proves wholly misleading when subject to philosophical critique. The two concepts diverge. They mark two phases of an historical process, which are still visible at the joints where the editors have stitched the epic together. The Homeric discourse creates a universality of language, if it does not already presuppose it; it disintegrates the hierarchical order of society through the exoteric form of its depiction, even and especially when it glorifies that order. The celebration of Achilles and the wanderings of Odysseus is already a nostalgic stylization of what can no longer be celebrated; and the hero of the adventures turns out to be the prototype of the bourgeois individual, whose concept originates in the unwavering self-assertion of which the protagonist driven to wander the earth is the primeval model. (Horkheimer and Adorno, *Dialectic of Enlightenment* (1944), 35)

The shattering brilliance of the comment sets the culture controversy in a new light. Culture as it came to be understood in the twentieth century derived, over the centuries, from the tensions intrinsic to classical civilizations – those containing the fusion of popular idealizations in the

---

[15] Raymond Williams's brief discussion of this development is particularly apt: *Sociology of Culture*, 15–16.
[16] Extract following is from *Dialectic of Enlightenment*, "Excursus I: Odysseus or Myth and Enlightenment," 34.

form of romantic myths and the universalizing culture of the epic form. This precisely is the dialectic that stands behind the very idea of culture as we now use it and, more poignantly, this is the reason the term is impossible to define.

Cultural meanings resist definitional constraints because at one and the same moment they disturb both the romance of the individual and the organizing principle of the universal. It could even be that this is one of the reasons why, in today's globalizing environment, so much doubt is cast on the autonomy of the nation-state. The effects of global processes – both economic and cultural; material and ideal – reconfigure the individual's access to meaning apart from the universalizing impulse of national cultures. When doubt is cast on the political idealism of a national culture, the individual is thrown into a sea of global differences on which each successive wave varies from the next, leaving the whole in search of safe interpretive harbors that never existed to begin with. Neither Herder and Kant in the eighteenth century, nor Marx and Arnold in the nineteenth, nor Hitler and Weber's Adorno in the twentieth were cut from the same cultural cloth. Yet, at the same time, it would be insane not to say that, differences being granted, they were not all discontented by the dialectic that Horkheimer and Adorno defined so clearly as having been unsettled from the foundations of civilizational time, with Homer and the other unstable fusions of the popular and the universal – the epics of Gilgamesh, Abraham, Israel, Jesus, Mohammed, and all the others.

It becomes clear, now, why definitions of *culture* fall flat upon the same cultural realities that so often cause an over-determined idea of social science to fall just as flat on its face. Whatever else a science of the social may do, it must at the least take account of, if not mimic exactly, Max Weber's idea of cultural science (which was not, it may be remembered, meant to exclude the sciences proper):

Thus for a science which is concerned with the subjective meaning of action, explanation requires a grasp of the complex of meaning in which an actual course of understandable action thus interpreted belongs. In all such cases, even where the processes are largely affectual, the subjective meaning of the action, including that also of the relevant meaning complexes, will be called the intended meaning. (This involves a departure from ordinary usage, which speaks of intention in this sense only in the case of rationally purposive action.) (Max Weber, *Economy and Society* (1913?)[17])

---

[17] Max Weber, "Basic Sociological Concepts," *Economy and Society, I* (Berkeley, CA: University of California Press, 1978), 9. The version of the text, translated by H. P. Secher, is of a revision of a 1913 essay found among the papers in *Wirtschaft und Gesellschaft* after Weber's death.

While it is far from evident that Weber, writing early in the twentieth century, cleared the ground for either cultural sociology or culture studies, he did fence off the two boundaries necessary for such an interpretative exercise: (1) that a science of cultural things must account for the cultural meaning of social things as distinct from natural ones; (2) that by one means or another culture may be studied only to the degree that it provides, as Clifford Geertz suggests,[18] a second-order interpretation of the first-order meanings the interpretation of which are, themselves, the practice of culture. From which, the transformative logic of cultures is that *the study of culture is a semiological interpretation of a primary semiotic performance.*

Such a view, admittedly hard for some to swallow, demands precisely what Weber could not accept – a relinquishment of the ideal of analytic definitions, hence also of formal protocols of operational research into the objective standing of social facts. Analysis does not so much disappear as recede into the cultural system of significations to which it refers and from which it arose to begin with. Horkheimer and Adorno reminded, in their post-analytic analysis of the dialectic, that the abandonment of the analytic does not mean than an analytic culture will abandon us. This precisely is at the root of their disgust at the degradations of mass culture – degradations that, in an earlier form were perfected by the Nazis from whom they fled.

Hence the irony of *culture*, the subject of study, is betrayed by the history of the term. Culture, whatever else it may be, is at least the proper subject of reflection and study for those who recognize the importance of understanding the central riddle of social studies in general, including the practical social studies of all who need to know why their lives are as they are. Yet, whether the riddle is taken as a question of social science or of the practical art of human self-understanding, the solution, if any, is available only in the paradox that one must turn back the clock of human time, returning to the far past to consider the near present. Which in turn, entails the methodological riddle that one cannot ever turn back to the far past without culturing a certain quality of mind in which might grow the imagination necessary to go back to come home.

This imaginative exercise upon which depends all social thinking, professional or practical, is never so well done than when it is done by the broad-minded social anthropologist. Whereas a sociologist is often captivated by the appearance of the present evidence of social realities, the anthropologist must face the past for what it is. Anyone, for that matter, who presumes, for whatever purpose, to visit from the present a

---

[18] Clifford Geertz, *The Interpretation of Cultures* (New York: Basic Books, 1973), 17–23.

purportedly primitive or traditional society in a past enduring to the present must question whether her presence on the ground of an active society allows her to see the human as such. Nikes on natives is common today. And if Nike pervades the times of all living peoples, however one might characterize the stage of their societal development, then in some aspect an intended consequence of global capitalism is to make us all primitives – this by virtue of erasing the practical differences among people. There is to be sure a material difference between life in the aboriginal Australian outback or the far Congo rainforest, but the material differences are made acute by the infusion of similarities of cultural desires. America is despised the world over not so much because of its economic imperialism as for its cultural intrusions. However those Nikes got on the feet of young men at war in the Sudan or Rwanda, even if they were unloaded second-hand from some well-intended relief agency, they are worn with meaningful understanding of all they signify – one of the many signs of first world cultural status manufactured by colored labor in the third and fourth worlds.

Thus, the irony thickens. Cultural time, under the pressures of global differences, turns the differences between past and present into a lark. Not only is the classical European distinction between cultural and material factors thrown into question, but so too that between the past and present. This might well be the social anthropological attitude come home to roost as the curve of modernization turns back upon itself. It was certainly the attitude Claude Lévi-Strauss conveyed on January 5, 1960 as he took his chair in social anthropology at the Collège de France:

This science [social anthropology] is too susceptible to those forms of thought which, when we encounter them among ourselves, we call superstition, for me not to be allowed to render to superstition an initial homage. Is it not the character of myths, which have such an important place in our research, to evoke a suppressed past and to apply it, like a grid, upon the present in the hope of discovering a sense in which the two aspects of his own reality man is confronted with – the historic and the structural – coincide? (Lévi-Strauss, *The Scope of Anthropology* (1960)[19])

Some on the more sociological side of things will surely quibble that Lévi-Strauss is referring here to myth, not culture as such. And therein lies the deep structural riddle of the meaning of culture: Is myth a *desideratum* of culture or the thing itself? Or, if not the thing itself, can it be said that myth is the central feature of culture? Or, more generally (and following Lévi-Strauss's argument in the pages following the lines quoted), is not

[19] Claude Lévi-Strauss, *The Scope of Anthropology* (London: Jonathan Cape, 1968), 7.

culture itself a semiotics, a system of significations, in and of itself? I distort perhaps; but no more than does Geertz.

The argument Lévi-Strauss took from Saussure was that social anthropology, like linguistics, could just as well be a semiology, a science of sorts of the system of signs by which meanings are distributed for production and consumption. But, the issue is better put as a first-order question: Is culture itself a semiotics? – which is to wonder whether there can be a science of communicable meanings if the system itself – culture, that is – is not itself constituted in first place as a system of meanings – which, in turn, leads back to the point Lévi-Strauss was making.

In a few lines of such poetic beauty as to rival the best writing in *Tristes tropiques* in 1955, Clifford Geertz in 1973 provided what remains one of the more explicitly succinct definitions of culture as a semiotic of meanings and one that cannot help but to bring Lévi-Strauss himself to mind:

Culture, this acted document, thus is public, like a burlesqued wink or a mock sheep raid. Though ideational, it does not exist in someone's head; though unphysical, it is not an occult entity. The interminable, because unterminable, debate within anthropology as to whether culture is "subjective" or "objective," together with the mutual exchange of intellectual insults ("idealist!" – "materialist!"; "mentalist!" – "behaviorist!"; "impressionist!" – "positivist!") which accompanies it, is wholly misconceived. Once human behavior is seen as (most of the time; there are *true* twitches) symbolic action – action which, like phonation in speech, pigment in painting, line in writing, or sonance is music, signifies – the question as to whether culture is patterned conduct or a frame of mind, or even the two somehow mixed together loses sense. The thing to ask about a burlesqued wink or a mock sheep raid is not what their ontological status is. It is the same as that of the rocks on the one hand and dreams on the other – they are things of this world. The thing to ask is what their import is: what it is, ridicule or challenge, irony or anger, snobbery or pride, that, in their occurrence and through their agency, is getting said. (Clifford Geertz, *The Interpretation of Cultures* (1973)[20])

Burlesqued winks and mock sheep raids? To what is Geertz referring? Nothing less than Geertz's most justifiably famous idea – that of *thick description* as the method of cultural study.

The locution, *thick description*, is used so commonly as to have lost its original meaning. This we know because many who use it take it to mean something like "close and thorough empirical research of all the facts." This, admittedly, is more an American error – blighted as we are with the necessity of generating programs of science that might issue in

[20] Clifford Geertz, "Thick Description: Toward an Interpretive Theory of Culture," *Interpretation of Cultures*, 10.

operational concepts yielding grounded explanations. But this is not what Geertz meant.

Geertz borrowed *thick description* from the Oxford philosopher Gilbert Ryle from whom came the burlesqued wink. From the outside, said Ryle, a wink does not reveal its meaning. It could be a meaningless twitch or a meaning-filled gesture – a burlesque upon the events passing before those gathered about. And, Geertz adds, the distinction here opens to other questions. Is the wink, if meaningful, a gesture according to a local code opaque to the outsider? Does it convey a particular message about the situation? Or might it be a convention of some sort not particularly tied to the context but only to ones like it? And so on. These of course are the questions asked by anyone who would study the cultures of people in respect to whom they cannot pretend to be native members. The sheep raid figure is, thus, an example by extension upon Ryle – that of a Jewish trader who was taken to be a Berber by the colonial French army who lost his sheep, but spared his life, because a joke was taken for serious by those unable or uninterested in doing a thick description of the events unfolding on a North African plain.

Thick description entails, in effect, a decoding of the meanings of human conduct occurring in public where actions of all kinds are susceptible to being mistaken and where, thereby, the meaning can make all the difference in the world at hand. In culture-filled public situations meanings are decided *not* by a hermeneutic of the actor's intention (or, even, by a probe to the inner meaning of the structured system), but by a reading of the cultural code at play in the situation. Though "reading" has been surcharged with jargon in recent years, there is a difference between a reading and a hermeneutic. Strictly speaking, *hermeneutics* probe for secreted intentions behind the scene; while *readings* take the surfaces of social things for what they are to decode their differential relations to the multiple but finite possibilities the culture allows; hence, Lévi-Strauss's idea that the study of culture is a transformational semiology. When faced with a wink, the question is not *What do these people mean when they do that?* Rather, it is *When they do* that, *which of the possible meanings are they signifying?* The difference between the questions is small, infinitesimally small perhaps, but it *is* a difference.

The thickness of the description must refer thereby not to operational concepts, strong protocols directing the science, the number of valid data and reliable interpretations of them. The thickness lies in the getting down to the small differences the wink could be among those it is not – down to, that is, the fine line in the gesture that reveals the cultural code as it pertains to concrete events. In other words, thick description is less about the mass of data than the fineness of the clue. Geertz has called the method "microscopic" which is to say: "Small facts speak to large issues, winks to epistemology, or sheep raids to revolution, because they are made to."[21]

The wink is neither a weed masking a true intention nor a seed of pure cultural understanding. It is merely (if that is the word) a flower in the garden of meanings, for which the seed was sown sufficiently long ago as to have grown up amid weeds without losing its bloom. Not even the anthropologist can know that there was in fact an original sower of the seeds, or for that matter a Manichean rival who sows the evil weeds. All that matters is that the events occur in public, which is to say: that they are meaningful in the sense that they signify something to those about. This is culture – and the challenge for its interpreter is reading the code by which the meanings are signified, an interpretative act that is thick, not by virtue of the mass of its detail, but by the specific gravity of its readings.

Call it what you will, culture by any other name is that social thing which cultivates the conditions for participation in some local social whole, no matter what its size or prominence in the flux and reversals of historical time. Culture cultivates the microscopic details of the social. How can it be otherwise? Social things are lived in the mini-spaces of the social whole the naked eye cannot see. Meanings are not general, but concrete. Signs are not neon displays over the squares of time in all the big cities, but the slightest gestures that signify the small difference in the possible meanings, many but limited.

Call culture a language if you want, call it system of signs (hence a primary semiotics), call it a means for producing myths in a people, call it a system of meanings – the meaning of culture, the thing as distinct from the word, is that social things mean; which, in turn, is to say that social things are signifying things, made for communication against all the odds.

[21] Geertz, "Thick Description," 23. For "microscopic" see 21.

3

Paris 1907 and why the sociological imagination is always unstable

The city of lights is, actually, a city of monuments upon which the lights shine. On a July evening when the sun sets late, the dusk lingers almost to midnight. For a time before the sun's final setting in the northern sky, the city lights brighten. In this weird and wonderful confusion of lights, the eye is drawn lazily down boulevards and along the Seine to cathedrals, bridges, towers, statuary, and all the relics that, for the stranger, make Paris unforgettable. The interior quarters on either side of the river compose, in effect, a monument of monuments, which is actually an illusion, a phantasmagoria of parts and pieces that belong to no reality in particular.

In 1902, when Durkheim returned to the city of his student days, Paris must have seemed just this way – real and familiar, as Paris is to French intellectuals; but also strange and different. He was, after all, a man for whom the memorable past was an object of discriminating fascination – his own lost past in the rural Jewish community of childhood; but also the past of ancient civilizations and cultures that served as goad and foil for the sociology of modern society he was inventing. In fact, Durkheim's sociological doctrine was, in its way, a light shed on the monument of a passing moral order. This is one of the reasons that, after the formative years in Bordeaux, Durkheim's return to Paris was a triumph of sorts. He was already famous beyond the circles of academic labor. He would soon become, if not the talk of the town, one of Paris's most controversial and influential figures. Apart from the quality of his scholarship, Durkheim's leading idea was morally imposing. It fed the longing in early twentieth-century France for some moral light to guide it through the dangerous back alleys of political conflict grown acute on a full century of social uncertainty and struggle. Anyone who has walked the back streets of Paris into the early morning hours just after the prostitutes retreat, making away for the butchers and fruit merchants breaking for early coffee knows the experience. The city lights tenderly outline the penumbra under which social changes lurk, testing the possibilities.

In this, Paris was like no other global city in the West. A century after Durkheim's return, this Paris was all but gone – only the monuments remain. Even in the postmodern quarter-moon, Paris remains a sociologically interesting memorial to the worlds modernity tried to go beyond. This is a fact of embarrassing proportions in that Paris itself, with its illustrious classical air, is one of the newest of all global capitals. Its grand boulevards were laid rather late in the nineteenth century over the cobbled layers settling one upon the other back through the remnants of medieval glory to Roman times and before.

For Durkheim, whatever aesthetic pleasures he may have taken from the city of lights, Paris's modern history must have seared the memory of events occurring in his youth – events that were themselves caught up in the transformations that made the city the phantasmagoria it is. The Paris Commune of March–May 1871 is known to have affected Durkheim. He was a boy at the time, still in Epinal. It would be another four years before he would come to Paris to prepare for the Ecole Normale Supérieure. Still, Durkheim and his generation had, if not exactly personal and direct experience of the rebellion and slaughter of the spring of 1871, at least a collective memory of the events no one in France could easily avoid. Today still, French people of a certain age will speak of the "events of May '68" which, in turn, were absorbed into the monumental history of the events of 1789 that repeated themselves farcically in 1848 and 1871. When, as an adult, Durkheim devoted himself to a science that might overcome social conflict, the collective memory of the slaughter of many thousands of innocent communards by the forces of bourgeois restoration was surely in mind. Even if 1871 in Paris may have been somewhat distant, what was not was the Franco-Prussian War of 1870–71 during which the Prussian army overran and annexed Durkheim's native Alsace.

Durkheim was brought up on civil strife and social violence. So was modern Paris, which under the reign of Napoleon III, was made over into the city of lights by modernity's first notable city planner, Baron Haussmann. He designed the Bois de Boulogne and the Luxembourg Gardens which were cut back to make way for his boulevards. Most notably, at the instigation of his patron, Haussmann designed the Arc de Triomphe at the Place de l'Etoile from which radiate twelve grand avenues, most importantly the Champs Elysées and the Avenue of the Grand Army. The aesthetic effect on latter generations is telling, but the original motivation was significantly to protect the Empire against urban rebellion by eliminating the small streets where revolutionaries could throw up barricades in favor of wide open boulevards through which suppressing armies could move with alacrity. Haussmann began these public works projects in the decade before 1871. Obviously that spring they failed for a while, before succeeding in May when the national guard of the Versailles government crushed the communards.

No one has written a more probing sociology of this period in Paris than Walter Benjamin, whose posthumous *Arcades Project* (*Das Passagen-Werk*), in all its sprawling aphoristic genius, captures precisely the reason, in his phrase, Paris was the Capital of the Nineteenth Century. The phrase is ironic. Paris was the emblematic head of high modernity in Europe, not because of its culture, certainly not for its industry, nor even for its lights. It was because, in Benjamin's analysis, it embodied the contradictions of modernity – or, in the words of his close friend Theodor Adorno, the dialectic of enlightenment in which the deeper structural struggle interior to modern culture between the particular and the universal took architectural shape. For Benjamin, the ironwork interior commercial passageways in Paris, constructed in 1822 and after, were the expression of the contradiction between modernity's aesthetic of productive power and its commercial force. As the ironwork was the foundation for modern urban architecture, a form aspiring to universal significance, so the small commercial establishments in the arcades were the local articulations of the commercial exchanges that lent specific gravity to the coming capitalist era.

In Benjamin's words, the cultural dialectic would find expression, on the one side, in Haussmann's remaking of the city – "Napoleonic imperialism, which favors investment capital" – and Charles Baudelaire's *flâneur* – in whom "the intelligentsia becomes acquainted with the marketplace." Between the grand boulevard and the arcade, culture becomes, not just a commodity, but a productive force – of which the principal yield is the phantasmagoria of modern culture itself:

Our investigation proposes to show how, as a consequence of this reifying representation of civilization, the new forms of behavior and the new economically and the new technologically based creations that we owe to the nineteenth century enter the universe of a phantasmagoria. These creations undergo this "illumination" not only in a theoretical manner, by an ideological transposition, but also in the immediacy of their perceptible presence. They are manifest as phantasmagorias. Thus appear the arcades – first entry in the field of iron construction; thus appear the world exhibitions, whose link to the entertainment industry is significant. Also included in this order of phenomena is the experience of the flâneur, who abandons himself to the phantasmagorias of the market place. Corresponding to these phantasmagorias of the market, where people appear only as types, are the phantasmagorias of the interior, which are constituted by man's imperious need to leave the imprint of his private individual existence on the rooms he inhabits. As for the phantasmagoria of civilization itself, it found its champion in Haussmann and its manifest expressions in the transformations of Paris. (Benjamin, *Exposé of 1939, Arcades Project*, 14–15)

Phantasmagoria are ghostly images arising from distorting light. Originally they referred to optical illusions deployed for public entertainment; in time, they described the clash of illusions, the reversal of the reality and the fantastic. They became in other words a figure describing vastly more strange and complicated versions of Marx's *camera obscura*. In the phantasmagoria, the imagination is a delirium fed by the false light of external culture.

This, it happens, is precisely the term Durkheim uses in *Suicide* to describe the risks moderns face in a world where economic progress and social conflict produce the Janus-faced effect of too much ego, too little social order. The phantasmagoria is exactly what Durkheim believed beset the individual when urban society failed to control the passions:

Social man necessarily presupposes a society which he expresses and serves. If this dissolves, if we no longer feel it in existence and action about and above us, whatever is social in us is deprived of all objective foundation. All that remains is an artificial combination of illusory images, a phantasmagoria vanishing at the least reflection; that is, nothing can be a goal for our action. (Durkheim, *Suicide* (1897), 213)

For Durkheim, as for Benjamin, the city of lights was the modern city of ghostly illusions.

Benjamin died by his own hand in the Second World War, in part because he could not imagine a way out of the phantasmagoria accentuated by the Nazis. Durkheim died during the First World War, in part because his faith in the focal light of social knowledge seems to have been shattered. Durkheim did not himself commit suicide, but his study of the core pathology of the modern world – for which Paris had to have been at least an emblem if not a microcosm – made of suicide the essential outcome of the anomic condition in which one finds oneself when the lights are too phantasmagoric:

Ultimately, this liberation of desires has been made worse by the very development of industry and the almost infinite extension of the market. So long as the producer could gain his profits only in his immediate neighborhood, the restricted amount of possible gain could not much overexcite ambition. Now that he may assume to have almost the entire world as his customer, how could passions accept their former confinement in the face of such limitless prospects? . . . Such is the source of the excitement predominating in this part of the society, and which has thence extended to the other parts. There the state of crisis and anomy is constant and, so to speak, normal. From top to bottom of the ladder, greed is aroused without knowing where to find ultimate foothold. Nothing can calm it, since its goal is far beyond all it can attain. Reality seems valueless by comparison with the dreams of fevered imaginations; reality is therefore abandoned, but so too is possibility abandoned when it in turn becomes reality. A thirst arises for novelties, unfamiliar pleasures, nameless sensations, all of which lose their savor once known. Henceforth one has no strength to endure the least reverse. (Durkheim, *Suicide*, 255–256)

In the *Arcades Project* Walter Benjamin did not, so far as I can see, take Durkheim into account. But he might as well have for, on the point of despair unto death, they both understood that, one way or another, Paris and all the other modern cities illuminated by an inflamed capitalist spirit, were, if not unreal, at least irreal – a fevered illusion. Benjamin took his life alone in a small village in the Pyrennees in September 1940. He saw no other way. Among his last words was a note conveying a final greeting to Adorno who had become one of his most intimate correspondents and who understood, as his writings with Horkheimer of a few years later would make clear, that modern culture – whether in the city of lights or Nazi furnaces – reached for an illusion that smoldered in its own setting sun.

Paris, 1907, was a year, well before the worst was to come to light, when the contradictions of that culture would become evident if not clear. That was the year when Picasso, having broken through the blue period, presented *Les Demoiselles d'Avignon*, which led to cubism and, in turn, the revolution in twentieth-century art. In the confusion of differences between radical modernism and postmodernism, it is almost impossible to locate a work like *Demoiselles d'Avignon*. What is known is that in the years leading up to it, Picasso had been under the influence of his friend, the poet, Apollinaire, who – with Alfred Jarry, the dramatist of the absurd (also an influence on Picasso) – effected a comparable revolution in the literary world.

Picasso's *Demoiselles d'Avignon* broke the mold of modern art by adding a dimension to the play of color on canvas where light meets the eye. *Demoiselles* was not phantasmagoric as *Guernica* would be, but it did break the visual world into its incongruent parts. The forms of women's bodies are naked to the sensual eye, but they are set against each other in what, to the realist, would be ironic, even laughable relations. Picasso's young women of Avignon were thus a turning point toward the unveiling of the necessary contradictions of modern culture.

In 1907, both Picasso and Durkheim walked the streets of Paris. It seems improbable that they knew each other. Picasso was young and bohemian. Durkheim was older, at the height of his adult and quite bourgeois powers. Still, it is entirely possible that they could have crossed paths in the morning hours, as Picasso made his way across town, from a night of drink and conversation in Montparnasse back to his studio in Montmartre as Durkheim made his way to the Sorbonne. They surely lived at different ends of the clock, as of the social register. Yet, both experienced Paris at an unusual time in the history of an unusual city.

Durkheim's *Elementary Forms* would come five years after Picasso's *Demoiselles*. All things being equal, both works served a similar effect – to set the elements of the world in their improper, but honest relations. And these two were far from alone. In 1910, just between the two works, Stravinsky's *Firebird* would debut to astonished acclaim in Paris. Two years before *Demoiselles*, in 1905, in Switzerland, an obscure twenty-six-year-old patent clerk, Albert Einstein, published a series of technical papers that revolutionized modern thinking about the physical universe, including most famously the special theory of relativity – a confluence of achievements so rare that, a century later, *Scientific American* (September, 2004) said of Einstein in 1905:

Besides special and general relativity, his work helped to launch quantum mechanics and modern statistical mechanics. Chemistry and biotechnology owe a debt to studies by Einstein that supplied evidence of the existence of molecules and the ways they behave. . . . What is even more amazing is that he purveyed many of these insights through a series of papers that appeared during a single miraculous year, 1905. No other comparable fertile period for individual scientific accomplishment can be found except during 1665 and 1666, the original *annus mirabilis*, when Isaac Newton, confined to his country home to escape the plague, started to lay the basis for the calculus, his law of gravitation and his theory of colors.

It would not be far-fetched to say, *mutatis mutandis*, that what 1905 was to science, 1907 was to culture. Though Picasso's achievement was the more widely known, also in 1907, in Geneva, Ferdinand de Saussure gave the first of the lectures that would lead in time to a revolution in the social theory of the arbitrariness of social relations, the *Course in General Linguistics*. Quite apart from what was developing in Durkheim's thinking in Paris, 1907, the works of Picasso and Saussure led, in time, to the intrusion of non-linear principles in cultural theory.

Paris, 1907, is of course an arbitrary, but one that stands for the unsettlements of modern culture. That year, when Picasso was still young and unknown, and Durkheim was older and famous already, both, along with others in very different places, were refiguring the world others saw as settled on orderly progress. For them the worlds were far less stable than the prevailing bourgeois dogma hoped. The Great War would turn social things toward the worst possible outcome, a worst that in 1907 would be more easily imagined from within the phantasmagoria that Picasso and Durkheim both understood, some-how, perhaps intuitively.

If, then, the world they saw is still the phantasm of lights and illu-sions Picasso conjured up in their different ways, then the lesson for all sociologies is, perhaps: Be not afraid! Be not afraid of relativism, for everything is in the relations that cannot be settled in real space with clean lines. The world of social things is, as Durkheim proclaimed in 1912, the world wherein whatever light we have along the way is lit in the light of social experience. If he was right, then ultimately it must be that the categorical light of social thought is, in the end, unstable. It may not quite go out entirely, but it changes as does the light in the dawn in Paris. As in the July evening, the artificial lights draw the eye to the monuments against the fading northern sun, so in the dawn the rising sun dampens the illusion of streets alive. Only the social beings sleep. The natural ones do not. Sleep is for those whose days come and go as do their lives.

Social theory and the relativistic paradigm (1974)*

> I can still remember that as a child my mother could not get me away from the puppet-shows in the Luxembourg Gardens. I could have stayed there spellbound for days on end. I didn't laugh, though. The spectacle of the guignol held me there, stupefied by the sight of these puppets who spoke, who moved, who bludgeoned each other. It was the spectacle of life itself which, strange, improbable, but truer than truth itself, was being presented to me in an infinitely simplified and caricatured form, as though to underline the grotesque and brutal truth.
>
> Eugene Ionesco[1]

There is a way of thinking about reality that is unique to the modern world – one than endured to the late-modern, even the postmodern. Its uniqueness lies in the broad consensus among scientists, thinkers, and artists with respect to natural and human reality – an understanding that, contrary to narrow-minded views of either modernity or of certain of its cultural achievements (like academic sociology), is more in tune with

---

* The essay was originally published as "Sociological Theory and the Relativistic Paradigm," *Sociological Inquiry* 44 (1974), 2: 93–104. It has been cut for context and the elimination of references of scant current interest. I have eliminated several sections referring to religious thinking because, having lost contact with religious studies in the last years, I can no longer vouch for the claims. Likewise a longish section on what was once called "sociological theory" is deleted because the themes are taken up elsewhere in this collection. Here and there additions are entered either to link the edited material or otherwise improve the sense of the essay for present purposes. For those who might wish their texts pure, there are always markers of one or another kind signaling the presence of an updating of some kind. A note at the head of the original text indicates that an earlier version was apparently presented at the 1973 meetings of the American Sociological Association. I have no recollection of those meetings to the extent of being a little surprised that, in 1973 even, such a thing would find a place on the program. It is possible that the use of the expression "paradigm" in a day when Thomas Kuhn was the rage lent the essay an aura of acceptability. I keep that term, even though one can now go for months without hearing a reference to Kuhn. In 1973, one could hardly get through breakfast without someone saying something about a paradigm of one or another kind. Also, for honesty's sake, I also keep the term "relativistic" which today I find callow and clumsy.
[1] Quoted in Richard Coe, *Eugene Ionesco* (New York: Grove Press, 1961), 16.

Ionesco's childhood experience of social life as a strange, improbable, truer than truth spectacle. . . .

Described most generally, the perspective is one that views all reality – natural and human alike – as, if not excactly relative, caught for better or worse in a web of relations without which it would make no sense. Conversely, this is a view – which, now in the twenty-first century, I persist in calling "the relativistic paradigm" if only to irritate those who consider relativism as at least a scientific, if not also a moral failure – is marked by a deeply held hostility to traditional epistemological objectivism.[2] The type of thinking to which I am referring can be seen in the many intellectual and artistic movements, avant-garde ideas, and cults that appeared early in the twentieth cenutry, about the time Durkheim and Weber were trying to settle academic sociology on solid ground. Among the examples of movements for which 1907 could serve as a kind of symbolic date of orientation would be: relativity theory (physics), expressionism and Cubism (art), Dadaism (art, poetry, drama, music), atonalism and experimentalism (music), complementarity and indeterminacy principles (physics), the apotheosis of the schizophrenic (psychology), surrealism (art, literature), absurdism (drama and literature), the apotheosis of the comic (art, literature, drama, religion). With the exception of the revolutions in art and micro-physics none of these can be said to constitute the dominant paradigm within their respective "disciplines."

At the same time, it can be said that each represents a well-defined sphere of legitimate endeavor in their respective "fields." And, more importantly, the commonalities among these movements are sufficiently clear so that they may be taken together as a single perspective. In this connection, we must note that the process of bureaucratic differentiation by which we are inclined to isolate these movements into distinct disciplines, departments, or professions is a result of the institutionalization of the same traditional rationality against which the new perspective has intentionally positioned itself. Pablo Picasso, Eugene Ionesco, John Cage, Werner Heisenberg and R. D. Laing can be located in distinct "fields" in only the most artificial and purely functional way. The substantive products of their work demand attention across traditional institutional barriers.

Moreover, the relativistic paradigm is not easily analyzed in a systematic fashion for the simple reason that fundamental to the paradigm is the conviction that reality itself is not self-evident and orderly as more traditional

---

[2] Among others, Karl Mannheim, who certainly was no fan of relativism, is among those who at least provide the tradition a degree of clear thinking on the question of relativism: Karl Mannheim, *Ideology and Utopia* (New York: Harvester, 1936), 55–108.

thinking has presumed it to be. Relativism, in each of its forms, is critical of traditional rationality. It stands against Newtonian theory, rationalisms of all kinds, uncritical realisms, strict tonalisms, objectivisms. Thus the relativistic paradgim is, if not dismissive, at least suspicious of rationally generated systematic explanation. To understand it we must attempt to view it from within traditional thought, realizing that we are likely to distort but that this is the only means we have to understand it. The terms by which the elemental features of the paradigm may be described could be taken from any of its several manifestations. I will take them from the thought-world of micro-physics because here they are concisely stated and empirically well-documented.

The three basic elements in the relativistic paradigm are: (1) *complementarity*, (2) *indeterminacy*, (3) *relativity*. These correspond precisely to the analytic phrases that appear in Ionesco's absurdism[3]: (1) "a world of infinite coincidence," (2) "the void at the center of things," (3) "the apotheosis of the platitude." Their corollaries appear in numerous other fields, of which the more striking is one of the more seemingly remote areas of human endeavor, particle physics; hence the elegance of the terms used for the three basic elements.

Complementarity in modern physics is, of course, the idea that electrons must be understood to have both the quality of waves and of particles. The result depends on the type of observation performed. This is an assertion based upon undeniable experimental evidence. It was first discovered to apply to light and, later, to matter. Complementarity was one of the several points at which micro-physics overthrew the rationalism of the closed, orderly, observable Newtonian world. We can no longer know reality in the classical way. Heisenberg said: "If two observational situations are in the relationship Bohr has called complementarity, then complete knowledge of one necessarily means incomplete knowledge of the other."[4]

This discovery in physics is equivalent to the more radical anti-logical absurdism in Ionesco. While absurdism is intentionally more radical, at least verbally, than anything in physics, its roots are the same. Ionesco's principal influence is from Stéphane Lupasco, the philosophical proponent of the principle of contradiction. Moreover, it seems that Ionesco's use of contradiction is directly related to quantum physics' doctrine of complementarity.

[3] The interpretations of Ionesco, including the reference to Stéphane Lupasco, are from Coe, *Eugene Ionesco*, 24–26.
[4] Werner Heisenberg, *Physics and Beyond* (New York: Harper and Row, 1971), 121.

Microphysics suggested that certain forms of energy shared simultaneously the contradictory properties of waves and particles; quantum physics gave it to be understood that the logically impossible could and did happen. The exact significance of these discoveries, whether to the scientist or to the professional logician, is irrelevant; what matters here is the impression that they left upon the consciousness of the intellectual or artist. And this impression was one of a major revolution striking at the very foundations of logical thought, and backed by those who hitherto had been the stoutest pillars of rationalism: the scientists.

Thus, for Ionesco – and absurdism in general – existence itself is merely given as pure fact. It has no inherent logic. It is absurd. Accordingly, artistic realism is seen as a form of classic rationalism and, from the absurdist point of view, is not only impossible but anathema. Human beings live in a world of infinite coincidence.

The artistic revolt against rationalism and its positive assertion of the principle of complementarity extends to art and music. In art, Picasso decisively left his classical period when he turned to Cubism, which may be understood as complementarity with respect to artistic space. The Cubist movement broke up space (to use Katherine Kuh's phrase) then rearranged the parts so that differing perspectives – such as the front and back of an object – are simultaneously juxtaposed. Antonina Vallentin has said: "Cubist painters claimed that they were conveying a new vision of reality – reality as it really was in the multiplicity of its aspects, not fixed and monolithic as it appeared to the human eye."[5] Cubism led naturally to the collage which was the classical artistic medium for expressing complementarity in the Dada, surrealistic and Pop art movements. Representational realism is replaced by a graphic portrayal of the contradictory complexity of a reality viewed as infinitely coincidental.

In music, the radical experimental musician John Cage employed complementarity in the sense that he rejected the classical form based upon rational relationships among ordered tones. Cage, instead, saw music in the juxtaposition of noise (or sound) and silence. In Cage's music (as in Bohr's complementarity and Ionesco's anti-logic) this juxtaposition of hitherto irreconcilable elements results in the undermining of the very heart of traditional "logical" epistemology, the subject–object dichotomy.

For, when, after convincing oneself ignorantly that sound has, as its clearly defined opposite, silence, that since duration is the only characteristic of sound that is measurable in terms of silence, therefore any valid structure involving sounds and silences should be based, not as occidentally traditional, on frequency, but rightly on duration, one enters an anechoic chamber as silent as technologically possible

---

[5] Antonina Vallentin, *Picasso* (Garden City: Doubleday, 1957), 113.

in 1951, to discover that one hears two sounds of one's own unintentional making (nerves' systematic operation, blood's circulation), the situation one is clearly in is not objective (sound-silence), but rather subjective (sounds only), those intended and those others (so called silence) not intended. If, at this point, one says, "Yet! I do not discriminate between intention and nonintention," the splits, subject-object, art-life, etc., disappear, an identification has been made with the material, and actions are then those relevant to its nature.[6]

From this Cage draws the rationally absurd conclusion: "A sound accomplishes nothing; without it life would not last out the instant."[7]

In theories of mind and the psyche (what once all too simply was called psychology), the principle of complementarity remains today, long after its heyday in the 1960s and 1970s, an interesting expression in the varieties of anti-psychiatry movements (which in the 2000s have gone underground in the varieities of new age therapeutic movements). But in its day, the idea that madness might be merely a medical category had an astonishing variety of forms in the work of David Cooper, Aaron Esterson, Gregory Bateson, Theodore Lidz, Thomas Szasz and, of course, R. D. Laing, who gave the movement its most dramatic and intentional expression. Laing attacked the rationalist distinctions between experience and behavior, the inner life and the outer world, psychiatrist and patient, sane and insane. Stated philosophically, but with the vocabulary that would appear in the 1970s and 1980s, Laing stood against the rational dichotomy between subject and object. Drawing heavily upon existentialist and phenomenological ideas, Laing juxtaposed being and non-being. Man "is enabling being to emerge from non-being."[8] Thus, the person's experience of relationship with another person juxtaposes the logically contradictory facts of the other's presence with his absence (negation).

In the 2000s such a line is hardly as surprising as it was thirty years ago, before the names Levinas, Lacan, Derrida, and Deleuze, among others, had come so remarkably to international attention. Thus it is striking just how well Laing's thinking endures:

All experience is both active and passive, the unity of the given and the construed; and the construction one places on what is given can be positive or negative: it is what one desires or fears or is prepared to accept, or it is not. The element of negation is in every relationship and every experience of relationship. The distinction between the absence of relationship and the experience of every relationship as an absence, is the division between loneliness and perpetual solitude, between provisional hope or hopelessness and a permanent despair. (R. D. Laing, *Politics of Experience* (1967: 37))

---

[6] John Cage, *Silence* (Middletown: Wesleyan University Press, 1939), 14.   [7] *Ibid.*, 14.
[8] R. D. Laing, *The Politics of Experience* (New York: Ballantine Books, 1967), 42.

Indeterminacy, the second element in the relativistic paradigm, may be seen as an (anti-)logical extension of the first. If complementarity reveals the anti-rational, absurd nature of reality, then indeterminacy specifies this fundamental assertion by describing – again, paradoxically – the content of the emptiness of reality which is there even though it cannot be there. Indeterminacy arises at the boundary between assumption and methodology. The assumption that reality is ultimately empty is the result of a positive method. Thus the distinction between method and assumption is obliterated. The result is not sheer nothingness, but a void that – in spite of its refusal to reveal itself – is the central feature of reality. The elliptical nature of these comments is clarified somewhat when one looks at the concrete applications of indeterminacy.

In physics, Heisenberg's indeterminacy followed from Bohr's complementarity.[9] Together these ideas were the core of quantum physics which may be summarized crudely as the conclusion that the micro-particles of which all matter is composed cannot be said to "exist" in any traditionally rational (Newtonian) static sense. Indeterminacy is based upon the method of observation. Its elemental fact is that the instrument of observation necessarily disturbs the observed particle. Thus, it cannot be known as such. P. W. Bridgman, the American physicist, has said:

[The physicist] has learned that the object of knowledge is not to be separated from the instrument of knowledge. We can no longer think of the object of knowledge as constituting a reality which is revealed to us by the instrument of knowledge, but the two together, object and instrument, constitute a whole so intimately knit that it is meaningless to talk of object and instrument separately.[10]

The implication is that the fundamental elements of nature are not really "there" in the traditional sense. They are indeterminate and can be known only as the scientist, in effect, creates them. Heisenberg has said:

The goal of scientific investigation is no longer a knowledge of atoms and their motions as such, independent of the formulation of our experimental investigations. Rather, we find ourselves, from the very beginning, involved in the give-and-take between nature and man, so that the customary division of the universe into subject and object – into internal and external world – leads us into difficulties.[11]

In absurdist drama, the spirit of indeterminacy is captured in Richard Coe's phrase "the void at the centre of things." Like Sartre in *No Exit* and Beckett in *Waiting for Godot*, Ionesco – throughout his drama – asserts the absurdity of life, typically framed in terms of its purest expression,

---

[9] Heisenberg, *Physics and Beyond*, 76–81.
[10] Arthur March and Ira Freeman, *The New World of Physics* (New York: Vintage, 1963), 161.
[11] *Ibid.*, 168.

death. "Death is the one constant theme which gives unity to Ionesco's theatre; sooner or later, the cadaveric quality of words are transmitted to the living organism, and there are few among his major plays with neither corpse nor killer."[12] As in physics, the indeterminate void at the center of reality must be seen in connection with the author's dramatic method. Thus, Ionesco's characters are "deliberately blurred in outline" and are "shifting and interchangeable."[13] More fundamentally we must note the absurdist's methodological attack on words. Antonin Artaud, the absurdist theorist, has said: "For I make it my principle that words do not mean everything and that by their nature and defining character, fixed once and for all, they arrest and paralyze thought instead of permitting it and fostering its development."[14]

However, also as in physics, this attack upon the rational method does not result in total emptiness. The void is there, but it leads to a something positive (although admittedly in an ambiguous sense). "Beneath the poetry of texts, there is the actual poetry, without form and without text."[15] The blurring of characters and the confusion of words that appear repeatedly in absurdist drama have the intended goal of confronting man with the absurd void, but also of pushing him through the void at least to the brink of the possibility of a reason beyond rationalism. In one brief passage, Ionesco goes even further, and suggests that the very ubiquity, the very omnipotence, of the absurd contains its own denial, and that "maybe there is a reason, over and above our reason, for existing. Everything is so absurd, that even that is possible."[16]

In art, the foregoing is replicated. Contradiction leads to void, but the void transcends pure nothingness. Dadaism – best known for its art but also a widely based movement expressing itself in music, poetry, and drama – is perhaps the most extreme expression of the void. Tristan Tzara, in his "Dada Manifesto of 1918," said: "DADA MEANS NOTHING. . . . If you find it futile and don't want to waste your time on a word that means nothing. . . ." Surrealism, the constructive corollary of Dadaism, is the clearest instance of this feature of the indeterminacy principle. For example:

Dali added collage to his painting, using pasted photo-engravings in order to accentuate the interplay of fact and fancy. By contrasting irrational content with unexpected realism, these artists made the impossible seem plausible . . . They virtually caused the unreal to appear "realer" than reality.[17]

---

[12] Coe, *Eugene Ionesco*, 70.   [13] *Ibid.*, 77.
[14] Antonin Artaud, *The Theatre and Its Double* (New York: Grove Press, 1958), 110.
[15] *Ibid.*, 78.   [16] Coe, *Eugene Ionesco*, 69.
[17] Katerine Kuh, *Break-Up: The Core of Modern Art* (New York: New York Graphic Society, 1965), 70.

With respect to music, John Cage's indeterminacy appears, again, in the central place he gives to *Silence* (the title of his best-known book). Cage's compositions are indeterminant. They are open-ended. The performers compose as they perform. The conductor basically provides the "raw materials" which are the range of possible sounds and the scheduled duration of silences.[18] The conductor merely keeps track of time (duration) for the performers. Thus, the restrictive rational organizing work of traditional composers and conductors is pushed to the background. The performers compose. They employ their sounds as methodological devices to make "meaningful" the void of silence. The performance is indeterminate. It is based upon silence. Yet it is creative. It requires participation.

This is a lecture on composition which is indeterminate with respect to its performance. That composition is necessarily experimental. An experimental action is one the outcome of which is not foreseen. Being unforeseen, the action is not concerned with its excuse. Like the land, like the air, it needs none. A performance of a composition which is indeterminate of its performance is necessarily unique. It cannot be repeated.[19]

Thus, with Cage as with Ionesco and the others, the "void at the center of things" is an absurdly positive construction deriving from the "infinite coincidence of all things."

In the theories of R. D. Laing, as noted, non-being and negation are at the center of being. This becomes for Laing the philosophical principle by which he redefines the normal. Normalcy is repressive. "What we call 'normal' is a product of repression, denial, splitting, projection, introjection and other forms of destructive action on experience. . . . It is radically estranged from the structure of being."[20] Accordingly, madness is seen as the personal method by which one may push through the absurdity of normalcy. The void is the non-being into which one descends in madness. Simultaneously, madness is the method through which one participates in the deeper reality.

Schizophrenia is "itself a natural way of healing our own appalling state of alienation called normality . . ." "Madness need not be all breakdown. . . . It may also be breakthrough. It is potentially liberation and renewal as well as enslavement and existential death." It is not an illness to be treated, but a "voyage." Socially, madness may be a form in which ". . . often though quite ordinary people, the light begins to break through cracks in our all too closed minds."[21]

---

[18] Cage, *Silence*, 36.   [19] *Ibid.*, 39.   [20] Laing, *The Politics of Experience*, 27.
[21] Robert Boyers and Robert Orrill, eds., *R. D. Laing and Anti-Psychiatry* (New York: Harper and Row, 1971), 137–138.

We come, third, to the very heart of the relativistic paradigm – the *relativity* principle itself. Here, better than in respect to the previous two elements, we may consider the positive and constructive aspects of the paradigm. This is its "content," if such a thing has substance. The relativity principle is, of course, close to complementarity and indeterminacy. However, it ranges well beyond these two by asserting that while all "things" are relative to each other it is still possible to describe a matrix in respect to which the parts of reality may be located. The most important feature of the matrix is that, being relative, it overthrows the rationalist distinctions between the "big" and the "small," the "greater" and the "lesser," the "higher" and the "lower," and so forth. In other words, while the principles of complementarity and indeterminacy rebel against the rationalist epistemological distinction between knowing subject and known object, the relativistic principle overthrows the rationalist ontological perspective that views the natural and human world in hierarchical terms. Relativity radically equalizes all things, persons, events, and facts in reality. All things become platitudinous and, simultaneously, the platitude reigns supreme. In Richard Coe's phrase relativity involves the "apotheosis of the platitude."

In physics, one need only allude to the most fundamental principle of the general theory of relativity – that time and space cannot be taken as independent fixed referential systems. One cannot say that a given body is here or that a given event occurs at this specific time. We are unable to measure, in absolute terms, the whereness or whenness of bodies except by comparing them with each other, as some have done:

> The essential formulation of the principle turns out to be the following: It is not, as Newton assumed, empty space but the matter distributed through space that determines, at each instant and at each location, a definite physical reference system. This amounts to saying that the motion of a body is describable by certain simple laws only when measured relative to all other matter in the universe.[22]

This is to say that the "existence" in space-time of any particular body forces us to think of that body relative to all other things in reality. Thus, we cannot meaningfully speak of an absolute objective system of nature in which there is an "up" or a "down" or a "big" and a "small" except in relative terms. The most recent extension of this principle is the theory of conformal invariance, described in 1973 by John A. Wheeler:

> In the past five years one of the greatest developments in elementary particle physics has been so called conformal invariance, the discovery that the equations of elementary particle physics possess a property that in effect is this: changing

---

[22] March Freeman, *The New World of Physics*, 94–95.

the scale in which you examine the phenomenon does not change the nature of the phenomenon. . . . This strange feature of nature that permits us to subsume the very large and the very small under the same kind of equation is something we don't yet understand, but it raises in one's mind the perpetual question: can it be true that what we think of as the very small and what we think of as the very large are really not so different?[23]

In absurdist drama relativity becomes the "apotheosis of the platitude." While in physics, bodies have no absolute, linear relationship with each other, likewise, in absurd drama words lose their absolute linear meaning. In a world where all words are relativized, then the platitude – the elementary particle of human verbal interaction – becomes all important. By "measuring it" over against the absurdity of all reality, the platitude becomes the key to whatever meaning there is in total reality. The philosophical background for this way of thinking is the College of 'Pataphysics to which Ionesco has affiliated himself.[24] It derives from the classic absurdist writer, Alfred Jarry. Its basic assumptions, according to Roger Shattuck, are:

'Pataphysics is the science of the realm beyond metaphysics; or, 'pataphysics lies as far beyond metaphysics as metaphysics lies beyond physics – in one direction or another . . . 'Pataphysics is the science of the particular, of laws governing exceptions. . . . A return to the particular shows that every event determines a law, a particular law. . . . 'Pataphysics is pure science, lawless and therefore impossible to outlaw. . . . 'Pataphysics is the science of imaginary solutions. In the realm of the particular, every event arises from an infinite number of causes. All solutions, therefore, to particular problems, all attributions of cause and effect, are based on arbitrary choice, another term for scientific imagination. . . . . For 'Pataphysics, all things are equal. . . .[25]

'Pataphysical thought, it may be seen, does not cower in the isolation of particulars from each other. Rather it employs positive imagination to frame the micro-particles of human experience in macro-cosmological terms. For example, Coe says of Ionesco:

By showing up the meaninglessness of conventional idiom, by shattering the hard crystallized phraseology of common speech, his achievement is to throw back into the melting-pot all those individual elements of which rational language is composed; and from there, a whole vocabulary can then emerge anew, scoured of its accumulated patina of overtones and associations: the long-awaited raw material for a new generation of poets to work upon.[26]

[23] Florence Helitzer, "The Princeton Galaxy," *Intellectual Digest* 3: 10 (1973): 25–32, at 29–30.
[24] Coe, *Eugene Ionesco*, 7–10.
[25] Roger Shattuck, "Pataphysics Is the Only Science," *Evergreen Review* 4, May–June (1960): 24–33, at 27–29.
[26] Coe, *Eugene Ionesco*, 44–45.

In the absurdist 'pataphysical point of view the relativity principle becomes quite explicitly a strategy both for drama and for life in an absurd world.

Life is, of course, absurd, and it is ludicrous to take it seriously. Only the comic is serious. The 'pataphysician, therefore remains entirely serious, attentive, imperturbable. He does not burst out laughing or curse when asked to fill out in quadruplicate a questionnaire on his political affiliations or sexual habits: on the contrary, he details a different and equally valid activity on each of the four sheets. His imperturbability gives him anonymity and the possibility of savoring the full 'pataphysical richness of life.[27]

Thus, we see the emergence of the fully serious comic clown. In rationalist thought, the clown is a lowly creature, the circus a band of deviants whose only purpose is to entertain the normal. In the absurdist frame of reference the situation is equalized. All men are clowns. The only choice is whether or not to take this fact seriously. The clown is the particular. The clown is the imaginary solution to the problem of the meaning of reality. The particular and the total are not different.

'Pataphysics had its direct influences on the world of art. The ideas of Jarry influenced Picasso during his early years in Paris.[28] More explicitly the Dadaists relied conclusively on radical ideas of not only Jarry but also Jacques Vache, another of the early 'pataphysicians.[29] Dore Ashton has said:

The Dada legacy passed on to contemporary artists is expressed in the hybrids produced, for instance, by Claes Oldenburg. A replica of a shirt, painted to look wrinkled and soiled, is enlarged to fill indifferent spaces. It is an object that has no attached value. It is there: meaningless, absurd, but there. Similarly, in the "happenings" there is no organic development, but a series of confused events aimed at the articulation of chaos. The use of countless rags, broken crockery, tin cans, and other throwaway material is an obvious arrow pointing to a negative polemic. Painting, sculpture, the dance, music are thrown into a happening at random. This is not the divine fusion envisioned by the Wagnerites, but, rather, a diffusion which these young protagonists consider characteristic of existence. Apollinaire's burlesque, and even Dadaist criticism, are dropped out in this process of condensation, of stripping in reverse. By throwing everything in, the young happening artist reaches the same point as the purist, who throws everything out.[30]

Only the comic is serious. Thus, we see in modern art the importance of the clown in Picasso, Rouault, and Chagall. More profoundly, we see

---

[27] Shattuck, "Pataphysics Is the Only Science," 29.

[28] Anthony Blunt, *Picasso's "Guernica"* (London: Oxford University Press, 1969), 8.

[29] Manuel Grossman, *Dada: Paradox, Mystification, and Ambiguity in European Literature* (New York: Bobbs-Merrill, 1971), 19–36.

[30] Dore Ashton, *A Reading of Modern Art* (Cleveland: Case Western Reserve University, 1969), 185–186.

the expression of the same theme in the psychological counterpart of the comic, fantasy. In fantasy and dream, the boundary between fear and fun, nightmare and creative imagination is perfectly fluid. These themes are ever present in Van Gogh, Picasso, Matisse, Miró, Lee, Oldenburg, and Dali. We may take the threads presented by the clown, the dream, and fantasy and weave a gestalt that allows no absolutistic hierarchical view of the world. Modern art rejects uncritical attention to landscape and perspective. It starts with the broken-up bits and pieces, the particles of existence and uses them to express the comic and fanciful, extra-rational possibilities in this chaos.

The Dionysian mood that appears in drama and art is found equally in music and theology where it is affirmed in an even more positive fashion. With John Cage it appears in his intentional use of everyday life's particular noises for musical creativity:

Wherever we are, what we hear is mostly noise. When we ignore it, it disturbs us. When we listen to it, we find it fascinating. The sound of a truck at fifty miles per hour. Static between the stations. Rain. We want to capture and control these sounds, to use them not as sound effects but as musical instruments.[31]

Religious thinkers active at the same time held a view similar to this, of which the theologian Harvey Cox is a striking example. In his book *Feast of Fools* he emphasizes the role of festivity and fantasy in leveling the social world. "Unmasking the pretense of the powerful always makes their power seem less irresistible."[32] Cox also emphasizes the creative possibilities of this relativizing experience:

Fantasy like festivity reveals man's capacity to go beyond the empirical world of the here and now. But fantasy exceeds festivity. In it man not only relives and anticipates, he remakes the past and creates wholly new futures. Fantasy is a humus. Out of it man's ability to invent and innovate grows. Fantasy is the richest source of human creativity. Theologically speaking, it is the image of the creator God in man. Like God, man in fantasy creates whole worlds ex nihilo, out of nothing.[33]

Finally, and again, R. D. Laing expressed much the same theme as that found in Cox, and already present in the earliest writings of Michel Foucault – the Holy Fool. Madness and sanity are relativized with respect to each other. Even more, the mad are those with the greatest possibility for finding essential humanity. In the "normal" world the schizophrenic is feared and isolated. In Laing's ideal world, the schizophrenic, whose life

---

[31] Cage, *Silence*, 3.
[32] Harvey Cox, *The Feast of Fools* (Cambridge: Harvard University Press, 1969), 9.
[33] *Ibid.*, 59.

is broken up into many, chaotic experiences, is the one who is most likely to attain true, transcendent selfhood. He does so by journeying back to life's elementary particles.

In this particular type of journey, the direction we have to take is back and in, because it was way back that we started to go down and out. They will say we are regressed and withdrawn and out of contact with them. True enough, we have a long, long way to go back to contact the reality we have lost contact with. And because they are humane, and concerned, and even love us, and are very frightened, they will try to cure us. They may succeed. But there is still hope that they will fail.[34]

Relativism, 2005

To read what one wrote more than thirty years before can be embarrassing. Some of the essay meets that standard. It seems to me strange, today, to speak of "fields" as though they were separate from each other, as if there were such spheres as art, science, thinking, and the like. Whether I was right to speak this way thirty years ago is a question apart from the fact that, undoubtedly, it is not in the twenty-first century. In point of fact, the spheres of human meaning are not nearly so distinct as once they were (which fact in itself has implications for Max Weber's struggle early in the twentieth century to account for the modern world as one of the spheres through which the meaning-seeker human traveled).

This may be why, more than four decades after the publication in 1962 of Thomas Kuhn's sensational book, *The Structure of Scientific Revolutions*, the concept *paradigm* no longer has the cachet it did in the 1960s and 1970s. In fact, the word has entered popular discourse as a kind of throwaway expression for "point of view" or the like, which in itself may be interesting. Kuhn's paradigm was not a point of view, pure and simple, but the fact that the notion has lost its steam may be due only partly to the drift of popular culture toward the lowest denominator. In fact, it does seem that there are fewer paradigms in the sense of strong research programs.

As the reception of Kuhn's concept spread it came to be viewed as more a sociology of science with affinities to the science studies of Robert K. Merton and his students. Interestingly, about the same time, the term began to turn back on sociology itself as there arose, in the 1970s, the habit of referring to academic sociology as a multiple paradigm science. Though this precise expression was given currency by authors like George Ritzer, among others, the idea without the language was found in one of

[34] Laing, *The Politics of Experience*, 168.

that era's most influential books on the state of sociology: Alvin Gouldner's *The Coming Crisis of Western Sociology*. From its publication in 1970
Gouldner's book served as a kind of manifesto of sixties radicals seeking
a place in academic sociology as relief from the failures of their political
work. There were other arguments of the same kind, but Gouldner's was
rooted seriously in the attempt to demonstrate that academic sociology
and Western Marxism were going through the same sort of decentral-
izing shift. The split within Marxism was that between the more vulgar
and scientific Marxism associated with Stalinism and the more humanistic and critical Marxism associated with Marx's writings of the 1840s.
In academic sociology, the split was seen as a breaking apart of the presumed hegemony of Talcott Parsons and the Harvard school of sociological functionalism. Ironically, Gouldner spared his teacher, and life-long
friend, Robert Merton, the wrath of this book's long and today strangely
wordy attack on Parsons. Still, Gouldner's hope was not so much for a
proliferation of competing schools as, in effect, an opening of American
sociology, in particular, to the critical elements in European thought, of
which critical theories of the Marxist kind were much in mind.

Today, early in the 2000s, where *paradigm* once was, *deconstruction* now
is. The latter term, no less popularized and degraded than previously the
former had been, is still of some symbolic value. One hears even football
announcers carrying on about how they would "deconstruct" the play on
the field. Silly though it may be, the fact remains that, however deflated,
when terms are broadcast in this way on open mikes, it means something
about the culture of the times. And it means something rather more
than the fact that about the same time "piss" entered acceptable popular
discourse. If "piss," then "shit" cannot be far behind. But "deconstruct"
and "paradigm" are horses of different colors. They arose in high culture
to find their ways in popular, if not quite mass, culture. Whatever people
may think the word means, popular uses of words in this way may deserve
a hearing and in this case the hearing would suggest that people are willing
at least to take things apart (*decompose*), perhaps even to let them stand
in their natural un-centered way (*deconstruct*) without assuming they will
be *destroyed*.

In this respect, academic sociology lags behind the popular imagination. Though there is a less menacing hegemony in the field, still a good
many of those who swim in the main stream long for the shore of an
orderly science – even a multiple paradigm one will do. Yet, it seems less
than likely, if only because now, nearly a half-century after sociologists
began to realize they were not of one accord, and a good century after
1907 when the relativism paradigm (if you will permit me) began to take
hold, social science (if not Science as such) has not gained an appreciable

foothold on the deck of public discourse. Social sciences make their contributions, but not so much as science as a source of informed comment on the uncertain sweep of social life.

It is, thus, a bit quaint I realize to reprint an essay under the banner of a relativistic paradigm. Still, quaint though it may be, one might wonder why it is that academic sociology, far from entering the fray of the movements described, is for the most part embarrassingly defensive even to the point of wanting its paradigms to ward off their worries about relativism. "Relativistic" is a terrible adjective, but relativism by whatever name is surely much the way the world is for better or worse. One might change the language. Changing the world, as Marx found out, is quite a more difficult thing.

4

Ferdinand de Saussure and why the social contract is a cultural arbitrary

If ever there were a ghostly presence in social theory, its name would surely be Saussure.

Ferdinand de Saussure (1858–1913), the Swiss linguist, is the founding father of structuralism by way of his theory of semiology as a general science of social facts. Those who are appalled by the so-called linguistic turn in social thought have Saussure to blame. Were he bodily here about, it is improbable that he would have minded one way or the other what people thought of him. This is a guess based mostly on the one reasonably well-known social fact of the man's biography – that whatever fame he was offered, whatever pleasures he experienced living abroad, Saussure was restless for little more than a quiet life in Geneva.

Ghosts are wisps of a sort that enter the skirmish to change the play while leaving little material trace. Thus lived Ferdinand de Saussure, one of the most important thinkers out of Durkheim's time and cultural sphere of interest, of whom little is known, which must be because he wanted it that way. In *Saussure*, still the best short book about the enigmatic linguist, Jonathan Culler sees a sign in the coincidence that Saussure was "born in Geneva in 1857, one year after Freud and one year before Durkheim." When the life itself is so plain, one looks for signs in the skies. They are there to be seen.

After an unremarkable childhood in Geneva, Saussure studied science at the local university. This slight mis-step of adolescence was soon retraced. From youth his competence in languages had been very well formed. When Ferdinand grew tired of science studies, he left Geneva for Leipzig to study philology. After mastering the subject, Saussure moved on to Berlin where he wrote *Mémoire sur le système primitif des voyelles dans les langues indo-européennes*. The book immediately drew high scholarly praise. Saussure did not like Berlin. He then returned to Leipzig where a member of faculty asked if he were, by chance, related to the great Swiss linguist of the same name. Saussure was twenty-one. One can only imagine the elder man's astonishment at the answer (if, that is, the young man bothered to claim his fame).

Tired of Germany, he moved to Paris late in the 1880s, where he became a most successful teacher at the Ecole pratique des Hautes Etudes. His subjects were Sanskrit, Gothic, and Old High German. One can only, again, imagine what qualities would allow a teacher of these subjects to be admired by students. By 1891, he grew tired of Paris and returned to a professorship at Geneva. One report has it that he refused a chair at the Collège de France in order to go home. He was just thirty-three. For the rest of his years, he pursued the life of a scholar and a teacher. In 1907, when Saussure was an elder in his profession, he was asked to teach an introductory course in general linguistics which, in relative terms, would have been somewhat like Princeton asking Einstein, in his more senior years, to teach the introductory course in physics. Saussure did the work, apparently with relish, from 1907 until 1911. He died in 1913. He was fifty-six. Even less is known of those last years in Geneva than of the middle years in Germany and France. Exactly nothing at all would be known of them had not students edited and organized notes from the introductory course Saussure took up anew late in his short life. These notes became the *Course in General Linguistics* – one of the most important books of the twentieth century, from which the author was himself largely absent.

How often, since Socrates, has this happened? Not more than once or twice a millennium it seems. Saussure was no Socrates. Still, both were, in effect, spooks of whom we know a great deal in the absence of their having written down anything to the point of their most influential teachings. More eerie still, Saussure had to have been an intellectual, if not personal, intimate of Durkheim's as of Freud and Marx. The *Course in General Linguistics* contains passages so similar in their formulation that the cynic would think they had been lifted straight from the writings of all three. In respect to his observation as to the coincidence of the birth years of the three of them, Jonathan Culler is clearly on to something apt in its weirdness.

A ghost, generically, is the presence of an absence. It might be said, apart from his biographical passings, that Saussure's semiology was itself a theory based on the presence of an absence. Strange though it may sound, the basic fact of language according to Saussure is that the linguistic sign, though fixed in relation to the community in which it is found, is not fixed in its relation to the thing signified. This is evident from the pliability of common words. The English language noun "sign" can refer equally to an array of public announcements of meaningful, if uncertainly so, contents – "food," "stop," "danger

ahead," "dancing girls," "yield," "gas" or any other indicator that
something meaningful lies ahead. Yet, there is no real-world thing –
social or otherwise – that determines the meaning to which a sign like
"sign" may point. Thus, a word-sign – let us say: "cliff" – is unrelated
to any real thing, fact, or condition that may lie ahead – let us say:
"an abrupt end to the surface on which you are traveling." This is the
signified to which the sign "sign" points. But the thing signified is
nothing at all in the real world. The sign, in Saussure's theory, is no
more than a conventional association of a signifier and a sound image.
In brief (too brief), a word like "goat" refers not to a critter in a pasture
but to a single sound of one syllable, *gōt* – a sound that conveys a
meaning to those accustomed to most variations of spoken English.
There are exceptions of course, as in the case of an Anglican priest
to whom I was once subjected for an hour of misery who, throughout
his sermon, pronounced the sign "goat" as if it required two sounds:
go-at instead the usual *gōt*. The ultimate proof of the arbitrariness
of meaningful signs is in the apparent comprehension of the regular
members of this man's congregation who, having committed themselves
to a life of faith, seemed to have adjusted themselves rather painlessly
to their priest's tedious irregularities.

In time, Saussure's argument about the arbitrariness of signs became
controversial. Jacques Derrida, in particular, accuses him of logo-
centrism, which is to say: phono-centrism – the prioritizing of spoken
over written language. Noam Chomsky, a structuralist of another kind,
differs with Saussure over the question of a deep structural grammar
that, in Chomsky's view, accounts for the articulation of the meaningful
speech sounds. Both have their points, but neither quite gives Saussure
credit for the sociology behind his scheme.

The key to Saussure's idea of the arbitrariness of the sign is the
prior distinction between *la langue* and *la parole* – between, that
is, the language itself as a system (*la langue*) and its performance in
speech *(la parole)*. The former is the repository of a language's contents
and rules – its *paradigms*; while the latter is the site of their articulation in *syntagmatic* utterances. This, roughly, is Chomsky's distinction
between *competence* and *performance*, whereby competence is a function of a deep grammar that lends structure to actual performances.
Hence, whichever poison you choose, the absences in the presence
of an actual linguistic performance, an utterance: The meanings conveyed are not accords with respect to empirical objects in the known
worlds, nor are they immutable covenants. Rather, they belong to a
dynamic and historical system in which the semantic contents and
grammars allow for the production of meanings in context, from which

the system itself is always and necessarily absent. In short, there is no room for the entire structure of language (*la langue*) in the performance of it (*la parole*); but there can be no performance without the whole of the language that provides not instructions for linking social facts with signifying things but a ruler for measuring their differences. The key to understanding what some fool means when he utters the sound *go-at* is realizing over time that he cannot mean to say *bōt* ("bōat") or even *bo-at* much less *kol* (that is "cow").

Saussure's *Course* is filled with technical discussion of such issues as these, but all of them come back to a few key points which can be awkwardly but well-enough summarized: Languages are social contracts, from which speakers draw the rules and contents by which they produce and receive meanings over time in settings. The merit of this attitude for a semiology of cultures is evident in Saussure's own words:

> The linguistic sign is arbitrary; language, as defined, would therefore seem to be a system which, because it depends solely on a rational principle, is free and can be organized at will. Its social nature, considered independently, does not definitely rule out this viewpoint. Doubtless it is not on a purely logical basis that group psychology operates; one must consider everything that deflects reason in actual contacts between individuals. But the thing which keeps language from being a simple convention that can be modified at the whim of interested parties is not its social nature; it is rather the action of time combined with the social force. If time is left out, the linguistic facts are incomplete and no conclusion is possible. . . . If we considered language in time, without the community of speakers – imagine an isolated individual living for several centuries – we probably would notice no change; time would not influence language. Conversely, if we consider the community of speakers without considering time, we would not see the effect of the social forces at work. . . . Language is no longer free, for time will allow the social forceps at work on it to carry out their effects. This brings us back to the principle of continuity, which cancels freedom. But continuity necessarily implies change, varying degrees of shifts in the relationship between the signified and the signifier. (Saussure, *Course in General Linguistics* (1907–11))

What is this if it is not Durkheim read by way of Marx with Freud in the deep background? *Meanings are arbitrary but not irrational. They are rational but not reasonable. They issue from a social contract which derives over time from the community. But over time, meanings create a history which has the mysterious effect of being absent to the presence in which meanings perform their signifying labor.*

What then, really, of Culler's vision of meaning in the near coincidence of birth years for Freud, Durkheim, and Saussure? It means they all, about the age of twelve, would have witnessed at a remove, and been affected by, the Franco-Prussian war and the Paris Commune of 1871. It means that, whatever they read or heard, they would

have come to university at a time when Marx's mature writings on economic values in the capitalist mode of production were widely known.
It means that all three, each the child of bourgeois values, would have
had to consider the riddle bourgeois culture was just then realizing
might not be easily resolved. If history is the progress of reason, then
why does irrational violence among men still get the upper hand?

In the absence of a record of Saussure's innermost thoughts, what
thoughts he may have held in common with his great age-peers can
only be adduced from a close reading of the *Course*, where (as Culler
explains so very well) Saussure, like Durkheim and Freud – all children of the terrors of 1871 – set their methods of social research against
the then still prevailing doctrine of the early political-economists –
against which Marx no less railed unrelenting to the same effect: The
individual is not the source of value (which is to say: meaning). The
community is. Social research is a matter of social facts, not psychological ones – so Freud, in granting at the first the semi-autonomy of
dream language and the structural dynamic of the psyche as outside
the pure self by virtue of being the site of struggle between nature and
society; so also Durkheim, in affirming the primacy of social forces
over the primitive individual; so too, needless to add, Marx in defining
economic values not according to their utility to individual consumers
but according to the system of social exchanges in which differences in
quality are determined by the equivalencies of the values established
by the social mode of production.

Saussure, the ghost, was the only one of the three to propose and outline a general social science. Freud and Durkheim withdrew to their
special sciences of psychoanalysis and sociology. Marx, one assumes,
had he not been more the child of 1848 than 1871, might have taken
the step Saussure took; certainly his followers did. But Marx himself
confined his announced program to a more or less false science of
historical materialism. Saussure alone envisioned a thoroughly systematic method of social science as the science of socially structured
meanings:

When semiology becomes organized as a science, the question will arise whether
or not it properly includes modes of expression based on completely natural
signs, such as pantomime. Supposing that the new science welcomes them, its
main concern will still be the whole group of systems grounded in the arbitrariness of the sign. In fact, every means of expression used in society is based,
in principle, on collective behavior or – what amounts to the same thing – on
convention. Polite formulas, for instance, though often imbued with a certain
natural expressiveness (as in the case of a Chinese who greets his emperor by
bowing down to the ground nine times), are nonetheless fixed by rule; it is this

rule and not the intrinsic value of the gestures that obliges one to use them. Signs that are wholly arbitrary realize better than the others the ideal of the semiological process; that is why language, the most complex and universal of all systems of expression, is also the most characteristic; in this sense linguistics can become the master-pattern for all branches of semiology although all language is only one particular semiological system. (Saussure on Semiology in *Course in General Linguistics*)

The fundament of the vision is the arbitrariness of the sign – free from necessary natural relations to social and natural things in themselves; fixed, but not immutable, in relation to the community formed by the social contract that lends them meaning.

Even Saussure's fellow traveler from Geneva, Rousseau, from whom the very idea of social contract is inherited, stumbled on this crucial point. The social contract cannot be viewed as the collective will of the community because such a view freezes it in the ice of an undecipherable unity of all individual wills. Rather, the social contract, Saussure saw, must be social through and through, which is only possible when the individual events of which the whole is composed are dislodged from a necessary relation to their natural worlds. It is impossible to have it both ways at once. If it is meaning one wants to explain (which in principle is the only thing a study of culture can want to be), then meanings cannot be fixed as if they were naturally occurring facts. Meanings are social facts, which means they assume their social value only in the exchanges members make when they accept the arbitrary but necessary condition of social participation: *The only way social participation can be meaningful is if participants accept the social obligation to suspend doubt as to the arbitrariness of the terms laid down by a contract that came before and will live on after the events at hand – which is not, by the way, to say that the contract never changes. It changes of course; but only in time which, as Saussure said, is the final arbiter of structured meanings.*

It is possible that Saussure was drawn back to Geneva from the glory proffered in Berlin and Paris because he accepted the responsibility to comfort Rousseau's ghost, which had to have been unsettled by the violations of the collective will in 1789, 1848, 1871, 1914, 1940 – just to mention the more dreadful failures of the social whole. This Saussure may have done by reversing, in a fashion, Rousseau's famous conundrum: "Man is born free and everywhere he is in chains." Saussure's corrective was: *Man is born enchained to a general will that is not his but he is free wherever he accepts the arbitrary general will as the resource, not the topic, of his freedom.*

Literary politics and the *champ* of French sociology (1981*)

A survivor's sad note, 2005

The essay following first appeared close to a quarter-century ago, in 1981, as the introduction to *French Sociology: Rupture and Renewal Since 1968*, a collection of readings representing the contesting positions in the field of French social thought. In the early 1980s, literary Paris was still embroiled in the cultural after-shocks of the events of May '68; hence the book's subtitle. Since then, much has changed of course. Yet the essay stands as it was originally published. The discussion of literary Paris was meant to be a structural analysis of a cultural field. Even though, years later, the individuals then prominent in the field are either gone or less salient than once they were, the structures of the cultural relations remain roughly the same, as indeed they had remained from 1907 when Durkheim was at the height of his prominence to 1968 when even the changes brought by that year left Paris altered but standing.

Roland Barthes and Jacques Lacan had died the year before the book was published. Michel Foucault would die in 1984. His former teacher, Louis Althusser, died in 1990 but his public life ended well before that in the tragic effects of mental illness. Others remain. Alaine Touraine, Michel Crozier, and Raymond Boudon are still active. Claude Lévi-Strauss may be less active, but then, early in the 2000s, he is approaching his hundred birthday.

Closer to disciplinary sociology, Pierre Bourdieu died in 2002 and, in 2003, Philippe Besnard died all too young. My essay and the book it introduced owe a great deal to both of these very good men. Bourdieu was far more than merely brilliant. He was a generous man who welcomed more or less well-meaning strangers without allowing their ignorance to

---

* Originally published as "Reading French Sociology," an introduction to *French Sociology: Rupture and Renewal Since 1968*, edited by Charles Lemert (New York: Columbia University Press, 1981). The current title is the one used for an early reprint in *Theory and Society* 10: 5 (Sept, 1981): 645–669. The essay was published in 1980. For the most part, the present tense remains. Deaths, such as Bourdieu's in 2002, are not updated.

perturb his good nature. Philippe Besnard, more than anyone else, made the phone calls and introductions that allowed me to do the research that led to this work. We were friends in those days and would have remained so, I suppose, had I not moved to other subjects and thus given up my annual visits to Paris. It was a great shock to learn just a few weeks ago (as I write in the summer of 2004) of Philippe's death. Yet, even after he, and the others, are gone, their work continues in its effects if not in its writing. In Philippe's case, no one did more to create and sustain an international group of scholars devoted to the study of Durkheim and his remarkable group of researchers. One member of the Groupe des études Durkheimiennes (one who had been more faithful than I) remarked that his death was "a terrible loss to us all, with no one to take his place." Philippe was never a star in the usual Parisian sense. He could have been, surely. Instead he limited his adventures in public culture in order to devote himself to the painstaking scholarship which he pursued with others whom he drew into a group, much as Durkheim had.

Pierre Bourdieu was a star. By the 1990s, he had assumed the status of a cultural icon in a field from which so many others had departed. Though surely, as always, there will come a day when the brilliance of his ideas will fade in the light of some other star, Bourdieu's writings are still as avidly read around the world as they had been in his lifetime; so too Foucault and others, many years after their passings. Which is to say that structures outlive the individuals by whom they are known. The field of French social thought, now dispersed into global space, is in many ways more active today than it was in the days when one still had to visit Paris to sip the juice of its fruit.

We who survive to recall an earlier time will pass along soon enough. Would that we were the stewards of our time as Besnard and Bourdieu were of theirs. Yet, even if we are not – even if we have not been given the talents bestowed on them – at least there can be the human satisfaction of accepting whatever role, small or grand, we may have for a while in the play and struggle that sustains the fields of cultural production.

(CL 2005)

Reading social theories is seldom a matter of reading. More often than one would like, it is impossible to pick up a book and read. We are obliged, usually, to begin quite far from the book at hand, with an understanding of the literary politics in which the book was produced. Reading ethnomethodology, for example, requires a healthy et cetera assumption. One must fill in what is missing as best one can, then wait for further clues. This, of course, happens only after one has gained considerable understanding of ethnomethodology's program. Likewise, one reads Foucault in stark horror at the peculiar illustrations, the surfeit of contradictory formulations, and the paucity of clear footnotes. It is quite some time before one realizes that this is part of his method. And, to read Habermas it is not enough to puzzle through the tangled sentences. In due time one realizes that those sentences can be parsed only when one sees Habermas's crypto-Idealist intent to totalize all the pure conditions of truth and, thus, in each statement, to have something to say about everything. Examples are easy to come by.[1]

And so, one must read quite a lot before one begins to read. The work of reading is conditioned by the relations of literary production. This essay applies this relatively straightforward principle to one of the more difficult contemporary literary fields, French sociology and social theory. Those of us exiled to life outside the Parisian literary world are often confused and put off by the secret codes which seem to govern those who write from within. What we gain in cheaper rents and fresh air, we lose in our ability to decipher what we read. Intricate sentences seduce us by their magnificant form, but we often are left limp for want of detectable substance. Arguments take place on these pages, and we are befuddled non-persons. We are invited to dinner and end up dumbly overhearing without understanding the hushed conversations of the real guests. Thus enticed, we crave a meager footnote and are given the stalest of morsels or, worse, nothing at all. I exaggerate, of couse, but these are common complaints.

I exaggerate to introduce my point. Reading the French is no more perplexing than reading any other body of literature made difficult by the complexity of its topic. In the case of French sociology, texts are doubly complex. As sociology, they reflect the complexity of the contradictions of the social world. As French, they reflect the intricacy of the Parisian literary world. The following is based on one simple assumption. Critical reading is from the literary field to the text. Understand Parisian literary politics and, in due course, the text will unravel. No stranger can ever perfectly master those politics in all their nuance. I doubt that many Parisians can either. But one can suggest the most general relations of force which explain, to some degree, why and how French social theory is as it is.[2]

---

[1] Problems in reading Foucault, ethnomethodology, and Habermas are discussed in: Charles Lemert and Garth Gillan, *Michel Foucault: Social Theory and Transgression* (New York: Columbia University Press, 1982) and Charles Lemert, *Sociology and the Twilight of Man* (Carbondale: Southern Illinois University Press, 1979), chs. 7 and 9.

[2] The French are properly sensitive to jet ethnographers (Chamboredon's term), like myself, who descend for a few weeks or months each year, then presume expertise on French intellectual life. In the Preface to *French Sociology* I have, at length, offered my apologies and excuses. In brief, they are: guilty, as charged; but perhaps a stranger, his errors aside, can see enough to be helpful to fellow strangers.

It is best to begin with the unique place of reading in French intellectual culture. As readers ourselves, it is important to understand that, in France, reading is much more than a neutral tool of intellectual work. In France, "being well-read" is an emblem. It is a necessary, and sometimes sufficient, badge of intellectual competence. Those who wear it authentically are those who have distinguished themselves in French schools. Traditional French education is built around the mastery of the great texts of French culture – their memorization, their explication, their emulation in the pupil's writing. Pupils who succeed in French schools are those who have most perfectly demonstrated a brilliant and compelling literary and oral style, the standard for which is France's literary culture.[3] In other words, the first condition of intellectual excellence is good speaking and good writing, which are inculcated by means of good reading.

The effects of such a system are well known. When combined with the centralization of France in Paris, the French schooling method generates a second dimension to the notion of Paris as a literary capital. In addition to being the institutional center of France's publishing industry, Paris is a literary capital in the sense that it is where the politics of French reading and writing are fought out. The literary version of the *tout Paris* phenomenon[4] is the daily struggle of writers to be read, of readers to appropriate what must be read. The literary *tout Paris* is that open, public place where everyone watches (i.e., reads) what everyone else is doing (i.e., writing). The café as a literary and artistic locus in which this watching – this regard – was direct and face-to-face is not so much dead as transformed by the same mass media which, similarily, transformed and replaced the salon. Before "all of Paris" authors face the scrutiny of an ambitious reading public created, in large part, by a perversely dense and imploded structure of publishing houses, reviews, newspapers, radio and television commentators which mediate between writers and readers.

The struggle involves writers' desires to be read, and readers' needs to be well-read. *Le Monde des livres, Apostrophes*, the F.N.A.C. and Beaubourg debates, *Le Nouvel Observateur, France Culture* – these are the new forums by which author-watching takes place, literary publics

---

[3] See Pierre Bourdieu and Jean Claude Passeron, *Les Héritiers* (Paris: Minuit, 1964); or the English translation: *The Inheritors* (Chicago: University of Chicago Press, 1979). Compare: Pierre Bourdieu and Jean Claude Passeron, *Reproduction in Education, Society and Culture* (London: Sage Publications, 1977).

[4] *Tout Paris* is roughly, "fashion-conscious Paris." I distinguish the *literary tout Paris* from *tout Paris* as such. Even though, in the following, the latter is used to describe the former, it is quite clear that literary fashions operate in a relatively distinct *champ*. I am not saying that literary fashions are merely based on or derived from Parisian fashion-consciousness in general. See Raymond Boudon, "The French University since 1968," *Comparative Politics* 89, October (1977): 89–118.

are fabricated, intellectual *vedettes* (stars) rise and fall. The Thursday evening edition of *Le Monde* (containing the special literary section) like *Apostrophes* (Friday evening's television debates among authors and other Parisian literati), were and are institutions exerting a formidable social force on readers and writers. It is not easy to ignore them, even when one knows better. Nothing in the English language literary world is quite comparable. Even the *Times Literary Supplement* and the *New York Review of Books* are unable to exert such dominance because in the English reading world there are rival, if lesser, literary centers diminishing the control of London and New York City. But in France, *tout Paris* is *tout*. Thus, among intellectuals in Paris, it is very difficult and frequently embarrassing not to have an opinion on what has been or is being written. A reader's standing is, therefore, linked by training and ethos to what he reads.

Therefore, French sociology, like the traditional lettered disciplines, is written by those who, by disposition, require themselves to be well-read, which means reading with an acceptable level of seriousness what others read and write. From the point of view of the author, this means that French writing is produced by those who have, in principle, read widely and well. Hence, as writing, it is very often shaped in and by a literary space unknown to most foreigners. This is the space between the surface of the published text and the social deep structure of the *tout Paris* debates that exert their pressure on the author. This is why – now from the point of view of the reader – many of us are frustrated by that large portion of French writing in the human sciences which makes constant – though often uncited – reference to what others are saying and writing. We search for frequently non-existent footnotes in order to identify opponents alluded to in the surface text. The Parisian author, unimpeded by the Anglo-American empiricism of the footnote, often finds documentation superfluous because "everyone knows" that the reference is to Sartre, or the humanist Marxists, or to Aron, or to whomever.[5] At the other extreme, once the opponent is named, he must be dealt with in no uncertain terms. Poulantzas's dissection of Miliband, Manuel Castells's dismissal of the totality of urban sociology, and Bourdieu's attack on American sociology of science are examples.[6] In France, there is no

---

[5] For an excellent example see: Michel Foucault, *Archaeology of Knowledge* (New York: Random House, 1972).

[6] See, for example: Nicos Poulantzas, "The Capitalist State: A Reply to Miliband and Laclau," *New Left Review* (1976): 63–83. And Manuel Castells, "Vers une théorie sociologique de la planification urbaine," *Sociologie du Travail* (1969): 413–433. And Pierre Bourdieu, "The Specificity of the Scientific Field and the Conditions of the Progress of Reason," *Social Science Information* 14: 5 (1975): 19–47.

middle ground. The opponent is either unnamed or, once named, the author's position is exposed and the opponent's must be undermined. The thoroughness of one's readings of others must be demonstrated in order to maintain the validity of one's claim to a voice in *tout Paris*. In America, by contrast, we deal with opponents either surgically in isolated review of literature sections or superficially in benign, parenthetical lists of divergent texts. In France, one hears the Parisian whispers behind the lines. One should read these whispers with appreciation for the plight of people who, possessing often sharply divergent views, must encounter each other daily on committees, in nearly adjacent offices, in the Maison des Sciences de l'Homme (MSH) cafeteria, in a Rue du Cherche-Midi bookstore.[7] There is, in so dense a sociological community, the tension wrought by an obligation to exhibit in one's own writing a comprehensive and competent reading of the very other whom one has known and will know personally all one's professional life. The line between the anonymous scholar and the public writer is poorly drawn. In its place one must develop a metatheory of reading which permits the author to depersonalize and abstract his readings of others. This is why the French collapse the semantic distance between reading and writing. A reading – of Marx or Freud – is often also a theory of writing.[8]

Thus is added another dimension to the problem of reading and writing in Paris. By force of habit one must read everyone; by circumstance, those whom one must read are immediate neighbors. The second complicates the first. Since everyone is reading everyone else, it is immediately clear to all who have been included or excluded, critiqued or praised, by a given author. Little is hidden. Reading must be performed with great agility. It is always possible that a given text is conditioned by Parisian literary politics. We English language writers appreciate too little the protection we have in the expanses of land and sea which separate us from each other. It is perhaps for this reason that our scientific writing and thinking are so often devoid of pathos and subtlety. We have smaller need, in our public texts, to manage our less public collegial relations. Doubtless this partly explains the greater dexterity (lapsing occasionally into involutedness) with which the French write. It is writing that must hide as much as it reveals; thus, writing which demands a specialized reading competence.

---

[7] A simple, but poignant example, is that the exterior picture windows of the offices of Boudon and Bourdieu face each other in the MSH (Maison des Sciences de l'Homme) building. I suspect, however, that this observation has only symbolic value.

[8] The obvious example is: Louis Althusser and Etienne Balibar, *Reading Capital* (London: New Left Books, 1970).

The *champ* of French sociology: its form

Often the French will speak of their educational and professional formation as a *trajectoire* . . . a career path. To see oneself on a trajectory is,
of course, common to middle-class mobiles everywhere, but in France
the sense of one's career path is conditioned, once again, by Paris. To be
French is to think of Paris as the center of France (at the least). Thus, a
universitaire desires to pass as quickly as possible through an early exile
in a provincial university to attain a post in Paris. Or, alternatively, if one
begins in Paris, to resist all temptations to accept a post in the provinces,
no matter how attractive the offer. Remember Durkheim's uncertainty
over the timing of his return to Paris from Bordeaux. In a letter (1902)
written to Lévy-Bruhl he reflected on the awkwardness of his candidacy
for the chair in education at the Sorbonne: "I will give the impression of
someone who seeks to use any expedient in order to insinuate himself in
Paris. I find the idea of giving such an impression repulsive, especially
since it does not correspond to my state of mind."[9] Even if one is content
in the provinces, he[10] must think of Paris; even if his trajectory leads of
necessity to Paris, he must wait for the proper moment.

Paris is at once the principal city toward which an ideal career trajectory must aim and, because it is the center, it is the place in which and
with respect to which the political struggles of the intellectual *arrivés* are
enacted. Put metaphorically, Paris is the center of an attractive field of
forces, attracting magnetically; it is, at the same time, a field of battle
among those attracted.[11] *Champ* is a term which can convey these two
ideas, but for English readers there is semantic deficit. "Field" as a translation for *champ* is semantically undercoded. We have too few meanings
for a single term. In academic circles we use field to define a discipline or
as a technical metaphor describing social relations as a field of force.[12] But
in French settings the first of these is uncommon, and a third is added:

---

[9] Steven Lukes, *Emile Durkheim, His Life and Work: A Historical and Critical Study* (London:
Penguin Books, 1973), 365.

[10] I use the generic masculine (he, his, him), recognizing the sexism involved. There is no
adequate English language alternative. One can use "one" just so often. The French are
fortunate in having the very flexible third person singular, *on*. [How times have changed!
CL, 2005]

[11] The play on the word *champ* could go on endlessly. Instead of field of battle, one could
use field of play (keeping European football, more than American baseball, in mind).
The concatenation of metaphors – magnetic, political, military, Marxist, sportive – read
collectively, is for our purposes as instructive as any attempt to organize an established
meaning. Pierre Bourdieu has used *champ* in an explicit and technical fashion. I am
indebted to him for instruction on the term's meaning. He is not, however, implicated
in the abuses of my informal usage.

[12] As in Kurt Lewin, *A Dynamic Theory of Personality* (New York: McGraw-Hill, 1935).

the idea of field of play or struggle, that is, a battlefield. The *champ* as a "force field" is a space of action, practices; as a "battlefield" it is a place of struggle. Paris – as literary capital, and as intellectual *champ* – is a field whereupon ideas and their authors arrive, conquer, hold the center for a moment, then inevitably fall. As Bourdieu puts it, "Epistemological conflicts are always, inseparably, political conflicts."[13] Knowledge and writing involve the protection of one's theoretical territory in a field of constantly changing boundaries and constantly revalued intellectual capital.[14]

Foucault well expresses this space of intellectual struggle in his analysis of the relationship between the manifest, ordered system of public discourse and discourse as it is practiced:

Behind the visible facade of the system, one posits the rich uncertainty of disorder; and beneath the thin surface of discourse, the whole mass of largely silent development (*devenir*); a "presystematic" that is not of the order of the system. Discourse and system produce each other – and conjointly – only at the crest of this immense system. . . . Behind the completed system, what is discovered by the analysis of formations is not the bubbling source of life itself, life in an uncaptured state; it is an immense density of systematicities, a tight group of relations.[15]

To see behind official and public writing and speaking not Life (nor Order, nor Truth, nor a transcendent Center), but disorder, density, multiple bonds of obligation, is to speak with great sensitivity of and from Paris. This sensitivity explains many of the content themes of recent French thought – the critiques of the Center and of historicism; the infatuation with structures; the suspicion of functionalism's faith in core values.[16] To read French sociology competently one must know something of the rules, strategies, and conditions which form this *champ*. I will discuss only three: the role of style and individuality, the organization of the sociological productivity, and the special problems of publishing. I select these because they are most specific to the French situation.

Style and individuality

On the surface, the idea of an intellectual field of action and struggle conditioning sociological productivity seems to contradict the familiar

13 Bourdieu, "The Specificity of the Scientific Field." Related is the idea of the political responsibility of the intellectual avant-garde; for example, Foucault's description of the intellectual as "one who makes use of his knowledge, of his competence, of his relation to truth in the realm of political struggle." See Michel Foucault, "Truth and Power Interview." Trans. Garth Gillan. In Lemert, ed., *French Sociology*, 293–302.
14 Boudon, "The French University since 1968."
15 Foucault, *Archaeology of Knowledge*, 76.
16 These themes are discussed elsewhere: Charles Lemert, "De-Centered Analysis: Ethnomethodology and Structuralism." *Theory and Society* 7 (1979): 289–306.

half-truth of French individualism. French individualism is finesse and style conditioned by the modes available for individual use.[17] It is always individualism within the rules of proper fashion. Yes, it is only at St. Germain des Prés that one sees young women with purple hair, but also only there that one sees *many* young women with purple hair. In the world of fashion bizarre styles are a produced effect. They must be bizarre to be noticed by *tout Paris*. Once noticed they are widely appropriated, thus necessitating a new fetishizable mode. It is not by accident that the neighborhood outlet store of a large fashion house such as Ted Lapidus or Yves St. Laurent is a diffusion, not a "branch". Styles are broadcast to all Paris, and once diffused, they have no vital connection (as does a branch) with their source, which then transmits another wave of modes the following season. Likewise in the world of ideas. Modes of thinking are diffused throughout a field and thus made available for individualized use. Though they will be replaced in another publishing season, when in vogue they serve to formalize the rules of individual contents, conducts, and contests. The French find pure voluntarism suspect.[18] Individualism is always proper behavior; thus, it takes the form of style, flair, accent – that is, the ability to nuance a given mode of conduct.[19] It is possible that only a Parisian could interpret Parsonian theory as "institutionalized individualism"[20] just as a Parisian, Lévi-Strauss, could speak of mythic structures producing the contents of men's minds without need of the "thinking subject."[21]

One must, therefore, read French sociology with constant reference to the importance of style as a medium for the individualization of general modes. When one compares the styles of François Bourricaud, Alain Touraine, Pierre Bourdieu, and Raymond Boudon, the respective nuances are apparent; Bourricaud's cool, gentlemanly detachment;

---

[17] See Jesse Pitt's discussion of the origins of the French notion of individuality and prowess: Jesse Pitt, "Continuity and Change in Bourgeois France," in Stanley Hoffman et al., *In Search of France* (New York: Harper and Row, 1965), 235–304.

[18] See, for example: Raymond Boudon, "Review Essay on Rawls' *A Theory of Justice*," *Contemporary Sociology* (1976): 102–109. Michel Crozier and Erhard Friedberg, *L'Acteur et le Système* (Paris: Seuil, 1977). Alain Touraine, *La Voix et le Regard* (Paris: Seuil, 1978).

[19] Compare: Pitt, "Continuity and Change in Bourgeois France," 241: "Prowess depends for its formulation and evaluation upon canons of value which are given to it by the Church – or by the traditions of the Nation-State. These are the principes. Prowess consists in the application of these principles to particular situations that result in elegant solutions where the immutability of principles, their sacred character, and the talent (grace) of the individual are clearly revealed. It is an 'act of faith' and reinforces the commitment of its author and of his witnesses to the true faith."

[20] François Bourricaud, *L'individualisme Institutionnel: Essai sur la Sociologie de Talcott Parsons* (Paris: Presses Universitaires de France, 1977).

[21] Claude Lévi-Strauss, *The Raw and the Cooked* (New York: Harper & Row, 1969).

Touraine's impassioned introspections; Bourdieu's insistent, cutting pursuit; Boudon's heavy formality. Differences, yes; but all of the *normalien* mode – brilliant, confident, articulate – a mode with respect to which the individual flair is a nuance calling attention to the modal type itself.[22] Of course, there are other modes of discourse: the textual empiricism of the Althusserian school, itself a derivation of the *normalien* fashion or, the informal rationality of Crozier.

Style, which is so often a stumbling block for foreign readers of French writing, can actually be an aid to the careful reader. With few exceptions one can be assured that the style is always less determining than the mode it accents. People who work in a field of struggle can never isolate themselves. The attention of a public readership, upon which success depends, requires the author to attract attention to himself, while simultaneously defining a recognizable intellectual space. That territory must be defended and the main line of defense is the acquisition of readers who must be able to understand the text.[23] Thus, no matter what the surface style, the non-native reader can safely assume that most French texts, one way or another, contend with ideas in vogue at the moment. As I will explain below, French sociology since 1968 deals with a reasonably limited set of problems: change, control, order, equality, structure, action. It could be said that sociology, by definition, deals with general topics such as these. True, but I note that in the United States these problems are considered only in the aggregate, with various parts of the sociological whole ignoring certain among them selectively. We have nearly pure subjectivist sociologies, such as ethnomethodology, that do not worry in the least about objective structures; and formal, objectivist sociologies

[22] Examples of the styles are in Lemert, ed., *French Sociology*. On the special importance of the Ecole Normale Supérieure (ENS) as a model for intellectual prowess in sociology (and generally) see: Terry Clark, *Prophets and Patrons: The French University and the Emergence of the Social Sciences* (Cambridge: Harvard University Press, 1973). For documentation of its importance in the Durkheimian School, see: Philippe Besnard, "La Formation de L'équipe de L'année Sociologique," *Revue française de Sociologie* 20: 1: 7–31. And: Victor Karady, "Durkheim, Les Sciences Sociales et L'université: Bilan d'un Semi-Echec," *Revue française de Sociologie* 17: 2 (1976): 267–321. On the continuing importance of the ENS as both a model for and certifier of membership in the French intelligentsia see: Pierre Bourdieu and Jean Claude Passeron, "Sociology and Philosophy in France since 1945: Death and Resurrection of a Philosophy without a Subject," *Social Research* Spring (1967): 167–212, especially their remark on p. 206: "In such an intellectual world, self-educated people and foreigners, i.e., those who have not been trained at this national school for the upper intelligentsia, the Ecole Normale (Supérieure), can, with a few exceptions, only hope to achieve a position which is respected rather than admired." On the *normaliens* in general for this period, see: Victor Karady, "Normaliens et autres enseignants à la Belle Epoque," *Revue française de Sociologie* 13: 1 (1972): 35–59.

[23] Technically, this involves the problem of the naturalization of the text in reading. See, for example, Jonathan Culler, *Structuralist Poetics* (Ithaca: Cornell University Press, 1975).

that can readily dismiss the subject.[24] The division of labor is clear. But in France one is obliged, whatever one's position, to speak to the field as a totality. Bourdieu and Passeron describe this obligation: "It will be understood that in a situation in which the intellectual is required to have a quasi-sociological knowledge of the entire intellectual field every intellectual act bears a load of over-determinants which at every instant compels every intellectual by virtue of his position in the whole to commit his entire position with respect to the whole."[25]

As a result, competent reading of French sociology (as of other French writings) can go quite smoothly if one first bothers to understand the total field in which a given text is situated. To isolate Bourdieu and Touraine from their field is to court readerly confusion. Bourdieu's sociology of education, by the standards of American or British sociology of education, will make only partial sense. Likewise, to read Crozier and Boudon merely as American-style writers is to risk naïve over-simplification. Boudon, for example, is not just a French theory constructionist. Diplomacy in international reading is strongly recommended. When confused – or, alternatively, uninspired – suppress imperialism and ethnocentrism, especially when reading the French. Read the idiosyncratic style as an index, coded by a field. Read from field to text. If you apply the standard of the BBC radio lecture, or the American positivism of clarity and evidence, the reading will go poorly. If, on the other hand, you assume that these people are writing from the midst of a literary field more intensely combative than ours – a field which, however foreign, is understandable – their writing will gain its own clarity: if not the light of a familiar beacon, the light of discovery.

The organization of sociological productivity

It would be a mistake to conclude from the preceding that sociology in France lacks its own specificity, that there is nothing determinate in sociology as it is organized. Sociology does exist as an intellectual force related to but independent of the Parisian intellegentsia. However, this has not always been so. As recently as 1945 Lévi-Strauss was able to say: "French sociology does not consider itself as an isolated discipline, working in its own specific field, but rather as a method, or as a specific attitude working toward human phenomena. Therefore, one does not

[24] For a more detailed discussion of this problem in American sociology see: Charles Lemert, "Language, Structure, and Measurement: Structuralist Semiotics and Sociology," *American Journal of Sociology* 84 (1979): 929–957.
[25] Pierre Bourdieu and Jean Claude Passeron. "Sociology and Philosophy in France since 1945," 204.

need to be a sociologist in order to do sociology."[26] Gone are the days
when sociology was considered a mere attitude, when a Durkheim had
to be bootlegged into Paris as a professor of education. The change was
not, however, easily achieved, nor is it as complete as some would like.

Jean Stoetzel demonstrated some years ago[27] that between the period
following Durkheim's death and the immediate post-World War Two
years, France's sociological productivity changed, in form and content,
from an essentially humanistic orientation (1918–29) to an empiricist
period (1945–54) in which, not incidentally, Stoetzel himself was a leading figure. In the earlier period, the humanistic methods of philosophical analysis and classical scholarship predominated. Stoetzel shows that
74 percent of all sociological works produced employed these approaches.
While in the empiricist period, after World War Two, empirical research
(including qualitative and quantitative investigations, statistical analysis and documentation) was the leading orientation (62 percent). Likewise, the contents of sociological work changed from an interest in moral
sociology, the sociology of religion, and social psychology to demogra-
phy and political sociology in the empiricist period; that is, from topics
directly derivable from a Durkheimian social philosophy to topics studied by means of direct observation and formal analysis. Stoetzel's empiricist period (1945–54) was also the moment when sociology in France
began to achieve a degree of institutional stability, following the institutional ups and downs of the interwar transition. Before World War
Two the various research groups (described by Terry Clark)[28] were often
isolated from each other and from international sociology. Though the
Centre Nationale de la Recherche Scientifique (CNRS) was founded
before World War Two (1937), it was not until well after it that sociology settled into the institutional form by which it is known today. It
was, for example, only in 1958 that Aron was able to institutionalize a
licence (roughly, an American BA) in sociology; and in 1960 that today's
leading journals were established – *Sociologie du Travail*, *Revue française
de Sociologie*, *Archives européennes de Sociologie* (*European Journal of
Sociology*).

However, in the early 1960s sociology found itself called by the planning spirit (planomania, to use Baudelot and Establet's expression) of an
economically renascent France. At this moment sociology entered into

[26] Claude Lévi-Strauss, "French Sociology," in Georges Gurvitch and Wilbert E. Moore, eds., *Twentieth Century Sociology* (New York: Philosophical Library, 1945).
[27] The following data on productivity are drawn from: Jean Stoetzel, "Sociology in France: An Empiricist View," in Howard Becker and Alvin Boskoff, eds., *Modern Sociological Theory* (New York: Holt, Rinehart and Winston, 1957).
[28] Clark, *Prophets and Patrons*. Compare: Victor Karady, "The Prehistory of Present-Day French Sociology," in Lemert, ed., *French Sociology*, 33–47.

what Diana Pinto calls its golden years.[29] Sociology had acquired a proper market. It was called to serve the reconstruction of France through *le planning*. At the same time, this calling, because it implied an illicit affair with the central state, was the object of criticism founded in a revitalized, post-existentialist Marxism. As the former led to funding for research and the creation of teaching posts, the latter prompted a popularity among students, many of whom were attracted to sociology as a critical weapon, just as others were summoned by the hope of public service careers. In this period, sociology participated in national planning, was itself planned,[30] and benefited from the Fifth Plan's focus on new educational institutions (such as the creation of the new university at Nanterre).

However, as Pinto argues, the sun seems to have set as quickly as it rose. By 1968 sociology was the object of derision on the part of the rebelling students. Cohn-Bendit, it should be remembered, was a student in sociology at Nanterre. Touraine, Bourricaud, and Crozier, then colleagues at Nanterre, were subjected to criticism, even ridicule. Others, like Bourdieu and Passeron, were more favored by leftist students (their *Les Héritiers* having been a source book for students protesting their poor educational and economic prospects). But the impression held by most a decade later is that sociology in France has not survived the 1968 crisis – at least not as the rich, golden boy of a new French society. In the late 1970s and early 1980s morale is low. There are virtually no new permanent research posts provided by the CNRS, posts necessary for the development of a new generation of sociologists. It is felt that the remaining patrons – Boudon, Bourdieu, Crozier, and Touraine – are less able, therefore, to build or even maintain the size of their research groups. Many doubted that those who left the established groups to found their own laboratories would succeed. Those who had permanent positions in teaching or research seemed to be resigned to, if not content with, entrenchment. Many of those participating in experimental teaching programs, such as ADSSA,[31] seem to be disappointed by its inability

---

[29] Material presented here on post-World War Two sociology is based on a number of personal communications and written sources, especially: Diana Orvieto Pinto, "Sociology as a Cultural Phenomenon in France and Italy: 1950–1972," unpublished thesis, Harvard University, 1977. I am particularly grateful to Diana Pinto for lending me a copy of her (then unpublished) thesis. And interviews with Jacques Lautman and Jean-René Treanton in May–June 1978 and May 1979. See also Michael Rose, *Servants of Post-Industrial Power? Sociologie du Travail in Modern France* (New York: M. E. Sharpe, 1979).

[30] See, for example: Michael Pollak, "La Planification des Sciences Sociales," *Actes de la Recherche* 2/3, June (1976): 105–121.

[31] ADSSA: Association pour le Développement des Sciences Sociales Appliquées. Crozier, Henri Mendras, Boudon, Bourricaud, Lautman, Jean-Daniel Reynaud, and Sainsaulieu are among the principals involved in this project that, though an independent, applied teaching center, offers a third-cycle doctoral degree through Sciences Po.

to attract students. An event of symbolic, if not substantive importance, was the campaign in 1978–79 to fill the chair at the Collège de France opened by Aron's retirement. There was much speculation as to who might be, in effect, crowned the new super-vedette of France's sociology. At first Bourdieu and Boudon, the two younger stars, were assumed to be the leading candidates. Later, it was rumored that Bourdieu withdrew and that Claude Lefort had entered the race. In the end, the post was given to a chemist – a defeat for sociology itself, as many saw it. As one young sociologist said (in 1979): "La sociologie française . . . C'est de la merde."[32] Though the extreme of cynicism, this remark well expresses the widespread pessimism.

However, what remains is that French sociology has achieved a certain institutional security which, in relative terms, may be no more seriously threatened by governmental indifference and student disaffection than sociology in America or Great Britain. It is not a good moment to be a sociologist anywhere, at least not from the point of view of financial and economic security. Therefore, the important fact is that sociology in France, after a late start, has achieved at least a threshold of institutional permanence. It is taught as sociology, and no longer as social philosophy. Sociological research is funded, if not at the level sociologists would like. A significant literature does exist in its name. Sociological journals like *Revue française de Sociologie, Sociologie du Travail, Actes de la Recherche en sciences sociales, Année sociologique, Cahiers internationaux de Sociologie, Social Science Information*, and the *European Journal of Sociology* do exist (granting the last-mentioned's increasing anglicization and – among all – a variation in quality). And, most to the point, sociology worthy of international attention is being produced and read, abroad as well as at home.

Sociology has its own territory in the field of French intellectual life. It is not merely a consumer of Parisian fads, it diffuses fads of its own. As a result, the work of any specific sociologist is potentially subject to two fields of action: that of the literary *tout Paris*, and that of French sociology itself. On the level of ideas, there is clear evidence of considerable inter-field exchange. Althusser, Foucault, Barthes, and, even, Derrida have been read by sociologists. At the level of choices, many sociologists, after achieving a measure of vocational stability, face a choice. Should they place their bets on sociology, or on a more public literary field? There are of course a number of ways by which one can manage this strategy. Some, such as Alain Touraine, seem to be turning more and more toward *tout Paris* – a natural consequence of his fluent literary style, excellent

---

[32] "French sociology . . . what a lot of shit."

television presence, and, most of all, the logic of his ongoing attempt to define and revise a sociology of action. Others, at the other extreme, keep themselves to more or less strictly sociological tasks (Renaud Sainsaulieu, Pierre Grémion, Mohamed Cherkaoui). Between the extremes are still other paths. Bourdieu generally resists the temptations to public writing and keeps himself to sociology, but a sociology he develops on his own terms. Some, while not exactly *tout Paris* authors, affiliate themselves with the independent intellectual traditions of political parties (Jean Lojkine, for example) or free-floating intellectual movements (Baudrillard). Others (e.g. Bourricaud) remain identifiably within the sociological field, while writing frequently for more general revues such as *Contrepoint*. And still others finesse the choice altogether: Boudon, by establishing himself in the international sociological world dominated by the United States, while maintaining strong intellectual and professional interests in France; and Crozier, by the prodigious feat of writing for both markets.

As Boudon explains,[33] this counteraction of two fields on a given sociologist has both negative and positive results. On the negative side, the presence of the *tout Paris* field can and has been a distraction from more traditional scholarly pursuits, a distraction Boudon characterizes as "a taste for tenuous and shattering hypotheses, obscurity, the cult of an esoteric and personal style, hasty and premature syntheses, the refusal to use common sense." To this I would add: a willingness to write too much, too rapidly – a characteristic any careful reader can readily confirm. On the other hand, however, Boudon admits that the existence of this alternative field has served to break up the internal tyrannies of the patron system, in which a single intellectual leader is able to dominate younger and/or less well-established co-workers, thereby narrowing the range of intellectual creativity and experimentation (to say nothing of work opportunities).

It is to this patron system that a few additional words must be directed. Terry Clark's *Prophets and Patrons* made much of the idea of a rigid patron system as the dominant institutional form of French sociology.[34] That his book has never been well-received in France may be due as much to the embarrassment it causes as to its uneven scholarly quality. Whatever can be said against the book – its naïve functionalist idea of institutionalization, its incomplete and faulty analysis of the Latin Quarter effect, its jet ethnography[35] – Clark has identified a major weakness of sociology as a French institution. Few would deny that the patron system in which a strong leader dominates a cluster still exists, however much it is modified

[33] Boudon, "The French University since 1968."   [34] Clark, *Prophets and Patrons*, ch. 2.
[35] For a detailed and aggressive French version of these (and other) criticisms see: Jean-Claude Chamboredon, "Sociologie de la Sociologie et Intérêts Sociaux des Sociologues," *Actes de la Recherche*, March (1975): 1–17.

and weakened. The model patron cluster arrangement in sociology was of course that of the original Durkheimians.[36] During the Durkheimian and post-Durkheimian periods it could be said to have been an appropriate, even necessary, system for sociology, lacking as it did more than a few prominent figures in stable and prestigious positions. Clark clearly holds a strong bias – no doubt of functionalist provenance – against so "uninstitutionalized" an arrangement in which the patrons are potentially so little regulated by universalistic norms in their dealings with cluster members, and in which the international norms of scientific sociology can be so easily avoided in favor of occasionally local and "deviant" standards of scholarship.[37] His bias notwithstanding, one can acknowledge the good sense of Clark's reservations without requiring the institutionalization of science as an organizational telos. Boudon,[38] for example, alludes briefly to the liabilities of the system: the creation of "closed shops"; the restrictions on the amount, diversity, and inventiveness of cluster members' research; the personal distance between masters and apprentices deriving from the latter's dependence on the former.

Clark,[39] writing in the early 1970s, predicted that four structural changes would be necessary to break up and ameliorate the negative effects of the sociological *patronat*: the decentralization of control away from the national ministries in charge of research; the destruction of the patron monopoly by means of the emergence of a middle-level of independent and highly competent sociologists; the decentralization of employment options for sociologists away from a few chairs at the Sorbonne or the Collège de France and from a limited number of research centers; and the deflation of the status of the patrons themselves. The key to transformation was to be found in changes such as those that had in fact taken place by the late 1960s: the establishment of independent teaching institutions (such as the Ecole des Hautes Etudes en Sciences Sociales); the qualification of younger sociologists, not beholden to a few patrons (made possible, in principle, by the third-cycle doctorate), and the provision of large numbers of posts independent of any single leader or group of leaders (again, in principle, provided by the permanent sociological posts in the CNRS). From the vantage point of the early 1980s it appears that the desired effects of these changes have taken hold. There is, at the moment, a large number of competent and/or

[36] See the special issues on Durkheim of the *Revue française de Sociologie*, 17: 2 (1976) and 20: 1 (1979).
[37] Clark, *Prophets and Patrons*, ch. 2 and p. 240. See also pp. 20–92.
[38] Boudon, "The French University since 1968."
[39] Clark, *Prophets and Patrons*, 90–92. See also: Boudon, "The French University since 1968."

bright sociologists who, in an earlier period, might have been absorbed into a cluster, but who now work in relative independence of the major groups, even when they bear some formal affiliation: one thinks in this regard of Jean Baudrillard, Philippe Besnard, Pierre Grémion, Manuel Castells, Jean Lojkine, Mohamed Cherkaoui, Christian Baudelot, Victor Karady, among others.[40] Beyond this, it is quite clear that if Clark's view of the patron stranglehold was once true, it was not nearly so by 1980. For, even among those who maintain positions within the major groups, there is considerable latitude. Members leave groups with regularity, often on entirely amicable terms. Recently, Sainsaulieu, Worms, and Grémion have shifted to more marginal positions on Crozier's Centre de Sociologie des Organisations (CSO). Passeron, Baudelot, and Robert Castel, to varying degrees, have disaffiliated themselves from Bourdieu's Centre de Sociologie Européenne (CSE).

Boudon's Groupe d'Etude des Méthodes de l'Analyse Sociologique (GEMAS) has never really attained a formal patron structure. And perhaps the most striking example of this trend toward decentralization is Touraine's Centre d'Etude des Mouvements Sociaux (CEMS), with which people of all manner of tendencies have maintained loose affiliation. Orthodox Althusserians (Manuel Castells), left-liberal Marxists (like Daniel Bertaux), orthodox party affiliated Marxists (Jean Lojkine), maintain a working relationship alongside a more tightly-knit inner circle of researchers. In all of these groups loyalists remain for a variety of reasons. One cannot but suspect that in some way they might be subjected to the presumed evils of a patron/cluster system, but it is undoubtedly the case that the traditional arrangement is weakened if not moribund.

Now, of course, one could treat these observations skeptically. It could be noted that it has long been the case that clusters arise, rebellions or disaffections take place, and then new clusters are organized.[41] In the 1930s Georges Friedmann, Raymond Aron, and Jean Stoetzel were colleagues in Celestin Bouglé's Centre de Documentation Sociale at the Ecole Normale Supérieure (Bouglé himself having come out of the Durkheim cluster). Then, in a subsequent generational wave in the 1950s and 1960s, former associates of Friedmann founded their own groups: Touraine's

[40] Castells and Lojkine are affiliated with CEMS, Cherkaoui with GEMAS, Karady with CES, Grémion with CSO, Baudelot left CSF and now teaches at Lille. Baudrillard teaches at Nanterre. Poulantzas taught at Vincennes. Besnard holds a research post at MSH.

[41] The following discussion of departures and generations is drawn mostly from: Rose, *Servants of Post-Industrial Power?*, 26. And from an interview with Jacques Lautman on May 8, 1978. See also Karady, "The Prehistory of Present-Day French Sociology," in Lemert, ed., *French Sociology*, 33–47.

Laboratoire de Sociologie Industrielle and Crozier's Centre de Sociologie des Organisations. (In addition, Jean Daniel Reynaud eventually took over Friedmann's chair at the Conservatoire National des Arts et Métiers.) Also in the 1950s and 1960s, Crozier, Lautman, and Bourdieu were involved in Aron's original Centre de Sociologie Européenne, the last-mentioned leaving Aron in 1968 to form a group of the same original name, with the subtitle Education et Culture. Bourdieu's departure thus was part of a third modern generational wave of the late 1960s involving departures from Touraine's group: Lucien Karpik (Ecole des Mines), Marc Maurice (who established the Laboratoire d'Economie et de Sociologie du Travail at Aix-en-Provence), and others forming a group at Jussieu. In the same period Stoetzel's protegés Boudon and Bourricaud formed GEMAS in 1971. There is nothing new in members leaving old clusters.

What remains to be seen is whether or not in the 1970s the latest wave of departures – Renaud Sainsaulieu, Pierre Grémion, Robert Castel, Manuel Castells, Christian Baudelot, for example – are able to emerge as patrons. Looking only at this prominent sample, it seems unlikely. Robert Castel has no such ambition; he describes himself as a sociological artisan. Manuel Castells has left Paris for a post in the US which, it is said, he will attempt to maintain while continuing his work in Madrid and Paris. Baudelot retains his teaching post at Lille, while on leave as a researcher in INSEE. Grémion seems for the moment to have settled into the role of a semi-autonomous, virtually private scholar. Only Sainsaulieu, at present, seems to desire the traditional *patronat*. He has just founded a new research group (MACI) and, it is said, has been offered the post as director of the Centre d'Etudes Sociologiques, but there are doubts that either of these moves can establish him as a major patron. Of course, it remains to be seen what will happen in the 1980s. But at the end of the 1970s, smart money would bet that the defeat of the Left, the paralyzing effect of the unionization of researchers, the virtual freezing of the sociology section of CNRS, the general disaffection with sociology on the part of students, and a conservative government are factors which will combine to limit the options of this generation of potential stars. The best prediction would be that the basic groups – CSO, CSE, CEMS, GEMAS – will remain much as they are, atrophying perhaps as younger members move to marginal positions or into university posts, and that in the near future no new comparably important clusters will arise.

Whatever the future, the picture at present is one of a few major groups continuing to dominate in terms of visibility, if not control. The domination will be more open, though effective nonetheless, mostly in the form of defining the terms of the public debates; that is, establishing the field of sociological discourse. In addition to the obvious institutional means, the visibility will continue to rely partly on access to the established journals, partly on access to the major publishing houses, and partly on access to *tout Paris*.

The publication system

This leads to a third aspect of the Parisian intellectual field worthy of comment. What does remain of the old system is the fact that marginal or non-affiliated sociologists seem to have a less than equal chance to gain a readership. The media (*Le Nouvel Observateur* and *Le Monde*, among others) control the visibility of published books. Publishing houses often work on the basis of special series controlled by one of the stars (Bourdieu at Minuit; Touraine at Seuil; Bourricaud, Boudon, and Poulantzas (before his death) at Presses Universitaires de France). Without access to the press, to a major publisher, to an established journal, or a group-sponsored publication (such as *Actes de la Recherche*), a younger sociologist works with a handicap. Hence, his obligation to pay attention to what is in the field of sociology proper or in the Parisian *champ* and to write with an eye toward the receivability of his work. This is precisely the "tight group of relations" of which Foucault spoke in the passage cited above: relations behind the public discursive system which limit and permit what can be done and said. Though being well-connected is a great advantage in other systems, such as the American, the system works differently in Paris. Sometimes even with certain publishing advantages one is blocked in the French system, as is illustrated by the case of one very able sociologist. In the spring of 1978 he spoke with profound discouragement of the fact that his latest book – on which he had worked for four years and which was published by a prestigious house – had been totally ignored by *Le Monde* and *Le Nouvel Observateur*. A few weeks after its publication he knew that it was doomed to failure for want of serious mention. Indeed, a year later, it had sold less than half of its modest first printing and was, scientifically and commercially, dead. In the United States – where reviewing is a more open, if slower process, where time passes between publication and distribution and reviewing, where only a relative few of the East and West Coast intelligentsia need worry about mentions in the *New York Review* – we have fewer such disappointments. More cumbersome though it is, our field is more open (for these and, of course, many other reasons). In France the field of literary action still controls both the stars and the lesser lights.

One of Terry Clark's intriguing (but undeveloped) observations was that the internal pressures of the patron system undermined the quality of research by compelling authors to heed national rather than universal standards for scientific excellence. Clearly, this does not apply to the major figures: Crozier's *Bureaucratic Phenomenon*, Boudon's *Education, Opportunity, and Social Inequality*, Bourdieu and Passeron's *Reproduction* and Poulantzas's *Political Power and Social Classes* are well-recognized by international standards. Clark's point was directed more at the secondary literature, especially that of cluster members. Here again, there is reason to hold reservations. Much is being done in France that would meet anyone's standard of excellence: Victor Karady's historical studies of French education, Philippe Besnard's work on Durkheim and the Durkheimians, Mohamed Cherkaoui's studies in social mobility and the sociology of education, Pierre Grémion's work on the state, Robert Castel's studies in the social history of psychiatric medicine[42] – to cite but a few examples – are likewise works that would stand any test.

But, on the other hand, there is a certain merit to Clark's remark. One need only browse in bookstores to encounter much foolishness going by the name of sociology: books which are at best articles, theses better left on advisers' bookshelves, diary accounts of visits to China, Africa, the Americas presented as sociological investigations, and so forth. Though I have no proof, it is difficult to avoid the impression that the ratio of texts published to sociologists employed is extraordinarily high. At least this impression is supported by the publishing records of the major figures. Ignoring altogether articles, interviews, lectures, and the like, the lists of publications of the major sociologists are prodigious: Touraine, at least twelve books since 1965 (four in 1976–77, two in 1978); Bourdieu, thirteen books between 1962 and 1975; Boudon, seven books between 1965 and 1971; Crozier, at least eight since 1964.[43] One marvels that so much is as good as it is and, accordingly, one need not be surprised

---

[42] Robert Castels, *L'ordre Psychiatrique* (Paris: Minuit, 1976). Robert Castels, *Le Psychanalysme* (Paris: Maspéro, 1973). And: Robert Castel, Françoise Castel, and Ann Lovell, *La Société Psychiatrique Avancée* (Paris: Grasset, 1979). Works of the others on this list are cited in Lemert, ed., *French Sociology*. Others who are frequently mentioned in this same connection and could be listed here are: Daniel Bertaux, Pierre Birnbaum, Luc Boltanski, Jean-Claude Chamboredon, François Chazel, Claude Gignon, Nicolas Herpin, Haroun Jamous, Lucien Karpik, Janina Lagneau, Bernard Lecuyer, Guy Michelat, Monique de St. Martin, Christian Topalov, Dominique Wolton. Since this list of – more or less – younger (born after 1933) sociologists is taken from mentions in my interview notes, it is nearly as arbitrary as the first.

[43] For detailed bibliographies of these four, see: for Boudon – the list at the end (311–314) of his *La Crise de la sociologie* (Geneva/Paris: Librarie Droz, 1971), and also *Effets pervers et ordre social* (Paris: Presses Universitaires de France, 1977), *passim*; for Bourdieu – *Current Research* (Paris: Centre de Sociologie Européenne, 1972), with a supplement for the years 1972–75; for Touraine – *Rapport sur les activités, l'organisation, et le programme du Centre d'Etude des Mouvements Sociaux* (Paris: CEMS, 1976); and for Crozier – *Liste des publications* (Paris: Centre de Sociologie des Organisations, 1978).

that so much is repeated. Perhaps this is simply the fate of intellectual stars anywhere. Thus the real cases in point are those younger sociologists of obvious promise who threaten to spend themselves in incomplete and unworthy publications. Manuel Castells is often mentioned in this regard. A good bit of his work is strongly criticized for its carelessness, among other things.[44]

As everywhere, it therefore happens that poor writing, unworthy of its author (to say nothing of a reader's time), is published. The interesting question is why and how it happens in France. There are two apparent explanations which are posed at the two extremes of the patron/field analysis presented above. One is Boudon's thesis that the *tout Paris* phenomenon saps the quality of scholarly sociology. Once one gains a place in the Parisian field of readers, one is tempted to protect that position. Opportunities abound for publication, newspaper and magazine interviews, television appearances, lectures. Once this path is chosen it is difficult to resist its allure and, accordingly, its dangers. The famous recent case of the New Philosophers – who, their critics have argued,[45] were merely a media event – is but the extreme end point of a trajectory through the *tout Paris* field. Only a very few (Aron, Sartre, for example) can follow this path without sacrificing quality, without becoming idiosyncratic and idiolectic. In less extreme cases, *tout Paris* creates the peculiar circumstance of public stars who in sociology possess little influence or lose whatever they once had. Thus, writers like the late Poulantzas, Edgar Morin, and Jean Baudrillard are today widely read outside of sociology, but ignored for the most part within. It is not simply that they do not produce quality work, but that they have ceased to do sociology. I doubt, therefore, with respect to Boudon's thesis, that the issue is quality nearly so much as loss to sociology. Baudrillard, for example, *maître assistant* in sociology at Nanterre, is an able and creative thinker, but his worldly success puts him beyond sociology, of which he has no need. In the process sociology has lost a potentially important author.

The other explanation is Clark's thesis that the tightness of relations within a patron/cluster sociological field prevents true creativity from emerging and fosters mimicry of the masters by their apprentices. Though evidence of this can be found in notable cases, I think that this thesis should also be revised. If patrons restrict the freedom of their followers,

---

[44] Ruth Glass, "Verbal Pollution," *New Society* (September 29, 1977), 667–669. Compare Emmanuele Reynaud's review of Castells's *The Urban Question*, in *Revue française de Sociologie* 15: 4 (1974), 617–626.

[45] The most extensive critique of the *nouvelle philosophie* (which includes references to others) is François Aubral and Xavier Delcourt, *Contre la nouvelle philosophie* (Paris: Gallimard, 1977).

it is even more the case that the general limitation of resources within sociology has limited the opportunities for publication. There are in France few journals of high quality. *Revue française de Sociologie, Sociologie du Travail, Actes de la Recherche,* and the *European Journal of Sociology* are usually considered in this class. In the case of the *Revue française de Sociologie,* there is no question that its quality has improved markedly in recent years. An index of this improvement is that, according to members of the Editorial Committee,[46] the rejection rate for submitted articles has climbed in the mid-1970s to an estimated 70 percent. But this should be compared to rejection rates of 90–95 percent in the same period for the two leading American sociological journals. Is this simply a question of demographics? Possibly. There are fewer sociologists submitting articles for a comparable number of issues. But it is also likely to be a function of the internal closeness of the Parisian sociological community. As noted above, authors must manage their collegial relations in their professional work. Even if reviews were done anonymously, it is very difficult to maintain that anonymity in a place like Paris or in a building like the Maison des Sciences de l'Homme. We who have learned how to identify anonymous reviewers of our submissions though separated from them by great distances might well appreciate the problems of those who must face their critics daily in the cafeteria. Thus, one is justified in thinking that this internal closeness, this nearly pure visibility, has its effects on the quality of work published. For example, book reviews in sociological journals tend to be cautious and deferential.[47] Academic Paris is a small town. One wonders how much more forceful reviews might be if the authors only had to worry about chance encounters at annual meetings. More to the point, what might be the effect on the pre-publication review process? Rejections and demands for revision are surely harder to express and insist on in this setting. Thus I would say that, if quality suffers, if universal standards are not always adhered to, it is because writers are deprived by their system of the fullest and freest possible criticism upon which all science depends. But, again a caveat. It is impressive, given the system, that as much is as good as it is. We should also ask if our more "universalistic" review system has actually produced proportionately better results.

The champ of sociology: contents

Those who come to French sociology from more bureaucratically segmented sociological fields, such as the American, must read the contents

---

[46] Estimates made by Philippe Besnard and Mohammed Cherkaoui in separate interviews and communications between May, 1978 and November, 1979.

[47] For examples see Sansaulieu's review of Bourdieu and Passeron's *Reproduction* and Baudelot and Establet's critique of the same book, both in Lemert, ed., *French Sociology.*

of France's sociology with self-restraint. Because of the forces and patterns described in the previous section, one cannot look for "fields" in the American sense of the term, that is, well-organized specialities. In only the rarest of cases does it make sense to label someone in France a "sociologist of X" (education, work, etc.). Of course, much sociological work in France is institutionally identified in this way. There are research institutes specializing in the sociology of work, of education, of leisure, and so forth. But when one looks at this "field" – now, in the French sense of the term – these are not boundaries but sites, that is, material and intellectual points from and around which more general sociological work is produced. Touraine might once have been called a sociologist of work or today might be labeled a specialist in social movements. But to maintain such a definition would require a very selective reading of his work, omitting all of the discussions of sociology and society as such (which would be the greater part of his *oeuvre*). Likewise Bourdieu and Crozier: are they simply sociologists of education and organizations, respectively? Obviously not.[48]

Instead of specialities, one must read for the ideas with respect to which sociological thought is expressed. For example, Jacques Lautman has said[49] that the sociologies of work and education, so important in France, are best understood with reference to important general ideas like class, power, organization, and equality. France's sociology of work[50] is, in Lautman's view, a concrete way of examining the problems of power and class struggle, while the sociology of education in France is basically an attempt to deal with equality. There is, of course, a sense in which this is true of all sociologies. But compare (while holding constant questions of style and quality of data) Baudelot and Establet's *L'Ecole capitaliste*, Bourdieu and Passeron's *Les Héritiers*, and Boudon's *L'Inégalité des chances* with Bowles and Gintis's *Schooling in Capitalist America*, Christopher Jencks et al.'s *Inequality* and Coleman et al.'s *Equality of Educational Opportunity*.[51] All concern equality and education, but the former, French examples were read in France with reference to problems of class conflict

---

[48] In this connection, the fact that no one would label Boudon a sociologist of anything specific, but a generalist, is another refutation of the view that he is merely an American in disguise.

[49] Interview on May 25, 1978.   [50] Compare: Rose, *Servants of Post-Industrial Power?*

[51] Christian Baudelot and Roger Establet, *L'Ecole Capitaliste en France* (Paris: Maspéro, 1971). Raymond Boudon, *L'inegalité des Chances: La Mobilité Sociale dans les Sociétés* (Paris: Armand Colin, 1973). Bourdieu and Passeron, *Les Héritiers*. Samuel Bowles and Herbert Gintis, *Schooling in Capitalist America* (New York: Basic Books, 1976). Christopher Jencks et al., *Inequality* (New York: Basic Books, 1972). James Coleman et al., *Equality of Educational Opportunity* (US Department of Health, Education, and Welfare, 1966).

and inequality, while the latter, American cases, for a long while were read mostly by specialists in educational policy concerned with school reform.[52]

Of course, not every French sociologist would draw up the same list of great ideas in the same way. But, allowing for differences of emphasis, a consensus of sorts can be found. Touraine, for example, has described the sociological *champ* as organized around two cross-cutting axes.[53] One axis – between the poles of action and crisis – describes the tensions between the historical actions of society (class struggle, institutionaliza-tion, organization) and the crises interfering with these actions (orga-nizational dysfunction, bureaucratic blockage, domination, and "deca-dence"). Splitting the former is another axis – between order and change – which locates on one pole the ordering mechanisms (repression, social rules, and reproduction) and, on the other, change processes (develop-ment, adaption, and modernization). Of special interest, however, is his view that he considers order and action to be the strengths of French soci-ology (while change a blind spot of American sociology, and crisis a weak point of French sociology).[54] Of interest here is the degree to which this scheme, though specific to Touraine, reflects more general views. If one had to reduce the general to a single problematic, it would be, in Boudon's words[55] the tension between "social determinism and individual liberty"; or, rephrased, between structural constraint and social action. Of course, one might object that, at this level of abstraction, the problem is no prob-lem at all, but merely the central and universal question of any sociology. The response is that there are many illustrations in the history of sociology and social theory in which the tension between structures and individual action has been ignored altogether: the subjectivism of American prag-matist sociology up to and including ethnomethodology, the economism of orthodox Marxian theory, the objectivist formalism of early structural-ist anthropology and linguistics, the uncertain, ambiguous place of struc-tures behind Weber's social groups, and so on. Thus I would argue that the specificity of the intellectual field in France's sociology, at the moment, lies in its attempt to transcend the old objectivist–subjectivist problematic with reference to the more concrete formulations like control–action.

It is here that French sociology is both a product and beneficiary of a wider intellectual and political-economic field. First, it is necessary to

---

[52] See, for example, Jean-René Treanton, "Autre Point de Vue," *Revue française de Sociologie* 13: 3 (1972): 420–435. On the provincial character of earlier American sociology of education see: Jerome Karabel and A. H. Halsey, eds., *Power and Ideology in Education* (London: Oxford University Press, 1977).

[53] Touraine, *La Voix et le Regard*, 103.

[54] The latter observation was made in an interview on May 9, 1978.

[55] Boudon, *Effets pervers*.

speak of the changes in France's intellectual field since World War Two
and their effect on sociology. The period with which this essay is primarily
concerned (the decade after 1968) is also the period during which the
structuralism of the 1950s and 1960s was gradually dismantled. It must
be understood, however, that structuralism itself was a reaction against
the earlier period of existentialism and phenomenology in which objective
structures were deconstructed and subjectivized. Recall, as one example,
Sartre's view of objective structures: "The structures of a society which
is created by human work define for each man an objective situation as
a starting point; the truth of a man is the nature of his work, and it is
his wages. But this truth defines him just insofar as he constantly goes
beyond it in his practical activity."[56] Structuralism, quite intentionally,
replaced a scheme in which structures were produced by man with one in
which man was produced by structures. Bourdieu, commenting on this
shift, has said:

> The debate recently developed, especially in France, about structuralism as a
> "philosophy without subject" misses what is truly original in this trend of research
> by attributing to structuralism what the founders of social science, Marx as well as
> Durkheim, always stated both in their theoretical writings and scientific practice:
> structuralism simply reaffirms the postulate of the systematic character, or the
> immanent intelligibility of the social world, thus divesting individual conscious-
> ness of the gnoseological privilege granted to it by the spontaneous theory of the
> social.[57]

Bourdieu's relocation of structuralism with reference to Marx and
Durkheim is important. That sociologists in France read structuralism
through the eyes of Marx and Durkheim explains both the interest it held
for some and the fact that it was never received in the most formalist form
(as it had been in anthropology, linguistics, and literary theory). Even
structuralist social theorists like Castells and Poulantzas rather quickly
rejected such formalisms as Althusser's early notion of a purely theoretical practice.

Thus, though the problematic of structuralism held a certain appeal –
as a means for rejecting the value reductionism of American functionalism, for avoiding the subject reductionism of existentialism and American pragmatism, for constructing a notion of action and practice free
of voluntarism, and so on – it was modified by more sociologically specific sensitivities. Marx and Durkheim were structural thinkers. However,
they were anything but formalists, in large part because they were also

---

[56] Jean-Paul Sartre, *Search for a Method* (New York: Vintage, 1963), 92–93.
[57] Pierre Bourdieu, "Structuralism and Theory of Sociological Knowledge," *Social Research*
35, Winter (1968): 681–706, at 684.

social historians and men concerned with practical action (revolution, pedagogy, social change). Secondly, the role of France's post-war political and economic situation is important. Crozier has recently claimed that the broad appeal of structuralism is explained by a French fear of change. He observes that "Lévi-Strauss himself made a point of insisting that structuralism could only deal with 'cold societies' where change did not take place."[58] The argument is that structuralism was an expression medium for a left, avant-garde rhetoric which, because it was ahistorical and formalistic, posed no threat to the established order. Crozier's hypothesis, though lacking in subtlety of analysis, is quite to the point of the effect of social conditions on intellectual movements. Risky though such speculations are, it does seem plausible that the tremendous economic and political changes in France since World War Two have had their effect. Just as it is so often said that the existential humanism of Sartre's generation might have been rooted in the Resistance experience during the war, why not consider a correspondence between structuralism and the fear of change in the period when France underwent rapid economic and political change – from a largely agrarian economy to industrialization, from disastrous political instability to the mixed blessings of Gaullist social control?[59] And why not, having begun to speculate, add the effect of the bouleversements of May–June 1968 as a factor supporting (if not causing) a renewed post-structuralist interest in social movement, action, practice, and history?

Which are the ideas prominent in sociology since 1968? Order, change, structure, practice, organizational stalemates (*blocages*) and collective action, the new middle classes,[60] historicity, counterintuitive effects (*effets pervers*), the state and control, class relations, power, equality, reproduction. Individual sociologists have selected and refashioned this list to their tastes, but these are the general concepts with which French sociology, taken collectively, has been preoccupied. These are ideas for which a ready market exists among those whose society has changed rapidly, boomed economically, then leveled off just as abruptly, leaving an enormous gulf of inequality between the well-off and the disadvantaged, whose protests

[58] "France's Cultural Anxieties Under Gaullism: The Cultural Revolution Revisited," mimeograph (Centre de Sociologie des Organisations, 1978). This paper was presented at the summer 1978 conference on Gaullism at Rockport, Mass.

[59] For background discussions of the growth of modern France see: Herbert Leuthy, *France against Herself* (New York: Meridian Books, 1957). John Ardagh, *The New French Revolution* (New York: Harper and Row, 1969). And Stanley Hoffman et al., *In Search of France: The Economy, Society, Political System in the Twentieth Century* (Cambridge: Harvard University Press, 1963).

[60] George Ross, "Marxism and the New Middle Classes: French Critiques," *Theory and Society* 5: 2, March (1978): 163–190.

made all the more visible the control mechanisms of the late capitalist state. For those unconvinced by this armchair sociology of knowledge, a simple commutation test might be more persuasive. Which are the ideas and topical domains left out (that is, relatively or completely ignored) by French sociology in the same period? Voluntarism, deviance, values, the family, social psychology – many of the staples of American sociology. Were these substituted for the former as a list of leading concerns, one would no longer have French sociology.

Perhaps, however, the best way to make the point is to turn to a more modest inventory of those sociological concepts invented or stylized for use in France in the 1960s and 1970s: in other words, to the distinctive features of the French sociological lexicon. As examples, one may take the following: Bourdieu's *habitus*, Boudon's *effets pervers* (counterintuitive effects), Crozier's *société bloquée* (stalled society, also a counterintuitive effect), Poulantzas's relative autonomy of the state, Touraine's *historicité*.[61] What these otherwise quite unrelated notions have in common is that each is intended to mediate the dilemma of structural constraint and practical actions. To varying degrees each rebels against formalist structuralism, and none returns to a simple subject reductionism. Bourdieu's *habitus* – the structured dispositions which inform practical strategies – clearly aims at describing an actor whose practices are indebted to the objective relations of society as they operate in specific historic contexts. Boudon's and Crozier's interest in counterintuitive effects are diagnostic concepts for explaining the frustrations of individual actors in the face of complexly organized, objective social structures. Touraine's *historicité* attempts to open a space for social actions which is determined neither by economic structures nor abstract cultural values, a space in which he proposes to find a society of social actors struggling against the established order for control of that society. And, even Poulantzas's anti-structuralist structuralism deploys the idea of the relative autonomy of the state by which he claims to avoid an absolute determinism of economic structures. By distancing somewhat the state from the ruling class, and politics and ideology from economic factors, he seeks to introduce the possibility for relatively autonomous historical action. Of course the ideas are applied to different substantive topics: social movements (Touraine), the state (Lojkine, Poulantzas, Grémion, Crozier), education (Bourdieu, Boudon, Baudelot and Establet), social class (Touraine, Bourdieu, Poulantzas), culture (Bourdieu), the new middle class (Touraine, the PCF, Mallet, Poulantzas),[62] social mobility

---

[61] These are not necessarily what the authors would consider their main contributions. They are distinctive with respect to the field.

[62] Ross, "Marxism and the New Middle Classes."

(Boudon), the city (Lojkine, Castells), among others. But what they illustrate is that concepts of enormously different provenance and purpose seem to hover about the same problematic: structural constraints on practical actions. However widely it is diffused across national borders, this problematic has its own specificity in France's sociology: the specificity of France's native concepts, its sociological inheritance, and its political-economic circumstances.

Conclusion

Certainly it cannot be claimed that French sociology has definitive answers to the problems besetting sociologies everywhere. What can be claimed is that among those sociologies outside the strict and direct domination of American sociology, France's is one of the most interesting. Having avoided the Scylla of mimicking American empiricism and the Charybdis of philosophical devolution, French sociology stands as a small but coherent body of research, the quality of which is frequently very high. Stylistically, its example of theoretical inventiveness and scope is well worth our while. Substantively, its consideration of such topics as inequality, critique, practice, structural analysis, social change, control, and the state, among others, deserves international attention. Those sociologies, such as the American, which have just lately discovered the full significance of certain of these topics would do well to heed the example of the French who, by virtue of intellectual heritage and political-economic circumstance, have long seen them as central. If the French do not give answers, they do give questions and, more than this, they offer the witness of their situation-bound solutions. The only positive thing I can, for the moment, think to say of the spread of international capitalism is that it has at least made national circumstances less determinant. As the present fiscal crisis deepens and as the control of national ruling classes gives way to the hegemony of international money interests, whatever differences separate others from the French will become even less important: hence, a reason to transcend sociological provincialism.

Part II

Durkheim's ghosts

5

Marcel Mauss and Durkheim and why the ghosts of social differences are ubiquitous

Marcel Mauss (1872–1950) was Durkheim's nephew. It was he who carried forward the spirit of his uncle's life's work after 1917 when Durkheim, shattered by the death of his son André on the Eastern Front, died (one supposes) of a broken heart. Or, it is possible that the Great War itself shocked Durkheim into the stroke from which he never recovered. Either way, whether it was the personal or the social tragedy in the years after 1914, Durkheim was in a fashion a doomed giant of French sociology. Had his son survived the war, the father still may not have survived the crushing evidence it represented: the war and its aftermath of the absurdities brought on by the Versailles Peace Treaty in 1919, which ignored the basic rule of social accords – that peace is permanently made only when the settlement obeys the rule of proportionality between victor and vanquished. Had he lived to see Europe in the 1920s even, much less the 1930s, the experience would have almost certainly swept away all confidence that industrial societies could recapture the moral cohesion lost to the decline of the traditional order.

Still, the nephew carried on as the leader of Durkheim's school. Marcel Mauss was its most generous and possibly most accomplished scholar among the Durkheimians to have survived the war. If his generosity exceeded that of the uncle and the scholarship was every bit as sterling, the nephew's qualities were nurtured by the relation he enjoyed with the uncle. Mauss was anything but a remote relation. He too came from Epinal. He followed his uncle as a student, as in his work as a scholar. He helped in the research that led to *Suicide*, as he did in the work of *L'Année sociologique*. Their intellectual kinship in the avuncular intimacies exceeded even the blood ties – and nowhere more so than in the short but grand essay of 1903, *Primitive Classifications*, which led to the uncle's rethinking of the slips and dislocations in his works of the 1890s.

When it comes to the dynamics of kinship structures in scientific families, the avunculate is one of the more unusual relations – and

especially so when kin relations are effectively patrilineal. None of
the other great turn-of-the-nineteenth-century social thinkers enjoyed
the benefits of a kin group like the Durkheimians. Weber's Heidel-
berg circle was the closest in kind, but very different in the sense that
it never enlarged itself to embrace the institutional forms whereby
a family becomes a school. Only the University of Chicago department of sociology in the 1890s did this, but at the equivalent opposing cost of sacrificing the family-like ties that sustain a school; as a
result, the expression "Chicago School" is at best a figure of speech
covering all manner of incommensurable attitudes. Freud, of course,
fathered a well-institutionalized school, but suffered the divorces that
established psychoanalysis as a kingdom of feuds. Du Bois, though
an organizational and political genius, worked always as a solitary –
longing perhaps for the father he never found, keeping all who would
come close to him at arm's length. Charlotte Gilman and Anna Julia
Cooper, whose fathers were brutes, worked alone. Not Durkheim! True
to his moral values, he gathered to himself a group of loyal and brilliant workers, of whom none was more loyal nor more brilliant than his
nephew.

Hence, again, the quirky force of the avunculate, which is a relation
of determined differences as to age and status that, in the difference,
allows and even inspires an unusual degree of intimacy. The nephew
thus, under the right conditions, is subject to the authority of the uncle,
but it is an authority determined not in the direct power relations with
the father, but at a social distance that transcends even geographical
proximities. Against structured rules of the group, the avunculate can,
and often does, create strange affinities in which a gift bestowed on
the nephew may well return, in time, to the uncle – for whom it may be
real, if not sufficient (in Durkheim's case), to heal the wound opened
by the loss of something precious.

The most enduring gift Mauss gave his uncle – one greater in value
even than the commitment to Durkheim's group after his death – was
the tug toward new thinking on an unsolved puzzle that began with their
joint work, *Primitive Classifications* in 1903. This text stood exactly
half-way in time between Durkheim's first work of classical proportion,
The Division of Labor in Society (1893), and his last, *Elementary Forms*
(1912). It may not have cleaved Durkheim's career in two but it did
represent an important change. The first book, *De la division du travail
social*, was a study of *l'organisation des sociétés supérieures*, while the
last, *Formes élémentaires de la vie religieuse*, was intended as a study of
le système totémique en Australie. Yet, neither book kept to the societal
form it claimed to examine – the earlier one on developed societies

turned largely on a mistaken interpretation of the more elementary ones, while the latter, though obsessed with ethnographic reports on the elementary Australian forms, earned enduring value as a contribution to the sociology of modern scientific knowledge.

It would be too strong to suggest that Mauss, who was just more than thirty years old in 1903, shoved his uncle into new terrain. Durkheim had long been preoccupied with the differences between elementary and superior forms of social organization – as had been all of the great European social thinkers of the day. *Can the social survive the modern?* This could well be the foundational question of social science at a time when the line between anthropology and sociology was, at best, a metaphor of scant institutional meaning. In the relation with Durkheim, Mauss was already, in 1903, as he would be the rest of his life, the student of elementary social forms – an expertise he honed, in the manner of the times, by the second-hand study of field reports. Durkheim was hardly an innocent to this practice, but it did not become salient in works of his own hand until the writings leading from *Primitive Classifications* to *Elementary Forms*. The field data that constitute the value of the former, much more scant and broadly drawn than those in the latter, led to a conclusion that could well be pasted into the final pages of *Elementary Forms* without causing notice:

> Primitive classifications are therefore not singular or exceptional, having no analogy with those employed by more civilized peoples; on the contrary, they seem to be connected, with no break in continuity, to the first scientific classifications. . . . We have seen, indeed, how these classifications were modeled on the closest and most fundamental form of social organization. This, however, is not going far enough. Society was not simply a model which classificatory thought follows; it was its own divisions which served as divisions for the system of classifications. The first logical categories were social categories; the first classes of things were classes of men, into which these things were integrated. It was because men were grouped, and thought of themselves in the form of groups, that in their ideas they group other things; and in the beginning the two modes of grouping were merged to the point of being indistinct. Moieties were the first genera; clans, the first specifics. Things were thought to be integral parts of society, and it was their place in society which determined their place in nature. (Durkheim and Mauss, *Primitive Classifications* (1903), 81–83)

"Things were thought to be integral parts of society." Social facts are things because social things *are* – are what? The social is the integral of things, which in turn are the content of thinking itself. To think concretely is to think with things transformed into signs lent meanings by the social group. It is seldom noticed, however, that the theory involves two slips of a necessary if unfortunate kind. Thought, if it is to think, must be outside the social, which is to say that the two must be distinct. Thus, in turn, things may be integral to society, but they are not the same sort of thing – otherwise they would be nothing, *no-thing* at all because things of whatever kind are attributions of distinctions of kind and quality.

Hence, the rule of social differences. For Durkheim it began with the necessary differences between social and natural things – thus to allow the autonomy of sociology as the science of social things. But this programmatic rule of differences could not account for the differences necessary for things to be thought. If social facts are things, then social things must be different. But their difference cannot lie in the operating procedures by which analytic science cuts them out of their naturally occurring relations. This was the error Durkheim made in *Rules* and compounded in *Suicide* where, in the overly analytic effort to demonstrate causal variations among the social types of suicide, he could not explain the fact that the types, far from being discrete, were not even continuous variables. The rule of social differences with Durkheim was thus the fly in the ointment of his early sociology which he meant to be a balm on the wounds of social divisions.

Durkheim could not solve the riddle of the rule imposed upon his sociology, not even in *Elementary Forms*, where he came upon the means but could not apply it. The means were collective representations. But the application of the concept in its strict semiotic sense had to await Lévi-Strauss who recovered the Durkheimian themes in Saussure to allow for differences as a transformational grammar. What Saussure understood, and Durkheim did not, was just this: Things become social things within a system of representations – by which signs are attached not to the objects they represent but to the signs by which they are brought into the cultural system. A cultural system of meanings is, thus, one in which the key operation is the wink – the slight, unspoken, recognition of differences. A suicide is a social thing only because suicides, whatever their despair, recognize their differences from the social whole, which they choose to quit, leaving behind the signs of their anger, self-hatred, love, or despair. Speaking is a kind of suicide in that the speaker kills all the other meanings that he could convey in order to let the one that remains have its significance. No other meaningful killing is quite so fine as self-murder – we kill ourselves – literally or figuratively – whenever we cut ourselves off from the others; and this is quite a different cutting off from that of analytic science, which is directed at the purported world of objects.

It is not that Mauss understood what his uncle could not. But it is that the early work with Durkheim, and that after his death, led Mauss in quite another direction from their joint effort in 1903 – and this line turned out to be independently important to the later history of French social thought. Mauss outlived Durkheim by a good third of a century. But after his uncle's death in 1917, among all the other works of his pen, he wrote but one short book, *Essai sur le don* (1925). And, what a work it was! No longer than *Primitive Classifications* and in some ways less disciplined theoretically than the work with Durkheim, this essay (translated as *The Gift*) did, however, lay the groundwork for a reinterpretation of the rule of differences. The thing to which Mauss's study attended was the coin of social exchange. What makes the gift a social thing, however, is that there are few other social things where the tactical dilemma of social obligation is more finely expressed. For it is the gift that stands at the crossroads of social exchange by which the rules of differences and moral obligations are practiced.

> To give something is to give a part of oneself. . . . one gives away what is in reality a part of one's nature and substance, while to receive something is to receive a part of someone's spiritual essence. To keep this thing is dangerous, not only because it is illicit to do so, but also because it comes morally, physically and spiritually from a person. . . . There is a series of rights and duties about consuming and repaying existing side by side with rights and duties about giving and receiving. The pattern of symmetrical and reciprocal rights is not difficult to understand if we realize that it is first and foremost a pattern of spiritual bonds between things which are to some extent parts of persons, and persons and groups that behave in some measure as if they were things. (Mauss, *The Gift* (1925), 10, 11)

Here, well after Durkheim's death, is the other shoe dropping on the sociological floor.

The sociological epistemology developed by the nephew and the uncle from 1903 to 1912 opened sociology to questions of social things as things knowable because they are transformable representations of society itself. But the risk they took was the one inherent in any and all constructionist theories of knowledge – from Kant and Hegel to Berger and Luckmann and their followers – to say that social things are constituted in practical reason is to speak a half-truth. As strong as the insight may be, the obstacle it creates is that of the unresolved differences between Kant and Herder, or Hegel and Marx, or Berger and Luckmann and Horkheimer and Adorno, namely: How is knowledge to maintain the dialectic of its own enlightenment? How, in other words, is practical knowledge's desire to universalize the other able to resist its need to acknowledge its difference?

The gift is the answer – or, if not the answer *tout court*, at the least the purest illustration of it. To give a gift, whether material or moral, is to give a part of one's own being. Gift-giving is, if not suicidal, at least sacrificial to the point of mortal danger. Thus, in gift-giving one puts her life in the hands of another. If the gift is not returned in time, it is lost – to the moral bond that constitutes the relation itself, which in turn is the moral bond upon which the social relies, without which there could be no thinkable social things.

What was added, in time, to Mauss's insight was that the danger in gift-giving is not that one does not recognize the obligation to return, but that the return may be attempted at the wrong moment. To give the self-same gift back in the instant it is given, rejects it and the giver. To give back in the same instant something else of comparable value, devalues the gift by not receiving it well, which is to say: by not holding it over time to allow the gift to separate from the giver. To repay a gift after too long a delay breaks the relation sealed by the giver by allowing the value of the gift to inflate too much, which has the effect of deflating the value of the relation to a degree that it cannot be reassessed. In a sense, it is almost worse to return the gift at the wrong time than not to return it all. This is the famous equation that Derrida was among the first to clarify but that also lay at the foundation of Bourdieu's theory of *habitus* as a practiced art. What goes wrong when the gift is not well exchanged is that the social differences upon which the social relation depends are destroyed. Giving aims to give oneself to the other. Returning the gift must affirm the difference from which the other gives – a difference that requires a deferral in time to achieve the separation by which the loss of the thing is lent its value as a representation of the social bond.

This is the core of a cultural semiotics. Collective representations are not abstractions. They thrive in the exchange of particular and well-timed repayments. And for social things to represent meanings – to have social value – their exchange must obey the rule that Marx described so beautifully in *Capital I* in his discussion of the commodity theory of values – that exchange depends on a qualitative difference expressed by a quantitative equivalence. As one cannot hope to trade a bushel of wheat for a bushel of wheat from the same field, neither can he return the sheep just given in the potlatch without violating the status of the giver by trivializing the value of the gift. So too, meaningful communication – whether in languages as such or signs of another order – will not work when the recipient repeats, word for word, what has just been said.

All traffic signals are subject to moving violation. This is how they work. The signal is a gift of an arbitrary kind for which is exchanged the sign of respect for the social convention. To ignore the signal is to create danger. To take it too literally is to tie up social traffic – in crowded places, just as dangerous. But to stop or go makes meaningful the red or green, which would be empty gestures were it not for the fact that, for whatever reason, drivers of cars understand the slight difference in color conveys the enormity of the social whole as it winks at us on the small corners of the daily round.

Durkheim's woman and the Jew as the pluperfect past of the good society (1995*)

More than any of the classic social theorists, Emile Durkheim devoted himself to founding and defining a sociology that could become *the* sociology of modern life. With the possible exception of Max Weber, none of them was as temperamentally suited to the precise definition as a way of beginning endeavors of this kind. By contrast, Marx and Freud were too much interested in getting to the mysterious bottom of things to allow their conscious logic to be the foundational pillar of any project.

Thus, again, an irony: that among those still-famous classic thinkers, the one who in his professional sociology most resisted the fantastic and the imaginary could not keep them out. Durkheim was, therefore, precisely correct (or correct enough) in his science. A sociology is, indeed, about facts that constrain the individual even when the individual resists them. There could be no sociology without them; of which there could be no better proof than Durkheim himself, who in his life as a professional sociologist wanted to be the one who proved there were social facts that did not rely for explanation on the individual. Yet, he was a practical enough moralist that he could not resist the constraining force of the moral riddle of modern life, which entails, among other things: *Modern societies are different from all others because, being divided themselves, difference is what makes them modern.* As science, modern sociologies were obliged, somehow, to explain difference with difference. As moral theories, modern sociologies had, somehow, to justify the good of difference as a (now) natural state of life. The riddle within the riddle was what to do with the different demands of science: *If science could produce the truth, then moral differences would fade; if, however, moral differences were taken with*

* Reprinted with permission and thanks to Dean Birkenkamp, who edited both the first and second editions of the book from which the essay is taken, namely: "Modernity's Riddle and Durkheim's Lost Fathers," *Sociology After the Crisis* (Boulder, CO: Paradigm Publishers, 2004) (revised edition; originally published by Westview Press, 1995). The selection has been edited to eliminate material that fits well in that book but not here. Portions of the essay were drawn from "The Canonical Limits of Durkheim's First Classic," *Sociological Forum* 9:1 (March 1994): 87–92.

final seriousness, none would be true. Difference, in other words, challenged the liberal, cultural foundations of modern life. . . .

Durkheim's solution to the riddle did not succeed because it could not – either in his sociology or in his moral theory of modern life. He did no better, no worse, than the other classic social theorists. But the earnestness with which Durkheim held to his conviction that a new science could solve the riddle of modern life illustrates best of all the depths to which this riddle structured modern culture. *Modern societies are different from all others because, being divided themselves, difference is what makes them modern.* Durkheim, like many moderns, believed that the differences that make and shake the foundations of modern life were a new, more progressive form of common life. He understood that the social differences were just as salient in modern times as the collective conscience was for its time. Yet the puzzle was how to recover the latter's original social good in the modern division of labor. For Durkheim, as for many moderns, the solution was to stipulate future progress as the final standard for the good society. The silent contradiction in that standard was that it could only be one projected back to an original good lost to the present. In Durkheim's case, the price of a real – that is, present and good – society was the denial of its very condition of existence, its differences.

If things social are different, then who am I? If my world is divided, then where do I fit in? For all practical purposes, the question only arises in modern societies because only then and there is difference considered a structured (that is, enduring, hence salient) feature of social life. This, then, is why the question – either way it is put – may be considered the riddle of modern life and thus of sociologies of all kinds. Were it the case that individuals lived amid social relations they had no reason to consider different (or, as it is often said, Other), then very probably the need for a sociology would not arise. For only when the structured social life is different (both from the individual and in and of itself) is there any reason to worry, one way or another, about its constraining power. If the social world appears to be the same as oneself, then it can be more safely assumed that one knows who one is. The riddle is acute and ubiquitous in modern urban life. Still, it can be found at all times and in all places even when conditions allow people to forget their common encounter with differences.

All human individuals do at some time in their experience encounter those elemental social conditions in which the social is not felt to be different. One such experience is, of course, that of infancy and early childhood. The other is in later life when the individual, having been told the tales of his family and community, "remembers" what it was like in earlier, simpler times. The former is direct experience; the latter indirect. The two are linked directly in social experience. Individuals tell and hear, thus imagine, that they remember the stories of earlier times because they all experienced such an earlier, elementary time – a time when, in Durkheim's terms, the collective consciousness was, for all intents and purposes, the same as the individual's: not different, thus not modern. In this sense, we were all once, to use the awkward but necessary word, primitives. . . .

Curiously, there are few children in most sociologies, and none at all in Durkheim's. Had it not been for Freud, there would have been few children at all among the classic social theorists.[1] But, it is clear why, except for those few in some of his suicide rates, Durkheim's sociology had no children. The child in his scheme would have been outside, before the social. The child was among those social things Durkheim could not have thought because of his view of man: "Man is double, that is because social man superimposes himself upon physical man." To which Durkheim adds immediately this astonishing remark:

If this dissolves, if we no longer feel it in existence and action about and above us, what is social in us is deprived of all objective foundation. *All that remains is an artificial combination of illusory images, a phantasmagoria vanishing at the least reflection;* that is, nothing which can be a goal for our action. Yet, this social man is the essence of civilized man; he is the masterpiece of civilization. Thus we are bereft of reasons for existence; for the only life to which we could cling no longer corresponds to anything actual; the only existence still based upon reality no longer meets our needs.[2]

For Durkheim, sociologically speaking, there is nothing real outside the social because there is no individual without the social. Man is either social, or some rudimentary physical creature left to the phantasmagoria of pure imagination.

For Durkheim, the pre-verbal child is not social, therefore not sociologically real. The idea is astonishing because the opposite could be just as true according to his theory. The small child is, in social fact, the individual most completely constrained by the social, beginning with the total social environment provided (in his middle-class European culture, surely) by that other social individual who, also, does not exist in his sociology: the mother-woman.

Here, Durkheim is faced with a particularly hard set of facts. Women exist. They certainly existed in his study of suicide rates. Yet, according

---

[1] In a sense Freud's oedipal child was not really a child. He was the projection of adult fears into the child's experience.

[2] Emile Durkheim, *Suicide* (1897). Trans. George Simpson (New York: Free Press, 1951), 213, emphasis added.

to his implicit theory of society as the collective conscience, it is only man who is double, only man who is civilized. Woman exists, but she is not social. "[The] two sexes do not share equally in social life. Man is actively involved in it, while woman does little more than look on from a distance"[3] Though more social than the child, the woman (without whom, in real life, the child cannot be social) is similarly outside social life, thus outside Durkheim's sociology.

Woman, in particular, must be less than social. Otherwise, society, as Durkheim thought it, could not be what he imagined it to be. For society to be *the* thing in itself – to be *sui generis*, thus the social fact of sociology – society must be one of two things: Either society is integral, that is, one in and of itself as in the elementary collective conscience, or it is sufficiently one as in his vision of a progressively moral organic society. Durkheim's society, thereby, could not tolerate real, unyielding, constraining differences. Durkheim's *sui generis* society was, thus, the elementary society of the lost past of modern society. Modern society depended, in his view, entirely on the ability of modern life to progress to an organic unity in which the differences felt in such social divisions as class struggle would be overcome in a greater bodily unity of equal, if separate, contribution. Thus, similarly, he says, of woman:

The female sex will not again become more similar to the male; on the contrary, we may foresee that it will become more different. But these differences will become of greater social use than in the past. Why, for instance, should not aesthetic functions become woman's as man, more and more absorbed by functions of utility, has to renounce them? Both sexes would thus approximate each other by their very differences. They would become socially equalized, but in different ways. And evolution does seem to be taking place in this direction.[4]

In modern life, the differences are overcome by functional equalities. In this case a woman has the aesthetic function, man the utilitarian. She makes the home and other things beautiful; he works and makes the world.

Thus the deep structural contradiction in Durkheim's sociology. He wants a sociology that will solve the riddle of modern life, one that overcomes differences while acknowledging them as real. But he cannot account for differences in society except by his unacknowledged leap of the imagination. Women, like class divisions, are not morally real. The differences they represent resolve themselves in social progress. But what is social progress? Nothing less than the achievement, in modern life, of that state of social consciousness which most nearly approximates the one now lost to consciousness, the elementary or primitive.

[3] *Ibid.*, 385.   [4] *Ibid.*, 385.

Durkheim's society was indeed a "phantasmagoria vanishing on the least reflection." However much he wanted it otherwise, Durkheim's theory of society was that of the social world lost to the present, recaptured in the hope of progress. But not real in the sense of being there, present. What was most real, for him and the social theorists, was a world divided by differences. Then, in Europe, differences of class. In the United States, this too, but also palpable differences of race. And, in both, differences between men and women.

With all the best intentions, Durkheim was forced to discredit two historic figures, both of whom were salient in his life and his society. Without this move, his sociology would have failed. But his discrediting was not harsh. Both of them were given their place – one as the heroic figure of the modern primitive; the other as the sign of the primitive modern yet to be. These figures were the Jew and the woman. The one was the figure of his own lost childhood, the other of society's future perfect. The collective conscience Durkheim knew as a child was that of Jewish life and law. He would not, however, have become a sociologist had he not renounced those traditions. This act may, or may not, have been the central drama of his early life. But it is unlikely to have been one whose effects were not powerful moral constraints on Durkheim the individual. In some important way, he became what he was because he had lost the collective conscience of his childhood, for which he sought a new morality in the science of modern life. But, Durkheim the child could not have been far away, ever.

Though Durkheim said nothing of his own childhood and little of children in his sociological writings, he said quite a lot about Jewish people and their traditions. In *Division of Labor*, for one striking example, the Jews were the basis for another of Durkheim's surprising omissions. The crucial technical feature of that book's argument was his use of laws as the visible index of the moral life of the two different forms of social life (a move made necessary by the significant fact that society "does not lend itself to exact observation nor indeed to measurement").[5] He, thus, stipulated penal laws, which were repressive in their effect, as the observable indicator of mechanical societies. He thought, in this regard, that the more primitive societies were rule organized, thus repressive of those who broke the mechanical form. Contrariwise, the more modern and organic societies, Durkheim thought, came into sight when the repressive rules of the most ancient societies made way for laws that served more to bind the

---

[5] Emile Durkheim, *The Division of Labor in Society* (1893). Trans. George Simpson (New York: Free Press, 1964), 64.

separated members to the whole. These, of course, arose as the division of labor became more and more organic. Functionally separated members meant that no one member was bound to the common conscience directly, for which the corollary: In the more modern, organic society no individual could insult the social whole gravely. The modern man, thus, was less susceptible to repressive punishment (which Durkheim described as the repulsive gesture of the collective conscience in primitive societies). Accordingly, in organic societies, the rule of law served more and more to restore the deviant member to the whole. In its most advanced form, contract law is the organic law par excellence. In Durkheim's own words in *Division of Labor*:

Social life comes from a double source, the likeness of consciences and the division of social labor. The individual is socialized in the first case, because, *not having any real individuality, he becomes, with those whom he resembles, part of the same collective type*; in the second case, because, while having a physiognomy and a personal activity which distinguishes him from others, he depends upon them in the same measure that he is distinguished from them, and consequently upon the society which results from the union.

The similitude of consciences gives rise to juridical rules which, with the threat of repressive measures, impose uniform beliefs and practices upon all. The more pronounced this is, the more completely is social life confounded with religious life, and the nearer to communism are economic institutions.

The division of labor gives rise to juridical rules which determine the nature and the relations of divided functions, but whose violation calls forth only restitutive measures without any expiatory character.[6]

On close inspection, there is something wrong here. It's all too neat. Where there is collective conscience, there is no individual; where there is division of social labor, there is, though in indirect relation to the social whole, no society. But if, in the simpler societies, there is no individual, how can there be a "similitude of consciences" – in either sense of the word?

Part of the problem appears in an odd literary fact of *Division of Labor*. The book contains very few actual social facts. Though published just a year before *Rules* and filled with clues that he was already planning his great empirical study of suicide,[7] *Division of Labor* relies on very few facts. The problem is not simply that it is a book of theory (in spite of the author's empirical intentions). Rather, it is that when he does refer to facts Durkheim gets them wrong. Most astonishingly he is wrong (or at least not exactly right) where he ought to have known better, but perhaps he was constrained by his theory to misrecognize the facts.

---

[6] *Ibid.*, 226, emphasis added.
[7] The opening chapter of Book 2 of *Division of Labor* is a virtual outline of the argument of *Suicide*.

Durkheim gets the facts of ancient Jewish law wrong at the crucial point in his argument. In order to prove the theoretical scheme (summarized in the passage just quoted), he turns to history. Given his theory, one would there expect empirical references to "primitives." Indeed, he begins the crucial section: "As far as we can judge the state of law in very inferior societies it appears to be entirely repressive."[8] Durkheim then refers to the unfreedom of the savage. But who is the savage? It turns out to be the original Jews, ancient Israel. His argument establishes the laws of ancient Israel as a principal illustration of repressive law ("the oldest monument of this kind that we have"). Durkheim then summarizes and discusses the four most juridical and priestly books of the Pentateuch – Exodus, Leviticus, Numbers, Deuteronomy – to support the conclusion that in them "restitutive law – cooperative law in particular – holds a very minor position."[9]

What is wrong is that this is not so. The priestly codes of ancient Israel were always developed against the foundational covenant that binds Israel to its God. In fact, it is hard to imagine any interpretation of the very scriptural texts to which Durkheim refers without ultimate reference to the original covenant. As it turns out, the predominant narrative of Exodus, the first of the books Durkheim cites, is restitutive: "Now therefore if you will obey my voice and keep my covenant, you shall be my own possession among all peoples; for all the earth is mine, and you shall be to me a kingdom of priests and a holy nation. There are the words which you shall speak to the children of Israel."[10] The repressive laws of the Pentateuch are morally and religiously incoherent without references to the contract God makes with Israel, and that contract, like modern contracts, is regenerative and restitutive. In fact, in the annual cycle of Jewish ritual life, regeneration and restitution are every bit as salient as atonement and punishment.[11]

Even if one were to allow for the likelihood that in Durkheim's orthodox childhood the collective conscience strongly emphasized the repressive rules in Jewish life, it is hard to imagine how he could have escaped instruction on Israel's founding contract. It is more likely that he

[8] Durkheim, *Division of Labor*, 138. The book's empirical section is chapters 4, 5, 6, and 7, which conclude Book 1 (in which the classic distinction between mechanical and organic societies and their laws is made). The passage quoted is in the conclusion to Book 1.

[9] Durkheim, *Division of Labor*, 138.

[10] George E. Mendenhall, *Law and Covenant in Israel and the Ancient near East* (Pittsburgh: The Presbyterian Board of Colportage of Western Pennsylvania, 1955). And: Norman Gottwald, "Israel and the Covenant," in *Light to the Nations* (New York: Harper & Row, 1959), ch. 5.

[11] See, for example, Mircea Eliade, *The Myth of the Eternal Return; or, Cosmos and History* (Princeton: Princeton University Press, 1954).

was driven in adult life to misremember, or misrecognize, his own Jewish past. The sociology of Durkheim's adult life took on moral assumptions that required a denial of his childhood – either of what he knew in fact, or of what he could have known had he been more free to look clearly. Durkheim was too careful a scholar to have made such a mistake without some good reason. That reason, very likely, was that his sociology was linked in important ways to his personal experience in childhood. It is perfectly clear that his personal story contradicts his sociology. Were it the case that the orthodox Jewish laws of his childhood had constrained so powerfully as to deny those under its influence "any real individuality," then it is improbable, if not thoroughly inconceivable, that Durkheim could have separated himself from the powerful societal force of those generations of rabbis and Jewish law. Conversely, had he, one would expect he would have been severely punished, if not by his father (who died young), then by that community. So far as I know, there is no evidence that he was. In fact, when he died, Durkheim was buried not among France's cultural saints in Père Lachaise in Paris but in provincial Epinal among those he had left to found sociology.

Such was the power of Durkheim's sociology. In order to make it what he thought it should be, he had to misrepresent the experience of his own childhood. The lost world he obliquely reconstructed in his book on the modern division of labor was a product of keen, but entirely modern, imagination. For there to be a society sufficiently *sui generis* to account for the independent power of social facts, there had to be, at least once, a collective conscience before the altar of which modern men learned the power of that society. Yet, for modern man to live as a free and rational individual, that original society must have been replaced by one that allowed an individual sufficient freedom to be "an autonomous source of action" and sufficient conscience (in both senses) to be a moral man.[12] Thus, again, the riddle of modern morality: *If things social are different, who am I?* I can only be who I am if I am free enough from the demands of the society to be autonomous, yet somehow moral. That is, the modern man can accept himself as different only by insisting that he is not fully social, not fully constrained by society.

Thus, Durkheim was left in a quandary he sought to repress behind his good theory. If, morally, modern society had lost its original power, then how could there be a sociology based on facts that constrained powerfully? If, in other words, we were to account for Durkheim himself – as sociologist, not as rabbi – we could only do so in one of two ways, neither fully

---

[12] "Man is a moral being only because he lives in society, since morality consists in being solidary with a group." See Durkheim, *Division of Labor*, 399, to which compare p. 403: "To be a person is to be an autonomous source of action."

satisfying. Either, his theory of sociology was wrong because, were it right, he would not have been what he was. Or, Durkheim was wrong about that which he ought to have known best – his childhood, his experience as a Jew. The latter is the only plausible choice. But its price is that one must suspect Durkheim's idea of sociology and, thus, very likely, sociology itself. That there is reason to do so became evident in his greatest book on the 1890s, *Suicide*, where the Jew reappears, misconstrued again, at a crucial juncture in that book's argument; and where one must accept as fact that Durkheim's sociology required, among other misadventures, the exclusion of women from society.

If *Division of Labor* is the book in which Durkheim outlines his moral theory of modern life and its uncertainties, and *Rules* is the book where he outlines his formal program for a sociology capable of resolving those uncertainties, then *Suicide* is the book in which both of these prior purposes come together. As he said in its preface, "The progress of a science is proven by the progress toward solution of the problems it treats."[13] Here he sought to prove two things at once: (1) that sociology's social facts could explain what was apparently the most unsocial of acts, self-murder; (2) that sociology's account of suicide in modern societies confirms the moral responsibility of modern societies to rebind themselves by securing a truly organic division of social labor. Yet, again, the two purposes do not suit each other exactly as Durkheim had hoped.

In order to demonstrate the power of sociology, Durkheim had not only to show that the most individualistic of human acts, self-murder, was caused by social forces but to prove that there was variation among the causes and types of suicide. The theoretical demands on Durkheim were strict: If in a divided modern society suicide and its causes did not vary, then, in the words of his definition of social facts, neither could meet the condition of being "general over the whole of a given society whilst having an existence of its own." In more formal language, unless suicide and its causes varied in a differentiated society, then they could not be variables, dependent and independent, in scientific sociology. Thus, the book's underlying argument (especially in its crucial Book 2, "Social Causes and Social Types") required him to set up his famous, but incomplete, fourfold table of suicide types. Each type of suicide was to correspond to a different cause:

First, *egoistic suicide* is principally illustrated by the greater rate of suicide among modern individuals in the liberal, more educated, more well-to-do classes. Protestants in particular. This is the type of suicide caused, he argued, not by knowledge or education itself but by the failure of modern society to integrate

[13] Durkheim, *Suicide*, 35.

the individual, thus to prevent him from becoming too individualistic, thereby escaping society's moral protection.

Second, *altrustic suicide* is, presumably, due to just the opposite cause. If egoism is too much individualism, altruism is too much society. The principal examples of altruistic suicide are cases of individuals who kill themselves for the sake of some powerful societal purpose – men in old age, women at the death of their husbands, followers or servants on the death of their chiefs.

Third, *anomic suicide* is most clearly and unambiguously illustrated by its association with times of economic crises. *Anomie* may lead to suicide when major disruptions in the social order inhibit society's ability to regulate the feelings and actions of individuals. Lacking moral guidance in difficult times, individuals are deprived of the moral preservation that might otherwise keep them from self-murder.

Fourth, *fatalistic suicide* is best known for being the most famous footnote in the early history of sociology.[14] While Durkheim devoted at least a chapter to each of the other types, fatalism appears in a footnote at the end of his discussion of anomic suicide. It was a logical afterthought (one defined "for completeness' sake") and significant for that fact alone. As altruism was to be the opposite of egoism, then, he reasoned, fatalism must be anomic suicide's opposite – instead of too little, too much regulation. Examples of fatalism were hard to come by, he freely admits, though he proposes suicides of young husbands or of married but childless women. In the footnote, he adds: "But it has so little contemporary importance and examples are so hard to find aside from the cases just mentioned that it seems useless to dwell on it." As before, Durkheim was forced by his scientific logic to mention even that which seemed useless.

But, in the passing reference to fatalism, was it useless? If that fourth causal type were not there, then what is one to think of the others? If he was correct in defining the preceding three – that is, if his logic rightly isolated those distinct types – then how could there not be this fourth? Had he set out to perform a purely inductive study in which he searched the empirical field for instances from which to infer the types, then the fourth logical type would not be required. But, he had already set out with the assumption that the types *must* exist if sociology is to work in a society of social differences. That fourth type just *had* to be there. Just as altruism (also, weakly developed) had to be there as the opposite to egoism. But the real test of the integrity of Durkheim's four types, and thus of his sociological method, is between those two most clearly modern types, egoistic and anomic.

The problem of Durkheim's method becomes all the more evident in his own summary of the three main types:

14 *Ibid.*, 276.

Anomie . . . is a regular and specific factor in suicide in our modern societies. . . .
So we have here a new type to distinguish from the others. *It differs from them in
its dependence, not on the way in which individuals are attached to society, but on how
it regulates them.* Egoistic suicide results from man's no longer finding a basis for
existence in life; altruistic suicide, because this basis for existence appears to man
situated beyond life itself. *The third sort of suicide [anomic, that is] . . . results from
man's activities lacking regulation and his consequent sufferings.* . . .

   Certainly [anomic] and egoistic suicide have kindred ties. Both spring from society's insufficient presence in individuals. In egoistic suicide it is deficient in truly
collective activity, thus depriving the latter of object and meaning. In anomic suicide, society's influence is lacking in the basically individual passions, thus leaving
them without a check-rein.[15]

Not only, as Durkheim admits, do egoistic and anomic suicide have kindred ties, but, for all intents and purposes, they may be the same. In
the one, society's collective activity is deficient; in the other, society lacks
influence. In the one, the individual is too little integrated; in the other,
he is too little regulated. In one (egoistic), the principal example is that
of the too successful economic man whose success may separate him
from society; in the other (anomic), the prime example is that same man
when he faces a collapse of his economic order. It is not that there are
no differences but that the differences are so slight. What might have
been the results had Durkheim had at his disposal a technology that
would have permitted a convenient regress of the causes against each
other? Did the individual economic man kill himself more or less often in
times of social disruption? One supposes more. But Durkheim does not
say.

   What can be said in retrospect is what is obvious from Durkheim's
unqualified use of the word "society" in this important summary statement. For it is in the modern divided societies, where suicide is the most
interesting sociological fact, that his lack of an explicit theory of society
is most a problem. If society is the general, powerful, and *sui generis* thing
he thought it was, then the problem of modern societies is that they are
too divided for such a *sui generis* society to be any one thing.

   Durkheim's society, thus, was a lost world he constructed in his sociological imagination, for which the most primitive societies (where suicide
is not a remarkable fact) were the dreamlike images. This was already
evident in *Division of Labor* and would become the central fact of *Elementary Forms of the Religious Life*. For Durkheim to argue strongly that
sometimes modern societies allow individuals too much autonomy (thus
accounting for egoistic suicide) and that sometimes individuals are insufficiently regulated by society (thus causing *anomie* and its consequences)

---

[15] *Ibid.*, 258, emphasis added.

was to argue little more than his general moral concern with modernity: The modern social division of labor sometimes causes individuals not to know who they are, or what to do, amid the differences it creates. For Durkheim to argue a strong causal explanation of the variable types of suicide, he would have had to have a stronger theory of society. He did not because the society he imagined, even in modern times, was the lost society of his – and modern man's – childhood.

Once again the Jew and the woman put Durkheim's sociology up against his moral concerns. In *Suicide* the Jew is the all-important figure who confirms the uniqueness of egoistic suicide. In the strongest, most confident, early part of his analysis of this type, it is the Jew who accounts for the unusually high rates of suicide among the educated, well-to-do Protestants. Durkheim here has no problem explaining the higher rates among Protestants relative to Catholics, for the latter are the less well educated, thus less likely to be separated from the social influence of the religious community. But, by this logic, Jews, being on the average even more literate and educated than Protestants, ought to have had even higher suicide rates. Instead, by his calculations, they had the lowest. This could only be, he concludes, because it is neither the religion nor the education that explains excessive individualism but the religious society. Jewish religious society is strong. Thus, among Jewish people, education serves to bind men to their community, while among Protestants it presses men toward individualism and separates them from the religious society. This is the crucial distinction because Durkheim's whole moral and sociological enterprise would be nonsense if, as he says, knowledge were "the source of evil [and not] its remedy, the only remedy we have."[16] Durkheim, therefore, was forced to conclude that the Jew was at one and the same time among the most intelligent, therefore most "modern," of men, and a "primitive" in certain respects. "The Jew, therefore, seeks to learn, not in order to replace his collective prejudices by reflective thought, but merely to be better armed for the struggle."[17]

The Jew, therefore, *must* have been for Durkheim the modern primitive. Otherwise, egoistic suicide would have been doomed as a type from the beginning. The cost, however, was that Durkheim, again, was required to renounce himself. If not himself, at least his childhood self. Once again, Durkheim's sociology could not explain Durkheim, the educated Jew, who sought to learn precisely in order to separate himself, and all

---

[16] *Ibid.*, 169.

[17] *Ibid.*, 168. In the passage immediately following, Durkheim explicitly describes the Jew as the modern primitive: "This is the reason for the complexity he presents, primitive in certain respects, in others, he is an intellectual and man of culture" (p. 168).

of France, from the "collective prejudices" of the traditional social conscience upon which his vague, but necessary, image of society depended.

Durkheim's science worked at the expense not just of his own original tradition but of the other figure for whom he could not account:
woman. Woman appears more prominently than one might suppose, given
Durkheim's prejudices. Yet, she, in her way, is the crucial test of the
theory. Were one to study the suspicion that the four types are logical and
non-empirical, it would be possible to test the lack of empirical salience in
Durkheim's types by looking for, then comparing, any category of social
facts that is constant to all four. If there were one, then it would be possible to determine if the facts associated with the multiple appearance of
the social category varied with the general type. There is one, and it is
woman.

She is, first of all, common to the two marginal types. The widow is
a prime example of altruistic suicide, as the barren woman is one of the
two meager illustrations of fatalistic suicide. But she is even more salient
in the other two types, where women create major technical problems
that Durkheim had to solve to save his theory. In his discussion of egoistic suicide, after the presentation of the Jew as the primitive modern, he
turns to the second major instance of egoistic suicide.[18] Just as, in the first
case, suicide is said to vary inversely with the degree of integration of religious society, so he finds it varies inversely with the degree of integration
of domestic society. For Durkheim, there is something about marriage
and family life that serves as, in his words, a "coefficient of preservation"
against suicide. It is not insignificant that it is here (in the opening section
of Book 2, chapter 3) that Durkheim performs his most subtle statistical
analysis. In fact, he invents the "coefficient of preservation" (crude by
modern standards, but still the only coefficient in the book) seemingly in
order to solve a problem in the evidence. The facts were that married life
appeared to protect individuals to varying degrees depending on a number of variables, including whether one lived in France or (if in France) in
the provinces or near Paris; whether there were children in the marriage
or the mate had died; and, of course, whether the individual was male or
female. Thus, Durkheim encountered a substantial number of variables,
which created technical problems because he (and Mauss) had to perform all the calculations by hand. But when he did those calculations he
found a persistent, and to him, surprising fact.

Women, at every turn, did not conform. Or, more exactly, it was necessary for Durkheim, the sociologist, to get them to conform, statistically

---

[18] A third type, which concerned political disruptions, was weakly developed relative to the
other two.

speaking. Among the ways in which the women represented by his suicide rates confused the picture were these:[19]

1. The coefficient of preservation (against egoistic suicide) varies between the sexes depending on the society and marital status.
2. In France, for example, marriage protects women less well than men (though it protects both better than the single life, which Durkheim's translator naively describes as "celibacy").
3. In general, the presence of children protects all married persons more than does simple marriage – considerably for men, partially for women.
4. Still with respect to egoistic suicide, the state of widowhood or widowerhood decreases the immunity for each spouse, but the decrease is in regular proportion to that sex's level of protection in marriage, that is, widowers have higher coefficients of protection than widows.
5. With reference to anomic suicide, marriage protects the wife more than the husband in societies where divorce is more common.

This last point (5) is, of course, cross-societal. How it was arrived at involves a story of its own, one that turns out to have powerful implications for Durkheim's method and theory. By contrast to 1 and 5, conclusions 2 through 4, generally, refer to France (though Durkheim is not entirely careful to limit his generalization). The issue arises because, in the second chapter on anomic suicide, he reports that in the Grand Duchy of Oldenburg, women were more favorably protected than in France, thus posing a problem of difference Durkheim could not neglect (even though he defers his account to the chapter on anomic suicide).

Oldenburg was an important subject in the argument as a whole for three reasons. First, it was the only governmental unit to have kept data that could be converted into the suicide rates represented in his coefficients of preservation. Durkheim, thus, set about to compile (literally, to retabulate, thus invent) comparable data for France so that he could counter the then prevailing argument that, among other things, insisted that marriage protected women better than men. Thus Oldenburg was crucial to his use of suicide rates, and his method. Second, however, the Oldenburg data contradicted the French, causing Durkheim to drop references to Oldenburg in Book 2, chapter 3, only to take them up again in Book 2, chapter 5, in the discussion of anomic suicide, where he returned to the data on egoistic suicide (which, in principle, ought to have described an entirely different type). There he accounted for the relative protection against anomic suicide of married women in the Grand

[19] The statistical analyses alluded to in the following occur in Book 2 of *Suicide*, chapter 3, for those concerning egoistic suicide, and chapter 5 concerning anomic suicide.

Duchy by linking their lower rates while married in Oldenburg to the practice of divorce, which was greater in that Protestant society than in Catholic France. Here the idea apparently was that in societies where there is *anomie* affecting (by divorce) both the conjugal and family societies, women are better off married, while without the anomic disruption the marriage makes less difference to them. Finally, from this humble statistical beginning, Oldenburg led to the conclusion that had a potent effect on Durkheim's moral recommendations at the end, about which more later.

In other words, straightforwardly put, women are different. More different than, according to the weak general theory of society, they should have been. If society is *sui generis* – one, general, and powerful – then why are women all that different? Worse yet, if the problem of modern society is anomic disruptions in the social division of labor, then why are not women, with their greater indifference to that society and its negative effects, the solution to its problems? Durkheim had an answer to the former question, but none to the latter (though, as the passage quoted on page 41 suggests, he seems to have been aware of its implications). In any case, Durkheim's discussions of the difference of women with respect to the two main types of suicide (and thus to the crisis of modern societies) show just how important the difference of woman was to him. These ultimately awkward discussions of women eventually raised serious and unanswerable questions about whether his types of suicide are, in fact, different empirical types. This in turn creates confusion not just for Durkheim's professional vision of sociology but for his practical, moral sociology.

If, as previously observed, there are no fundamental differences among the types of suicide, then there can be no plausible sociology for modern societies. No such differences would mean no variables, which, in turn, would mean both no scientific method and nothing to say about the fundamental social fact of modern society. What, then, would become of his claim that *social facts* give conceptual life to differing variables and, therefore, to the four distinct types of suicide? The bind is tight. The way out puts the differences among his logical types in grave doubt. For one, Durkheim himself admits that neither the logical afterthought (fatalistic suicide) nor altruistic suicide has any importance to modern society.[20] In addition, as I suggested earlier, the two principal illustrations of the two main types of suicide are, essentially, two sides of the same coin. If

---

[20] Of altruistic suicide, Durkheim says (*Suicide*, 373) that it "certainly has no share in the present progress of suicide" and that the egoistic and anomic are the only forms "whose development can be regarded as morbid, and so we have only them to consider."

excessively individuated economic man is the token of egoism, and the economic man crushed by political and economic crises is the token of *anomie*, then are not these two recto and verso of the same type? Is not, thus, society's inability to prevent excessive individualism essentially the same as society's failure to regulate its members sufficiently? Or, if they are different, why is it, in the end, when considering practical solutions to the divisions of modern life, Durkheim advises that both egoism and *anomie* "might be dealt with by the same treatment"?[21] These, in themselves, raise questions hard to answer.

Finally, it is woman who puts Durkheim's whole enterprise in doubt.[22] It is she who not only links the discussions of the two main types of suicide but also forces him to concede (just after he admits the two types are "kindred") that in respect to her the two types have the same cause and, thus, are the same.[23] When Durkheim returns to the question of widowhood (and to the Duchy of Oldenburg) in the chapter on anomic suicide, he refers back to the discussion of the same subject with reference to egoism, and says: "The suicides occurring at the crisis of widowhood, of which we have already spoken, are really due to domestic anomy resulting from the death of the husband or wife."[24] Is he not saying that egoistic suicide (which ought to be due to a discrete independent variable) is "really" a case of *anomie*? As generous as one might want to be toward Durkheim, it would be hard to conclude otherwise.

Durkheim surely knew better, just as in some way he knew better about the primitive modern Jews. He made a serious effort to explain this anomaly. But that explanation could be found only by resorting to the weakest, most gratuitous aspect of that theory. When he did, it quickly became evident that even that aspect was more an entailment than a gratuity. The aspect in question was his much-debated theory of the *double man* – one part social, the remainder a rudimentary, passion-filled, and not particularly real individual. Obviously, this crude idea was a

---

[21] Durkheim, *Suicide*, 383.

[22] My interpretation of Durkheim's dealings with women was worked out before I was thoroughly familiar with Jennifer Lehmann's impressive work on the subject. Her studies are far more extensive than mine, especially on Durkheim's attitudes toward feminism. See Jennifer M. Lehmann, *Durkheim and Women* (Lincoln: University of Nebraska Press, 1994). The major difference between us is that she tends to see his trouble with women as a series of contradictions in his logic, while I see it more as the inevitable consequence of his modernizing project. The problem was not Durkheim's alone. See also Jennifer M. Lehmann, "Durkheim's Theories of Deviance and Suicide," *American Journal of Sociology*, 100: 4 (1994): 904–930. And: Jennifer M. Lehmann, *Deconstructing Durkheim* (London: Routledge, 1995).

[23] Durkheim, *Suicide*, 258. Here he attempts, vainly, to distinguish the two types after admitting they are "kindred."

[24] *Ibid.*, 259.

consequence of his sociology. If sociology existed for and because of social facts, then it surely could not admit as fact those elements of the individual outside the constraining force of society. Thus, the double bind of his general theory of *modern* societies: On the one hand, if we *must* define them, they are like the elementary society in their moral force; on the other, since we know they are divided by differences, then somehow they must eventually progress to a state where the moral demands of society and the individual moral responsibilities of free individuals might discover a steady state of mutual satisfaction. In other words, again, the consequence of resorting to the lost past for a theory of society required a projected, and parallel, resort to a progressive future. At no point are the implications of this bind more terrible than with respect to woman.

The only plausible account Durkheim could give for the difference of women (thus, by implication, for the difference between the two suicides) was in his double-man philosophy. Women, in short, are the lesser social creatures. In fact, the "man is double" idea is introduced first, and necessarily, at the end of the second chapter on egoism at precisely the point where he must account for the striking difference of women. Just after saying "social man is the essence of civilization," he adds his cumulative explanation for those facts that, with respect to suicide, women seem less affected, one way or another, by family life. Durkheim, then, with the double-man idea in mind, enumerates all the lesser creatures of the social world: children, the aged, animals, and women:

Suicide is known to be rare among children and to diminish among the aged at the last confines of life; physical man, in both, tends to become the whole of man. Society is still lacking in the former [children] . . . ; it begins to retreat from the latter [the aged]. . . . Feeling a lesser need for self-completion through something not themselves, they are also less exposed to feel the lack of what is necessary for living. The immunity of an animal has the same cause. . . .

This is also why women can endure life in isolation more easily than man. When a widow is seen to endure her condition much better than a widower and desires marriage less passionately, one is led to consider this ease in dispensing with the family a mark of superiority. . . . Actually if this is her privilege it is because her sensibility is rudimentary rather than highly developed. As she lives outside of community existence more than man, she is less penetrated by it; society is less necessary to her because she is less impregnated with sociability. She has few needs in this direction and satisfies them easily. *With a few devotional practices and some animals to care for, the old unmarried woman's life is full.*[25]

---

[25] *Ibid.*, 215, emphasis added (as though it were necessary).

Quite silly in our time, but, in his situation, Durkheim has no choice. It is either women or his sociological enterprise. Women have to be inferior. Nothing else can explain the evidence of his suicide rates. Nothing else can save the difference between his types and thus his sociology. It now becomes clear that the man in his "man is double" idea is not a linguistic convention. He is in fact gendered, not generic.[26]

Durkheim's real question is, therefore, What is man? To which the answer is: He is double. But not as Durkheim had hoped. Gendered man, as the embodiment of civilization, is moral. But, as a real individual in need of marriage for protection, he is physical. What then, one wonders, is the relation between the physical needs of man and those of woman if she is the one who is primitively social and moral? Well, it seems, he is sexual, while she walks the dog – he marries, she does not. "Woman's sexual needs have less of a mental character, because, generally speaking, her mental life is less developed."[27] The "generally speaking" might be a hint that Durkheim senses that what he has had to say does not quite add up.

Where it adds up least, however, is at the very end of *Suicide*. After having presumably demonstrated the social fact of the new science he defined in *Rules*, Durkheim comes back explicitly to his moral vision for the future. There, in the final chapter of Book 3, he returns to woman. In the chapter's recommendations for solutions to the current state of modern society, Durkheim returns to advice he had previously given in the conclusion to *Division of Labor* and, more conspicuously, would give in his famous 1902 preface to that book, "Some Notes on Occupational Groups." Having diagnosed the anomic (and/or egoistic) ills of the modern society, he *must* return to the question of his first book. How, exactly, will the modern division of social labor progress to the point where man will be even better off in his independence than he was in his original dependence on the collective conscience? The answer he provides here, and elsewhere, is that man will benefit from the greater maturity of corporate society:

[A] more perfected division of labor and its accompanying more complex cooperation, by multiplying and infinitely varying the occupations by which men can make themselves useful to other men, multiplies the means of existence and places them within reach of a greater variety of persons. The most inferior aptitudes may find a place there. At the same time, the more intense production resulting from

[26] On the issues invoked by this distinction, see (among the many feminist discussions available): Diana Fuss, *Essentially Speaking* (Routledge, 1989), especially chs. 1, 2.
[27] Durkheim, *Suicide*, 272.

this subtler cooperation, by increasing *humanity's* total resources, assures each worker an ampler pay and so achieves a balance between the greater wear on vital strength and its recuperation.[28]

Or, as he said earlier: "The corporation has everything needed to give the individual a setting, to draw him out of his state of moral isolation." In the end, Durkheim can resolve the crisis only with reference to the generic man of *humanity*. He thus keeps close to the convictions he had already formed in his first book. As in the appearances of difference between his two modern forms of suicide, which were most striking in the case of egoistic and anomic economic man, he proposes a solution within the economic order.

Yet, in the previous section he had already begun by admitting: "There is one form of suicide, however, which could not be halted by this means; the form springs from conjugal anomy. We seem here confronted by an antinomy which is insoluble."[29] The confronting problem is the one expected. The "two sexes do not share equally in social life." But, in these concluding pages, Durkheim seems to take a somewhat different attitude toward women, for here appears the passage, quoted much earlier, in which he hints that at least some part of the solution to modern life lies with, if not woman, some new division of labor between men and women:

The female sex will not again become more similar to the male; on the contrary, we may foresee that it will become more different. But these differences will become of greater social use than in the past. . . . Both sexes would thus approximate each other by their very differences. They would be equalized, but in different ways.

One wonders, after reading the whole of the book, how Durkheim imagines that woman, in her difference, might become equal if her social nature is so rudimentary? He has no definite answer, but like a true liberal, he has a qualified wish:

Only when the difference between husband and wife becomes less, will marriage no longer be thought, so to speak, necessarily to favor one to the detriment of the other. As for the champions of equal rights for women with those of man, they forget that the work of centuries cannot be instantly abolished; the juridical equality cannot be legitimate so long as *psychological inequality* is so flagrant. Our efforts must be bent to reduce the latter. For man and woman to be equally protected by the same institution, they must first of all be creatures of the same nature.

[28] *Ibid.*, 386, emphasis added. The quotation following is earlier in *Suicide*, 379.
[29] *Ibid.*, 384. Other quotations in this paragraph are in the same place, 384–386. Emphasis, further on, on "psychological inequality" is added.

Is it by chance that the first professional sociologist now resorts to a psychological explanation for woman's inequality?

For Durkheim's theory to add up, he must abandon a good bit of both its scientific and moral content. He seems to recognize, in the end, that woman's difference cannot be attributed to her lesser nature. It might even be, he suggests, that the sexual division of labor needs to stand alongside the corporate life as a possible resource for the progressive division of labor that will heal the hurts of modern life.

He does not say more. Just the same, one learns a great deal about his sociology from the two shadowy figures that haunt his plans for that sociology.

The Jew represents, without fully containing, the primitive past of modern man – the past of the child, and of the childlike time of society, when rules constrained to good moral effect. The Jew, for him, is the primitive modern, chief among those mythic figures from which he draws his imaginary vision of society itself. If the Jew of his past pushes Durkheim somehow into a dream of what modern morality might be, the woman pulls him beyond what he is able to imagine. She alone is the individual who cannot be explained by his science, nor healed by his morality. Yet, she, were she to become equal in her way, might help define the future of hope of a divided society.

If things social are different, who am I? Durkheim's answer might be said to have been: As the Jew, I am the same in a different world. As the man who needs a woman to complete my moral soul, I am, in my difference, dependent. The Jew and the woman – the primitive modern, and the social future perfect – explain the difficulties of this man's earnest and honest desire to invent the original professional sociology.

The sociology Durkheim invented was an act of the social imagination in which he sought to reconcile his modern world to those of his lost Jewish fathers and of his silent, necessary mothers. Faced with the same modernist riddle, most of his successors shared Durkheim's noble, unsettling dream.

6

Jacques Derrida and why global structures had to die when they did

Jacques Derrida was born in 1930 of Jewish descent in Algeria. This was just five years after Frantz Fanon was born in Martinique. Derrida did not quit his native land until 1949, when he moved to Paris for studies at the Ecole Normale Supérieure. This was just before Fanon would settle in Algeria and rise to fame. One source claims that the experience of moving from the colony to the capital left him feeling "a little bit black, and a little bit Arab."

One can imagine what might have become of the culture of the ideas associated with Paris in 1968 had Fanon lived to join Derrida, the child of Algeria, and Foucault, who was living in Tunisia that year. Fanon would surely have joined the whirlwind his earlier writings helped stir from afar. On the other hand, Derrida and Foucault, in particular, among the other notables of 1968, might have been called by Fanon to make earlier mention of the liberation struggles of the colonies – struggles they understood, as did Bourdieu – first-hand and very well. To those innocent of the history of the last years of France's colonial empire, it might not occur that the writings of the grand and exciting intellectual figures of 1968 in Paris were as determined as they were by the decolonizing experience. When, among other seemingly abstract allusions, they spoke of the critique of the Subject or of decentering, or even of the deconstruction of the organizing culture of Western philosophy, they may have referred to Hegel, Husserl, Heidegger, and Hippolyte, but they had well in the mind the colonies in which they had grown up or lived in their youth.

Derrida, Foucault, and Bourdieu (whose sociology grew out of field work in Algeria) were, more than others of their generation, children after a fashion of, if not exactly the colonies, the colonized experience. They in their different ways understood, either first-hand or by observation, what it meant to be a subject subjected to the regimes of a colonizing power – a subjugation made all the more acute by the differences inherent to colonial statuses. This, of course, is what Fanon wrote of with such raw intensity. Still, Derrida, Foucault, and Bourdieu understood the realities, as they did the necessities, of decentering – a term associated with Derrida primarily but applicable just as well to Foucault's irregular method and Bourdieu's search for a way between object and subject.

Of the three, not to mention the others of those heady times, none was more prescient, if somewhat oblique, to the relation between philosophical thought and global politics as they came determinedly to a boil in the mid-1960s. Hence, Derrida's lines in 1966, said to be the manifesto of the post-structuralist departure:

Something has perhaps occurred in the history of the concept structure that could be called an "event," if this loaded word did not entail a meaning which it is precisely the function of structural – or structuralist – thought to reduce or to suspect. Let us speak of an "event," nevertheless, and let us use quotation marks to serve as a precaution. What would this event be then? Its exterior form would be that of a *rupture* and a redoubling. . . .

Up to the event which I wish to mark out and define, structure – or rather the structurality of structure – although it has always at work, has always been neutralized or reduced, and this by a process of giving it a center or of referring it to a point of presence, a fixed origin. The function of this center was not only to orient, balance, and organize the structure – one cannot in fact conceive of an unorganized structure – but above all to make sure that the organizing principle of the structure would limit what we might call the play of structure. . . .

It was necessary to begin thinking that there was no center, that the center could not be thought in the form of present-being, that the center had no natural site, that it was not a fixed locus, but a function, a sort of nonlocus in which an infinite number of sign-substitutions came into play. This was the moment when language invaded the universal problematic, the moment when, in the absence of a center or origin, everything became discourse. . . .

When and where does this decentering, this thinking the structurality of structure occur? It would be somewhat naïve to refer to an event, a doctrine, or an author in order to designate this occurrence. It is no doubt part of the totality of an era, our own, but still it has always already begun to proclaim itself and begun to *work*. (Derrida, from *Structure, Sign and Play* (1966))

Everything, and everyone, is there in these lines – Saussure, Lévi-Strauss, Hegel, Heidegger, Husserl, Nietzsche, Freud, even Marx, on without end. Were one to engage anew to understand the origins of the philosophy initiated by Derrida, and others of his day, and how it was a departure from structuralism without really letting go of structures as relations always open to disruption, you could do no better than to lock yourself up alone to meditate, Buddha-like, on these few lines.

The rest of Derrida's essay, which was delivered before an international audience at Johns Hopkins Univerity in Baltimore, is an extended critical appreciation of Lévi-Strauss, the inheritor of the mantle of both Durkheim and Saussure. Therein, Derrida criticizes the elements in Lévi-Strauss's structuralism that are susceptible to being taken as a formal science of cultural facts – the side of Lévi-Strauss's writings that come to mind for those who see his structuralism as the dichtomized other to Sartre's existentialism. Derrida, by contrast, affirms the side of Lévi-Strauss's thinking that derives more directly from the last texts of Durkheim on collective representations and the lonely text of Saussure on the cultural arbitrary.

Play is the disruption of presence. The presence of an element is always a signifying and substitutive reference inscribed in a system of differences and the movement of a chain. Play is always play of absence and presence, but if it is to be thought radically, play must be conceived of before the alternative of presence and absence. (Derrida, *Structure, Sign and Play* (1966))

Where in this is the critique of global structures? Perhaps the simplest way to answer is by imagining Fanon in Baltimore in 1966, rather than Washington to die in 1962. Had he been there, he would have likely spoken out of the terror of his own colonized experience of Negritude – of the wretchness of being absent to the pervading presence of the colonial regime, of being deprived the game of hide-and-seek by which participation gains its power, of being so absent to the Global Presence as to be nothing at all, until such time as the global structures recede before the social facts of modernity's structured contradiction – a culture based on free play; a political economy founded on a grinding center.

They are both dead now. Derrida died forty-two years after Fanon – in 2004 in Paris, of a cancer as terrible as the one that killed Fanon. No one among the philosophical agitators of 1968 took death more seriously as a philosophical topic than did Derrida. None, that is, except the one, Fanon, who did as much as any writer to stir up the colonial rebellions that led to the revolutionary moment in the capitals of the European Diaspora. Odd that these two Africans – one by birth, the other by blood – would have been so matched as they were in life. Derrida, the native of Africa, was the first among the French literati to draw the connection between the decentering colonial world and the eccentric future of philosophy. Fanon, the blood African, was the one among the great decolonizing theorists to write so bloodily of the blood they knew all too well from the cruelty of the colonial system.

When the cultural front of the resisting colonies joins the cultural front of a colonizing capital, the juncture is explosive because colonization in the modern West was done in the name of the silence that kills. Why they came together just then – in the intense heat of world affairs that culminated in 1968 – is a question that can be answered much as we answer the question of human mortality. Why do we die on a certain date? Why does a global structure die in a certain year? The answer to both is, of course, that neither individuals nor structures die once and for all at a given when. Both are born for death which is the only necessity they can be sure of. The difference is that the structures are more skilled in pretending the day or year will never come.

The uses of the French structuralisms (1990*)

Some years ago, Raymond Boudon, one of France's most distinguished sociologists, published a critique of structuralism with the title *A quoi sert la notion de "structure"?* In English the French title translates, "What use is the notion of structure?" However, the book's eventual English-language publishers, presumably afraid of killing their product with such a negative title, named the book *The Uses of Structuralism*.[1] Boudon's book was indeed quite negative. He argued that French structuralism was not useful because it was little more than a reiteration of all structural logics back to the Greeks. Writing early in the 1960s, before post-structuralism had fully surfaced, Boudon saw only one side of the then very new movement. The uniquely different features of structuralism were invisible, hence useless, to him.

Most of the troubles some still have with French social theories – even now a good four decades after Boudon wrote – are condensed in Bourdon's title, which as time has passed was obviously overly-condensed. Yet, the core fact stands – that structuralism is more a movement than a thing unto itself; as such it has revealed itself to be a bit of moving target. At first, as structuralism pure and simple, it appeared in the 1950s and early 1960s as a formalism that seemed to reduce the human sciences to pitiful abstractions – Lévi-Strauss's universal binary oppositions,[2] Althusser's scientific Marx,[3] Barthes's zero-degree writing and formalistic

---

* Reprinted with permission from George Ritzer, ed., *Frontiers of Sociology* (New York: Columbia University Press, 1990), chapter 9. The selection has been edited, mostly to remove the empirical illustration based on the Vietnam War, which appears in the original where it seemed more apt that it does here. Also, I must confess that I've toned down some of the statements that made the various postmodernisms more of a departure from the earlier structuralisms than I now think they are. An earlier version was presented at a conference on the state of social theory held at the University of Maryland in 1988. A much different version appears in *Postmodernism is Not What You Think: Why Globalisation Threatens Modernity* (Paradigm, 2005), 2nd edn, ch. 6.
[1] Raymond Bourdon, *The Uses of Structuralism* (London: Heinemann, 1971).
[2] Claude Lévi-Strauss, "The Structural Study of Myth," *Structural Anthropology*, ed. Claude Lévi-Strauss (New York: Anchor, 1967).
[3] Louis Althusser, *For Marx* (New York: Vintage, 1970).

semiology.[4] At a second moment, roughly from the late 1960s into the 1970s, post-structuralism burst on the scene, incorporating Nietzschean and psychoanalytic concepts. The target was different, yet it retained clear affinities with the structuralism it attacked. Then, a decade or so after, late in the 1970s and into the 1980s and 1990s, postmodernism as a theoretical scheme gathered force from numerous sources – thus presenting still another target both different from and continuous with the earlier structuralisms. It is difficult to take accurate interpretative aim at such a thing which, true to its nature, is simultaneously different and the same.

For some, matters are made worse by the seeming obscurity of the writing and the (admitted) perversity of some of the ideas. The French structuralisms clearly mean to challenge what, through the course of modern (if not also classical) thought, has been taken for granted. Michel Foucault understood quite well the problems his interpreters faced:

I understand the unease of all such people. They have probably found it difficult enough to recognize that their history, their economics, their social practices, the language (*langue*) they speak, the mythology of their ancestors, even the stories that they were told in their childhood, are governed by rules that are not all given to their consciousness.[5]

Though it may not speak well for academic sociology, Foucault's observation about people's natural desire not to perturb the cultures with which they have grown up, gives reasonable account for why, at least in the social sciences, there are no organized schools of research indebted to post-structuralism or, for that matter, any of the structuralisms.[6]

Yet, notwithstanding the lack over such a long time, there is still now in the 2000s good reason to consider the prospects – that is: the serious uses of the structuralisms for academic social sciences which have, in the breach of four decades, done much good work but hardly broken the mold of their very often classically stodgy ways of thinking about the

[4] Roland Barthes, *Elements of Semiology* (Boston: Beacon Press, 1970).
[5] Michel Foucault, *Archaeology of Knowledge* (New York: Random House, 1972), 210–211.
[6] A number of writers have proposed a revision of sociology along post-structuralist lines. Richard Harvey Brown has made the most sustained effort. See: Richard Harvey Brown, *Society as Text* (Chicago: University of Chicago Press, 1987). See also: Ino Rossi, *From the Sociology of Symbols to the Sociology of Signs* (New York: Columbia University Press, 1983). And: Charles Lemert, "Language, Structure, and Measurement; Structuralist Semiotics and Sociology," *American Journal of Sociology* 84 (1979): 929–957. It is also true that the work of Pierre Bourdieu, for example: Pierre Bourdieu, *Outline of a Theory of Practice* (Cambridge: Cambridge University Press, 1977), and Anthony Giddens, for example: Anthony Giddens, *The Constitution of Society* (Berkeley: University of California Press, 1984) bear obvious theoretical affinities to post-structuralism. Yet, neither could be said to be post-structuralist strictly speaking and neither has yet engendered a school. [Which may be to say that "schools" are engendered more by formal sciences than by traditions of social thought. For example, it certainly is the case that Robert K. Merton at Columbia led a school of social research that was indebted to his own brand of structural thinking, which, we might add, was an influence on Boudon among other French sociologists. CL/2005]

realities they study and the methods they use. The witness of Durkheim should here be inspiring. In the span of his own all-too-short career he saw the deficiencies of his earlier method of the 1890s and reinvented himself in the last decade of life. The irony of it is that a second look at the structuralisms – which are still very prominent in other fields – may be a way of keeping faith with the master himself, Durkheim, who after all was as much the source of these lines of thought as was his ghost-partner, Saussure. This alone warrants the consideration – not to exclude of course the tangible benefits that may devolve to the work we do.

The pursuit of the latter-day utilities of the structuralisms may profitably begin with a justifying remark by the modern founder of the earliest wave of the movements. In the introduction to *The Raw and the Cooked* Lévi-Strauss says:

By pursuing conditions where systems of truth become mutually convertible and can therefore be simultaneously admissible for several subjects, the ensemble of these conditions acquires the character of an object endowed by a reality proper to itself and independent of any subject.[7]

At first reading, structuralism did indeed begin with an attack on subjectivist thought that, at the time, was well-ensconced in the prevailing culture of European modernism. Early structuralism thus had all the appearances of an objectivist swing against subjectivist extremes. There was, however, much more to the story. As we now know, the post-structuralist departure was anything but a turn back to subjectivism. It was, if anything, an appreciative move taken in recognition of the ground-clearing work Lévi-Strauss and others had done to set the issues straight, thus to open a new path altogether.

    Post-structuralism was thereby born along with, and as a part of, structuralism. Derrida, speaking in 1966 at the first major international conference on structuralism, began with the now-familiar words that recognized the duality and duplicity of structuralism:

Perhaps something has occurred in the history of the concept of structure that could be called an "event," if this word did not entail a meaning which it is precisely the function of structural – or structuralist – thought to reduce or to suspect. Let us speak of an "event" nevertheless and use quotation marks to serve as a precaution. What would this event be then? Its exterior form would be that of a *rupture* and a redoubling.[8]

---

[7] Claude Lévi-Strauss, "Overture to *Le Cru et le Cuit*," *Structuralism*, ed. Jacques Ehrmann (New York: Anchor, 1970), 44–45.
[8] The lecture was given in October 1966 at the Johns Hopkins University conference, the proceedings of which were edited by Richard Macksey and Eugenio Donato, *Structuralist Controversy: The Languages of Criticism* (Baltimore: Johns Hopkins University Press, 1972).

The words are opaque of necessity, as we now know. They intend to announce an event that ends events. They claim that the idea of structure had come to a point that would end both structure and event, yet would keep them in quotation marks as necessities, redoubled beyond this rupture.

For those not committed to its language and program, post-structuralism may seem, in Derrida's word, to be nothing more than a play on words. But that is the essential point. In a culture like modernity's where words are ignored by being treated as mere vehicles for prior human meanings, there is a need to take the language we use seriously but in a way that is serious with respect to the social facts of language. Which is to say that language (as practiced and performed), since the days of Saussure, has come to be thought of as a kind of play – a game really of hide-and-seek in which the meanings absent to articulated speech are the differences that set the value of the meanings meant. The whole point thus is to take language seriously as the play it is, to liberate the play of words and ideas.

This was the shift in Western thought Derrida announced. For this purpose he required the prior existence of structuralism, just as structuralism entailed, in Derrida's view, post-structuralism. The "post" in post-structuralism was a tactical joke, a playfully serious trick. Structure, Derrida went on to say, had served to limit and confine modern thought. "Event" – the concept structuralism sought to eliminate – was the false alternative, the artificial hope for emancipation from this confinement. Event was, after all, the codeword of existentialism – and a cognate to other subjectivist ideals – the ideally free subject, consciousness, rational choice, subjectively intended meaning, the essential nature of "Man," and so on.

Structuralism, insofar as it led to post-structuralism, was its own gravedigger. These two awkwardly bound perspectives attacked the formative conviction of modernist thought, that the world could be viewed through the lenses of the subject–object dichotomy. Structuralism, with all its first appearances of objectivism, was the beginning of the end for objectivism and subjectivism. At least this was the claim of Derrida and others who were central to the post-structuralist movement in the late 1960s and through the 1970s – Foucault, Lacan, Kristeva, Barthes, among others. . . .

As for the third of the structuralisms – the one too often called epithetically "postmodernism" – the meaningful duplicity of the line of thought is attenuated in the fact of its intellectual history. If there is such a thing as postmodern social theory, then it was originally identified with two thinkers whose allegience to the French post-structuralists was irregular in the one instance and nearly all but lacking in the other. I refer here to two important texts of 1979: Jean-François Lyotard's *The Postmodern Condition* and Richard Rorty's *Philosophy and the Mirror of Nature.*

Lyotard began with a statement consistent with Derrida's in 1966. "Our working hypothesis is that the status of knowledge is altered as societies enter what is known as the postindustrial age and cultures enter what is known as the postmodern age."[9] Rorty states that the "therapeutic" aim of his book is "to undermine the reader's confidence . . . in 'knowledge' as something about which there ought to be a 'theory' and which has 'foundations.'"[10] His view is comparable to Lyotard's that the conditions of knowledge have fundamentally changed because in the postmodern era knowledge, most especially "scientific knowledge, is a form of discourse."[11] These assertions built upon ideas that had developed in the preceding two decades. They were, therefore, consistent with Derrida's definition of the post-structuralist event within structuralism: "This was the moment," according to Derrida, "when language invaded the universal problematic, the moment when, in the absence of a center or origin, everything became discourse."[12]

One way or another, everything in the three structuralisms comes back to language, or more accurately, to a specific commitment to the idea that language is now necessarily the central consideration in all attempts to know, act, and live. Though there are substantial disagreements within the structuralist line, all three movements – structuralism, post-structuralism, and postmodernism – intend to replace modernist principles of positive knowledge in the sciences, the social sciences, and philosophy with a new approach based on language. This conviction distinguishes this line of thought from others, like Habermas's, that similarly accept the importance of language.[13] This is the stake in a prospective use of these ideas in sociology.

The place of language as such among the social facts of human community has long been a mystery most often put to the side, until, among

---

[9] Jean-François Lyotard, *The Postmodern Condition: A Report on Knowledge* (Minneapolis: University of Minnesota Press, 1984), 3.

[10] Richard Rorty, *Philosophy and the Mirror of Nature* (Princeton: Princeton University Press, 1979), 7.

[11] Lyotard, *The Postmodern Condition*, 3.

[12] Jacques Derrida, "Structure, Sign and Play in the Discourse of the Human Sciences," in *The Structuralist Controversy*, ed. R. Macksey and E. Donato (Baltimore: Johns Hopkins University Press, 1970), 280.

[13] See Richard Rorty, "Habermas and Lyotard on Postmodernity," in *Habermas and Modernity*, ed. Richard Bernstein (Cambridge: MIT Press, 1985). See also Fredric Jameson, "Foreword," in Lyotard, *The Postmodern Condition*. And Fredric Jameson's (1984) Preface to Lyotard's *Postmodern Condition*.

others, Durkheim almost inadvertently turned to the question of collective representations about the same time that Saussure, in Geneva, proposed semiology as a general science of social facts as meanings. That these two kernels did not blossom on the ear for a good while, until Lévi-Stauss and Barthes, first in the 1950s, took them up again, should not be reason to refrain to taking them seriously in their re-emergence. Again, the "event" that Derrida calls attention to while transcending.

Derrida's idea is that this event was *"the moment when language invaded the universal problematic, . . . the moment when . . . [a] . . . everything became discourse . . . [b] . . . a system in which the central signified . . . [c] . . . is never absolutely present outside a system of differences."*[14] The three ellipses (marked [a], [b], [c]) each contained significant qualifications. When the material is excluded, as above, the argument is relatively neat. But in each of these places Derrida's actual text strains the reading by introducing heavy qualifications that make a philosophical statement, namely:

[a] *"in the absence of a center or origin,"*
[b] *"provided we can agree on this word [discourse] – that is to say,"* and
[c] *"the original signifier."*

Each qualifying phrase contradicts a reader's attempt to understand the event Derrida announces as a positive, factual moment in history. The first, [a], and the third, [c], introduce philosophical claims that cannot be proven, and each is so sweeping as to be beyond argument. The absent center, for example, refers to the assumption that prior to post-structuralism all traditional thought, including modernism, relied on a restrictive, transcendent principle. This, of course, is less a point of fact than of interpretation. Even as a point of interpretation it would have been hard to argue convincingly in 1966 that this was the essential nature of modernist thought. It is hard enough to argue the point in 1990. The second qualification, [b], *"provided we can agree"* on the meaning of the term *"discourse,"* is both an acknowledgment of the strangeness of his idea to his readers and an expression of his now-famous deconstructionist principle that we must use familiar language to express the totally unfamiliar.

The overall effect of the passage is to subject the reader to an insistence triply qualified, presented in the guise of an argument. It is not an argument that one can "follow" along a direct line of clear and distinct logical understanding. It is not a statement open to logical or empirical verification, but an invitation to enter a different, postmodern (that is, in 1966, post-structural) language within which one finds

---

[14] Derrida, "Structure, Sign and Play," 280.

that everything is language. The argument which is not an argument is found only in a series of juxtaposed, different elements – conditional "perhaps"/proclamation, structuralism/end of structuralism, post-structuralism/continuity of structuralism, argument/insistence. One wants to ask, what does Derrida mean? To which he would reply, if he were to reply at all: I am playing, seriously. "Play is the disruption of presence," he says near the end of the text.[15] All attempts to be clear are based on the philosophical presumption that meaning and reality can be present to consciousness. To "make clear" is to reflect or, in Rorty's term, mirror nature. These are attempts to get around language which exists, so to speak, on its own terms.

Post-structuralism and postmodernism, though in different degrees and ways, each seek to destroy the ideal of pure, meaningful communication between subjects as a corollary to the disruption of the metaphysical distinction between subjects and objects. This is the way in which language invades the universal problematic. Language is assumed to be that one social thing which when it is made the center of things disrupts everything, including the possibility of a center of things. Language looks to the future. Thus Derrida ends this essay with a hesitant, fearful anticipation of a liberating birth, cloaked in a language one understands, barely:

I employ these words, I admit, with a glance toward operations of childbirth – but also a glance toward those who, in a society from which I do not exclude myself, turn their eyes away when faced by the as yet unnameable which is proclaiming itself and which can do so whenever a birth is in the offing, only under species of a non-species, in the formless, mute, infant, and terrifying form of monstrosity.[16]

Any attempt to develop a post-structuralist, or postmodernist, sociology requires a willingness to face this monstrosity of language. According to such a perspective, when language is taken seriously for what it is, the social world is seen in a particular way. It is no longer possible to view the world as internally and necessarily coherent. To take language seriously, as the structuralisms do in their manner of writing as in their philosophy, is to decenter the world, to eviscerate it of grand organizing principles (God, natural law, truth, beauty, subjectivity, Man, etc.) that mask the most fundamental truth of human life, differences. Those who have followed recent developments in postmodernist feminist theory and literary theory realize that this conviction is filled with political intent.

---

[15] *Ibid.*, 292.   [16] *Ibid.*, 293.

Aware that women writers inevitably engage a literary history and system of conventions shaped primarily by men, feminist critics now often strive to elucidate the acts of revision, appropriation and subversion that constitute a female text.[17]

Scores of people are killed every day in the name of differences ascribed only to race. This slaughter demands the gesture in which the contributors to this volume are collectively engaged: to deconstruct, if you will, the ideas of difference inscribed in the trope of race, to explicate discourse itself in order to reveal the hidden relations of power and knowledge inherent in popular and academic usages of "race."[18]

Modernism is taken as the centered, hierarchical, Europeanized, dominant world against which the principle of difference is thrust to assert the realities of those whose daily lives are marked by the experience of difference – women, non-whites, working class, the third world.

The question for sociology is: What is it about language that permits such a long excursion from Lévi-Strauss's rediscovery of linguistics in the 1950s to today's politics of difference? And what are the prospects in this for sociology?

Against philosophies of the Center, modernism in particular, post-structuralism introduced an intellectual politics based on the now-famous concept of decentering. It is not always understood that decentering is less a philosophy, or a rival concept to those of modernism, than a practice. This is, in part, the point of post-structuralism's unsettling approach to writing.

From one point of view, decentering is a reasonably precise philosophical concept conveying Derrida's and Foucault's original attacks on centered philosophies, most especially phenomenology's extreme subjectivist philosophy of consciousness.[19] This is the sense most accurately associated with the rejection of Enlightenment theories of knowledge. From another point of view, decentering suggests a broad political opposition to all traditional and modern social forms, philosophy included, in which structures serve to inhibit social freedom. It is advisable, therefore, to think of these structuralisms as first and foremost a form of knowledge derived from a political practice. This attitude conveys not only post-structuralism's attempt to overcome philosophy for political purposes but also its claim that discourse and writing must be taken as the subject matter and means of intellectual work, which soon enough brings

[17] Elizabeth Abel, ed., *Writing and Sexual Difference* (Chicago: University of Chicago Press, 1980), 2.
[18] Henry Louis Gates, *"Race" Writing and Difference* (Chicago: University of Chicago Press, 1985), 6.
[19] Foucault, *Archaeology of Knowledge*.

us to consideration of the troubling idea of the Text (put as it often is, after Barthes, to emphasize a certain technical if not quite methodological status).

Roland Barthes defines the Text as "that *social* space that leaves no language safe or untouched, that allows no enunciative subject to hold the position of judge, teacher, analyst, confessor, or decoder. The theory of the Text can only coincide with the activity of writing."[20] This statement is linked to the claim that decentering is an ongoing intellectual practice deriving from the theoretical decision to interpret the Text in relation to other texts, rather than in relation to its author. For Barthes this involves the distinction between the work and the Text:

> The work is concrete, occupying a portion of book-space (in a library, for example); the Text, on the other hand, is a methodological field. . . . This opposition recalls the distinction proposed by Lacan between "reality" and the "real"; the one is displayed, the other demonstrated. In the same way, the work can be seen in bookstores, in card catalogues, and on course lists, while the Text reveals itself, articulates itself according to and against certain rules. While the work is held in the hand, the text is held in language.[21]

The work, therefore, is seen as the unit of modernist writing in which writing is a transitive activity – the production of literary objects by subjects, authors. Thus, the privileging of the Text over the work is another instance of the philosophical side of decentering, here the rejection of the purportedly modernist belief that the social world is inhabited by self-conscious subjects who project meaning into their works. It is a rejection of subjectivism as a cryptometaphysics.

This move replaces the original modernist couplet – *subject* (author)/ *object* (work) – with something else which itself has the appearance of a couplet *practices* (writing)/(intertextual) *field*. But the relationship of text to its intertextual field is active, creative, and practical. Practices/field has the form but not the substance of a conceptual dichotomy. It looks the same but is different – post-dichotomous. Texts are products of intransitive writing, they are outside the subject–object dichotomy. "The Text cannot be thought of as a defined object."[22] It is, as noted, a methodological field, while the work is a concrete object. Texts, therefore, play in a forever open and open-ended field which they produce and by which they are produced, and in which they must be interpreted.

The important thing to keep in mind is that from within a post-structuralist view of social things, this reorientation is a general social

---

[20] Roland Barthes, "From Work to Text," *Textual Strategies: Perspectives in Poststructuralist Criticism*, ed. Josue Hariri (Ithaca: Cornell University Press, 1979), 81, emphasis in original.
[21] *Ibid.*, 74–75.   [22] *Ibid.*, 74.

theoretical move – and one that, while refusing to separate the empirical and the theoretical, affirms the mutual necesssity of both. Though it remain close to the language of text and discourse, a post-structuralist move would situate itself as just as robust a theory of society as any other – or, in the 2000s, even more robust of view of the social as system of global differences. The critique of the subject-author is an instance of opposition to all forms of social domination. Much of Foucault's writing on various topics, from *The Order of Things* to *The History of Sexuality*, is in opposition to dominations represented by the engendered, Europeanized humanism which, in another context, is characterized by the term "patriarchy." The link between a general social theory and the problem of the author is apparent in Foucault's "What Is an Author?"[23]

> We are accustomed . . . to saying that the author is a general creator of a work in which he deposits with infinite wealth and generosity, an inexhaustible world of signification. We are used to thinking that the author is so different from other men, and so transcendent with regard to all languages, that as soon as he speaks meanings begin to proliferate. . . . The truth is quite contrary . . . the author does not precede the works, he is a certain fundamental principle by which, in our culture, one limits, excludes, and chooses. . . . The author is the ideological figure by which one marks the manner in which we fear the proliferation of meanings.

In this respect, post-structuralism is a social theory articulated within concrete studies of literary, historical, and philosophical questions.

Post-structuralism is very much a product of the political and social events leading to and ensuing from May 1968 in Paris. Foucault's sexual politics,[24] Lacan's engendering of psychoanalysis,[25] Kristeva and Irigaray's feminist theories,[26] Derrida's politics of difference,[27] Deleuze and Guattari's schizoanalytic politics all are rooted,[28] one way or another, in the late sixties revolutionary politics that challenged the world-centered ambitions of post-war Gaullism. If, at that same moment, left intellectuals in the United States sought a coherent New Left alternative to both Old Left Marxism and Johnson–Humphrey liberalism, French intellectuals searched for an alternative that rejected traditional communist and socialist party politics and was post-Marxist without being anti-Marxist. In the one joint programmatic statement of the post-structuralist movement, when Foucault, Barthes, Derrida, Sollers, and Kristeva allowed and caused their separate projects to be joined in an edition of *Tel Quel* titled

---

[23] Michel Foucault, "What is an Author?" in *Textual Strategies*, ed. Hariri, 158–159.
[24] Michel Foucault, *History of Sexuality, Vol. 1* (New York: Pantheon, 1978).
[25] Jacques Lacan, *Ecrits: A Selection* (New York: Norton, 1977).
[26] Toril Moi, ed., *French Feminist Thought: Politics, Patriarchy, and Sexual Difference* (New York: Basil Blackwell, 1987).
[27] Jacques Derrida, "Racism's Last Word," in *"Race," Writing, and Difference*, ed. Gates.
[28] Gilles Deleuze and Félix Guattari, *Anti-Oedipus: Capitalism and Schizophrenia* (New York: Viking, 1977).

Théorie d'ensemble (published not incidentally in the early autumn of 1968), these politics were quite explicit. The introduction stated that their joint project was, in part, "to articulate a politics logically bound to a dynamically nonrepresentative writing, that is to say: analysis of the confusion created by this position, explication of their social and economic character, construction of the relations of this writing with historical materialism and dialectical materialism."[29] It would be an uncomfortable stretch to consider this a social theory in the usual sense, but that theory is there, however faintly. It is the basis for a positive connection with social theoretical work in sociology.

In more sociological terms, the implication of this attitude toward writing as an intellectual practice is that action is oriented to an open field of play that lacks inherent, limiting rules. Rules become resources in Giddens's sense; limits are social arbitraries serving only to define the possibilities of transgression in Foucault's sense; the field defines the conditions and terms of practices in Bourdieu's sense. The structured field is viewed as open, that is, characterized by differences, absence, play. Hence the various descriptive terms one associates with post-structuralist thinkers: discursive formation (Foucault), intertextuality (Barthes), *la langue* (Saussure), *champ* (Bourdieu). To these sometimes implicit visions of a field of play are juxtaposed the correlative notions that describe intransitive actions: practices, writing, speaking, habitus.[30]

On first examination, this would appear to be an interesting theoretical model in the form: *Think of social action as intransitive practices in a dynamically open field of play.* But this would not be a sufficient interpretation of post-structuralist thinking. Models, in its view, are modernist attempts to mirror the social world. Models depend on the assumption that the social (or natural) world can be represented, that is, "presented again" in the language of knowledge. Post-structuralism, implicitly, and postmodernism, explicitly, reject the Enlightenment ideas that knowledge is an autonomous and constituting feature of social life.

The notion that our chief task is to mirror accurately, in our Glassy Essence, the universe around us is the complement to the notion, common to Democritus and Descartes, that the universe is made up of very simple, clearly and distinctly knowable things, knowledge of whose essences provides the master vocabulary which permits commensuration of discourses.[31]

[29] *Tel Quel, Théorie d'ensemble* (Paris: Editions du Seuil, 1968), 10.
[30] In reference to the concepts presented in this paragraph see: Giddens, *Constitution of Society*; Foucault, *Archaeology of Knowledge*; Bourdieu, *Outline of a Theory of Practice*; Roland Barthes, *Elements of Semiology* (Boston: Beacon Press, 1970); Barthes, "From Work to Text."
[31] Rorty, *Philosophy and the Mirror of Nature*, 357.

There are no post-structuralist models. "Let us wage a war on totality; let us be witnesses to the unpresentable; let us activate the differences and save the honor of the name."[32] Postmodernist knowledge, such as it is, is the consequence, not a representation, of action in a field of play. What is at stake is a social science willing to tolerate the idea of working in a confusing, different social space that is neither epistemological nor political, but both while also neither.

In a certain sense this is not an alien idea to sociology. We have been, from the beginning, the most artificial of disciplines and the clumsiest of sciences because sociology is, by its nature, a situated practice. It is only in recent years that sociologists have reincorporated ideas from ethnomethodology and other parasociological sources (including some of the post-structuralist literature) to recover the centrality of what Giddens describes as the double hermeneutic, the fact that theories of society interpret that which they also help constitute, even while interpreting.[33] Though post-structuralism makes a more radical claim than such indigenous sociological practices as ethnomethodology and Giddens's structuration theory, it bears this point of positive comparison with those aspects of sociology that forthrightly work within a recognition of the unique double nature of sociological knowledge. Ideas like the "double hermeneutic" and "writing as intransitive practice" are similarly comfortable with the uncomfortable social space in which knowledge is no longer the foundation of that which is, where instead language both is the universal problematic and, insofar as "knowledge" is concerned, is all that is.

In post-structuralist perspectives, the generic name for this knowledge which is (nothing but) language is discourse. Discourse expresses, and is, the inherently transgressive quality of post-structuralist intellectual politics, as one can see in Hayden White's definition:

A discourse moves "to and fro" between received encodations of experience and the clutter of phenomena which refuses incorporation into conventionalized notions of "reality," "truth," or "possibility." . . . Discourse, in a word, is quintessentially a *mediative* enterprise. As such it is both interpretive and preinterpretive; it is always about the nature of interpretation itself as it is *about* the subject matter which is the manifest occasion of its own elaboration.[34]

Post-structuralist social theory, whether avowedly sociological or not, is discursive in this sense of transgressing the subject matter it interprets by constantly reflecting on the necessity and nature of interpretation itself.[35]

[32] Lyotard, *The Postmodern Condition*, 82.   [33] Giddens, *Constitution of Society*, xxxv.
[34] Hayden White, *Tropics of Discourse* (Baltimore: Johns Hopkins University Press, 1978), 4.
[35] Compare Giddens's idea of discursive consciousness: Giddens, *Constitution of Society*, 41–45.

Of course, there are problems with a proposal to make discourse both the subject matter and the medium of sociological analysis. A discursive sociology, as we have already seen, would require an uprooting of deeply ingrained convictions: belief in the subject–object dichotomy and other classical dualities; loyalty to the ideal of sociology as a well-founded, scientific source of knowledge; expectations that good work will produce identifiably worthwhile political and intellectual outcomes.

The far more serious problem with a discursive sociology in the post-structuralist tradition is that posed by taking discourse as an object of study. It is one thing to accept a discursive, transgressive method as the condition of sociological practice, another to deal with evident dilemmas in the discursive analysis of discourse. Sociologists and other intellectual practitioners can be discursive in the sense of appropriating the attitude of constant, as White puts it, to-ing and fro-ing with the real world. Social theory as reflective, intransitive action is thinkable even if objectionable to some. But what are the limits of discourse as an "object" of study? This question demonstrates the severity of the challenges posed by post-structuralism. One must bracket even the term "object." But what do the brackets mean? Does a discursive social theory mean there are no "objects," that is to say, no contents to intellectual practices? Is such a practice forever doomed to a world of talk about talk itself, of the interpretation of interpretation, of a program without performances? The problem is acute when one considers the question, is there in the "real" world non-discursive social action? It is one thing for a discursive intellectual work to treat other discursive materials of the same sort. This is what the post-structuralists mean by intertextuality in the strictest sense of the concept.

The success of post-structuralism in literary studies may rely considerably on the fact that, in this area, other texts are the proper subject matter. The most compelling successes, in my opinion, of applied post-structuralism have been among feminist, third world, and Afro-American critics who uncover the discursive power of hitherto silent, oppressed women, black, or third-world writers.[36] In a case like Henry Louis Gates's 1988 discussion of the confluence between the African Esu-Elegbara and the Afro-American signifying monkey figures in two separated but historically bound cultural systems, the analyst is applying a discursive method to texts that are found to be surprisingly discursive themselves. Both figures served to contain and express the doubled cultural experience of

---

[36] Gates, *"Race" Writing and Difference*; Henry Louis Gates, *The Signifying Monkey: A Theory of Afro-American Literary Criticism* (New York: Oxford University Press, 1988); Hazel Carby, *Reconstructing Womanhood: The Emergence of the Afroamerican Woman Novelist* (New York: Oxford University Press, 1987).

those who are simultaneously African and in some fractured way American. The figures were discursive in that they mediate the divided social reality of people for whom colonial oppression and slavery were the decisive social attributes. This discovery of the discursive, and political consciousness of so-called non-literate or otherwise excluded people is parallel to similar discoveries of the study of oppressed women, the working class, and other victims of colonial domination, and this literature – of which E. P. Thompson's *The Making of the English Working Class* is a *locus classicus*[37] – is familiar and assimilable to even normal sociological thought.

The greater difficulty concerns the hint strong within post-structuralist thought that everything social is discourse. Are there no events in the "real" world that lack this trangressive, mediative quality? This, of course, is a very familiar question, arrived at by a different route. What is to be said of the silence of oppressed people? Is their silence merely a latent discursivity, covered by false consciousness? It is one thing to say that certain slave narratives are discursive, and another to suggest that all which is said by or inscribed on behalf of slaves is discursive, and still another, by extension, to suggest that slavery is nothing but discourse. This is the question that separates a prospective sociological post-structuralism from the actual post-structuralist literary criticism. Sociologists should have little difficulty accepting the idea that there are hidden or underlying variables behind surface appearances. But they will have trouble with the suggestion that those variables are exclusively discursive. Is there nothing in the "real" world but texts and discursive talk? Literary theorists and others, including social historians, can plausibly study nothing but texts. Can sociologists? Or, better put, what does it mean to propose that sociology be the discursive study of nothing but discursive texts?

In a different guise, this is the familiar problem of the presumption of a necessary difference between theory and concrete empirical data. Most sociologists could, if pressed, consider the proposition that theory is the discursive property of any sociological work. This would amount to little more than granting that in theory, whatever else we do, we state and describe both a statement about the "real" world and the rules by which we arrive at that interpretation. Usually, however, even in a radical version of this conviction, sociologists hold to the existence of a "real" world outside of the discursive sway of theory. The world's "reality" is taken, normally, as the source of concrete empirical data. This conviction, we

[37] Cultural studies, a movement with strong ties to sociology and to post-structuralism, expressly takes Thompson's work as among its classical references. See Stuart Hall, *Culture, Media, and Language: Working Papers in Cultural Studies, 1972–79* (London: Hutchinson, 1980).

can now see, would be treated with great skepticism by post-structuralism and postmodernism. The idea of a freestanding reality as the source of empirical data partakes of the modern-ist distinction between the knowing subject and the world of objects, and relies on a belief in attainable knowledge as the arbiter of that distinction. We might grant, therefore, that post-structuralism would have this particular philosophical attitude toward the division of theory and data. But, can we grant that sociology can get along without freestanding data, that is, without data from the world as the resource of theory? Viewed through the lens of a post-structuralist critique, we can see that the question need not be posed so narrowly. We can agree that data are necessary to even a post-structuralist sociology and still accept the proposition that those data are neither necessarily of an order different from theory nor non-discursive.

7

Gilles Deleuze and Félix Guattari and why structures haunt instruments and measures

One of the more elementary tools of analytic science is the ruler – the very simplest of all instruments used to measure whatever thing or state of things is thought to be in need of analysis according to rates, velocities, temperatures, pressures, volumes, masses, weights, densities, lengths, widths, and so forth. The ruler is also one of the first tools children learn to use, even before they attach themselves to electronic tools of various obsequious kinds. The ruler seems so innocent. All it requires is to be settled gingerly up against a thing the length of which one wishes to know for whatever reason. Yet, even that gentle touch of proximity involves a cut of refined cruelty. If the thing is, say, a household pet or a favorite doll these things are immediately decomposed into parts that no longer present little kitten or teddy as they are known. The child, for instance, learns, when first she is taught to use the ruler, that things of all kinds are not really kittens or teddies but units of silly kinds. *Inches?* – like inch worms? *Centimeters?* – like caterpillars? It doesn't make too much sense at first until the schools demand acceptance of the logic of examining whole and real things by breaking them down into impossibly abstract units.

It all begins there – the learning of analysis according to measures made by instruments. Modern science, to say nothing of modern life, would be impossible were it not that the vast majority of neurologically healthy members understand this system – a system that is represented as though it were essentially true (hence, natural) when in fact it is unique to modern societies. This does not mean that other-than-modern societies do not measure. We know, from Stonehenge, that they did and do. But the modern ones hold measures dearer to the cultural heart. Their dependence on regularized and global market transactions requires as a first language the mastery of a universal standard of value. Trusting the standard measures is, thereby, a requirement for participation. Whatever else modern cultures are, they are first and foremost cultures of measurement.

Still, as pervasive and miraculous as the culture of measurement has been – bestowing, as it has, countless benefits on the robust minority in the northern veneer of global life – the fact remains, little commented upon, that measurement by instruments always comes up against a limit that cannot be ignored. Behind, beyond, underneath, or below the surface of things measured (including one's personal worth) there is always another story; always some hidden, unruly possibility; always another dimension that cannot be measured in so many units of calculably fungible coin, inch, gram, mph, whatever. The ultimate question to ask of the instrumental limits to measurement is, simply: Is there an instrument, perhaps one yet to be invented, that might be able to measure such depths, uncertainties, and remainders? No other question is harder to ask from within a culture of measurement – this because the asking implies the possibility that the things to be measured are not measurable.

Gilles Deleuze (1925–95), one of the French philosophers most admired in his day and especially by Foucault and Derrida, and Félix Guattari (1930–92), a psychoanalytically trained political activist and educator, wrote two of the most radiantly obscure works at the decentered heart of the post-structuralisms. It was not just that they combined psychoanalytic, philosophical, and Marxist politics in works like *Anti-Oedipus: Capitalism and Schizophrenia* (1974) but that they considered the relations among things without regard to the normal order of analytic categories. They were, in other words, ferocious opponents of the cultural rulers. What they did – notably in their second major work, *A Thousand Plateaus* (1980) – was to take the photographic image that froze for others to see the figures by which the analytic order is revealed as a dubious negative of deep and uncertain remainders of visible social things. They thus opened the possibility – not the first to do it; but the first to do it in ways that could not be gotten around – that there may not be a naturally available order to the inner, inferior, eventual structure of social things:

A rhizome as subterranean stem is absolutely different from roots and radicles. Bulbs and tubers are rhizomes. Plants with roots or radicles may be rhizomorphic in other respects altogether: the question is whether plant life in its specificity is not entirely rhizomatic. Even some animals are, in their pack form. Rats are rhizomes . . . The rhizome itself assumes very diverse forms, from ramified surface extension in all directions to concretion into bulbs and tubers . . . We get the distinct feeling that we will convince no one unless we enumerate certain approximate characteristics of the rhizome. . . . A rhizome ceaselessly establishes connections between semiotic chains, organization of power, and circumstances relative to the arts. (Deleuze and Guattari, *Thousand Plateaus* (1980), 7)

The rhizome is opposed to the root. The rhizome, a naturally occurring biological form, is a root system or colony that grows underground, sending up sprouts here and there, resisting uprooting or mapping or penning up.

The question of instruments is whether it might be that culture is more rhizomatic than rooted – that culture spreads its tendrils in the dark clay drawing its energy down from the light above ground to grow every which way in dark; and thus that culture is not a root that reverses the symbiosis by tapping deep for a final organizing truth brought upwards in search of the light.

If so – and all it need be is a possibility – then we can grasp the limits of instrument-reliant measurement. It is not that nothing can be measured. But that, when it comes to measuring meanings (cultures, that is), those meanings may be absent, not because our tools are bad, but because they thrive underground, appearing here and there to haunt the surface of things. In the garden of cultures the worst weeds are rhizomatic, choking out the carefully pruned plantings. People with lawns, for example, think of the local rhizomes as weeds that distort the pure truth of their greenery. It is possible, however, that the weed is the flower itself – or, at least, as much a flower as there is. That is the haunting uncertainty of instrumentation in the measurement of social things.

Structures, instruments, and reading in social and cultural research (1982*)

(with Willard A. Nielsen, Jr.)

The basic, though certainly not only, question of measurement theory is: How do we read? The warrant for this idea arises from the way empirical researchers do their work – or, better put, write and read what work is done.

Reading, for one example, involves a literature. Those engaged in social scientific measurement refer constantly to their literatures, but always in a haphazard way. Unfortunately, reviews of the literatures are seldom more than weak contexts for an author's own position. Accordingly, those who bemoan the fact there has been little cumulation of knowledge "in the literature" might consider their own reading practices. It is not that they do not read in the senses of passing the eye, and occasionally the mind, over texts in order to cull what can serve present empirical purpose. Rather, we have in mind the kind of serious reading that invovles what we dare to call an explicit-for-sociology theory of reading that would encourage a reading of literatures (the source of ideas, concepts, variables, etc.) with positive reference to measures.

In empirical social research the actual literatures are different in kind – generally non-fictional, often formally put, typically lacking in the poetic imagination – but they are literatures nonetheless. In fact, the literatures of the typical social researcher are frequently more interesting and varied according to genre that those of, say, a specialist in Elizabethan theatre. Social research involves, thereby, the assumption that measuring is the

* Reprinted with permission from Ino Rossi, ed., *Structuralism and Sociology* (New York: Columbia University Press, 1982), chapter 12. Thanks are also due to Willard Nielsen who did much of the hard work on the medical/nursing literature and contributed to all other aspects of the work on equal terms. Willard Nielsen was one of the most accomplished graduate students I had the privilege of working with in the 1970s. After finishing studies toward the PhD in sociology at Southern Illinois University, Nielsen went on to study in the History of Consciousness Program at the University of California at Santa Cruz. Today he lives in California, customizes and restores motorcycles, and teaches at local colleges. (I should confess that I have made a few alterations in the writing here, which may not quite reflect the way in which Willard or I would have written when we were together in the late 1970s. CL/2005)

reading of more natural literatures that are gathered and collected to be made ready for use in the second-order literatures social researchers write-up (as the saying goes) – namely: letters, documents, reports to census takers, answers to survey questions, self-assessments, behaviors written into economic trend reports, market indicators, SES profiles (etc.), ritual dances, and so forth. Hence, the reader of a secondary literature (what other social researchers have written) is bound to a reading of primary literature (what the all-purpose and legendary actor says or does).

The relationship between the two – between reading and measurement– is one in which the secondary literature serves as the basis upon which an "instrument" is constructed, while the primary literature is the field into which "data" are cut (or, in the long run, the field from which butchered evidentiary bits and morsels are cooked into data tasty to the analytic palate). We are not speaking metaphorically when we say that reading is the fundamental work of sociology.

In order to make our case concretely, we have selected a secondary literature which puts our proposal to a test. We shall discuss the literature on the presumption of compliance as the normal type for the nurse (RN)–medical doctor (MD) relationship in hospital settings.[1] These literary materials are well-bounded and extensive (as the citations we provide show). However, from the beginning, they seem to render our proposal of a structural reading theory impotent. This literature debates the idea that the RN–MD relationship in hospitals is typically and appropriately the compliance of RN behaviors to MD's orders. This proposition is aggravating to a structural reading because it implies that the fundamental issue is sociopsychological: that the explanation for RN behavior is an attitude (compliance or non-compliance). Where more than diadic social structural features are considered (structure of medical vs. surgical wards,[2] structure of hospital administration,[3] etc.) structural factors are often relegated to the background. Even when given the role of independent variables,[4] their independence is purchased at the price of a formalism which destroys the positivity of the crucial relationship between

---

[1] The terms "nurse" (RN) and "medical doctor" (MD) are shorthand notations for persons who perform certain medical tasks. The holding of an RN or MD is not paramount for our discussion.

[2] Rose L. Coser, "Authority and Decision-making in a Hospital: A Comparative Analysis," *American Sociological Review* 23 (Feb 1958): 691–700.

[3] F. L. Bates and R. F. White, "Differential Perceptions of Authority in Hospitals," *Journal of Health and Human Behavior* 2 (1961): 262–267. And: Grace Sills, "Nursing, Medicine, and Hospital Administration," *American Journal of Nursing* (Sept 1976): 1423–1434.

[4] A. B. Flood and W. R. Scott, "Professional Power and Professional Effectiveness: The Power of the Surgical Staff and the Quality of Surgical Care in Hospitals," *Journal of Health and Social Behavior* (Sept 1978): 240–254.

"observed" behaviors of RNs and MDs and the structural factors of ward or hospital organization. Thus, this literature, by ignoring or formalizing structural effects, challenges the structuralist problematic by virtue of being an essentially (if not avowedly) sociopsychological literature. The challenge to a structural theory of measurement and explanation is most acute in the face of this sort of literature, as opposed to literatures limiting themselves, however important their problems, to questions of state–class relations, class conflict, or social mobility. We add (perversely, but not facetiously) that the literature of RN behavior serves us well because it is a garden variety. This literature is manifestly dull, sometimes laughable. In short, it is the stuff most sociologists read and with which they are obliged to work.

Sociologists use "instruments" to "measure" "observables" in order to *produce* "data" for "explanations" – a reasonable statement rendered powerless by recent sociology. Sociologists know – now more than ever – that "instruments" cannot be operations linking observables to facts.[5] The weakness of our instruments is not a question of observer-subject effects, the inexactness of error term descriptions, or the imprecision of data taking; it lies in the language of instrumentation.[6] Instruments are theories or products of researchers' formal discourse. With the demise in the 1960s of overt and crypto operationalism, the ideal of a positive relationship between a measured datum and an observed real world (RW) stimulus-response unit was itself destroyed. There exists no positive relationship between words and things. The RW is at best a Presumably Real Social World (PRSW); and measurement reads this illusion.

The most stunning demonstration of this fact is found in recent advances in measurement error theory.[7] It is assumed that the stochastic disturbance term "measures" the deviation between the languages of

---

[5] D. Willer and M. Webster, "Theoretical Concepts and Observables," *American Sociological Review* 35 (1970): 748–757. And: Hubert M. Blalock, Jr., "The Measurement Problem: A Gap between the Language of Theory and Research," in *Methodology in Social Research*, ed. H. M. Blalock, Jr. and A. Blalock (New York: McGraw-Hill, 1968), 5–27.

[6] Aaron Cicourel, *Method and Measurement* (New York: Free Press, 1964). Hubert M. Blalock, Jr., *Theory Construction: From Verbal to Mathematical Formulations* (Englewood Cliffs, NJ: Prentice-Hall, 1969). Johan Galtung, *Theory and Methods of Social Research* (New York: Columbia University Press, 1969). Charles Lemert, "Language, Structure, and Measurement; Structuralist Semiotics and Sociology," *American Journal of Sociology* 84 (1979): 929–957.

[7] P. M. Siegel and R. W. Hodge, "A Causal Approach to the Study of Measurement Error," in *Methodology in Social Research*, ed. Blalock and Blalock, 28–59. John Sonquist, *Multivariate Model Building: The Validation of a Search Strategy* (Ann Arbor: Institute for Social Research, 1970). Blalock, "The Measurement Problem."

theory and research. If, for example, our variable is "*X*," then, normally:

$$X_{\text{measured}} = T_{\text{true value}} \text{ of } X + e_{\text{disturbance term}} \qquad (7.1)$$

Even though (7.1) states explicitly, through the stochastic term *e*, that all relevant features of *X* are unknown, it creates the illusion that the variable is measured completely and accurately. However, "any measure is subject to both errors incurred through definition of a less than completely valid measure of a theoretical construct and error incurred through an operational measure which is not perfectly reliable."[8] Therefore, (7.1) must be rewritten as:

$$X = (C + v) + e \qquad (7.2)$$

where, "*C*" equals the value assumed by the theoretical construct we are measuring, and *v* represents departures of the true values of the measured variable from the values of the theoretical variable we are attempting to operationalize.[9] Through the arbitrary *theoretical* decision to accept the stochastic disturbance term of (7.1) as incorporating both errors to which Siegel and Hodge refer, there exists no sound *methodological* device for the determination of *v* in (7.2). Measures of illusions are themselves illusory.

Criticisms of empiricism,[10] while salutory, are often merely a displacement of the problem. Recognizing that words and things do not necessarily have anything to do with each other, they turn to words – but without a serious theory of words and texts. Galtung is an excellent example.[11] He is ready to abandon the notion that measures can detect actors' "real" intentions, and turns to actors' words as such, hence transforming "the problem from the problem of correspondence between thoughts and words to the problem of how representative the interview situation is as social intercourse."[12] This is a sophisticated formal version of the ethnomethodological principle of the validity-destroying effect of the context embeddedness of social discourse. Neither seems to fully admit that the gulf between PRSW things and measures (hence, data) is unbridgeable even by the partial reformist strategies of humanistic or technical "sensitivity." This is evident when Galtung's implicit theory of measurement is restated with reference to the RN–MD literature (see figure 7.1).

A measured datum available for use in a compliance theory of RN–MD relations is the measurer's coded sign for a real-world impression, or text (the written entry by RNs of their behavior: administration of a specific drug to a patient). The impression (RN's chart entry) is a product of a

[8] Siegel and Hodge, "A Causal Approach," 55.   [9] *Ibid.*
[10] David Willer, *What Is Exact Theory?* Mimeograph. University of Kansas, n.d. Sonquist, *Multivariate Model Building.*
[11] Galtung, *Theory and Methods of Social Research.*   [12] *Ibid.*, 124.

behavioral response (RN drug administration) which in turn is created by the action of a stimulus (MD's order) on a responding object (RN as addressees of MD's orders). Though few today would admit it (for an exception see Salancik)[13] this amounts to the same thing as an earlier naïveté: that a datum is a one-to-one emblem for a stimulus. In more general terms, this is the position that observables produce measured data. This can be seen more clearly when the concept "*data*" is clarified. A datum is a measured unit. If – as everyone seems to agree – a datum is unable to stand for a real world thing, then *how* does it mean?

A datum is an expression vehicle for a content. When an RN enters the "fact" that she administered a drug of a certain dosage to a certain patient at a certain time subsequent to and directed by an MD order, a sociologist is warranted – let us assume – to enter a purely sociological mark in his records (perhaps on a standardized observer's check sheet, or simply in a field notebook). This mark becomes an encoded sign only in the context of a theory; that is, the formal discourse which led the sociologist to believe certain things which became his proto-"instrument"; for our example, sociologist presumably believes: (1) that there is something interesting about RN–MD relations, a problem of some kind; (2) that whatever is interesting is contained in RN response-to-MD sequences; (3) that certain behaviors – administration of drug, entry making – are a way of observing the RN-to-MD response; (4) that the specific behaviors could legitimately be recorded in a sociologist's preliminary text, perhaps by means of a simple x in the "RN makes chart entry" column of the sociologist's log book. This x or check-mark is a proto-datum which becomes a true datum only in the context of "data" – that is, a larger number of x's in the same column which at some subsequent point have been certified by sociologist's technology as valid, reliable, and significant. This certification, of course, is possible if the aggregated x's, rewritten as numbers, are supplied proper contents. This content is of course generated from the same theory which generated the instruments by which the datum and its fellow significant data were collected. In our example, a given x in the proper column becomes an expression unit for the meaningful content: //compliance// (for example, Rank and Jacobson).[14] In other words, the x-marks in the "RN makes entry" column are – both prospectively and retrospectively – expression units for the content

---

[13] Gerald R. Salancik, "Commitment and the Control of Organizational Behavior and Belief," in *New Directions in Organizational Behavior*, ed. B. W. Staw and G. R. Salancik (Chicago: St. Clair Press, 1977), 1–54.

[14] S. G. Rank and C. K. Jacobson, "Hospital Nurses' Compliance with Medication Overdose Orders: A Failure to Replicate," *Journal of Health and Social Behavior* 18, June (1977): 183–193.

Galtung:	Stimulus	→	Object	→	PRSW Response	→	Impression	Measurement → Datum
Example:	MD's Order	→	RN as addressee	→	RN behavior¹: Administration of Drug	→	RN behavior²: Chart Entry	→ Compliance datum
			.		.		.	→ .
					.		.	→ .
					.		.	→ .
					N		N	→ N

Figure 7.1: Traditional measurement theory

//compliance//. They are thereby sign functions existing exclusively in sociologists' texts.

A measurement theory such as Galtung's relies on an unjustified procedure. It must arbitrarily and without explanation exclude certain entirely possible meanings from the x-marks. The very drawing of an "RN makes entry" column (an element in an instrument) is, we know very well, designed to "infer" the content x-marks can have, //compliance//. Since the placing of the x in some other column ("no chart entry," "sequence incomplete," "other," etc.) is the equivalent of the content "non-compliance," instruments so designed can only collect positive entries. They solve the problem of the datum's unrepresentiveness of a real world thing by the use of contents from the instrument (its columns, and the theory according to which they were written).[15] Although a sensible beginning, the strategy soon collapses because it ignores a crucial possible content: the RN's intentions, which could of course be marked, for example, by such entries as "patient in bed 12 resting comfortably at 12:30 a.m.," which, in the context of an inappropriate MD medication order for 12:30 a.m. could supply to a datum the content, //non-compliance//. But in a scheme like Galtung's such data contents cannot be generated because the logic of the instrument requires a correspondence between data logged by a sociologist and the observed, pre-established behaviors. In other words, possible contents are arbitrarily excluded at the point of measurement by the instrument's assumption that a behavior is equivalent to a datum whose content can only be //compliance// or //non-compliance//. These unexplained exclusions are the monologicity of positivist measures. All the talk of indirect measurement, auxiliary theory, disturbance term, and the like do nothing to change the situation. The exclusion of possible contents is the necessary consequence of the refusal to recognize the extent to which empiricism and its avatars (like operationalism) remain the driving force behind any theory of measurement which holds that data values correspond to and are generated by

[15] We refer here to the distinction between words and things and the assumption that real worlds do not exist for sociology.

(however obliquely) real world events. If words have nothing to do with things, they have nothing to do with things. Words (even sociologists' words) have only to do with words. The solution is not in the refinement of measures, but in a proper theory of words and their relationship to each other – that is, of the intertextual relationship between sociologists' and actors' words. This, we believe, is managed only by a theory of reading which explains sociologists' readings of PRSW texts. Texts are, to use Umberto Eco's words, "multi-level discourses."[16] Texts are not composed of straightforward syntagmatic links between words, or simple denotative contents necessarily associated with terms. Texts are not read automatically (as in positivist measurement), but on the basis of a reader's competence, that is, his learned ability to properly associate possible contents with expressions addressed to him.[17] Thus, when an MD writes a medication order such as: "Valium 5mg. p.o. Q.i.D. x 1 mo.," the nurse must know that this means //give a certain tablet at a certain dosage four times a day for one month//. A competent RN-reading of this text involves the RN's training, including knowledge of the effect of the dosage on the patient. In effect, this is knowledge of the chemical and physiological implications of the behavioral response to the MD's medication order text (e.g., an improperly administered medication may lead to a coma, mental stress, etc.). Likewise, the RN knows, also on the basis of training, that the administration of a drug requires an appropriate chart entry, which includes knowledge (however conscious or pre-conscious) that the social structure of the medical ward would collapse if RNs fail to make such entries. Were all RNs to refuse to chart drug administrations, this would require the presence at all times of MDs or some other more reliable representative thereof. Thus, all MD orders are read with reference to competent knowledge of drug order codes, physiological effects of drugs, social effects of chart entries, and hospital organizational rules, among other pertinent knowledges.

With respect to measurement, the problem for the sociologist is to read these RN readings. Sociologists at this point are in exactly the same situation as the RN. They must read with reference to their competent knowledges: namely, the literature on hospital structures, formal organizations, medical systems, compliance relationships, status attributions, and so on. Sociologists' literatures are multiple – including, of course, at least: (1) materials published in sociological journals or books published

---

[16] Umberto Eco, "Possible Worlds and Text Pragmatics: 'Un Drame Bien Pari-Sien,'" *Versus: Quaderni di studio semiotico* 19–20, July–August (1978): 5–72.

[17] We use the generic masculine in knowledge of the sexism involved, but in ignorance of an adequate substitute. (2005/CL: a time- and culture-bound note, left as it is in respect for my own slowing learning and the real facts of the times.)

in the name of sociology (e.g., the RN-to-MD compliance literature); (2) general documentation provided by private and public agencies (such as government statistics on health care system structures, costs, training needs, etc.); (3) oral texts provided in conversation by nurses, medical doctors, patients; (4) newspaper accounts of events in hospital settings, and so forth. Though the first (to which we restrict ourselves) is primary, the others are equally – or in certain instances more – important. These literatures are the only resources available for those who desire to create instruments to measure "events" in the PRSW. Sociological instruments of whatever kind (survey instruments, field notebooks, experiment protocols, interview schedules) are exclusively and necessarily constructed on the basis of a reading of literatures. It is, therefore, surprising that there has never been an explicit theory for the reading of these texts. It is assumed, apparently, that sociologists possess a native skill by which they read out instruments from literatures – an assumption which naïvely entails the corollary: literatures are neutral resources which do not complicate the measurement process. These assumptions explain why all the attempts to control for measurement error concentrate on the observer or his instrumentation, as if the reliability and validity of instruments were only problems and as if instruments were created without difficulty. Since this is patently absurd, we must turn to a theory of reading able to suggest the way an instrument can be read from literatures (remembering that, for the sake of our example, we refer only to formal sociological literatures).

The first and fundamental principle of reading is that the reader and the text are bound to each other by a common set of historically relative conventions. Texts in an unknown foreign language cannot be read. A reader's basic competence is the ability to recognize at least something familiar in the texts: its language, its contents, its grammars, its connotations, and so forth. This mastery is never complete precisely because the reading, the text, and their social formation are historic conventions. We know this from the fact that certain literary forms (the novel, for example) once did not exist, may not exist in the future, and during their tenure have changed considerably. One cannot read Flaubert and Balzac as one reads Butor or Updike. The contents of reading competencies change. This leads to a second principle: readers, texts, and readings are socially produced. Neither the author nor the reader is able to write or read in mutual or respective isolation from their social circumstances. Reading is the product of the relations of literary production. Though the situation is even more complex than this, we shall work with these elementary principles, drawn quite clearly from post-structuralist reading theory.[18]

---

[18] Jonathan Culler, *Structuralist Poetics* (Ithaca: Cornell University Press, 1974).

To simplify a bit: a literature is encoded by the same social and productive relations which determine readers' reading. Reading competence is the ability to recognize enough of these codes in order to make some sense of the text. Readings are never perfect because, (a) there is no reason to decode a text perfectly and (b) the code is constantly changing even as it is read.[19]

All this is particularly true of a sociological literature which aims, presumably, to describe the very social conditions in which it is itself produced. Thus, a literature must be read with reference to what we know of the society in, by, and for which it was produced. In brief, we know that all sociological literatures written since the 1950s in advanced capitalist societies were produced under the following social conditions: increasing structuration and centralization of social functions in state and corporate organizations; decreasing autonomy of individuals as workers, producers, inventors of social norms; decreasing significance of nation-state distinctions as a result of increasing internationalization of capital; increasing fiscal crisis in the late capitalist world; increasing formalization, routinization, and control in individuals' work and personal lives. Consequently, no sociological reading of a literature can produce competent instruments if it fails to permit a reading of at least the following "levels": individual intentions and behaviors, organizational constraints thereupon, socioeconomic constraints on both actions and organizations. Simply put, readings must consist of social structural (organizational and socioeconomic constraints) and actor-related (intentions and behaviors) factors.

Turning to the RN–MD literature, we see that texts exist which are pertinent to all these levels, even though any given text tends to be a selective reading. Some limit their reading to the RN–MD diadic relations.[20] Others read only the personality traits of RNs;[21] still others read only RN decision-making abilities.[22] At another level, there are studies, such as Coser's which pass beyond social psychology to the social structure of medical and surgical wards. Coser's claim is that the RN's interaction with the MD is a function of the differing structures of

---

[19] Umberto Eco, *A Theory of Semiotics* (Bloomington: Indiana University Press, 1976), 213.
[20] Rank and Jacobson. "Hospital Nurses' Compliance with Medication Overdose Orders." Leonard Stein, "The Doctor–Nurse Game," *Archives of General Psychiatry* 16, June (1967): 699–703. C. K. Hofling, E. Brotzman, S. Dalrymple, N. Graves, and C. M. Pierce, "An Experimental Study in Nurse–Physician Relationships," *Journal of Nervous and Mental Disease* 143 (1966): 171–180.
[21] S. Reich and A. Geller, "Self-Images of Nurses," *Psychological Report* 39, October (1976): 401–402.
[22] J. A. Alutto and J. A. Belasco, "Determinants of Attitudinal Militancy among Nurses and Teachers," *Industrial and Labor Relations Review* 27, January (1977).

surgical and medical settings (high in the former, low in the latter).[23] At a still "higher" level, Flood and Scott read encroachment behaviors as a consequence of the social structure of the hospital as a formal organization in which hospital administration and physician components are the only independent variables of significance, leaving the nursing administration component in a necessarily insignificant position.[24] Then, at the level of the socioeconomic setting, there is an abundant literature which might read any particular topic (RN–MD relations) in the context of social and economic structures determining hierarchical control mechanisms (thus, presumably, obliging RN compliance).[25]

Of course, the literatures just cited are intended as "readings" of the PRSW. By listing them in this manner, we show that they were in fact selective readings and provide a literature with which to begin anew, in hopes of showing how to avoid their errors. We know now why the existing RN–MD literature is so selective. These readers did not begin by constructing instruments with reference to the social codes organizing their literature. For example, Coser limits herself to the relationship between role behavior and medical-surgical wards without the least explanation, as if nothing else mattered.[26] Thus, the literature she cites refers predictably to the social order of the ward and little else. This selectivity was due to an uncritical employment of the traditional theory of measures. Believing that RW "stimuli" are the sources of "data," she simply selected an unexplained "interesting" problem.

To avoid this trap, we must deal with the problem of an instrument's selectivity – the problem of parsimony. Having claimed that all the pertinent structural levels must be read, we are open to the charge that everything must be read – clearly an impossible task.

This requires us to be more precise in describing the nature of the instrument as a reading of a literature intended for a reading of a PRSW. The inadequacy of the traditional theory of measures (exemplified by Galtung's model) is that too few contents are available for expression units. Having derived the possible contents from a selective reading of the literature (e.g., deciding that compliance–non-compliance are the contents to be "discovered" behind RNs' behaviors), traditional measures

[23] Coser, "Authority and Decision-Making in a Hospital."
[24] Flood and Scott, "Professional Power and Professional Effectiveness."
[25] For example: Vicente Navarro, *Medicine under Capitalism* (New York: Prodist, 1976). H. B. Waitzkin and B. Waterman, *The Exploitation of Illness in Capitalist Society* (Indianapolis: Bobbs-Merrill, 1974). Sills, "Nursing, Medicine, and Hospital Administration."
[26] Coser, "Authority and Decision-Making in a Hospital."

cannot collect contents which do not fit the instrument, even though in the literature these other contents are available. This inadequacy can be solved by a description of the form of an instrument.

What, after all, is an instrument but a collection of types derived from a literature? The //complying nurse// is a type, as is its opposite. But we know that other types exist. Two can be given as examples: One is the //influencing nurse// who is neither purely compliant nor noncompliant.[27] This is the nurse who, by subtle games,[28] influences MDs to change or even discover the proper order to be given. The other is the //competing nurse// who disregards the compliance game altogether and operates,[29] in some circumstances, more or less independently: in effect, ignoring MD orders. The problem for measurement is that these types are not observable in the PRSW. It is possible to observe entries in a chart and suspect that the entry is: (1) a true entry reflecting strict compliance (complying type RN), (2) a true entry of a drug administration, but as a result of an MD order the RN influenced (influencing type RN), and (3) a modified or falsified entry reflecting a situation in which, for example, the nurse withheld the drug because she knew that the patient, on this evening, had no need of a sedative (competing type RN). It is totally irrelevant that one of these might be more probable than the others. The mere existence of any one, including the "extreme" third case, in any literature whatsoever is enough to make it a possible type behavior obligating an instrument to anticipate it.

But how? We must ask what an instrument actually observes. Not contents. And not types. Both are generated by a literature. What is observed is simply an expression token. The observation of an RN chart entry is, from the point of view of an instrument, only an expression vehicle for a content and a token of a type.[30] It is neither the content (//compliance//) nor a possible type (//professional// nurse). Only an expression token that is a concrete instance of a behavior is observed. The token behavior could be exactly the same in all three cases, but the type and content could

27 William A. Rushing, "Social Influence and the Social-Psychological Function of Deference: A Study in Psychiatric Nursing," *Social Forces* 41 (1962): 142–148. Stein, "The Doctor–Nurse Game," 699–703. Robert A. Hoekelman, "Nurse–Physician Relationships," *American Journal of Nursing* 75, July (1975): 1150–1152.
28 Stein, "The Doctor–Nurse Game."
29 Rank and Jacobson, "Hospital Nurses' Compliance with Medication Overdose Orders." Rushing, "Social Influence and the Social-Psychological Function of Deference."
30 The following discussion depends on the distinction between a token, found in a PRSW, which is read by a type, a theoretical instrument. This usage (drawn from Eco, *Theory of Semiotics*) serves here to make the point that stimuli from a "world" do not generate data; it is only the instrument which reads tokens of an empirical field which is itself established by a reading of the same literature that generates the types. One has tokens only on the basis of types.

vary. //Compliant//, //influencing//, and //competing// nurses could enter the same words in a chart, but as a result of different motives.

The problem is that those motives cannot be observed in any strict fashion (RNs will not tell us, they do not know themselves, they know and tell us lies to protect themselves, etc.). Galtung wisely urges us to read only the expression (his "impression") text; but he is totally wrong to assume that we can infer from a behavior expression a meaningful content to the behavior. He is wrong because we know from a "reading" of the literature that other contents are available for the same token expressions.

Since we have only the literature from which to collect these contents, we must begin there. But let us recall that a literature is a coded product of a social formation and a set of productive relations; and let us recall further that the literature used is only partially sociological texts: it could include documents, letters, nurses' autobiographies, and so forth. Thus, the literature's code is, taken as a whole, an ensemble of behavioral types, any one of which could be enacted and expressed by a concrete token on a given observed hospital ward. We also know therefrom that any and all of the three types, //compliant//, //influencing//, and //competing// are themselves products of social and economic relations: formal organization relations we would like to read. This entails two additional concepts: *ratio difficilis* and disambiguation.

A *ratio facilis* is a well-established conventional relationship between an observed token and its type.[31] This is exactly what we have in all the traditional literature which assumes (see figure 7.1) that an /RN chart entry/ is a proper token of the //RN-complying-professional// type. However, if we allow only instruments based on a *ratio facilis* we shall be no better off than traditional measurement theory. We shall measure only what the conventions of our literature tells us ought to be there (in other words, by allowing only *ratio facilis* we run the risk of perpetuating the status quo and discovering nothing new). A *ratio difficilis* is, on the other hand, a relationship between an established type and an unexpected, hence unique, content. Instruments must be able, in principle, to produce surprising results (discoveries); otherwise they are not measuring, only mapping. A complying RN token is scientifically meaningful only if we have some reason to believe that it is not a //competing// or //influencing// RN token. Since RNs cannot or will not tell us which token they are enacting, we can only explain the RN behavior by means of an instrument able to collect (i.e., produce) a *ratio difficilis*. This amounts to

---

[31] We are, of necessity, omitting much that could be included here: especially, the theory of signs and sign functions, connotation, and denotation. Also, we are abbreviating by collapsing somewhat the relationship between expression types and expression tokens. Again, see Eco, *Theory of Semiotics*.

an instrument which so incorporates all social structural dimensions and their combinations as to yield, at least: an //RN-competing-professional// type, and an //RN-influencing-professional// type, alongside the expected //RN-complying-professional// type.

Since it is always possible that the literature does not contain a possible type available for a *ratio difficilis*, and since the PRSW cannot itself tell us of this relationship, the possibility of discovery in social science rests entirely on a structural reading of the literature. Discovery is possible only when one reads from structures to behaviors and not vice versa (as in traditional measurement). Though the structures in the literature (knowledge of economic and social relations, organizational forms, etc.) may not tell us in so many words what we ought to produce – in a specific case study, a certain *ratio difficilis* – those structures can tell us that such a relation might be discoverable. For example, knowledge of the changing status of nurses may be found in Johnson and Martin;[32] Minehan;[33] new forms of professional behavior for nurses involving increasing autonomy in Davis;[34] Maas;[35] changes in sex composition of the nursing field with the inclusion of males in various statistical abstracts, effects of feminist ideology on female RN in Ashley; Bakdish; Moniz;[36] increasing caution of MDs in the face of malpractice suits in newspapers; increasing medical and hospital costs in our bank accounts, and increasing size of administrative components in hospitals and welfare organizations in Blau.[37] All these structural effects must be included in the instrument (the means of primary observation). Without them there are no surprises (hence nothing is measured). With them at least the possibility of discovery, upon which science is founded, exists.

We are still faced with the problem of parsimony. The above suggests that virtually everything must be incorporated in instrumentation. This, to be

---

[32] M. M. Johnson and H. W. Martin, "A Sociological Analysis of the Nurse Role," *American Journal of Nursing* 58 (1958): 373–377.

[33] Paula L. Minehan, "Nurse Role Conception," *Nursing Research* 26, September–October (1977): 374–379.

[34] Margaret K. Davis, "Intrarole Conflict and Job Satisfaction on Psychiatric Units," *Nursing Research* 23, November–December (1974): 482–488.

[35] M. Maas, J. Specht, and A. Jacob, "Nurse Autonomy: Reality Not Rhetoric," *American Journal of Nursing* 75, December (1975): 2201–2208.

[36] Jo Ann Ashley, "Nurses in American History: Nursing and Early Feminism," *American Journal of Nursing* 75, September (1975): 1465–1467. Diane P. Bakdish, "Becoming an Assertive Nurse," *American Journal of Nursing* 78, October (1978): 1710–1712. Donna Moniz, "Putting Assertiveness Techniques into Practice," *American Journal of Nursing* 78, October (1978): 1713.

[37] Peter Blau, "A Formal Theory of Organizations," *American Sociological Review* 35: 2 (1970): 201–219.

sure, is impossible. How, then, is one to perform a parsimonious reading out of instruments? One must read with reference to points of ambiguity in the literature. If RN–MD relationships are read from the point of view of traditional expectations about ward and hospital organization, there is little possibility of ambiguity. We expect (hence we find) compliance. Ambiguity becomes possible only when one can recognize that //RN-professional-quality medical care// could just as well be marked by //RN-competing// (or //RN-influencing//) as by //RN-complying//. And again, we can only anticipate this relationship if we have read the literatures to discover a possible structural explanation for an //RN-competing// with MD type. If we know that RNs increasingly define themselves as coequal professionals – that MDs, for fear of malpractice suits, might desire to diffuse and share legal responsibility; that hospital costs require a transfer of certain functions from high paid MDs to lower paid RNs, etc. – then we can discover an ambiguity in the traditional reading.

An ambiguity is not an explanation. It merely requires us to structure our instrumentation in a way that it can produce "explanatory" "data." What, after all, is explanation but the disambiguation of an intelligible ambiguity? But how is an ambiguity discovered? Only by knowledge of alternative explanations for a given observed behavior. This knowledge cannot be given by the RN (by the RW). It is found only in the literature which permits us to reconstruct the possible and probable social structures determining behaviors.[38] Social structures, as opposed to behaviors, exist only in literatures; they can never be observed. Thus, in the literature, read structurally, one finds the point at which measures must be made and instruments created; that is, the point at which rival social structural *"explanations"* tell us that things might not be as they appear. In our example, we shall of necessity limit ourselves to a small portion of the structural effects necessary to discover an ambiguity in need of disambiguation: the structural effects having to do with RNs' definition of their professionalism, and RN and MDs' participation in a system which, in principle, serves to provide quality patient care.

Ambiguity can arise only when it is recognized that the behavior to which the //professional RN// type corresponds can also be explained by apparently "non-professional" types. Both can be marked by other contents and types existing in the literature, such as: //therapeutic harmony// and //providing quality patient care//.[39] Our thesis is that in order to talk of professionalism among nurses the analysis must be expanded. We must go beyond the traditional equivalencies established (in one part of

---

[38] See: Eco, "Possible Worlds and Text Pragmatics."
[39] See: Johnson, and Martin, "A Sociological Analysis of the Nurse Role."

the literature) among //professional RN//, //complying RN//, //therapeutic harmony//, and //quality patient care//. This involves discovering in the literature possible substitutions for any one of these type contents when substitution would allow us to account for otherwise confusing facts – such as the fact that //competing// nurses do not always lose their jobs and sometimes are respected by MDs. In other words, we must reread all the literature which assumes that //complying RN// and //professional RN// are synonymous.[40]

We have discussed and summarized a sample of the social structural (SS) effects which correspond to three types (//influencing RN//, //complying RN//, //competing RN//) each of which are taken as probable contents for an observed expression behavior //RN chart entry//. And by doing so, in effect, we create an ambiguity: Which SS path provides the type best able to explain the //RN chart entry// token? Figure 7.2 illustrates a possible disambiguation.[41]

Let us suppose, on the basis of reading of the literature, that an axis is formed by two content types – U_1: //complying RN// and U_2: //competing RN// which are mutually exclusive types of professionalism. Whatever else //complying// and //competing// nurses are, they are not the same. But we know that neither type of nurse intends to be non-professional (especially in a world of increasing professionalization). We know that a prevailing, socially structured, definition of the two types as professional does exist. However, we also know that some conventions change. There is permeability between the two types and the marker //professional//.

[40] D. Froebe and R. J. Bain, *Quality Assurance Programs and Controls in Nursing* (St. Louis: C. V. Mosby, 1976). Barbara Bates, "Doctor and Nurse: Changing Roles and Relations," in *Dominant Issues in Medical Sociology*, ed. H. D. Schwartz and C. S. Kart (Reading, Mass.: Addison-Wesley, 1978). L. Pearlin and M. Rosenberg, "Nurse–Patient Social Distance and the Structural Context of a Mental Hospital," *American Sociological Review* 27, February (1962): 56–65. Hoekelman, "Nurse–Physician Relationships."

[41] This is only one methodological possibility. Figure 7.2 is based on Eco, *Theory of Semiotics*. The following symbols appear: U_1, U_2, α_1, α_2, β_1, β_2 λ_1, λ_2; and are explained by the terms following the symbols. However, λ_2 is not explained. It can signify anything as long as it opposes directly the signification of λ_1. Hence, λ_1 and λ_2 form an oppositional axis as do $\alpha_1 - \alpha_2$, $\beta_1 - \beta_2$, and U_1, $-U_2$. This indicates that "things" in themselves signify nothing. Therefore, the signified is defined only in relation to what it is not (e.g., a //complying RN// is not a //competing RN//). Part A indicates the potential ambiguity: How can a //complying RN// and a //competing RN// signify //quality patient care//? Part B offers one explanation for this ambiguity. The abbreviations mtn and mtl refer to metonymical assimilation and metaphorical substitution, respectively. Hence, the first part of B (to the left of the arrow) reads: the //complying RN// (U_1) via metonymical assimilation of the content of //non-professional RN// ($mtn\alpha_1$) is then rhetorically equivalent ($\equiv$) to //quality patient care// (λ_1,). The remainder of the equation is translated in the same manner. Part C shows the result of Part B. The content of //influencing RN// collapses the opposition of α_1 to α and therefore obliterates the opposition of U_1 to U_2.

This constantly shifting, unstable set of relationships is susceptible to metaphorical substitution or metonymical assimilation.[42] A metaphoric relationship exists when one type (//professional//) can be substituted for another (//complying RN// or //competing RN//); and a metonymic relationship exists when the latter two types can be assimilated to each other. These possible relationships of substitution and assimilation are, obviously, only evident from a knowledge of all possible social structures which could determine a behavior. A selective reading of the literature could lead (and has led) to the assumption that RNs are merely subprofessionals, hence, not capable of autonomous decision-making because their training is "inferior." This entails the further assumption that only the MD can provide //quality patient care//, the RN being a mere auxiliary. Read in this way, the literature yields the "explanation" that //conforming RN// and //professional RN// are synonomous and that no substitutions can be made. In this formulation, they must be directly, and without ambiguity, assimilated to //quality patient care// ($U_1(\text{mtn}\alpha_1) \equiv \lambda_1$). However, it is now well known (by our reading of accounts of poor MD patient care, films such as *Hospital*, notices of MDs losing malpractice suits, and other more formal literatures) that MDs, if left to their own devices, do not automatically provide //quality patient care//. This entails, further, the possibility that //quality patient care// *might* be provided equally by continuous and competent nursing.

This, in turn, raises the prospect that a non-conforming RN, for example //competing//, could both provide //quality nursing care// and be //professional//[43] (see Fagin 1975; Churchill 1977; Bandman and Bandman 1978). In this case, //quality patient care// can be assimilated metonymically to //competing RN// ($\lambda_1(\text{mtn}\alpha\ U_2)$). But this assimilation depends on the possibility of a metaphoric substitution of //competing RN// for //complying RN//. The result is attained by the addition of another marker to our reading of RN behaviors, namely: //autonomous decision-maker// which is assimilated to //professional RN// after it is substituted for //harmonious team worker//. Ultimately (see figure 7.2), //autonomous decision-maker// becomes a weak metaphoric substitution for //influencing RN//.[44]

This is a structural effect. There is evidence that nurses actually produce new RN //professional// behaviors, such as modeling their

[42] Eco, *Theory of Semiotics*.
[43] See: Claire M. Fagin, "Nurses' Rights," *American Journal of Nursing* 75, January (1975): 82–85. Larry Churchill, "Ethical Issues of a Profession in Transition," *American Journal of Nursing* 77, May (1977): 873–875. B. Bandman and E. Bandman, "Do Nurses Have Rights? No and Yes," *American Journal of Nursing* 78, January (1978): 84–86.
[44] See: Rushing, "Social Influence and the Social-Psychological Function of Deference." Stein, "The Doctor–Nurse Game." Hoekelman, "Nurse–Physician Relationships."

A. The Potential Ambiguity

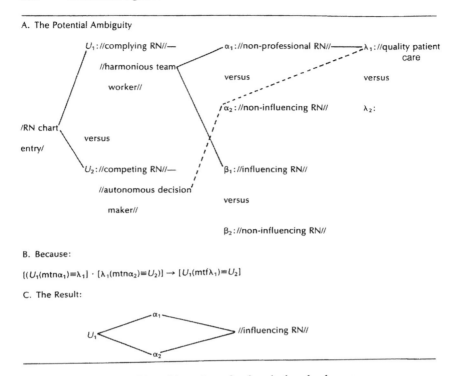

B. Because:

$$[(U_1(mtn\alpha_1) \equiv \lambda_1) \cdot [\lambda_1(mtn\alpha_2) \equiv U_2)] \rightarrow [U_1(mtf\lambda_1) \equiv U_2]$$

C. The Result:

Figure 7.2: Disambiguation of a rhtorical code change

//professional// behavior after that of MDs by performing nurses' ward rounds as a replication of doctors' rounds.[45]

It is apparent that the explanation for new behaviors of this sort is contained in the shifting structural relationships between RNs' understanding of their professionalism, the changing structure of hospital wards, modification of the MD role in patient care, and so forth. We could never "*explain*" (or even "*measure*") these behaviors, which all of us can observe without the benefit of either sociology or "structuralism" and without a coherent reconstruction of the structural field of the RN–MD relationship. Furthermore, what is explained is that //autonomous decision-maker// is not and need not be automatically assimilated to //competing//;

[45] Johnson and Martin. "A Sociological Analysis of the Nurse Role." Judith N. Cates, "Images of the Health Professionals," *The Sociological Quarterly* 6, Autumn (1965): 391–397. Froebe and Bain, *Quality Assurance Programs and Controls in Nursing*. E. Lewin and J. Damrell, "Female Identity and Career Pathways: Post-Baccalaureate Nurses Ten Years After," *Sociology of Work and Occupations* 5(1) (1978): 31–54.

and, accordingly, that //harmonious team worker// holds no necessary relationship to //professional RN//. Indeed when read in this way, one can see that the latter relationship is not only not "natural" but may even be an instance of another content //domination//, the explanation of which would involve still wider investigations of the RN–MD structural field (the structures of hospital administration, capitalist health care systems, etc.). This shows that one ambiguity leads to another and, as a result, the reading of structural effects is continuous (as it should be in any true science). But the continuous revision of sociological reconstructions of this structural field are not arbitrary. They move in a positive fashion, from ambiguity to ambiguity. Of course, ambiguities are only the beginning points of analysis by which parsimonious measurement becomes possible. Though instruments and, thereby, readings are constantly revised, the result is a non-positivist, positive reading of the structural field upon which explanation depends.

8

Roland Barthes and the phantasmagoria of social things

In *The Work of Mourning*, Jacques Derrida's collection of personal tributes to fallen friends, the most unusual of the essays is the one on Roland Barthes. Derrida did not express for Barthes quite the same overwhelming feeling as he would at Louis Althusser's funeral, nor even the same degree of intimacy he felt for Deleuze, nor the respect he conveyed for Foucault, nor the loss he felt for Levinas. From the beginning of "The Deaths of Roland Barthes" Derrida confesses that he cannot quite find the right form. For him the plural *deaths* points to the impossibility of the situation. He wants his words to be not about Barthes but *for* him. But *he* is not there. The words, therefore, are trapped in a philosophical view Derrida revised from Levinas who in turn reworked it from Heidegger – that death is the limit and the beyond of time. He asks the impossible of his words for Barthes:

So where do they go? To whom and for whom? Only for him in me? In you? In us? For these are not the same thing, already so many different instances, and as soon as he is in another the other is no longer the same, I mean the same as himself. And yet Barthes himself is no longer there. We must hold fast to this evidence, to its excessive clarity, and continually return to it as if to the simplest thing, to that alone which, while withdrawing into the impossible, still leaves us to think and gives us occasion for thought. (Derrida for Barthes, *The Work of Mourning*, 35)

For Derrida, death is not occasion for thought of the one dead, but of the fact that we are left by death with the impossibility of thinking except for the other who is not there.

Roland Barthes (1915–80) was not nearly so attentive to death as a subject of philosophical work, though those who knew him and those who have studied photographs of him realize that he was a man who enjoyed the pleasures of this life against the negative of loss. His father died when he was an infant. He was attached thereafter to his mother whose own death in 1977 was a loss he, literally, could not bear. Is it possible that he stepped in front of that van on Rue des Ecoles on

February 25, 1980, then allowed his chronically diseased lungs to give up in the few weeks remaining? It is a gratuitous speculation, often made, but made because, as his death was true to the impossibility of words – words like those Derrida offered him in his final absence. Barthes well understood the fragile structure under which meanings are arranged for one and all.

The ironic stylistic touch in Derrida's meditation is that he composed it – if that is the word for a series of fragments – around a rereading of two of Barthes's books. Not just any two, but the first and the last. The first had been in 1953, *Writing Degree Zero* – Barthes's first foray, with *Elements of Semiology*, into the formal semiology of languages he would later abandon. The reason, one supposes, that Derrida was comfortable with this among Barthes's texts was not that it seemed to anticipate his own ideas on writing but that it describes writing in the terms that suit the death of the writer. Writing, says Barthes, "is not so much a stock of materials as a horizon, which implies both a boundary and a perspective; in short, it is the comforting area of an ordered space." The comfort is in the limiting beyond of writing – the space of secrets, death itself, the occult, and utopia.

The other book Derrida chose was Barthes's last, *Camera Lucida*, which was published in 1980 just before his death and is a meditation of sorts on his mother who had died three years before. Derrida said in his words for Barthes that he read these two books back-to-back as though they were one. If, ever, there was any one then, besides Derrida, to whom it would occur to do such a thing, that one was Barthes himself. But the connection to be drawn between readings of writings out of context is one for which the theme of *Camera Lucida* is apt – the photograph. The photograph and, by extension, the novel work according to the play between points of attention in the image and the composition as a whole. The eye is drawn to a point (*punctum*) within the study (*studium*) itself. In being drawn visually to a point interior to the work we ourselves are drawn into the image by our desire to add to it what we bring which, as it happens, must already be there. Derrida, quoting while presenting Barthes:

What is to be heard in "composition"? Two things that compose together. First, separated by an insuperable limit, the two concepts compromise with one another. They compose together, the one *with* the other, ... the "subtle beyond" of the *punctum*, the uncoded beyond, composes with the "always coded" of the *studium* (*Camera Lucida*, 59, 51). It belongs to it without belonging to it and is unlocatable within it; it is never inscribed in the homogeneous activity of the framed space but instead inhabits or, rather, haunts it: "it is an addition [*supplement*] . . . . : it is what I add to the photograph and *what is none the less already there*" (*Camera Lucida*, 55). We are prey to the ghostly power of the supplement; it is this unlocatable site that gives rise to the *specter*. (Derrida for Barthes, *Work of Mourning* for *Camera Lucida*)

The photograph, like (but not exactly like) the novel or the musical composition, is a play of supplements added into the images evoked by the eerie necessity that they are already there.

Is it too much to extend this idea to culture – to that array of socially meaningful things in respect to which Barthes, following Saussure, proposed a sociology of signs? What Derrida, in spite of himself, does *for* Barthes is to tie the parts of a diverse writing life into the continuous, rhizomatic growth of ideas in Paris in that day, but also into the absent presence of the dark soil of Barthes's imagination.

Another of Barthes's early books was *Mythologies* (1957), a stunning series of cultural studies in the form of a semiology of popular culture. In that book's theoretical essay, "Myth Today," Barthes both takes up and anticipates the same kind of structuralist semiology that Lévi-Strauss was inventing. "Myth Today" famously turns on a photograph that stands as the proof text for his view, shared by Lévi-Strauss, that myth *is* a semiology.

I am at the barber's, and a copy of *Paris-Match* is offered to me. On the cover, a young Negro in French uniform is saluting, with his eyes uplifted, probably fixed on a fold of the tricolor. All this is the *meaning* of the picture. But, whether naively or not, I see very well what it signifies to me: that France is a great Empire, that all her sons, without any color discrimination, faithfully serve under her flag, and that there is no better answer to the detractors of alleged colonialism than the zeal shown by this Negro in serving his so-called oppressors. I am therefore again faced with a greater semiological system (*a black soldier is giving the French salute*); there is a signified (it is here a purposeful mixture of Frenchness and militariness); finally, there is the presence of the signified through the signifier.

In 1957, France's colonies were already separating themselves. Fanon was moving toward *The Wretched of the Earth* and death, at the moment when the colonial system was dying. The figure of the Black colonial saluting the French flag was, at the time of the writing, fraught with meanings, to which Barthes alludes, but gently. The pride of France, which had built its cultural prowess on the absence of its colonies, was dying. The image is an illusion – a phantasmagoria of the shifting light of history.

This is the wink of thick description. The signified – the meaning, that is – is the presence of loyalty to France and her military force conveyed by the one signifier, the Black man of the colonies, who during the wars of colonial liberation would be – and any French

person to see the magazine photograph could not but have known this –
the least likely to salute. Signs work always in the excess created by
those who desire to bring the meanings to them that are already there.
Signs are meaningful only because they participate in the ubiquitous
irony of meaning – that signs do not mean unless they are other, which
opens the comforting space into which the other can add that which
is already there. This is the truth of death. It is always there in the
comforting space of language in which the limit of an absence is the
condition for cultural meaning.

The wink is thick because it is much like the photograph in being
a dispersal of light, long dead, trapped in the negative image that is
brought back to life, long after the death, by the viewing of the image
captured. The nation-state and its societal community are like the
photograph in which a flag is the point of light to the composition it
claims to frame. The work of mourning is continuous with the work of
signification, which is to say that social things are meaningful phantasmagorias, as Durkheim was beginning to understand as he moved
toward his own death.

Language, structure, and measurement as a semiotic of differences (1979*)

In sociology there is a necessary bond between language, structure, and measurement. This is well illustrated by a familiar text from James Coleman:

The extraordinary complexity of structures of relations between people makes the task of measuring them a difficult one. . . . [T]he conclusion was reached that quantitative measurement, to prove theoretically useful, had better be carried out in direct conjunction with the theory within which it is intended to be used. On an intuitive level, it comes down to the simple fact that there is no use developing a concept of "segregation" or "stratification" unless there are some definite causal relations in which the concept plays a part; and once such causal relations are made explicit, they dictate many of the decisions about how to construct a measure of the concept.[1]

Coleman is saying that a social structure is, above all else, a concept in the sociologist's technical vocabulary, not a self-evident real-world object. The causal relations in which the concept participates are specific to science, not "reality." Since, in Coleman's view, measures are largely defined by these concepts, measurement (like structure) is an aspect of sociological language and not primarily the literal representation of an existing social object. If measures are derived from theoretical concepts, measurement values are necessarily determined more by sociological language than by presumably real empirical facts. In other words, social structures exist in the theoretical language which establishes the conditions of their measurement.

This view is widely held especially by those who are best known for their interest in the formal measurement of social structures. It is essentially the same as Blalock's view of indirect measurement and auxiliary theory: he argues that measurement theory must be included in the abstract theory

* Reprinted by permission from *The American Journal of Sociology* 84: 4 (1979): 929–957 where it appeared as "Language, Structure, and Measurement: Structuralist Semiotics and Sociology." The essay is unchanged save for minor editing.
[1] James Coleman, et al. *Introduction to Mathematical Sociology* (New York: Free Press, 1964), 430–431.

188

of structural relations.[2] Like Stinchcombe,[3] Blalock makes the structural variable a theoretical definition, not an empirical sign.[4] And Parsons's analytic realism methodology hinges entirely upon the establishment of structures within a pre-empirical theoretical lexicon: "A structure is not an ontological entity but is strictly relative to the investigatory purpose and perspective."[5]

This discussion is commonly joined by sociologists whose interests are otherwise quite different from those of Coleman, Blalock, Parsons, and Blau. Since the appearance of Cicourel's *Method and Measurement*,[6] ethnomethodologists have explicitly concerned themselves with the relationship between language and the sociological measurement of structures.[7] Ethnomethodology has claimed that measurement becomes a universal and necessary feature of both professional and practical sociological talk when measurement is understood as that social process whereby encoded norms are employed to make sense of the social world.

We call attention to the phenomenon that formal structures are available as accounts of professional sociology where they are recognized by professionals and claimed by them as professional sociology's singular achievement. These accounts of formal structures are done via sociologists' mastery of natural language. . . . This assures to professional sociologists' accounts of formal structures its [sic] character as a phenomenon for ethnomethodology's interest, not different from any other members' phenomenon where the mastery of natural language is similarly involved. Ethnomethodological studies of formal structures are directed to the study of such phenomena, seeking to describe members' accounts of formal structures wherever and by whomever they are done, while abstaining from all judgments of their adequacy, value, importance, necessity, practicality, success or consequentiality. We refer to this procedural policy as "ethnomethodological indifference."[8]

---

[2] Hubert M. Blalock, Jr., "The Measurement Problem: A Gap between the Language of Theory and Research," in *Methodology in Social Research*, ed. H. M. Blalock, Jr. and A. Blalock (New York: McGraw-Hill, 1968), 5–27.

[3] Arthur Stinchcombe, *Constructing Social Theories* (New York: Harcourt, Brace & World, 1968), 28–29.

[4] See: Charles Lemert, *Sociology and the Twilight of Man: Homocentrism and Discourse in Sociological Theory* (Carbondale: Southern Illinois University Press, 1979).

[5] Talcott Parsons, "Some Problems of General Theory in Sociology," in *Theoretical Sociology: Perspectives and Developments*, ed. John C. McKinney and Edward Tiryakian (New York: Appleton-Century-Crofts, 1970), 27–68, p. 35. Cf. Peter Blau, "Parameters of Social Structure," *American Sociological Review* 39: 5 (1974): 615–636.

[6] Aaron Cicourel, *Method and Measurement* (New York: Free Press, 1964).

[7] For examples see: Harold Garfinkel, *Studies in Ethnomethodology* (Englewood Cliffs: Prentice-Hall, 1967). Harold Garfinkel and Harvey Sacks, "On Formal Structures of Practical Actions," in *Theoretical Sociology*, ed. McKinney and Tiryakian. Cicourel, *Method and Measurement*. Aaron Cicourel, *Cognitive Sociology* (New York: Macmillan, 1974).

[8] Garfinkel and Sacks, "On Formal Structures of Practical Actions," 345.

It is true, of course, that ethnomethodologists use non-standard meanings for measurement and social structure. However, it is clear that by making language a primary theoretical topic they are considering the same problematic as Coleman and others.

It is, therefore, the catholicity of the language/structure/measurement problem that occasions its reconsideration in this paper. I will argue, however, that neither of the two general points of view mentioned above is satisfactory. The first, of which Coleman is typical, may be called *formalism*. Here "structure" usually refers to macro structures. Language is that which must be purified in order to make measurement possible. The second approach, of which ethnomethodology is typical, is commonly identified as hermeneutical or interpretative sociology.[9] Here structure is a weak term, often referring to an aspect of the individual's interpretative repertoire, such as an actor's ability to recognize and organize "socially acceptable behavior"[10] or "joint lines of action."[11] However, the weakness of this usage is somewhat repaired by a strong analysis of the way in which language determines all measurement procedures.

Both approaches see the measurement of structures as problematic. However, the formalists see technical sociological language as that which can overcome measurement problems, while interpretativists see language itself as the problem which dooms all measurement to endless self-examination. This is the difference between an occasionally humble heroism and a faintly optimistic fatalism. Accordingly, while considering the same general issue from different perspectives, each emphasizes a different aspect of the problem. The formalists, though naïve as to the complexities that prevent language from achieving any pure formal state, have properly emphasized the fact that the concept structure must, in sociology, get at macrosocial structures in a clear and precise way. The interpretativists (especially ethnomethodologists), though seemingly uninterested in the complexity of structures in a macro sense, have properly insisted on the relativity that language necessarily imposes on any scientific discourse.

The problem with which I will deal is: How can sociology measure complex social structures while retaining a proper respect for the contextual relativity that language imposes? Because I think that formalism

---

[9] The classification used here is roughly comparable to others in use. For example: Helmut Wagner, "Types of Sociological Theory," *American Sociological Review* 28, October (1963): 735–742. Jack Douglas, *Understanding Everyday Life* (Chicago: Aldine, 1970). Jürgen Habermas, *Knowledge and Human Interests* (Boston: Beacon Press, 1971). Lemert, *Sociology and the Twilight of Man.*

[10] Cicourel, *Cognitive Sociology*, 11.

[11] Herbert Blumer, *Symbolic Interactionism: Perspective and Method* (Englewood Cliffs: Prentice-Hall, 1969), 17.

and interpretativism give unsatisfactory answers, this article will seek a solution in a third alternative, the structuralist social theory that derives from Ferdinand de Saussure.

Semiotics is the study of signs and their meaning. Semiotics is related to linguistics, but language is only one of many sign systems. In addition to such sign systems as Morse code, highway signs, and fashion codes, one may properly include measurement codes employed by sociologists as a topic of semiological research. Structuralist semiotics is a prominent tradition of semiological research that ought to be of special interest to sociologists. Ferdinand de Saussure – the founder of European semiology (as distinct from what in America Charles Sanders Peirce called semiotics) – is generally considered to be the founder of structuralist linguistics[12] and of structuralist semiotics.[13]

Saussure worked out his social theory of signs with reference to the famous distinction between *la langue* (language) and *la parole* (speaking). The latter refers to the observed data of linguistic research, the actual speech of language users. However, left to itself, *la parole* overwhelms the linguist with a large number of disorderly facts. When one takes into account the variety of words, phonemes, and tonal emphases actually used by even the most elementary of speakers (strangers, children), it is apparent that speaking involves a virtually unlimited number of events. Science is inundated. Order is difficult to achieve.

Saussure overcame this superabundance of fact and established linguistics as an orderly science by means of the concept *la langue*, which he viewed as the social system of conventions from which *la parole* draws its elements. "Language [*la langue*] is a well-defined object in the heterogenous mass of speech facts. . . . It is the social side of speech, outside the individual who can never create or modify it by himself; it exists only by virtue of a sort of contract signed by members of the community."[14] Though, for Saussure, linguistic observation must take its units

---

[12] Noam Chomsky, *Language and Mind* (New York: Harcourt, Brace, Jovanovich, 1972). Roman Jakobson, *Main Trends in the Science of Language* (New York: Harper & Row, 1973). Jonathan Culler, *Saussure* (Glasgow: Fontana, 1976). Giulio C. Lepschy, *A Survey of Structural Linguistics* (London: Faber, 1970). Wallis Reid, "The Saussurian Sign as a Control in Linguistic Analysis," *Semiotext(e)* 1: 2 (1974): 31–53. Michel Foucault, *Archaeology of Knowledge* (New York: Random House, 1972).

[13] Roland Barthes, *Elements of Semiology* (Boston: Beacon Press, 1970). Umberto Eco, *A Theory of Semiotics* (Bloomington: Indiana University Press, 1976).

[14] Ferdinand de Saussure, *Course in General Linguistics* (New York: Philosophical Library, 1959), 14. It is almost certain that Saussure, who lectured in Paris at the Ecole des Hautes Etudes from 1881 to 1891, was influenced by Durkheim. In this passage one sees the probable influence of Durkheim's conscience collective. Their views of social fact are, also, nearly identical (compare Saussure *Course*, 77, with Durkheim, *The Rules of Sociological Method*, p. 13). The crucial difference is that Durkheim provided no technical concept

from speaking (*la parole*), linguistic analysis can define these units as facts only by locating them in *la langue*. With Saussure linguistics, in effect, becomes an implicitly sociological exercise insofar as facts are explained by a social convention, by a community's most elemental social structure: its language.

The *la langue/la parole* distinction is supplemented by another crucial dichotomy, *paradigm/syntagm*.[15] Roughly described, Saussure's paradigms are the content of *la langue*; that is to say, the series of formal structures (verb forms, word variations, grammatical rules, phonetic signals, etc.) from which the speaker selects the units that are formed into actual speech chains (syntagms) which are the substance of speaking (*la parole*). The syntagms are what the listener is aware of (as is, of course, the linguist); the paradigms always remain absent to observation. The latter are the structures which combine in an extremely complex manner to form the structured social convention, *la langue*.

Thus, for Saussure, linguistic measurement is a description of the place of observed units of speaking (*la parole*) in a social structure (*la langue*). It is here that one begins to see the value of Saussure's alternative to formalist and interpretativist sociologies. His notion of *la langue* resembles ethnomethodology in that it pictures social structures as conventions and thus as negotiated. However, unlike ethnomethodologists (and interpretativists in general) Saussure shares the formalist interest in providing formal descriptions of macrosocial structures. With respect to language, *la langue* is a formal macrostructure insofar as language structures are not considered immediately susceptible to manipulation by speaking individuals. In short, Saussure's position retains the social naturalism that interpretive sociology has always considered a fatal omission of formalism, but does not reduce the formal study of social structures – to a metaphoric microsociology of intentions (the fatal flaw of interpretativism, in formalism's eyes).

The value of Saussure to sociology rests upon our ability to think of sociological measurement as a language-specific semiotic process able to generate formal descriptions of macrostructures. In order to develop this possibility, it is necessary to begin with a discussion of Saussure's theory of the sign (the unit of linguistics) and its value (the sign's measurability).

comparable to Saussure's *la parole* and therefore did not explicitly explain the technical basis for the measurement and analysis of the relationship of individuals' motives to social structures. The advantage of Saussure's implicit social psychology will be illustrated below.
15 The paradigm/syntagm distinction is roughly comparable to more familiar dichotomies such as code/message, competence/performance, and metaphor/metonymy. See: Barthes, *Elements of Semiology*, 18–20.

This requires an examination of two additional Saussurian ideas: (1) the arbitrariness of the sign, and (2) the differential character of linguistic value.

Arbitrariness

"The linguistic sign unites, not a thing and a name, but a concept and a sound image."[16] This is Saussure's simplest definition of the sign, the unit of structural linguistic research.

The sign is nearly as important for what it is not as for what it is. It is not a way of naming objects in the real world. The term "cow" is not the name for a class of milk-producing bovine creatures. For Saussure, it is instead a psychological construct by which the speaker unites his or her acoustic impressions of certain phonemes with the concept *cow*. The "real" cows people take their children to gawk at have no necessary connection with the linguistic sign. Saussure, at this point, is both anti-empiricist and anti-naturalist. Methodologically, his unit of analysis does not pretend to present properties of the external world. Philosophically, he does not believe that the natural object-world is of primary interest.

This is not to say, however, that Saussure is a psychological reductionist or a methodological individualist.[17] The sign is not arbitrary in the sense of allowing any speaker to use any combination of sounds he chooses as a signifier. "The signifier, though to all appearances freely chosen with respect to the idea that it represents, is fixed, not free, with respect to the linguistic community that uses it."[18] The sign is a social event in that speakers must use the linguistic conventions established by a community of speakers. These conventions include phonic and lexical items and

---

[16] Saussure, *Course in General Linguistics*, 66.

[17] This is a problem in Saussure. On the one hand it can be said that he avoids psychological reductionism by founding the acoustic impression in sound. The impression thus derives from the material fact of speaking itself, while simultaneously being associated with a concept. There could be no sign if one were to consider concept, acoustic impression, and sound in isolation from each other. At the same time, there is a marked psychologism here. This is one of the points at which Saussure's concept sign has come under attack. Derrida (*Of Grammatology* (Baltimore: Johns Hopkins University Press, 1976)), while recognizing the importance of Saussure's concept, argues that it retains an essentially metaphysical taint. Eco (*A Theory of Semiotics*) claims that it lacks the precision necessary to explain its role in semiosis and that it is better replaced by the concept sign-function. However, since the present discussion concerns other, more general, features of Saussure's theory, these criticisms are not of direct importance here, though they would be in a complete development of Saussure's social theory. That Saussure is not a psychological reductionist can be readily seen by comparing his views with, for example, Homans's (George Homans, *The Nature of Social Science* (New York: Harcourt, Brace & World, 1967)) explicit methodological individualism.

[18] Saussure, *Course in General Linguistics*, 71.

syntactical rules. The sign is the unit of the speech chain (the syntagm) which draws its substance from the paradigms of a given language (*la langue*).

Behind Saussure's theory of the sign is an assumption of considerable importance. Language is not directly the product of subjective intentions. Even the sign articulated by an individual is formed with reference to social conventions. Thus, Saussure's idea of arbitrariness has two dimensions: (1) Signs are arbitrary insofar as they are social conventions. (2) They are arbitrary insofar as they are composed of elements (a concept and a sound image) that have no necessary or natural connection to each other. Neither of these ideas is entirely foreign to sociology.

The first dimension (that units of social behavior are arbitrary because of their origin in societal conventions) has been long accepted by various interpretative theories. In this view the observed units of social behavior ("indexical expressions," "behavioristic specimens," "joint acts," "frames," etc.) are the products of social negotiations. Thus, since they are not given, they are not readily formalizable. Harold Garfinkel's well-known definition of ethnomethodology is a convenient illustration: "[T]he term 'ethnomethodology' . . . refer[s] to the investigation of the rational properties of indexical expressions and other practical actions as contingent accomplishments of organized artful practices of everyday life."[19] In other words, the contingent nature of social behavior limits measurement to indices of the actor's intended meaning. Though nuance is necessarily overlooked here this is, roughly, the position of all interpretative sociologies from symbolic interactionism, through Goffman, phenomenology, and ethnomethodology to Habermas's "depth-hermeneutics."[20]

The formalists, on the other hand, beg the question of the contingency of social behavior with respect to hidden cultural meanings in order to

[19] Garfinkel, *Studies in Ethnomethodology*, p. 11.
[20] Jürgen Habermas, "Summation and Response," *Continuum* 8 (1970): 123–133. Though I take ethnomethodology as a representative of interpretativism, this is not to say that differences within this larger perspective are negligible. Ethnomethodology is of primary interest here because it has made explicit prior interpretativists' implicit discussions of the language/measurement/structure problem. For discussions of the place of ethnomethodology in this tradition see: Paul Attewell, "Ethnomethodology since Garfinkel," *Theory and Society* 1 (1974): 170–210. And: Charles Lemert, "De-Centered Analysis: Ethnomethodology and Structuralism," *Theory and Society* 7 (1979): 289–306. For discussions of Habermas's place in interpretativism see: Habermas, "Summation and Response," Jürgen Habermas, "Toward a Theory of Communicative Competence," in *Recent Sociology, No. 2*, ed. H. P. Dreitzel (New York: Macmillan, 1970), 114–148. Habermas, *Knowledge and Human Interests*. And: Charles Lemert and Garth Gillan, *Michel Foucault: Social Theory and Transgression* (New York: Columbia University Press, 1982).

clear the way for the designation of formal units of analysis which are presumed to function as measures of properties of a real world. Though it is seldom recognized, this position is arbitrary insofar as the theoretical variable is not a natural fact but the theorist's definition of an indicator. Take, for example, Stinchcombe's description of a variable as ". . . a concept which can have various values, and which is defined in such a way that one can tell by means of observations which value it has in a particular occurrence."[21] The key words are "defined in such a way." Formal variable definitions are arbitrary in the sense that they are determined by the internal logical or mathematical requirements of the theoretical system, not their representative exactness. "The values of the structural parameters, which provide us with a mathematical explanation of the empirical relationships, cannot be determined from the data alone."[22] Though in another respect (to be discussed) this position contradicts itself, here formalism is surprisingly similar to Saussurian semiotics in that its unit of analysis (the formal variable) does not name real-world properties.

Where Saussure and both sociological approaches are in accord is on the idea that, in the social sciences, an absolutistic theory of measurement cannot yield theoretically useful results. Unless one is willing to settle for a naïve empiricism such as operationalism, social research must admit some degree of arbitrariness into its theory-construction strategies in order to deal with a complex social world that does not give up its facts to a direct measurement. Interpretativism attacks this problem by emphasizing the arbitrariness by which the observed units are constructed, while formalism takes the alternative of concentrating on the arbitrariness of the theoretical constructs (variables) by which facts are explained. Unfortunately, neither of these tactics is satisfactory by itself. The former has not yet shown how the arbitrariness of its units can be explained formally with reference to structures. The latter (formalism) has not been able to deal with the contradiction involved in describing structures by means of arbitrary theoretical variables derived apart from the direct measurement of given (and absolutistic) units.

The Saussurian alternative is not, however, merely a convenient historical reference for a synthesis of ethnomethodology and formalism. Saussurianism, while touching on similar issues, leads sociology to a complete reformulation of the relationship among structures, measures, and facts. The value of such a reformulation depends on the assumption that social behavior follows laws similar to those of language behavior. The development of this assumption for sociology derives from the second major

[21] Stinchcombe, *Constructing Social Theories*, 28–29.
[22] Hubert M. Blalock, Jr., "The Formalization of Sociological Theory," in *Theoretical Sociology*, ed. McKinney and Tiryakian, 284.

part of Saussure's theory of signs, the differential character of linguistic value.

Differential values

One consequence of the arbitrariness of the sign is that it is present to observation as a unit of speaking, but cannot be explained scientifically without reference to the structure of its language (*la langue*), which is absent and not directly observable:

[W]e must first be convinced that the concrete entities of language are not directly accessible. If we try to grasp them, we come into contact with the true facts. Starting from there, we can set up the classifications that linguistics needs for arranging all the facts at its disposal. On the other hand, to base the classifications on anything except concrete entities – to say, for example, that the parts of speech are the constituents of language simply because they correspond to categories of logic – is to forget that there are no linguistic facts apart from the phonic substance cut into significant elements.[23]

In other words, the articulated sign is the unit of observation, but the "true facts" of language are found in the paradigms making up the structure of *la langue*. The former is present, the latter absent.[24]

The effect of this interpretation is that the linguistic value of the term "cow" is only partially found in its signifying function (that is, in the linkage between the phonic signifier "cow" and the signified concept *cow*). Value depends also on the relations between any enunciated term and (a) the other elements with which it is combined in an actual speech chain, and (b) those paradigmatic elements which were omitted from the utterance. Therefore, the value of "cow" is based upon its differences from other linguistic units. When "cow" appears in the sentence "I milked the cow," its value is different from that in the sentence "The cow milked me." The different combination in the latter case does nothing to the sign "cow" itself, but it dramatically alters the value of the term by connoting a highly unusual cow, such as one that might appear in a dream or a children's book. Even when "The cow milked me" connotes "The cow swindled me," the cow is transformed into a figurative creature to which human intentions are imputed. In addition, the value of "cow" in an utterance depends on the fact that the term "cow" appears, while innumerable possible alternatives have been omitted: such as, "I milked the *goat* (or *kitten, welfare office*)" and "The *gynecologist* (or my *husband*, the *nurse*) milked me."

---

[23] Saussure, *Course in General Linguistics*, 100.   [24] *Ibid.*, 123.

For the present, the most intriguing of these differential relations is the latter, that between the present enunciated term and its absent paradigmatic possibilities. In this connection, Saussure attempted to relate linguistics to other social sciences that concern themselves with value (economics, sociology, anthropology): "Instead of pre-existing ideas then, we find . . . values emanating from the system. When they are said to correspond to concepts, it is understood that the concepts are purely differential and defined not by their positive content but negatively by their relations with the other terms of the system. Their most precise characteristic is in being what the others are not."[25]

The argument now rests on the plausibility of Saussure's generalization. Is the value of social action also determined by a differential system? Is its character described best differentially, that is, as being what other unactuated possible actions are not?

In sociology the debate boils down to two basic positions. One (the formalist) assumes – in contradiction to the arbitrariness of its variables – that the value of a given behavior (or pattern of behaviors) is a self-evident property of a social world. It is therefore observable (though usually by indirect measures). "The reason for having theories of social phenomena is to explain the pattern in observations of the world." For such a statement to hold, it must be assumed that the actions observed are in no final sense mysterious. This permits the classification of observed action values with respect to variable categories. In other words, the scientific values (those which constitute the measurable features of variables) are taken as accurate representations of human values. The "meanings" of behavior patterns in a social group are described by the empirical measures of that behavior. This amounts to the assumption that the value of an action is inherent as a property of the observed actor. There is no insurmountable problem of interpretation. The actor does not hide any significant values from the observer.

There is, as I have already suggested, a contradiction here. It is important to distinguish between the measured value of observed behaviors, which is an aspect of measurement, and the relationship between indicators and variables, which compose a theoretical system.[26] The former relationship (observations to measures) concerns values and is not considered arbitrary; the latter (indicators to variables) concerns the units of analysis and is arbitrary. For a theorist such as Blalock this distinction points to the often overlooked fact that theory constructionism is anything but empiricist. On the contrary, it places so much emphasis on

[25] Ibid., 117.
[26] See discussions of auxiliary theory: Blalock, "The Measurement Problem."

the problems of the theoretical system itself that empirical values become a secondary consideration. Thus is created the contradiction between the relativism of the theoretical system and the cryptoabsolutism guiding empirical research. This contradiction is the source of the flaw in formalism, which has relied upon formal language as the necessary precondition for replication studies. Replication is understood as the procedural requirement for the accumulation of knowledge – that is, for the maturing of sociology as a science. However, this procedure is undermined by the fact that replication is sought by means of arbitrarily derived abstract theories which rest on the flimsy justification of the scientists' own theoretical judgment. Were formalism to take the other course of gaining formality (and the possibility of replication) in the absolutism of given social facts (where theory is merely the name for observations), it would be trapped in the naïve operationalism which virtually every major contemporary formalist desires to avoid.[27] The significance of this flaw is found in the fact that formalism, in spite of its good intentions, has not come anywhere near to becoming a formal science based on replication studies.[28]

Interpretativism, on the other hand, has frankly conceded that one cannot easily measure the value of behaviors because value is a function of subjective meaning which is not directly observable. Blumer's position is typical: "The position of symbolic interactionism . . . is that the meanings that things have for human beings are central in their own right. To ignore the meaning of the things toward which people act is seen as falsifying the behavior under study."[29] The value of a unit of behavior is subsumed under its meaning to the actor and, therefore, cannot be easily counted.

What is clear is that neither of the two sociological views of value is as complete as Saussure's. Both assume that the value of a social act is representative of a natural property of social life and therefore can be represented as a value in sociological propositions. In the formalist view, value is inherent in the behavior itself. The question of its origin is ignored so that attention can be given to its formal (often mathematical) representation within a theoretical system. In the interpretative position, the value of a social act is created by the actor. Though this makes representation

27 Talcott Parsons, *The Structure of Social Action* (Glencoe, Ill.: Free Press, 1937), 72. Blalock, "The Measurement Problem," 7–9. Coleman, *Introduction to Mathematical Sociology*, 63. (Cf.: Abraham Kaplan, *The Conduct of Inquiry*. (Scranton, Pa: Chandler, 1964), 39–42.)
28 Hubert M. Blalock, "Thoughts on the Development of Sociology," *ASA Footnotes* 1: 2 (1973): 2.
29 Blumer, *Symbolic Interactionism*, 3.

within theory more difficult it is clear that interpretativists are not reluctant to represent meanings in verbal theories. In both cases, value is seen as a positive feature of the social act (given in one, created in the other). Both positions are, therefore, quite different from Saussure's, wherein value is a purely negative entity, determined entirely by the differential system. In other words, for Saussure the value of a unit of action is dependent upon the social structures of which that unit is a part; the individual cannot be explained without the social. Measurement can proceed only by the description of the values formed in social structures.

The Saussurian alternative is summarized in two principles, both of which are applicable to sociological measurement: (1) that neither the units of observation nor the measured facts derived therefrom are direct representatives of a real empirical world; and (2) that, nonetheless, measurement is possible by the derivation of negative values from a differential structure. Saussure resolved the seeming contradiction here by his strongly sociological (and Durkheimian) concept of *la langue*. If the signs which become units of linguistic measurement are not representatives of reality (are not names for things), then what is being measured? Since it is the society that creates *la langue*, then to describe linguistic units (signs) with reference to that convention is also to examine a real social structure.

Obviously, this works very much to the convenience of one who is studying language. But the question that remains is: Can such a program be generalized to extralinguistic phenomena? In other words, is structural explanation possible in sociology?

Structural explanation and sociology

Science measures in order to explain. Measurement (however it is defined) can have no other scientific purpose. The usefulness to sociology of a structural semiotics of explanation depends on the answer to two questions: (1) Is the structural explanation derived from Saussure sufficiently original to improve upon practices currently used by sociologists? (2) Is it sufficiently explanatory to be sociological?

Originality

Why bother with Saussure if the same results could be achieved by an elaboration of the existing formalist or interpretative theories? The question arises because there are obvious similarities.

Saussurian semiotics is similar to formalism in that both are structural. When Coleman insists on lodging measurement within formal theory or when Homans and Blalock insist that explanatory theory is a system of "propositions that interrelate variables,"[30] they are using a kind of structural explanation. In formalism, the structure is a theoretical system of concepts and propositions within which values associated with empirical observations are interrelated. The empirical instance is always referred back to a structure, just as Saussure refers *la parole* back to *la langue*. The limitation of the formalist method is that it cannot explain the structures (deductive systems) it creates. Whereas a Saussurian approach would begin with the assumption that even scientific language is necessarily referrable back to social conventions, formalism must refuse this step because of the damage it would do to the precision of formal statements. One cannot easily maintain the generality of a formal statement if its source is the relativity of a community's conventional language. As a result, formalism buys precision at the high cost of empirical accuracy. "The cost of greater simplicity is the sacrifice of realism."[31]

On the other hand, if Saussurian thought corrects formalism by introducing language, how does it differ from those interpretative approaches, such as ethnomethodology, which base themselves upon the centrality of language to sociological measurement? When Garfinkel defines ethnomethodology as the "investigation of indexical expressions" he necessarily makes sociology responsible to language.[32] Moreover, he does so in a fashion that appears to permit a Saussurian analysis of the indexicality of everyday life phenomena in terms of a description of the differential elements (paradigms) constituting language itself. Garfinkel's description of formal structures in accounting discourses[33] and Cicourel's lists of interpretative procedures[34] seem to take this form. However, what prevents these major ethnomethodological positions from achieving the explanatory scope of Saussure is (not incidentally) the same thing that requires them to use a diminished and social-psychological concept of social structure. The interpretative position has arrived at language through the back door. It begins, not with language (*la langue*), but with a dominant feature of everyday life: the motivatedness and constructedness of social behavior as seen in speaking (*la parole*). "Whenever and by whomever practical sociological discourse is done, it seeks to remedy the indexical properties of practical discourses. . . ."[35] Sociological reasoning – though

[30] Blalock, "The Formalization of Sociological Theory," 274.   [31] *Ibid.*, 296.
[32] Garfinkel and Sacks, "On Formal Structures of Practical Actions," 338. (Cf. David Sudnow, ed., *Studies in Social Interaction* [New York: Free Press, 1972], 31.) Cicourel, *Cognitive Sociology*, 11. (Cf.: Lemert, "De-Centered Analysis.")
[33] Garfinkel and Sacks, "On Formal Structures of Practical Actions," 355–356.
[34] Cicourel, *Cognitive Sociology*, 51–58.
[35] Garfinkel and Sacks, "On Formal Structures of Practical Actions," 339.

bound to language and, therefore, given as a property of all social creatures – is a remedial enterprise. That is, it remains a hermeneutical practice, not an explanatory discipline. Ethnomethodology shares the fate of all hermeneutical methods: an inescapable bondage to the intersubjective history in which social reality is assumed to be constructed.[36] Thus, whereas Saussure explains individual actions (*la parole*) by reference to a social structure (*la langue*), interpretativism reverses this order. When social structures (including *la langue*) are viewed as the product of intersubjective scheming, one necessarily undermines the theoretical autonomy of complex social structures. The latter are virtually lost to precise theoretical work because of the overwhelming importance given to intersubjective motives.

Applicability

To pass from Saussure's originality to his applicability is to question the usefulness of structural explanation in sociology. Since "structuralism" is in direct and intentional conflict with causal explanation, it challenges the only strong theory of explanation sociology has ever used.[37]

Structural linguistics cannot ask why (what caused?) the speaker to utter (select) certain phonemes and words. To do so is to turn away from *la langue* to the question of a speaker's motivations and, thereby, to move explanation outside linguistics proper to ethics or psychology.

Structural explanation rests upon the description of the systems of differences from which utterances are selected. What permits explanation is the idea that the scientifically interesting facts are those of the social structure, *la langue*, not *la parole*. Thus, structural explanation does not

---

[36] See: Habermas, *Knowledge and Human Interests*. Jürgen Habermas, "A Postscript to Knowledge and Human Interests," *Philosophy of the Social Sciences* 3 (1973): 157–189.

[37] To be more precise one must say that structuralism challenges all historicist methods. See: Foucault, *Archaeology of Knowledge*. Claude Lévi-Strauss, *The Savage Mind* (Chicago: University of Chicago Press, 1966). Louis Althusser, *For Marx* (New York: Vintage, 1970). Causal reasoning is here taken as the sociologically most important type of historicist reasoning. Stinchcombe has suggested that all three basic sociological strategies (functionalist, historicist, and demographic) are historicist. Stinchcombe, *Constructing Social Theories*. (Cf: Lemert, *Sociology and the Twilight of Man*.) Even though it is the formalists who have sponsored causal explanation. For example: Homans, *The Nature of Social Science*. Stinchcombe, *Constructing Social Theories*. Hubert M. Blalock, Jr., "Theory Building and Causal Inferences in Methodology," in *Methodology in Social Research*, ed. Blalock and Blalock, 155–198. Those interpretativists who have attempted more than descriptive studies have fallen back on a type of causal reasoning. For example: Blumer, *Symbolic Interactionism*. The argument that predictiveness, not causality, is the standard of explanation in sociology does not threaten this position, since predictiveness is also a variant of historicist reasoning in the broad sense. Jack Gibbs, *Sociological Theory Construction* (Hinsdale: Dryden, 1972).

seek the origins of linguistic behavior because all of the usable elements of speaking behavior are assumed to have been defined by the social community.

Whether this can work in sociology depends on the relationship between the particular structure language and social structures in general. If the social formation of language follows unique and non-general rules, structural explanation does not apply. If, on the other hand, social structures generally can be viewed as a set of absent, predefined, differential elements, structural analysis may well be a useful form of sociological explanation.[38]

What exactly is a social structure such as a given stratification system? In the formalist approach, it is a system of concepts imputed by the sociologist to a set of data that is assumed to reflect an unequal effect of social norms and material conditions on social behavior. In the interpretative approach, such a social structure is the sociologist's second-order construct for a primary social construction. Both are causal explanations. In the formalist case, one assumes that a class of individuals is "acted upon" by structured causal forces which the sociologist formally specifies in terms of a system of propositions. In the interpretative case, social individuals are viewed as creators of a stratified social structure which reflects their understanding of a meaningful life. Stated generally: in the former case, stratification causes behavior; in the later, interpretative behavior causes stratification. Neither can escape the stern linearity of causal reasoning wherein social structures and individual, intersubjective behaviors must be conceived as belonging to two separate orders of reality. More to the point, both partake of the assumption of causal analysis that measures of structures and behaviors must be stated in terms of positive values. In effect, this assumption is linked to a broader philosophical belief that social facts (structures and behaviors) have a positive existence.

But do they? In what sense is the "existence" of a stratification system positive? Where does "upper middle classness" exist except in the language of sociology? For people "living" within a given stratification

---

[38] Though the statement sounds extreme it is supportable. Two issues are involved: First, one must note that causality is very much bound to classical metaphysical principles that require all thought to derive from some central, first principle. See: Derrida, *Of Grammatology*. Foucault, *Archaeology of Knowledge*. Therefore, to the extent that social science wishes to be empirical it must, at least, explain how it deals with this corrupting influence. Second, to say that sociological explanation is structural is not to say that causal or historicist reasoning has no place in sociology (e.g., Saussure's distinction between diachronic ["historical"] and synchronic ["structural"] linguistics). One might consider the same sort of division of sociological labor. Causal and historical studies would belong to a diachronic sociology that would study the origins of and changes in social structures.

system, that structure exists not as an evident positive fact, but as a concrete set of limitations and possibilities. A structure "functions" as a series of differential choices (made, makeable, or only imaginable) presented by means of various normative and material paradigms containing differential possibilities and prohibitions with respect to self-esteem, manners, income, housing, standard of living, etc. Nor is it self-evident that "behavior" is positive. In the structuralist view, behavior is theoretically negative in the sense that a given behavior is an activated formal possibility, not a positive intentional content generated by an actor. It is the selection of a form from structured paradigms. The forms selected are not free-standing (positive) objects, since they are determined only by their difference from other forms of normal behavior, which exist only in the social structures.

By contrast, linearity and positivity are necessary and concomitant features of causal reasoning. The attempt to explain the formal properties of causal relations requires positive theoretical objects, separated linearly from each other and, in principle, "possessing" different "forces." The result is ultimately fatal to any non-abstract explanation of complex structures because one has no alternative but to reduce the complexity of structures to insufficiently subtle formal propositions. Saussure provides a way to avoid this trap.

Described in terms of its semiotic[39] (and most basic) function, measurement is the application of a standard conventionalized code to a series of observations. Causal measurement, therefore, seeks to generate positive facts that are taken as names for "observed" real-world properties. The names are given by presumably standard (formal or "natural") codes that are believed to be capable, in turn, of generating the positive values which are explained by a theoretical structure. Structural measurement, in contrast, seeks to isolate arbitrary, negative facts observed not in a presumptive real world, but in concrete events constituting articulated texts of social behavior, which are observable only after measurement. The measure, in this latter case, is not an abstract standard but a conventional code in the form of a system of differences.[40] Structural measurement, therefore, seeks to locate articulated behaviors in a particular semantic field.

In causal reasoning, positive entities are measured; in structural reasoning, differences are measured. In the former, science imagines linear

[39] Semiotics, the science of signs and signification, studies all linguistic and extralinguistic (fashion codes, animal communication, medical diagnosis, etc.) systems of signification. See: Barthes, *Elements of Semiology*. Saussure, *Course in General Linguistics*. Eco, *A Theory of Semiotics*, 1–29. Below, it will be shown that scientific measurement and explanation constitute a semiotic process in that they involve the encoding of empirical signs.

[40] Eco, *A Theory of Semiotics*, ch. 2

spaces in which objects move with respect to paths. In the latter, science imagines temporary semantic fields that locate the positions of encoded signs of practical behaviors (that is, tokens).[41] In the one case, measurement is the act of projecting a standard code along an axis of observations; in the other, measurement refers observed distinctions back to the social structures by which the distinctive units are observed. Causal measurement, therefore, requires abstract context-free codes that deny even their own conventional nature.[42] Structural measurement, in contrast, requires temporary scientific standards predefined by the same social structures they measure. In other words, a causal theory of measurement (such as, for example, Blalock's) is a theory of observational strategies, while a structural theory of measurement is a theory of intercode (interstructure) relationships. Or: the former is a theory of scientific procedures, the latter of social structures.

Therefore, since extralinguistic social structures are conceivable in Saussure's sense and since Saussure does offer the outlines of a theory of explanation, structural reasoning could assume a central place in sociological work. Sociology, thereby, would be concerned primarily with the analytic description of the paradigmatic differences and negative values that constitute social structures.

Structural explanation as semantic encyclopedia

Finally, one must ask whether structural explanation can produce general scientific statements. The proper criticism of interpretative sociology is that it can generate only second-order descriptive texts which are not sufficiently more general than the first-order texts (everyday behavioral events) it studies. It is too concrete. Formalism seeks to correct this deficiency by translating verbal texts into formal, mathematizable lexicons which are then manipulated into general propositions. The proper criticism of formalism is that it gains general explanations while losing the richness (and "reality") of descriptive detail. It is too abstractly general.

Structuralism is an alternative that retains the concreteness of interpretativism and the generality of formalism. This accomplishment is based upon a frank reappraisal of explanation. Explanation is understood – from the structuralist point of view – as a semantic process that generates a

---

[41] The concept token and its correlate type are necessary to overcome the linguistic and sociological realisms which assume that empirical signs represent real-world objects. See: Eco, *A Theory of Semiotics*, 178–188, 217–260.

[42] The sociological problem of context-free abstractions is discussed in: Cicourel, *Cognitive Sociology*. Habermas, "Toward a Theory of Communicative Competence." Habermas, "A Postscript to Knowledge and Human Interests." Eco, *A Theory of Semiotics*.

certain type of statement: namely, one that meaningfully encodes already encoded measurement values. Explanation is a semantics of sociological signs. If, then, explanation is the production of sociologically *meaningful* (*"valid"*) *statements*,[43] the problem of generality in explanation must be reformulated with reference to a semantic theory.

It is necessary, at this point, to shift from Saussure's classical semiotics to more recent work in structuralist semiotics. The most cogent and pertinent to sociology is that of Umberto Eco, who has distinguished between dictionary and encyclopedic semantic theories.[44] In these terms, formalism provides a dictionary-like generality: that is, its statements are abstract, context-free definitions. (Interpretative explanations are undercoded descriptive texts; that is, context-absorbed commentaries.) Structural explanations are, in contrast, encyclopedic texts having the following features: Though concrete, they are more general than interpretative descriptions. They are not, however, abstract like formalist dictionaries. An encyclopedia provides contexts. Their mathematizability is potential, even probable, but not necessary.

Since it is impossible to develop all of the logical details of this alternative, it is best to explain encyclopedicity by means of an illustration, presented in contrast to both formalism and interpretativism.

The structure of formal organizations is an excellent empirical example. When sociologists discuss formal structures in this setting they must consider a general, macro feature of social organization. At the same time, formal structures in organizations cannot be isolated from their impact on such concrete behavioral problems as informal structures, personality needs of members, and decision-making processes. Given the broad consensus on this point,[45] one would expect sociological explanations

---

[43] Quotation marks and italics are used in this section as diacritical marks with intentional, technical purposes. Quotation marks denote terms used in a more or less sociologically normal manner. Terms thus marked are assumed, however, to be either problematic or in need of further explanation which cannot be given here. Italics mark terms used in a semiotically technical fashion specific to this text. Thus, meaningful here refers not to a common-sense qualification of statements but to the task of a semiotic semantics to generate meaning in statements. Likewise, "valid" is the sociologically encoded term which (in spite of its problems) serves the same semantic "function" as semioticians' meaningful. Thus, xxxx denotes a technical usage explained in this text (e.g., measurement, type, token); "xxxx" is a usage encoded elsewhere and not explained here (e.g., "knowledge"); "*xxxx*" represents a usage encoded here and elsewhere (e.g., "literature").

[44] Eco, *A Theory of Semiotics*, 98–100.

[45] Mason Haire, ed., *Modern Organization Theory* (Huntington, N.Y.: Krieger, 1975), 4–12. Alvin Gouldner, *Patterns of Industrial Bureaucracy* (Glencoe, Ill.: Free Press, 1954), 27. Peter Blau and Richard Schoenherr, *The Structure of Organizations* (New York: Basic Books, 1971), 4–12. Robert K. Merton, *Social Theory and Social Structure* (Glencoe, Ill.: Free Press, 1957), 195–206. Egon Bittner, "The Concept of Organization," in *Ethnomethodology*, ed. Roy Turner (Baltimore: Penguin, 1974), 69–81, 69.

of formal structures to revolve around the incongruity between general structures and concrete individuals. However, they do not. Sociologists usually establish a division of labor between the study of formal and informal organizational features.[46] While studying the one, they relegate the other to the background. Thus, a formalist such as Blau[47] studies formal structures, dismissing for the occasion the question of individuals' intentions. Conversely, an interpretativist such as Bittner[48] considers practical negotiations of formality in organizations while ignoring formal structures as such. This is not merely a matter of personal preference. It results from different measurement tactics. Codes used determine what can or can not be measured. I will illustrate this problem before demonstrating the advantage of an encyclopedic explanation.

Formal dictionaries

Blau has written some of the most explicit attempts to formalize theories of social structure.[49] With reference to organizations, he has said: "Formal structures exhibit regularities that can be studied in their own right without investigating the motives of the individuals in the organizations."[50] The unasked question is: What are the risks taken when one makes such an arbitrary procedural distinction? Take, for example, one of Blau's general propositions about structures and one of its derivations: "Structural differentiation in organizations enlarges the administrative component, because the intensified problems of coordination and communication in differentiated structures demand administrative attention. . . . One derived proposition is that the large size of an organization indirectly raises the ratio of administrative personnel through the structural differentiation it generates."[51] It is, of course, possible that the relationship between organization size and the size of the administrative component is explained in part by members' sense of social distance from the organizational structure itself. In this case, it is likely that the increase in the administrative component is due, in part, to the managerial problem stemming from a decrease in members' sense of inclusion

[46] Peter Blau and Richard Schoenherr, *The Structure of Organizations* (New York: Basic, 1971), 4–12. Peter Blau, "A Formal Theory of Organizations," *American Sociological Review* 35: 2 (1970): 201–219.
[47] Blau, "A Formal Theory of Organizations."
[48] Bittner, "The Concept of Organization."
[49] Blau, "A Formal Theory of Organizations." Blau, "Parameters of Social Structure." Blau and Schoenherr, *The Structure of Organizations*. Peter Blau and Otis Dudley Duncan, *American Occupational Structure* (New York: Wiley, 1967).
[50] Blau, "A Formal Theory of Organizations," 203. Cf. Blau and Schoenherr, *The Structure of Organizations*, 6.
[51] Blau, "A Formal Theory of Organizations," 213.

in the democratic process of shaping the organizational structure. Poorly integrated members must be managed, requiring a larger administrative component. Blau himself must have something of this sort in mind when he talks about "the intensified problems of coordination and communication in differentiated structures."[52] Elsewhere he states that the loss of democratic process in an over-organized society is "the challenge of the century."[53] But what is this problem of communication or possible malintegration, if it is not a problem of individuals' motives which Blau, in this instance, has decided not to examine?

If, therefore, motives are likely to have an effect on the size of the administrative component, one must question the value of any "deductive theory of the formal structure of work organizations."[54] That, on methodological grounds, eliminates this topic from consideration. Here, again, one sees the contradiction within formalism wherein arbitrary (in Saussure's sense) theoretical values are used to explain absolute empirical values: "*Strange as it may seem,* the higher-level hypotheses that explain the lower-level propositions are accepted as valid purely on the basis that they do explain them, in the specific sense that they logically imply them . . . ; whereas acceptance of the lower-level propositions that need to be explained is contingent on empirical evidence. . . ."[55] The strangeness, scientifically speaking, of this procedure is that the higher-level hypotheses, being abstract dictionary entries, lack a context (logical or empirical) by which they can be explained. Thus, dictionary explanations rely upon the imposition of abstract theoretical codes on data generated by contextless measures. In other words, formalism tends to produce formal explanations and precise measurements of only one feature of organizations: formal structures which have as their distinctive feature that they are analytically context-free in the same sense as the measures by which they are defined.

Therefore, it is not surprising that Blau's definition of social structure is stated in terms of its formal measurability: "[B]y social structure I refer to population distributions among social positions along various lines — positions that affect people's role relations and social interaction. This intricate definition requires explication, and *I will use the term structural parameter to clarify it.*"[56] Even though he states elsewhere that "social structure is defined by the distinctions people make,"[57] the fact remains that his deductive theory is constructed entirely without reference to these decisions. In fact, he comes very close to saying that structural parameters (that is, scientists' code) create particular social behavior: "The

[52] *Ibid.,* 212–213.   [53] Blau, "Parameters of Social Structure," 633.
[54] Blau, "A Formal Theory of Organizations," 201.   [55] *Ibid.,* 202, emphasis added.
[56] Blau, "Parameters of Social Structure," 616, emphasis added.   [57] *Ibid.,* 616.

assumption is that the differences in group affiliation and status created by structural parameters affect role relations and the social interaction in which these relations find expression."[58] Given other assumptions, this expression is not as elliptical as he might think.[59] Inasmuch as structures can only be "observed" parametrically, and since the information produced thereby is explained only by context-free hypotheses, this is equivalent to saying that, sociologically, these structures are created by their measures. This is what is meant by general theory purchased with dictionary-like abstractness. The cost is that particular social contexts are stipulated. They are not a positive source of sociological information.

Interpretative commentaries

Bittner and Garfinkel[60] are useful examples of interpretativists who have studied formal organizational structures. Bittner discusses the same problems as did Blau – the relationship among size, complexity, and administration in formal organizations:

It is often noted that the formal organization meets exigencies arising out of the complexity and large scope of an enterprise. The rationally conceived form orders affiliations between persons and performances that are too remote for contingent arrangement, by linking them into coherent maps or schedules. This integration transcends what might result from negotiated agreements between continuous elements, and lends to elements that are not within the sphere of one another's manipulative influence the character of concerted action. . . . A rational principle of justice may prevail in the entire structure while governing differentially correct associations between particular performances and rewards. The varieties of demeanors that are appropriate to a particular status within the system may be perceived as variations of a more general pattern.[61]

Non-ethnomethodological readers of such a text often and understandably miss the point that this is merely a specific type of interpretative explanation based on data generated by a measurement technique. Two features distinguish this statement from that of Blau on the same structural topics. First, organization is explicitly a cognitive attribute. As such, it becomes both a topic and a resource. The concept "organization" is used to study organizations and their structures. "[T]he study of the methodical use of the concept of organization seeks to describe the mechanisms of sustained and sanctioned relevance of the rational constructions

---

[58] Ibid., 617 emphasis added.   [59] Ibid., 617, n. 5.

[60] Bittner, "The Concept of Organization." Harold Garfinkel, "Good Organizational Reasons for 'Bad' Clinical Records," in Studies in Ethnomethodology, ed. Garfinkel, 186–207. The article cited here (Garfinkel), though published under Garfinkel's name, is the product of research conducted jointly with Bittner. Thus, Garfinkel is taken as an empirical complement to Bittner.

[61] Bittner, "The Concept of Organization," 78.

to a variety of objects, events and occasions relative to which they are not invoked."[62] Second, organization is a cognitive attribute of both common-sense actors[63] and professional sociologists. As such it is highly contexted.

These two features are what lend to the above passage both its explanatory claim and its status as a context-absorbed commentary. Formal organization structures cannot be literally defined[64] because they are understood, above all, as the workers' cognitive instruments for providing a "rational principle of justice" in the face of organizational complexity ("differentially correct associations between particular performances and rewards"). Thus, the text provided above works within the context of sociologists' use of the concept "organization"[65] in the same way as other studies are contexted with reference to common-sense concepts of organization used by interviewers in a psychiatric clinic.[66]

If, as was argued above, explanation is the theoretical encoding of already coded measurement values, interpretative commentaries are (given their own logic) explanatory. Bittner therefore uses the concept "organization" as "a generalized formula to which all sorts of problems can be brought for solution."[67] Both sociologists and organization workers are engaged in an explanatory enterprise. The only difference is that the (ethnomethodological) sociologist assumes a relatively non-privileged responsibility to account for the explanation itself, while the actor, so to speak, simply uses the concept "organization" to measure (encode organizational reality). The crucial point is that, in this sense, all social activity is measurement.[68]

The result of interpretative explanations of this sort is a semantics of the very feature of formally structured organizations that formalism is forced to abandon: the particular motives of workers. Thus Garfinkel,[69] in a study performed with Bittner, offers explanations for the poor quality of records kept by workers in a psychiatric clinic. These records are inadequate only when administrators, sociologists, and others with an actuarial interest bring a context-free concept of organization to them, expecting to find information useful to their (context-free) needs for comprehensive demographic data and medical histories. The records are bad only because they are not useful to formal theories of organizations. If, however, it is understood that clinical records are constructed as a therapeutic contract between the clinic and patients one sees them differently.[70] Not only are they in another sense good ("orderly and understandable")[71]

[62] Ibid., 76.   [63] Ibid., 74–77.   [64] Ibid., 71.   [65] Ibid., 69–70.
[66] Garfinkel, Studies in Ethnomethodology.
[67] Bittner, "The Concept of Organization," 76.
[68] For example: Cicourel, Cognitive Sociology, 91.
[69] Garfinkel, Studies in Ethnomethodology.   [70] Ibid., 199.   [71] Ibid., 202.

but their value opens an entirely different structural feature of the organization to those who read them in this light. The structured relationship between the differential interests of researchers and medical practitioners becomes clear.[72]

At this point one comes to the problem that concerned Blau: the relationship among complexity, size, and administration. An organization of relatively large scale faces the organizational problem of providing actuarial records for administrative purposes (external funding, third-party payments, institutional research, etc.). This formal requirement is in conflict with a physician's need (based on ethical and legal considerations such as the threat of malpractice suits) to maintain a record of his faithful compliance with normal therapeutic procedures. Organizations thus face the cost problem. On a fixed budget it may not be possible to maintain two separate sets of records without increasing the administrative component.[73] Implicit in Garfinkel's argument is that organizations will arrive at a point where the cost of the administrative component becomes prohibitive, thus permitting bad clinical records to be kept by those with contractual rather than actuarial interests in them.[74]

The distinctive feature of this explanatory commentary is that it measures with constant reference to workers' motives. Its deficiency is that the clarity of these measures cannot be matched by attention to general, formal features of organizations. Though Garfinkel does attend to structural features,[75] he does not do so with as much precision as Blau.

The crisis for sociologists in this incongruity between formalist and interpretativist measures is that, just as Blau can be criticized for ignoring workers' motives, so Bittner and Garfinkel can be properly criticized for slighting relatively non-motivated features of organizations. We can be certain that the cost factor controlling the relationship between administrative and medical components is due in large part to social forces that are not available for interpretative explanation: the state of the economy, the extent of rationalization in the social system, the availability of trained administrators, the market price of computer systems, and so forth.

Encyclopedic texts

A common problem for both of the preceding types of explanation is motives. Formalism ignores them. Interpretativism gets caught in them. Structuralist semiotics reduces this difficulty by showing how *behavior*

---

[72] *Ibid.*, 207.   [73] *Ibid.*, 192.
[74] *Ibid.*, 200. Cf. Blau, "A Formal Theory of Organizations," 214–216.
[75] Garfinkel, *Studies in Ethnomethodology*, 200.

can be read as motivated yet not a *"product"* of motives. The interpretativist's overly strong theory of motives is an unwarranted subjectivization of *behavior*. More seriously, it cannot lead to adequate measurement because when motives are taken as the "origin" of behavior, they are mysterious and unobservable. Interpretative processes (Mead, Blumer), typifying processes (Schutz, Berger, Luckmann), rational reflexive negotiating and interpretive procedures (Garfinkel, Cicourel) are not made available to view, though their products (negotiated, concerted rational behaviors) are. Interpretativism's fear of "reducing" meaning to behavior has apparently led to its overly strong theory of motives. A semiotic theory of explanation shows that one can measure behaviors as systematically significant expressions of motives without stipulating the latter as the exclusive cause of the former.

A semiotic measure of motives through behaviors is analogous to Saussure's linguistics which ignored the origins of speech, while using speech (*la parole*) as the behavioral products (signs) through which one reads the sense of utterances. Utterances are rendered *meaningful* not in a psychology of motives, but in a sociology of conventional linguistic structures (*la langue*). This alternative is crucial because an overly strong theory of motives as origin cannot yield a comparably strong theory of structures. When measurement is tied to motives, measurement (hence explanation) becomes metaphorical at that point at which one encounters unmotivated structures (such as the effect of the "market" on cost of administration).

The semiotic approach conceives of *"behavior"* as a *behavior function* (BF): that is, as the articulation of a motive (a significant *content*) with an "act" (a structurally provided expression unit). Motives, thus, are measured with reference to structurally provided acting *types*. Just as Saussure defined the sign of articulated speech utterances as the product of a motivated speaking individual, a BF would be the function of motivated actors. However, for Saussure, the speaking itself (*la parole*) was unmotivated insofar as the speaker has few degrees of freedom to modify and correct *la langue*. Saussure's speaking (*la parole*) is the borrowing of elements from language. Motivation therefore is assigned to the necessary but insufficient role of selection (as opposed to origination). These motivations could, in Saussurian thinking, be taken as the topics of a social psychology of speaking, but not of linguistics. Similarly, one can assign to social psychology the task of explaining motives without assuming that this task exhausts the obligations of sociology *tout court*. Sociology explains structured behaviors.

A BF, semiotically understood, is the product of a motivated selection of unmotivated *types* of behaving. *Types* (the primary topic of sociology) are "created" not by intentions of individuals but by the conventional

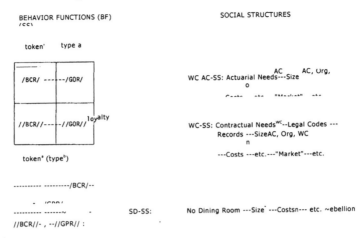

Figure 8.1: *Fro. 1.-Code:* / . . . / = expression unit; // . . . // = content unit; BCR = bad clinical records; GOR = good organizational reasons; GPR = good physicians' reasons; AC = administrative component; WC --_ workers' (physicians') component; *etc.* = other structural features not discussed here; other SS signs are explained in the text. Broken line around lower BF represents "possible BF not selected."

arrangements of the social group. Social structures provide the paradigms ("syntactical" and "lexical" – that is, norms and acts, respectively) from which actors select "normal" BF *expressions*.

I shift now from an actor's to an analyst's perspective. Social analysts would begin measurement by taking observations of BFs. It is here that I rely upon the semiotic proposals of Umberto Eco.[76]

Figure 8.1 presents some of the concepts discussed by Blau and Garfinkel but rewrites them in a form consistent with Eco's structural semiotics. This figure illustrates the analysis of only one "slice" of an actual BF and only several aspects of the available social structures (SSs). It is not a complete explanation. Nonetheless, one sees that BFs are observed as *expression* units (specific bad clinical records – /BCR/) which are *tokens* of a BF *type* (good organizational reasons – /GOR/). In the latter connection, it is assumed that a given bad clinical record (/BCR/) is merely the "*articulation*" of a *type* of behavior (writing bad clinical records for good organizational reasons – /GOR/). The /GOR/ type is provided by structural features of organizations (in this case, psychiatric/medical clinics). The structures, though positive in the sense that they provide types to BFs, are not "positivistically" positive in the sense that they are not considered available to observation. The SSs are absent to the BFs

[76] Eco, *A Theory of Semiotics.*

they form, just as Saussure's *la langue* is absent to the linguist observing *la parole*. The SSs are positive only in the sense that *types* – thus *token expressions*, thus BFs – can be explained only with reference to SSs. Contents are not the written marks on clinical records. These marks are expressions. Content describes the semantic content ("meaning") of a /BCR/. It is the token contents that are measured and explained, but they are observed as *expressions* of normatively defined (that is, structured) *types*.

It is important to note that this analysis is already at a certain level of generality. I have used Bittner and Garfinkel as resources to establish the expression type "bad clinical records" (/BCR/). Ordinarily social research would begin at a more concrete point, prior to sociologists' knowledge of this particular BF. The "badness" of these records is already a sociologically encoded expression type. Normally, research would begin where Bittner and Garfinkel began one day: reading records (/BCR/s) that made little sense given the assumption of good (well-structured) formal clinical organizations.

Measurement (the explanation of the /BCR/-BF) is possible, however, only with "knowledge" of formal organizations as such: that is, their social structures (SSs). Depending upon the topic at hand and the state of sociology's structured knowledge of that topic, this knowledge need not necessarily be gained *de novo*. In the present case, we have good sociological reasons to "know" (from Bittner, Gouldner, Merton, Blau, and others from the "*literature*") that such a token BF as "bad clinical records" (/BCR/) might be "explained" (*measured*) with reference to such structural features as: exact degree of organization's differentiation (complexity), size of organization, cost of administrative component, size of administrative component, size (and cost) of worker component, and the pertinent ratio relationships linking them. I am not questioning the usefulness of these formal explanatory concepts. I am doubting that their use in either formalist or interpretativist measures can lead to an "adequate" and "complete" sociological explanation.

The major problem of an encyclopedic *measure* is evident at this point. How does one introduce a principle of selectivity? Without such a method for engendering parsimony, one would quickly be overwhelmed by the multitude of possible SSs providing *types* to even a single BF. Eco offers such a method. It is not necessary to "list and to structure all the possible occurrences of a given item but only those which are *culturally* and *conventionally* recognized as the more statistically probable."[77] This would involve a preliminary explanation of the "literature" pertinent to the topic at hand. In this case, "*literature*" would include sociological literatures of the organizations, formal self-descriptive literatures

[77] *Ibid.*, 110.

of the organizations themselves, and workers' informal literatures (e.g., "bad" clinical records). The preliminary explanation of these literatures would yield a description of conventionally probable SSs available to provide types to the observed BF. The descriptions would be produced by means of all available and appropriate reading methods (descriptive statistics, analytic readings, and observational readings). This method for introducing parsimony (only partially illustrated here) is warranted by the fact that social structures are scientifically interesting only as features of sociologists' structural theories. Both interpretativists and formalists agree on this point.[78]

On the other hand, the hedge against the possible abstractness of sociologists' *readings* of probable SSs is found in the fact that the readings are done empirically (*contextually*). One does not "search the literature" prior to investigation. The readings are over against observed BFs such as a /BCR/ token. The *readings*, however, are not hermeneutical but structural. One does not attempt to discover the "inner meaning" of the observed BF, only (at the outset) its probable structural origins.

The result of structural readings of this sort would be an encyclopedic semantic tree (such as figure 8.1) displaying the SSs probably explanatory of the observed BF. Insofar as the *literatures* read are themselves encyclopedic descriptions of possible BFs, such a tree is, in effect, a second-order encyclopedia that reduces sociological and "natural" *literatures* to a relatively more formal and more general theory of the semantics of the observed BF.

It is important to note, however, that the final explanatory "*tree*" (and its accompanying text) cannot select probable explanatory SSs on merely formal statistical or mathematical grounds. Instead, such selections are made comparatively, by determining the differential value of probable explanations. For example, in figure 8.1, the status deprivation SS (SD-SS) would describe an aspect of the structural arrangements of status prerogatives in organizations. In a clinic this could involve questions of: the "quality" (honorific appropriateness) of the medical staff's dining facilities, including presence or absence of a separate dining room; convenience of eating schedules; cost of food, heat, lighting, cooks, building space, etc.; relationship of these to overall cost factors in the organization (budget, size of administrative component, size of organization, etc.). Here the explanation of the /BCR/-BF might be that physicians write bad clinical records to rebel against "inadequate" treatment (no separate dining room because of cost factors). In other words, the SD-SS explains the

[78] Garfinkel and Sacks, "On Formal Structures of Practical Actions." Blau, "Parameters of Social Structure."

//BCR// as a token of a *type*: good physicians' reasons to rebel (//GPR// rebellion).

Let us assume, however, that the "correct" explanation is along the lines made available to us by Bittner, Garfinkel, and Blau: namely, that //BCR// is explained by size of administrative component and size of organization (assuming that patients are not members). One could only "know" of the existence of this structural branch by determining its negative relation to the "rebellion" SS explanatory tree (SD-SS), as well as other statistically possible explanations not illustrated here. Stated in the simplest of terms, the /BCR/-BF must be measured differentially by a comparison of, in this case, the two alternative structured type BFs (here loosely labeled *rebellion* and *loyalty*).

The loyalty type must then be *measured* differentially, comparing the administrative (AC-SS) and workers' (physicians' [WC-SS]) structural branches. These designations are shorthand versions of the structural details that would have to be provided (depending, of course, on the state of the "*literature*"). I am here relying (without explicit justification) on Bittner and Garfinkel's descriptions. The point I wish to make is that the //GOR// loyalty type BF can be established only by a description of the AC-SS and WC-SS branches. Following Blau, Bittner, and Garfinkel, one assumes that the AC-SS branch would include: (a) organization's actuarial needs for good clinical records, (b) size of administrative component, (c) size of organization, (d) relative size of worker (physician) component, (e) relative costs of (d) and (b), and so forth. Likewise, the WC-SS would presumably include: (a) ethical and legal codes determining physicians' sense of contractual responsibility, (b) structured access of physicians to record-keeping procedures, (c) size of administrative component, (d) size of organization, (e) relative size of worker component, (f) relative costs of (e) and (c), and so forth. With reference to these branches, it is clear that Bittner and Garfinkel's explanation[79] requires a description of both branches. Similarly, both are necessary to incorporate motives into Blau's (1970) structural theory. Again, the explanatory value of the WC-SS is determined by its differential relationship to AC-SS.

At this point, the question is: Does this merely generate a way of rewording Bittner and Garfinkel? The test is whether or not such a semantic encyclopedia (figure 8.1) would be expandable when necessary to provide access to the kind of "information" provided by Blau. Among other things, this is the question of generality. Blau studied 1,500 agencies; Bittner and Garfinkel, one. Can these two types of "information" be used in the same explanation (provided, of course, they are "properly" collected)?

---

[79] Garfinkel, *Studies in Ethnomethodology*.

Assuming that /BCR/ as a general phenomenon in clinics and agencies of all sorts is a sociologically interesting question (which it is), one could not possibly stop at the AC-SS and WC-SS explanations here described, any more than one can trust Blau's explanation without accounting for the bad records from which (in part) his data were drawn.[80] I take just one instance: cost of administrative component relative to size of organization. It is clear that one would indeed need to describe the *statistically probable*[81] structural features of administrative cost in the same manner as the illustrated SSs have been described. This would include not only cost relative to administrative and organization size (which Blau studied), but also the cost features of the WC-SS (cost of physicians' salaries, cost of recording procedures [tape recorders, computers, typing pool, etc.], "cost" of intruding on physicians' felt need to protect a contractual therapeutic relationship, etc.). In short, one can arrive rather quickly at macro questions such as "market" and "state of economy" structural conditions, structural factors that even Blau's theory omitted. The interesting point is that Blau, having chosen to ignore workers' motives, could not measure certain structural factors.

I will conclude, and briefly summarize, by referring to the way in which a semantical encyclopedia would provide for "replication." The standard sociological format for *replication* studies is a test of the extent to which interexperimental "data" support the original dictionary entries. Because of their use of contexts, encyclopedic explanations are insufficiently abstract to be used in this kind of comparison. However, this does not exclude the possibility of tests of inter-"experimental" reliability.

A sociologically useful semiotics of the type described here would depend on the legitimacy of understanding the absent-to-view world of social structures as a primary "empirical" *resource* available to be "*read*" as one reads an encyclopedia. One takes to an encyclopedia questions that are seldom answered by any single entry. To expect any one article to answer a question is to treat an encyclopedia as though it were a dictionary. Normally, encyclopedic "answers" are provided by a search of structured relationships appearing in the differences among aspects of "knowledge" found in different articles. The encyclopedia explains nothing itself. Explanation is given only in a *structural reading*, which leads to an explanatory rewriting. The rewrite (a second-order encyclopedic text) may well be stated in highly formal, even mathematical, codes expressing correlations, factor magnitudes, and paths.[82]

---

[80] Blau, "A Formal Theory of Organizations," 204.   [81] Eco, *A Theory of Semiotics*, 110.
[82] Eco (*ibid.*, 122–124) has illustrated the use of formal semantic informal processing methods for the analysis of complex n-dimensional semantic problems.

Encyclopedias are organized in a way that presupposes their usefulness in the construction of these rewrites. An encyclopedia (as opposed to a dictionary) works only because it is organized around its own internal index and cross-referencing system. Thus, *"replication"* would be based on the writing of sociological texts so that they are available for "reliable" secondary readings and rewrites. In other words, the sociological writing of an encyclopedic tree (see figure 8.1) is also in part the displaying of an index of material borrowed from and, thus, cross-referenced to other *"literatures"* (sociological, everyday life, etc.). What is displayed is an explicit code governing BF *types* and conventional *social structures*. This is the sense in which an encyclopedia is both context-specific and general.

Part III

Culture as the ghost of primitive transgressions

9

Michel Foucault and why analytic categories are queer

Queering is political before it is sexual. To queer is to upset the apple cart of received opinion. In the modern world, the dominating received opinion is that, behind the visible troubles, the world is orderly, thus open to investigation. Analysis is the generic method that corresponds to this opinion. Analysis is the action whereby the world of real things, including social ones, is cut into parts the analyst realizes may not be normal in the cut-apart state. Yet, the cutting into working categories is deemed necessary for analysis – hence, truth and knowledge – to proceed. Knowledge, thereby, warrants the pain inflicted.

Cutting things apart hurts the things, especially when they are social. Social things are things, cultural and material, created to support the need of human beings to gather themselves into groups for survival's sake. Analysis thus cuts up the groups by cutting out social things from their natural state of human community. People bleed and die when this happens. This fact poses a dilemma for the liberal political ideas of modernity. Received opinion in modern culture is that it is not nice to hurt people – unless, that is, some wider utility is served. This is to say that knowledge is always political. Liberal doctrines of the modern world object to explicit attempts to involve knowledge in politics. They exclude from this rule their own politics of cutting up things to study them.

Liberal doctrine is thereby in a moral quandary. To admit that its cuttings have political consequences is to leave blood on the cutting room floor. To deny the political truth behind analysis is to throw the method into doubt. To queer such a culture is, one would think, an easy thing to do. All one has to do is to call it out. Yet, over centuries, few have dared to do this – in part, one presumes, because it is plain that the risk is that of getting yourself cut apart, if not burned at the stake.

To queer modern culture is to await the time when it is safe. The analytic and political instability of the modern hegemony in the 1960s were such a moment. Many stepped into the breach: Fanon, posthumously;

Lacan, wise-crackingly; Barthes, elegantly; Derrida, philosophically; Deleuze, unrelentingly; and others. Foucault did too, of course – not exceptionally, but distinctively. He wrote the history of received opinion and legitimate discourse in modern times. What he wrote was on the surface a kind free-verse poetry that, standing back, calls attention to the facts few dared call out before. What he wrote inspired the anger and confusion that besets those who dare to queer received opinion.

Here are plain the facts, if there are such things, of the man's life, written for an encyclopedia of the social sciences published by the Presses Universitaires de France.

1. Biography

Paul Michel Foucault was born 1926, at Poitiers. He died 1984, apparently of AIDS, in Paris. In 1945, after an irregular formation in provincial schools, Foucault attended Lycée Henri IV, Paris. There he first encountered Jean Hyppolite whose interpretations of Hegel inspired Foucault's own philosophical inventions. While a student at the Ecole Normale Supérieure (1946–1950), he suffered social and mental difficulties. Still, his original caste of mind benefited from exposure to Louis Althusser and Georges Canguilhem, who influenced Foucault's early histories of the human sciences. Also, he began seriously to read Frederic Nietszche, Georges Bataille, and Maurice Blanchot who were crucial to his historical and literary methods. In 1951, Foucault, having failed once, achieved the *agrégation de philosophie*. In a curious anticipation of things to come, he drew a question on sexuality for the oral exam.

Foucault began his university career at Lille in 1952. But in 1955, he turned to service in France's cultural missions at Uppsala, Warsaw, and Hamburg. The Uppsala stay (where he began the archival work for the history of madness) owed to the recommendation of Georges Dumézil. In 1960, Foucault returned to France to teach psychology in the philosophy program at Clermont-Ferrand.

Folie et déraison. Histoire de la folie à l'âge classique appeared in 1961. It was the principal thesis for his *doctorat d'état*, awarded that same year. In 1962, *Maladie mentale et psychologie*, a substantial revision of an earlier work, appeared; as did *Raymond Roussel*, an important issue of his early interest in literature. In 1963, Foucault published still another of his studies of the early modern age, *Naissance de la clinique. Une archéologie du regard médical*.

While teaching at Clermont-Ferrand, Foucault lived in Paris where his literary reputation flourished. From 1965 until late 1968, Foucault lived in North Africa while teaching at the university in Tunis. Still, in 1966, *Les Mots et les choses* became an immediate best-seller in France. Importantly, Foucault was only passingly in Paris during the events of May 1968. He was, however, active in the defense of students opposing Tunisia's oppressive regime. Thus began the political engagement that, in the public eye, made Foucault heir apparent to Jean-Paul Sartre.

Late in 1968, Foucault joined the nuclear faculty of the new university at Vincennes, established in response to the spring protests. *L'Archéologie du savoir*, an awkward and exceptional book of theories, was published in 1969. Soon after, Foucault dropped the programmatic themes of his early archaeologies. In 1970, he was elected, in effect, to Hyppolite's chair at the Collège de France. His inaugural lesson, *L'Ordre du discours* (1971), concluded according to the form with tributes to his masters – Canguilhem and Dumézil, but Hyppolite, above all, as the one from whom he had borrowed "the meaning and possibility of what I am doing."

In the early 1970s Foucault worked for prison reform through the Groupe d'Information sur les Prisons. In 1975, *Surveiller et punir*, widely considered his best book, added intellectual weight to his politics. Then, in 1976, *La Volonté de savoir* announced the departure into the histories of sexuality. Though they would develop slowly and differently, the histories of sexuality, like the study of incarceration, lent focus to the body as the precise object of power relations in the modern age. In the decade of life remaining, Foucault was seldom out of the public eye. Though he wrote and spoke prolifically, he would not publish another major book until the very end.

After 1970, Foucault traveled abroad more, in part to seek relief from the demands of his high cultural office. In San Francisco, during extended visits to the University of California at Berkeley in the 1980s, he enjoyed freedom for homosexual pleasures supplemental to his twenty-one-year bond with Daniel Defert. The experiences may have led to infection. Just days before death, early the summer of 1984, Foucault saw the first copies of *L'Usage des plaisirs* and *Le Souci de Soi*. A fourth manuscript in the sexuality series may exist. He demanded no posthumous publications.

2. Context

Foucault's intellectual position is at once easy and impossible to define. He hated ideological Marxism, but in definite ways completed Marx's critique of capitalism by accounting for the subtler, cultural exploitations of economic power. He despised all the prominent subjectivisms, notably those of Sartre and Merleau-Ponty, yet he invented a theory of micro-politics that described the subjugation of the modern self. He had no interest in postmodernism, yet he undoubtedly inspired many who march under that slogan. He was not a structuralist, but it is impossible to understand his thought apart from the lineage of Durkheim, Lévi-Strauss, Braudel, and Dumézil. Feminism was among the very few things he did not understand; yet, more even than Lacan, his theories transformed third-wave feminism.

The definite indefiniteness of Foucault's position in the fields at play in late modern social theory was no accident. He meant, in the phrase of his friend Roland Barthes, to approach the zero degree of writing from whence the intentions of the author are suppressed in favor of the surface of things themselves. His books are difficult, but, unlike Jacques Derrida, Foucault had the gift for poetry he thought necessary to his method.

One might say that his position was uniquely French. He was, indeed, a product of the forces of his day – recovery from war, loss of colonial empire, 1968, new social movements. Yet, these were world-wide forces. Foucault was among the few to respond in a thoroughly original way.

3. Contributions

Michel Foucault's enduring contribution to the human sciences is the relief he offers from debate over methodological positivism. Since Durkheim, sociology dreamed of being a positive science of social things. Since Weber, sociology has been troubled by the unknow-ables behind positive knowledge – interior meanings, counterintuitive structures, unconscious collective resistances. Foucault's method is, at once, positive and negative. He sought, in his word, to reconstruct the Unthought, the "unconscious of knowledge" – by which he meant the rules of social formation whereby social things become objects. His method was sternly empirical. He worked the archives. The results, however, are shocking because they derive from a synthetic anterior of social relations. Thus, in *Folie et déraison* (1961), *Naissance de la clinique* (1963), and *Surveillir et punir* (1975) he showed how moder-nity arose by the unconscious creation of objects that did not exist in the classical age – mental illness, the diseased body, the incarcerated criminal. Many dispute Foucault's facts. But his Nietzschean method refuses the will for truthful facts to uncover instead the rules of their formation. In *L'Ordre du discours* (1971) he listed his own rules of soci-ological method: reversal, discontinuity, specificity, and exteriority. He meant to approach social facts as historically concrete occurrences, without prior expectation of causal continuities or interior meanings. If the cost of the method is a diminished logic of proof, the gain is in turning the human sciences to the deeper and less apparent. In this respect, the method owes as much to Freud and Marx as to Nietzsche.

Foucault's most important conceptual contribution is to the theory of social power he construed upon the famously duplicitous term, power/knowledge. In the last books, *L'Usage des plaisirs* and *Souci de Soi*, he used the term "governing" to much the same effect. Against Marxist ideas of power as the downward force of the dominant classes, Foucault proposed the lateral play of power at every level of the social body. Hence, in the capitalist age, power works as much through the practical knowledge (*savoir*) of daily life as through top-down domination.

Nearly as important is the series of concepts entailed by the theory of power, notably: micro-politics, the subjugated body, and the carceral society. Foucault's life work was a social history of the origins of the modern age. Whatever his subject – the birth of madness, the medical gaze, the panoptical prison, the sexual self – Foucault studied pre-modern cultures in order to isolate the strategic social and political problem of the modern. Weber asked, Why do men obey? Foucault's answer was, Because they have been subjected bodily to the gentle persuasions of modern reason. Thus, *Les Mots et les choses* (1966), his history of the human sciences, is a key text. Modernity is the age of the social and clinical sciences that diffuse the knowledge (*savoir*) by which individuals govern themselves, for better or worse.

4. Relevance

Foucault's notions of social power and the body have transformed the theory of domination as, in particular, they have challenged feminist social theory. His idea of the carceral society is central to debates in criminology. His studies of sexuality are the founding texts of queer theory. His methodological influence is ubiquitous.

For years to come, Foucault will remain the exemplary model for post-disciplinary social studies. Though contested by experts, his ventures into the histories of crime, medicine, psychopathology, social science, and sexuality are models of work that can be theoretically imaginative and empirically grounded without undue regard for the bureaucratic disciplines. Finally, Foucault, the poet, may yet inspire the literary culture C. Wright Mills once said was lacking in sociology.

At the least, he brings the sociological imagination back in as empirical work.

5. Foucault's major works

Folie et déraison. Histoire de la folie à l'âge classique, Paris, Plon, 1961; trans. Eng. R. Howard, *Madness and Civilization* [abridged], New York, Pantheon, 1965.

Naissance de la clinique, Paris, PUF, 1963; trans. Eng. A. M. Sheridan Smith, *Birth of the Clinic: An Archaeology of Medical Perception*, New York, Pantheon, 1973.

Let Mots et les choses. Une archéologie des sciences humaines, Paris, Gallimard, 1966; trans. Eng. A. Sheridan, *The Order of Things: An Archaeology of the Human Sciences*, New York, Random House, 1970.

L'Archéologie du savoir, Paris, Gallimard, 1969; trans. Eng. A. M. Sheridan Smith, *The Archaeology of Knowledge*, New York, Pantheon, 1972.

Surveillir et punir. Naissance de la prison, Paris, Gallimard, 1975; trans. Eng. A. Sheridan, *Discipline and Punish: The Birth of the Prison*, New York, Pantheon, 1977.

La Volonté de savoir, Histoire de la sexualité I, Paris, Gallimard, 1976; trans. Eng. R. Hurley, *The History of Sexuality, Vol. I: An Introduction*, New York, Pantheon, 1978.

L'Usage des plaisirs, Histoire de la sexualité, II, Paris, Gallimard, 1984; trans. Eng. R. Hurley, *The Use of Pleasure*, New York, Pantheon, 1985.

Le Souci de soi, Histoire de la sexualité, III, Paris, Gallimard, 1984; trans. Eng. *The Care of the Self*, New York, Pantheon, 1984.

Pierre Bourdieu's aesthetic critique of sociological judgment (2000*)

Reading Pierre Bourdieu's and Loïc Wacquant's "On the Cunning of Imperialist Reason"[1] is like reading someone's email. Behind the seriousness of the presenting message, unforgivingly displayed in black on white, the reader senses, without fully understanding, the less well formulated thoughts, even feelings, of the sender. It is truly a strange world in which people can become acquainted with each other across very significant differences of time and space (both real and social, hence virtual) – thus to sense when something is not quite right in the message sent. Such an experience – whether of my communications with colleagues down the hall, or between Bourdieu and his worldwide following – is often unnerving. This does not mean that the message does not matter. It may mean, however, that the work of any intellectual is always potentially open to some public or another which may very well expose the ruse, or cunning, behind the seriousness of the work. If so – if, that is, all intellectuals whether those of world fame like Bourdieu or ones of modest, if any, reputation are thus exposed to the hazards of their own public

* Reprinted with permission from *Theory, Culture, & Society*, 17: 1 (Feb. 2000): 97–106. The original essay was entitled "The Clothes Have No Emperor: Bourdieu on American Imperialism" which was part of a symposium prompted by an earlier essay by Pierre Bourdieu and Loïc Wacquant, "On the Cunning of Imperialist Reason." Their essay, while very much in the vein of Bourdieu's writing and thinking, bore the cutting edge of Wacquant's brilliantly ferocious attitude toward opponents, especially the Americans who he generally holds in contempt, an attitude that is generously reciprocated by those who have had dealings with him. Yet, I chose to write in response to Bourdieu and not Wacquant, if only because at the time I found the relations of this essay with his general position interesting. Though Wacquant's way of treating other people never ceases to amaze me, I do think he is one of the most brilliant and serious commentators on various subjects, including the way Americans think. Thus, so far as one is aware of his motivations, the downplaying of his contributions which were in fact impossible to discern save by formal critical methods, for which I had no taste at the time. The present version is sharply reduced in size, omitting the references to race theory and focusing instead on the principles of Bourdieu's method.

[1] Pierre Bourdieu and Loïc Wacquant, *An Invitation to Reflexive Sociology* (Chicago: University of Chicago Press, 1992).

communications – then we all must be troubled, in new as well as the old ways, about imperialisms of all kinds.

The essay in question was originally "Sur les ruses de la raison impérialiste," a note published in Bourdieu's marvelously original journal of research and opinion, *Actes de la Recherche en Sciences Sociales*. Those who know this journal know that it has been filled, over the years, mostly with first cuts of Bourdieu's own researches, alongside contributions from his co-workers in France and, occasionally, from those abroad whose ideas are similarly sympathetic. *Actes* is a marvelous magazine because, in addition to being so thoroughly original in format and content, it has long served in France as the platform for Bourdieu's intent to remake sociology as a public activity. I do not remember when the first number of *Actes* appeared, but I know that it was already well in evidence in 1978 when I began a study of French sociology and social thought. Those were the days just before Bourdieu's ascension to Raymond Aron's chair at the Collège de France, when the new French thinking was still the rage – when, for strangers from abroad, Foucault was still the more prominent figure. Yet, even then (as, even before then, in the now famous studies of students and schools that were so central to the revolutionary movements in France in the 1960s), Bourdieu was determined that his sociology be noticed and that it make a political as well as intellectual difference. Today, in the mid-2000s, Bourdieu is gone from us, having followed Foucault, Barthes, Lacan, Althusser and so many others off the stage of public intellectuals able, in this life, to make their views known. Yet, like many of the others who went before him, Bourdieu remains, in death, a social theorist who is, at once, influential in France and most interesting to foreigners.

Over the years, Bourdieu had aimed for nothing less than what he declares in many places, but never so succinctly as in *Acts of Resistance*: "I would like writers, artists, philosophers and scientists to be able to make their voice heard directly in all the areas of public life in which they are competent."[2] Here Bourdieu advances a theme not entirely different from Foucault's ideal of the concrete intellectual: Do your work where you work, do it competently, thus to challenge and change the world. Like Foucault, Bourdieu proposes that politics require truth and that only the most concrete of intellectual labors will tell global truths. It is evident that Bourdieu considers the sociologist first among equals in these labors. The vocation of the public intellectual is decidedly not a calling of the autumn of one's scientific work when fresh ideas come

---

[2] Pierre Bourdieu, *Acts of Resistance: Against the Tyranny of the Market* (New York: New Press, 1998), 9.

slowly. This is the reason for doing such work, even in one's youth, even before it is possible to know that the work will make the difference intended.

Such a calling has always been more available in Europe, and especially in Paris, than in the United States where the pretenses of academic science have bled so much of the intellectual courage from sociology. Bourdieu is well aware of this cultural difference but uncharacteristically exposes himself to the embarrassment of confusing local news with comment-worthy general truth. When Bourdieu complains on the pages of his magazine of the *ruses*, or cunnings, of American cultural imperialists, he is (to use his word) smuggling a truth back into France where, he must suppose, there is a market in news of the obvious.

American imperialists of my acquaintance are more likely to suppose that his complaint about our imposition of local truths on global reality is one of the more intractable, and unappealing, responsibilities of Empire. We Americans, of course, did not invent imperialism, any more than we invented America. All we are doing is taking the turn history offers us to imperialize by the means available. Faced with our own galling incompetence to project either military or economic power on the evidently less mighty, we resort to culture. Vietnam, Iran, Somalia, Kosovo, Iraq, Sudan, among too numerous others, are global places where, in deploying our war machinery or economic demands, short-term successes have run aground of long-term foolishness. We resort, thus, as the powerful must, to doing what can be done. Hence, jeans, hamburgers, pizza, and, at the extreme of our embarrassment, *Baywatch* (which is said to be the single most universally attended cultural event in human history). To be sure, our corporations and bombers do plenty of damage on their own – and may well regain the upper hand. But, for the moment, it is our culture for which we Americans are known and, in the more refined establishments, despised. If there must be an emperor, at least he ought not be such an empty suit.

Against the larger record of imperial mischief, the damage done by our sociological over-generalizations is of tiny consequence. It is true that we Americans behave as imperialists must, even in the innocence with which we suppose our social scientific ideas are astonishing and valid for the species at large. But this does not certify the observation as news. Perhaps we are a bit derivative in some things, and more than a bit dull in others. And, certainly, we Americans should be more embarrassed than we usually are by the advantages that issue from our global privilege. But even if we are not sufficiently humble, we are not stupid. I simply cannot imagine anyone who can passably pronounce the name "Bourdieu" who would disagree with the general point he makes.

To call attention to truths so self-evident as these is to say that the clothes have no emperor – a locally clever, but globally uninteresting insight. Still, Bourdieu's essay is interesting in other ways. When one so terrifyingly intelligent as Bourdieu does not anticipate that his local communications are likely to find their way on to the global screen, then it is right to wonder if the incautious act is one arising, not from malice, but from a more primary innocence of method. As I have confessed, I know of no sociologist whose method so inventively weds thought to fact to political punch. Thus, even when Bourdieu trips over the obvious, he has a very great deal to teach us about the possibilities and limits of intellectual work in a world so peculiar as the contemporary one.

In 1982, in his inaugural lecture at the Collège de France, Bourdieu daringly opened his most prestigious public pronouncement to date by describing the sociologist as a "terrorist inquisitor." He meant to say that the sociologist is, or ought to be, the worst nightmare of those with investments in the established order (the doxologists, if I may pervert the slur he so often uses):

One cannot go into sociology without tearing through the adherencies and adhesions by which one ordinarily belongs to groups, without abjuring beliefs that are constitutive of belonging and without disowning every link of affiliation and filiation.[3]

Insofar as it is possible, this indeed is what Bourdieu has sought to do. To this end, his genius lies in knowing that one cannot be a terrorist inquisitor while cherishing orthodox principles. Hence, the importance of his most original concept. The *habitus* serves to smash the chains of objectivism and subjectivism – of, thereby, all the rigidifying analytic forms that would organize the social study of the world into safe, but boring, hence dangerous, categories.

In one of the more beautifully composed passages in the whole of sociological literature, Bourdieu describes *habitus* as "systems of durable, transposable *dispositions*, structured structures predisposed to function as structuring structures."[4] The line may be said to be beautiful because it demands so much in so few words; because it inspires the reader to abandon formalities, while providing an alien, but habitable enough, terrain. The statement makes no sense so long as one attempts to parse it according to the usual categories – objectivism/subjectivism, structures/agents, determinism/freedom, and so on. The language turns one's thinking

[3] Pierre Bourdieu, *In Other Words: Essay toward a Reflexive Sociology* (Stanford: Stanford University Press, 1990), 177–178.
[4] Pierre Bourdieu, *Outline of a Theory of Practice* (Cambridge: Cambridge University Press, 1977), 72.

upon itself, requiring the reader to yield the terms of convenience. She must learn to live in a startlingly familiar conceptual space that demands emotional openness. That space turns out to be the space of practical life.

When people work for bread and care for their babies they never think of themselves as suspended between dichotomous spheres – between, that is, objective structures determining their fate and subjective energies driving their free actions. Perhaps they should, if they could, but they cannot. This was the false hope C. Wright Mills, among so many others, laid upon the supposition that imagination added to fact would yield liberating action. Bourdieu's *habitus* assumes, among very much else, that in the practice of social life we are suspended in the betweens where the larger forces and the particular freedoms play indeterminably against and with each other.

In practice, it is the habitus, history turned into nature, i.e., denied as such, which accomplishes practically the relating of these two systems of relations, in and through the production of practice.[5]

There are durable structures, but they are encountered as transposable. If this were not so, those with little hope of making their bread or, in some tragic cases, of saving their babies would not carry on as they do – very often in ways as courageous as they are inventive.

The natural drift of mind nurtured in the categories Bourdieu would remove into the forgotten of conscious life is toward the missing space where structure once was. We act on dispositions *in* and *amid* the forces at play in a given *champ*, or *field*. It is what we do, but on closer inspection *field* turns out to be a figure of speech of a necessarily different kind. Where *habitus* compresses the categories of thought, *field* opens the relational space on which those practices unfold. Beginning with *La Distinction*,[6] Bourdieu began to use *field* as the conceptual orthogonal to what I suppose to be his second most inventive concept, *social space*. The real, he says in a number of places and ways, is relational, hence spatial. "The notion of *space* contains, in itself, the principle of relational understanding," which in turn entails the surprising, but potent, principle that, in effect, the most real structures of social life have no palpable substance:

Apparent, directly visible beings, whether individuals or groups, exist and subsist in and through difference; that is, they occupy relative positions in a space of relations which, although invisible and always difficult to show empirically, is the

---

[5] *Ibid.*, 78.
[6] Pierre Bourdieu, *La Distinction: Critique Sociale du Jugement* (Paris: Editions de Minuit, 1979).

most real reality . . . and the real principle of the behavior of individuals and groups.[7]

To work for bread to feed the baby is to come against the hard reality of forces beyond the range of vision that ease or frustrate the work. The work itself moves ahead according to those dispositions by which we know, without really knowing, where in the field at hand there might be whatever chances of success as may exist. The proof is always, and only, in the pudding.

The problem with Bourdieu's commentary on the evils of a society other than his own is, I believe, part and parcel of his method which, in turn, demands that ideas, facts, and actions are all part of the same sociological parcel; hence, Bourdieu's reflexive sociology. Though some (notably, Alexander)[8] consider the attempt a failure, Bourdieu is at least bold in his conviction that reflexivity imposes upon sociology an unusual set of possibilities and obligations. One cannot be a terrorist inquisitor without simultaneously terrorizing the field of relations that account for one's self. "Far from being a specialty among others, [the sociology of sociology] is the necessary prerequisite of any rigorous sociological practice," which practice he defines, oddly, as "participant objectification."[9] Thus, in *Homo Academicus*,[10] his study of the social space to which he belongs, the title means to say that to study the powers at play in the space of French academic life is to study the type of person who would enter the game. Though he claims he withheld the book from publication for fear of the "extraordinary danger"[11] of losing control of what he wrote, Bourdieu hardly could have refused either to release or to write such a book in the first place.

Whatever his failures, Bourdieu has raised the stakes in all discussions of the public intellectual. When Foucault turned the tables on the universal intellectual, he was acknowledging the truth of power in the modern age – that modernity does its work in the micro-physics of daily life. One cannot profess the universal truth of the modern age because modernity as such presents as a thoroughly beautiful truth, under the cover of which it does its dirty tricks. Hence, the concrete intellectual is the only one who can tell that truth requires slow, local work upon the seemingly disjointed events of practical life – in hospitals, confessionals, courts, prisons, classrooms and all the rest.

---

[7] Pierre Bourdieu, *Practical Reason: On the Theory of Action*. 1994. (Stanford: Stanford University Press, 1998), 31.

[8] Jeffrey Alexander, *Fin-de-Siècle Social Theory* (London: Verso, 1995), 179–186.

[9] Bourdieu and Wacquant, *An Invitation to Reflexive Sociology*, 68.

[10] Pierre Bourdieu, *Homo Academicus*. 1984 (Stanford: Stanford University Press, 1998).

[11] Bourdieu and Wacquant, *An Invitation to Reflexive Sociology*, 62.

Bourdieu, on the other hand, while maintaining his own refusal of the ideals of the universal intellectual, seeks a new ground for the sociologist. The work itself is concrete – always directed at conjoined spaces of a given field, or several fields, of social power – the social space of academic life, the field of cultured taste, the elite schools and the state, the field of television and its effects. Yet, Bourdieu wants also to describe these spaces as such – to demonstrate the dispersion of social positions in the relations that constitute the virtual whole of space itself. In this, Bourdieu has taken up a near impossible challenge as must be apparent to any reader of this page who has not already studied one of Bourdieu's graphic portrayals – such as the one on page 296 of *La Distinction: critique sociale du jugement*,[12] without which very little else in the book makes as efficient good sense as with it.

How indeed is it possible to describe any complex but local or regional social space in all of its concrete detail while presenting the whole of that space? The challenge rests on Bourdieu's refusal to engage the descriptions from within the distinction between objective and subjective validity protocols. How does he do it? By what he calls a "discursive montage," which in effect amounts to a very great deal of gracefully composed ordinary language set against and amid as many graphics as he can convince his publishers to print (which, he notes, in the case of the English edition of *Distinction* is not always easily done).[13] There is no question that Bourdieu, a student of the arts, proposes an essentially aesthetic judgment as the prior, if secreted, principle of his critique of social judgment. His conception of *habitus* bears an admitted debt to the principle of axiality in art historian Erwin Panofsky's studies of classical sculpture.[14] The *habitus* is, in effect, an imaginary plane of practical action that defines the volume of social spaces.

Bourdieu's sociology is very considerably a work of art in that it makes demands, as many now recognize, as much on the imagination as on the seeing eye. And here is where the trouble arises. Unlike any purely visual work of art – whether three-dimensional as in sculpture, or textured two-dimensional as in painting – the sociological imagination must rely, or so it seems, on untextured two-dimensional media discourse, usually printed, occasionally illustrated with numerical or pictorial graphics. Whether this is so of necessity or convention is another question. Natural scientists, especially molecular biologists, rely nearly as much on virtual images, usually reconstructions of sub-visual events beyond any technology of

---

[12] Pierre Bourdieu, *La Distinction*, 296.
[13] Bourdieu and Wacquant, *An Invitation to Reflexive Sociology*, 66, n. 8.
[14] *Ibid.*, 166 (among other instances)

visual enhancement to see, as they do on texts whether numerical or prose. Sociologists, and with rare exceptions, all public intellectuals rely, for the most part, on print. Their opportunity to appear in other media – as speakers before live audiences, on television or radio – is almost always derived from having pre-existing public reputations based on authorship. This is so even when one's guarded appearance on television is meant to terrorize the medium itself.[15]

I do not pretend, within the confine of this printed space, to define what a visual sociology might be, or *if* such a thing could be. But it is not a pretense to observe that Bourdieu is one of the few to press the discursive limits of sociology, and to do so on the basis of principles so evidently sound. The plain truth is that the objectifying structures of social life are *never* visible; hence the subjectification of practical life always creates the quandary of not quite ever knowing; thus, the necessity of some virtual axis of sociological practice such as the *habitus*. But, the concept, *qua* concept, bears more information than print can possibly support. Or, to put it another way, it demands a competence, at least, in poetry, in a field more accustomed to literal prose. Bourdieu, therefore, must press the limits of his sociological aesthetic by means of the ideals of social space as relations – presented most alluringly in the occasional graphics he can smuggle past cost-conscious publishers.

[15] Pierre Bourdieu, *On Television*. 1996 (New York: New Press, 1998).

10

Simone de Beauvoir and why culture is a semiotics of the Other

Simone de Beauvoir (1908–86) is one of the more puzzling figures on the horizon of France's politics and culture. The puzzle is that she is not as much the haunting figure she ought to be. Her many and various writings – fiction, memoir, theory, history, politics – are not, even in feminist theory, as prominent as one would expect.

It has proven all too easy to consign her great book of 1949, *Le deuxième sexe*, to a pantheon of philosophical texts everyone should know *of* but none are required to read. It is true, of course, that early in the 2000s there is much in *The Second Sex* that has been superseded – not least of all by subsequent feminist writers in France who, often without regard for the specifics of Beauvoir's ideas, went on to shake the foundations of social theory with psychoanalytically inspired works of telling importance. It is indeed difficult to turn back to a book of 1949 while skipping over Julia Kristeva, Luce Irigaray, Hélène Cixous, among others who bring to feminist theory many the same qualities of literary and philosophical range that make Beauvoir's book both inspiring and daunting to read. So little time; so many books to read. But the issue is not one of the economies of reading time.

In an interview for *Society* magazine in 1976 (roughly the twenty-fifth anniversary of *The Second Sex*), Beauvoir herself states that she did not believe that her book was in any way a source of the women's movement that arose in the 1960s.

The current feminist movement, which really started about five or six years ago, did not really know the book. Then, as the movement grew, some of the leaders took from it some of their theoretical basis. But *The Second Sex* in no way launched the feminist movement. Most of the women who became very active in the movement were much too young in 1949–50, when the book came out, to be influenced by it. What pleases me, of course, is that they did discover it later. Sure, some of the older women – Betty Friedan, for example, who dedicated *The Feminine Mystique* to me – had read it and were perhaps influenced by it somewhat. But others, not at all. Kate Millett, for example, does not cite me a single time in her work [*Sexual Politics*]. They may have become feminists for

235

the reasons I explain in *The Second Sex*; but they discovered those reasons in their life experiences, not in my book.

She was not the kind of person to engage in false humilities. It is perhaps true that second-wave feminism neglected her work. Certainly, Betty Friedan's *The Feminine Mystique* is as far different on the side of journalism as Luce Irigaray's *This Sex Which is Not One* is on the side of post-academic irony.

One might say of Beauvoir that her place in the revolution in French social theory is ambiguous if not ambivalent. *Second Sex* is far from being a dead book. In a sense, it is one yet to be recovered for more than its symbolic value. *Second Sex* belongs, ironically, not so much to the generation of Friedan's *Feminine Mystique* (1963) or Millett's *Sexual Politics* (1970), nor even to that of Irigaray's *This Sex Which is Not One* (1977) or Kristeva's *Revolution in Poetic Language* (1974). These are among the works that were at the center of second-wave feminism or on the late, left-margin of psychoanalytic thinking that led to its unraveling. To the extent that they were intentionally feminist or otherwise radical departures from modernist thought, they were among those efforts, typical of the 1960s and 1970s, to rethink modern thought but still to rethink it on its own terms. Friedan's powerful essay is still read today because it reminds of a time when, in her famous line, woman's problem had no name. In effect, the writings of this era, much like the early politics of the liberation movements that devolved from them, were engaged in naming the hidden realities of woman's position for what they were. It may seem bizarre to lump such different attitudes as those of Irigaray and Kristeva in this process, but the lumping is possible because at the crucial moments, at least in their writings of 1970s, both reverted to the categories at hand – power as the raw force of subjugation, semiotics as desire for the unattainable other. It would not be long before the beginnings would become something else.

It may seem a quibble to suggest a difference between even Irigaray and Kristeva and what came after in their own writings and those of others, but the difference is discernible and critical. It is a departure no less than the one that grew on Foucault when he turned, after 1970, to the long, winding, uncertain path toward the history of sexuality, the politics of sexualities, and his all-too-early death. One speaks of Foucault as a founder of queer theory, not because he used the term *queer* as it came to be. Nor even because, one assumes, he was at all points fully aware of the implications of every theoretical move he made. He would have no sooner associated his genealogical method with queer theory, than he was drawn to think of himself as a postmodernist. Yet, the effect was there and evident. Queering is less about sexuality than about an attitude toward the language one uses in an effort to escape the subjugations of modern power/knowledge that so gently lull even its radical critics into a false hope of its transcendence.

The distinction between second- and third-wave feminist theory is not so much the latter's intensification of the latent ironies of the former as in the emergence of a new, more radical semiotic of culture. By this is meant: an attitude that – far from using language as its primary topic or a semiotics as its method – considers language, as Derrida said in 1966, the universal problematic that changes everything. Thus, some of the writers who are associated with third-wave theory may not even engage in the fine discourse of the Lacanians or post-structuralisms. Some do; some don't. One who does, but not to the exclusion of other purposes, is Judith Butler whose *Gender Trouble* (1990) is, if there is but one, the *locus classicus* of queer theory. This because Butler therein calls into question the very category from which feminist theory took its departure. But she did so in a way that, of course, took seriously the beginnings of the movement – that is: by defining the term historically, even biographically, as unstable.

Butler and others on the philosophical wing of the third wave went far beyond earlier theories of the social construction of gender, which in a sense even radical second-wave thinkers like Dorothy Smith were drawn to as a kind of counter-essentialism of woman. Butler's idea of gender insubordination is one that is far closer to Derrida (though without calling too much attention to the proximity). She calls into question the originality of gender itself by the striking path of considering sex-differences according to the realities of sexual play itself. Thus, rather than establish sexualities as still another category whereby the oppressed resist power-knowledge (culture, that is), Butler incisively attacks the idea that homosexual practice is a mere imitation of the dominant heterosexual culture. She says, in brief, that everything in the sphere of sexual play is an original performance not a copy of an essential original. Gender thus is not one. It is many – like social performances of all kinds. And, if sexual practices, whether homo- or hetero-, are the beginnings of gender trouble, then in the long run all such social categories are themselves copies without originals.

There must be now some who may be reading along with faint or fervent conviction who begin to wonder where the connection is to Simone de Beauvoir in 1949. It is not, surely not, in the manner by which *Second Sex* laid out its sprawling, far-from-delicate argument. Nor is it that the work contains the early blossoms of thinking to come. But she does plant fertile seeds that, if they blossomed in others at a later time, it was because they shared the soil that would become the garden of the new that would not come into its own until after Beauvoir's death in 1986.

Second Sex was the first book of the post-war era to define woman – neither according to her essential attributes (this had been done many times before) nor according to her subjugation to man's world (this too was by then a familiar idea) – but according to the web of her uncertain relations as Other to man.

If woman seems to be the inessential who never becomes the essential, it is because she herself fails to bring about change. Proletarians say "We"; Negroes also. Regarding themselves as subjects, they transform the bourgeois, the whites, into "others." But women do not say "We," except at some congress of feminists or similar formal demonstration; men say "women" and women use the same word in referring to themselves. They do not authentically assume a subjective attitude. The proletarians have accomplished the revolution in Russia, the Negroes in Haiti, the Indo-Chinese are battling for it in Indo-China; but the women's effort has never been anything more than a symbolic agitation. They have gained only what men have been willing to grant; they have taken nothing, they have only received. . . . . They live dispersed among the males, attached through residence, housework, economic condition, and social standing to certain men – fathers or husbands – more firmly than they are to other women. If they belong to the bourgeoisie, they feel solidarity with men of that class, not with proletarian women; if they are white, their allegiance is to white men, not to Negro women. The proletarian can propose to massacre the ruling class, and a sufficiently fanatical Jew or Negro might dream of getting sole possession of the atomic bomb and making humanity wholly Jewish or black; but woman cannot even dream of exterminating the males. The bond that unites her to her oppressors is not comparable to any other. . . . Here is to be found the basic trait of woman: she is the other in a totality of which the two components are necessary to one another. (Beauvoir, *Second Sex* (1949), xxii–xxiii)

On the surface the passage seems only slightly distinguishable from Friedan, even earlier feminist theorists. But in the footnotes, with references rich to Lévi-Strauss, Lacan, and Levinas, there are hints of the other reading the book deserves.

Where Beauvoir's critique of woman's position is queer is in two enveloping facts of its coming into being. The book itself is truly and honestly the first to acknowledge that the otherness of woman is like but unlike the position of others oppressed – similar, but different. In this otherness is the distinctive social consequence of woman's social position – being thus an Other unlike any other. In this also she is closer spiritually to Fanon than to Friedan, thus closer to Butler and the third-wave than were those who came after her in France. But also, second, there is the important fact of the book's authorship – that it was written as part of what became one of the most important, if under-recognized, political memoirs since Rousseau's *Confessions*. *Second Sex*, while not autobiographical on the surface, was in its reflexive effects on the author. Beauvoir has said that she learned her feminism *in* the writing of the book, which is to suggest that one cannot appreci-ate Beauvoir's feminist theory without reading her several volumes of memoir from *Memoirs of a Dutiful Daughter* (1958) to *Old Age* (1972) and *Adieux: A Farewell to Sartre* (1984). Many have chronicled their lives after the fact, near the end. Few have used memory to shape their lives. Of Beauvoir's remembrances the most enduringly important to her feminism is *La force de l'âge* (1960). *The Prime of Life* draws upon her prime years of youth and schooling, the early days with Sartre, the war and her early literary successes. Many criticize her in retrospect for having made so much of her relation with Sartre, as if the liberated woman ought be utterly void of passion for men. Yet one who reads the book sympathetically finds in *The Prime of Life* a true and honest account of the woman's standpoint – not the idealized story of the rad-ical who overcomes, nor a tale of the pure freedom of liberation from all that oppresses. Rather, this and other of her memoirs are filled with the pain as well as the pleasure of life with men, Sartre and Nelson Algren notably of course, and women, her mother and her struggle, always unresolved, to transform her bourgeois upbringing into a life practiced as a truly independent woman. The feminist theory is thus always referred to the woman's actual, incomplete practical work to define her standpoint.

In the work as a whole Beauvoir offers an honest view of culture – as it is and as it affects her – but the offering does not seal the gaps, nor cover the differences. The differences are plain to see. Her writing was not a semiology but her descriptions of the cultures through which she lived lay bare a structure of differences as she encountered people, whether high or low in the scheme of social things. Woman is an Other unlike any other, yes. But the difference she embodies, with all its failures and promises, is a difference that, contrary to received opinion of her, queers any thought of woman as the modern heroine of human liberty. One complains only about her overplaying of woman's uniqueness among others facing long histories of exclusion. It is true, for example, that she did not experience the semiotic of culture as did Fanon. But she understood, as did he, that her otherness was one that deprived her of the very subjecthood for which she lived her life with more attention to its meaning value than is possible for those who live inside the cloister of bourgeois culture.

Beauvoir lived long enough to participate in the revolution that erased the difference, without erasing woman. Fanon did not live to see the same in respect to the colonized other. That is a difference – real, concrete, historical, personal; yet, also political.

Power-knowledge, discourse, and
transgression (with Garth Gillan) (1982*)

"I am supposing," Foucault writes in *Discourse on Language*, "that in every society the production of discourse is at once controlled, selected, organized and redistributed according to a certain number of procedures, whose role is to avert its powers and its dangers, to cope with chance events, to evade its ponderous, awesome materiality."[1]

There are, Foucault goes on to say in *Discourses*, rules of exclusion: prohibitions, rejections, and divisions; restrictive limitations on the exercise of discourse: rituals, fellowships of discourse, and doctrines; internal limitations upon discourse: commentaries, authors, and disciplines.[2] These operations in the construction of discursive practices are concealed behind a number of philosophical themes dominant in Western thought: the founding subject, experience as origin, and universal mediation. What is concealed in these concepts and operations? Are they not merely impurities that affect ideal truth in its passage to the concrete? Are not the distortions of discourse the marks of the historical contingency of truth? Do not these distortions leave untouched the conception of truth as ideal, as the telos of all human discourse, and the ultimate ground of all knowledge?

* Reprinted from Charles C. Lemert and Garth Gillan, *Michel Foucault: Social Theory & Transgression* (New York: Columbia University Press, 1982), chapter 3. Garth Gillan, then professor of philosophy at Southern Illinois University/Carbondale was a life-line to the worlds of European social and philosophical thinking. He is a man of many interests and commitments – father and husband, sheep rancher, psychoanalyst, deacon in the Roman Catholic Church, minister to Spanish-speaking migrant workers, musician – just to mention those things of which I am familiar. Yet, most astonishing of all is the experience I had in 1970s of spending summers and whole years in Paris while Garth remained at home on his farm in Southern Illinois, then returning to Carbondale for our regular lunches to learn from him what was going in Paris. The book was a joint effort. I believe the selection is from a portion for which he was the principal author. In either case, going back over the joint project I see now, so many years latter, how much my writing was influenced by Garth.
[1] Michel Foucault, *The Discourse on Language*. Translated by Rupert Swyer. Printed as an Appendix to *Archaeology of Knowledge*. (New York: Random House, 1972), 216. *Discourse* was Foucault's inaugural lection at the Collège de France.
[2] *Ibid.*, 216–224.

For Foucault, the possibility of asking these questions is an indication that these distortions have produced a will to truth distinct from desire and power. The dangers and risks of discourse are concealed in the concept of true discourse. Discourse, animated by the will to truth, is a form of dissemblance. The will to truth distorts itself in order to reappear in the guise of ideal truth. In their dialectic, true discourse and the will to truth conceal the truth. "True discourse, liberated by the nature of its form from desire and power, is incapable of recognizing the will to truth which pervades it; and the will to truth, having imposed itself upon us for so long, is such that the truth it seeks to reveal cannot fail to mask it."[3] Foucault's theory of discourse, therefore, involves violence and transgression. An original transgression: the concealment of the will to truth in the ideal of true discourse. A secondary transgression: the concealment of the will to truth in the very concept of truth. A third transgression: the violence done to the taboos erected in the first two transgressions by "the political history of the production of 'truth.'"[4] Discourse, power, and knowledge involve a history of transgressions.

True discourse only surfaces in a form twisted by violence. The face it turns toward men, "wealth, fertility and sweet strength in all of its insidious universality,"[5] is the calm exterior visage of power. The domineering free gaze of the clinic is matched by the cold, calculating gaze inhabiting Bentham's panopticon. The reverse side of the liberation of truth is the subjection of all to its gaze. Subjection and freedom intermingle. Power-knowledge is originally a violence done to the truth in which truth appears as ideal, original, and innocent. Transgression takes the form of knowledge and power.

Is it possible to expand this circularity of transgressions and use the will to truth against itself? Is it possible to unmask the concealments, elisions, productive prohibitions, positive repressions, which are the political technology of power-knowledge? Archaeology, or what, after *The Archaeology of Knowledge*, Foucault calls genealogy, is the transgressive knowledge in which the taboos thrown up around the will to truth are violated. The genealogy of knowledge transgresses the divisions of the true and the false, reason and madness, by the attempt "to remould this will to truth and to turn it against truth at that very point where truth undertakes to justify the taboo, and to define madness."[6] Nietzsche, Bataille, and

---

[3] *Ibid.*, 219.

[4] Michel Foucault, "Power and Sex," trans. David J. Parent. *Telos* 32 (1977): 152–161.

[5] *Ibid.*, 220.

[6] *Ibid.*, 220. In 1976 Foucault offered a clarification of the distinction between archaeology and genealogy. In "Two Lectures" (Michel Foucault, *Power/Knowledge: Selected Interviews & Other Writings 1972–1977*, ed. Colin Gordon [New York: Pantheon, 1980], 85) he said:

Artaud are the sentinels that guard the bridges over which the dialectic of transgression passes. The concept power-knowledge is the result.

Thus, the critical theory announced in Foucault's Collège de France inaugural address, *Discourse on Language*, becomes quite explicit in subsequent studies. History, unmistakably, is a critical exposition of the constitution of knowledge through the techniques of power. In *Discipline and Punish* Foucault unmasks the power over and knowledge of individuals in the semio-techniques of disciplinary codes. In *The History of Sexuality* he discloses the control over human populations and the objectification of self-consciousness at work in bio-power. Foucault's history is a critical analysis of the socially contingent nature of truth gained by crossing the divide between the true and the false. The historical reality of the will to truth is its complicity with power and not its neutrality or freedom from evaluative judgments. Every conception of ideal truth, including the dream of value neutrality in the social sciences, is a falsification of the operations of true discourse. Ideal truth does not liberate discourse from power, but tightens power's control. The taboo under which power and knowledge are placed reinforces an oppression made more effective because it cannot be criticized.

History is a critique of truth's distortion. But, equally, history is produced by transgressing a taboo that can never, finally, be criticized. History's truth is immanent, not transcendental. As such it must struggle, without hope of pure freedom, against the primal fact of all truth, distortion. Power-knowledge, remember, involves three transgressions. In the first two the will to truth is hidden behind discourse and truth itself. In the third, the historian, in a political act, overcomes the concrete taboos by which truth is hidden. But the taboo cannot be removed. It is reinforced in transgression. As a result, critical knowledge is not, for Foucault, the restoration of a primeval innocence or a primitive originality in which one can look upon the visage of truth without a veil. The "history of the production of truth" is not a return to an original peace free of violence or repression. Transgression, for Foucault, entails no pristine true discourse. Transgression is an original feature of the will to knowledge. It is also a feature of the recounting of its history. Transgression is the eternal

"If we were to characterize it in two terms, then 'archaeology' would be the appropriate methodology of this analysis of local discursivities, and 'genealogy' would be the tactics whereby, on the basis of the descriptions of these local discursivities, the subjected knowledges which were thus released would be brought into play." It is hard to tell whether this is a retrospective adjustment in Foucault's vocabulary or a reflection of the fact that, after *Archaeology of Knowledge* (New York: Random House, 1972) his main studies – *Discipline and Punish: The Birth of the Prison* (trans. Alan Sheridan [New York: Vintage, 1977]) and *History of Sexuality, Vol. I. An Introduction* (trans. Robert Hurley [New York: Random House, 1977]) – were indeed more regional and explicitly political, hence genealogical. In any case, we hold the view that genealogy is basic, and that the distinction appears to be spurious.

return of the truth upon itself, a primitive circularity in which distorted truth only meets up once again with distorted truth. Here is Nietzsche's *Eternal Return of the Same*. The history of the production of truth is thus not a perspective outside of the circularity of knowledge, but the worm hidden in the breast of truth.

In the concept of transgression, Foucault's relation to Bataille is evident. But Foucault does not give to transgression the same positive significance that the term had for Bataille. For Bataille, in *Death and Sensuality*, humanity has placed upon sexuality a primitive taboo. The knowledge of life, then, was the violent act of crossing that barrier. However, in spite of the critiques that have suggested there is an unspoken naturalism in Foucault's writings, particularly in his earlier works, *Madness and Civilization* and *The Birth of the Clinic*, transgression for him does not entail the hypothesis of an original state. The will to truth exists as a transgression upon its ideal possibilities.

All of this takes place within language. In the effort to speak, the Subject does not encounter within himself an irreducible center of certainty, but a contest thrown up by the limits of his being and the void created by the death of God, the ultimate representation of limit. In language the Subject is up against his own finitude and the fact that he is stripped of transcendence.[7] In a post-Sadean language, the concept of transgression says that meaning is confronted not as an absolute transcendence grounding language, but in the limits of meaning. Language is the existence of sense in the recognition of limits defined by "the limit of the Limitless."[8] But sense is not created by remaining within limits, such as the analytic of finitude, as if they constituted a new set of positivities within which humanity is reconstituted. Sense is, rather, in the excess that transgresses those limits.

For Bataille, eroticism arises when sexuality crosses the limits erected by the taboo on sexuality. Eroticism both crosses and sustains the limit of the taboo. The limit is an internal necessity for transgression. At the same time, it is the recognition that, in crossing the limit, the taboo is not eliminated. Transgression is the movement that creates, in the absence of an absolute Limit, a limitlessness essential to the transgression of limits. The dialectic is engendered by its own internal elements. But, then, this is no longer a dialectic. Language at this point is non-discursive. It is neither positive, nor negative, because it neither affirms, nor denies division, separation, or distance. Language recognizes only the "existence of

---

7 Michel Foucault, "A Preface to Transgression," *Language, Counter-Memory, and Practice: Selected Essays and Interviews*, ed. Donald Bouchard (Ithaca: Cornell University Press, 1977), 30–31.
8 *Ibid.*, 32.

difference."[9] The language of transgression confronts and interrogates limits. Contestation occurs without resolution; hence, "the Nietzschean figures of tragedy, of Dionysus, of the death of God, of the philosopher's hammer, of the Superman [Overman] approaching with the steps of a dove, of the Return."[10]

The language of transgression must be distinguished from the analytic of finitude described in *The Order of Things*. The finite in the language of transgression does not rest upon the positivity of finitude. In contrast, the analytic of Man's finitude, rejected by Foucault, is basic to Man as an object of knowledge in the social sciences. The nineteenth-century analytic is founded upon a field of positive data, the data of life, labor, and language. Man's finitude is the limit drawn by the recognition of the factual character of his existence. This finitude is determined by optic regions, life, labor, and language, in the knowledge of which Man can be grasped. Whether it is "the anatomy of the brain, the mechanics of production costs, or the system of Indo-European conjugation,"[11] life, labor, and language define what is possible and impossible for men. These positive regions not only determine the finite limits of Man, but are the expression of his finitude. They are positivities formed from the limits of "the spatiality of the body, the yawning of desire, and the time of language."[12] Man's finitude mirrors the finite content of the areas of knowledge through which he is known. The limits in the analytic of finitude are positive limits within which Man appears as an object of knowledge.

Transgressive knowledge, by contrast, is not a knowledge of finitude, nor an anthropological thought that in the absence of God has Man as its epistemological center.[13] The absence or death of God is, for Foucault as it was with Nietzsche, the rejection of the theological nature of Western thought. Transgressive thought does not presuppose an optic ground for the divisions of reason and madness, the true and the false. For Foucault, transgression does not signify a thought that determines limits, as if what can be known about man contains, *a priori*, all the limits to be placed upon his existence. An *a priori* knowledge of human finitude does not result in a determination of the epistemological limits of man's knowledge. Transgressive thought is as far from philosophical anthropology as it is from theology. Transgression represents "the still silent and groping apparition of a form of thought in which the interrogation of the limit

[9] *Ibid.*, 36.   [10] *Ibid.*, 38.

[11] Michel Foucault, *The Order of Things* (New York: Vintage Books, 1973), 314.

[12] *Ibid.*, 315.

[13] *Ibid.*, 340–343. Anthropology in Foucault's works refers not to the academic discipline of that name, but to the "analytic of man" described in *The Order of Things*. Anthropological thought is the discursive formation characteristic of Western modernity that makes Man the object and subject of knowledge.

replaces the search for totality and the act of transgression replaces the movement of contradictions."[14]

The terms limit, excess, and transgression appear, mostly, in Foucault's philosophical texts, but the concepts are essential to a reading of his historical studies. From *Madness and Civilization* to *The History of Sexuality* Foucault analyzes the limits placed upon reason and madness, the true and the false, by tracing the history within which those limits were constituted. The division of reason and madness appears first in the political and economic crises surrounding the rise and dissolution of confinement in the seventeenth and eighteenth centuries and the isolation of madness within the empirical forms of unreason by means of bourgeois social order. The division is completed in the moralization of madness effected through the moral therapeutics practiced in the asylums of Tuke and Pinel. With *The Birth of the Clinic* the claim of the clinical gaze to be the recovery of original experience is shattered. Foucault relativizes this privileged limit by means of a history of the dispersed events that constituted the clinic: the founding of the French Royal Society of Medicine, the control of epidemics, the financing of hospitals, the practices of pathological anatomy, the liberalization of medical perception in the transgression of modesty in the examination of women, and the conceptualization of the medical gaze as a field of free economic exchange. In *The Order of Things*, the history of the human sciences as a chronicle of accumulated knowledge is dissolved into a history of the discursive systems in which science arises in knowledge, *savoir*. The appearance of Man as an object of the social sciences is not the triumphant achievement of a scientific methodology, but is due to the sudden appearance of a configuration of the concepts life, labor, and language in the nineteenth century. The knowledge of individuals gained through the localization of disease in the visible body and knowledge of the individual body arising through pathological anatomy is extended in *Discipline and Punish*. The penal practices born through the penal reforms of the seventeenth and eighteenth centuries lead, not to rehabilitation, but to a micro-power invested in disciplines borrowed from the penitential practices of individual confession, the pedagogy of the Christian schools of the nineteenth century, the political ideology of the open republic. All are symbolized in the universally dominant case of Bentham's panopticon. The penal practices of the eighteenth and nineteenth centuries spawned a series of individualizing disciplines in which the prisoner is isolated and his behavior fragmented. As semiotechniques, they signify the individual in his specificity. The individual is thrown back into a self-conscious remorse. Through the practices of

[14] Foucault, "A Preface to Transgression," 50.

incarceration and attendant judicial measures, the seizure of the individual as the object of knowledge accompanies a normalization of reason. Reason is the norm. By means of the extension of carceral disciplines, society at large comes under the discipline of the rational norm. In *The History of Sexuality*, the myth of Victorian repression hides the true function of the discourse of sexuality. That function is not liberation, but the creation of a discourse able to dispose of sex in such a way that sexuality is the manifestation of social control and power over life.

Reason, from *Madness and Civilization* to *The History of Sexuality*, is found in the strategies, disciplines, technologies, and tactics which power exercises on the body. In that fundamental fact, there is a transgression on the divisions that constitute the macro-history and the macro-power of rationality: madness and reason, the true and the false, body and soul, the individual and society, power and knowledge, words and things, the confined and the free, repression and liberation, politics and transcendent religion, the state and the family, life and death. Having transgressed its own nature, reason placidly aligns itself with one side or another of the dichotomies it has given rise to by its violence. The history that transgresses these divisions is a micro-history that discloses the small, dirty details of mechanisms dispersed throughout the social body, and installed here and there in institutions; mechanisms that create a schedule and spatial order for bodily actions.

Where is this history located? It is in economic history, but a history not exhausted by the multiple transgressions of exchange. It is in political history, yet one not confined to the confrontation of classes. It is in social history, nevertheless, not one found in the rise and death of institutions. It is in intellectual history, but not a history for which ideas are the original signs of reality. Foucault's history is not traditional. It is located where knowledge has the body in its grip; where, in the time and space of the body, relations of power pinpoint a field of objectivity. How do events produce effects? How is history effective so that it can trace the "descent" and the "emergence" of cultural acquisitions, economic attitudes, political dispositions, and moral values? How is it possible for the ruptures, reversals, discontinuities, and transformations located in a series of events to possess materiality?

To familiar questions, Foucault gives a single, unfamiliar answer: because events are inscribed upon the body. The inscribed body is the space wherein the Hydra of history can look in all directions simultaneously. Foucault, however, does not develop a philosophy of the body in which history would take on flesh as it did for Merleau-Ponty. The inscribed body is the correlate of the concept of genealogy. "Genealogy, as an analysis of descent, is thus situated within the articulation of the body and history. Its task is to expose a body totally imprinted by history and the process of history's destruction of the body."[15]

The body is the space in which it is possible to find, not the traces of past events, but the play of forces in which the surface events of history are distortions of "lost events."[16] Foucault is following Nietzsche very closely here. "Descent" and "emergence" are Nietzsche's *Herkunft* and *Entstehung*. But the tapestry woven from those terms is Foucault's. The descent or emergence of an idea, a trait or characteristic, a social discipline, or rational conception, is the manner in which they are events subject to the reversals, discontinuities, forces of domination, risks and wagers, accidents and chances in which every event is caught. The body is inscribed with the play of creation and destruction, or risks and wagers, in which there is the reality of loss and not the forgotten plenitude of sensible meaning. The body is not the land flowing with milk and honey, but the plain of desolation, the desert in which history wanders.

The Birth of the Clinic is Foucault's first obvious history of the body. The clinical gaze is inscribed in an epistemic field constituted by the placement of death within the organs of the living body by pathological anatomy. The body is the field of objectivity in which the visibility of the body is known through its invisibility, the anticipated inner space of the body revealed to vision by autopsy. Beginning with Bichat, life is defined by death. Disease is a possibility installed in life, its contrary. The truth of disease is revealed in death. Life and the living body are only known against the backdrop of death. The body is also the space traversed in transgressing the shame involved in the palpation of the unclothed body. That transgression of modesty is the action of a *libido sciendi*, a desire to know whose manifest form is an encroachment upon bodily space.

The clinic is born in a gaze whose domain is the threat of destruction leveled against the living body. The clinic necessarily entails death and transgression. The medical gaze locates and individualizes disease in the body by holding the body in subjection. For the clinical gaze to know is for it to dominate the bodies of those condemned to death and poverty. The clinic's ability to locate disease in the body is made possible by the poor, who, with their bodies, pay an interest on capital advanced in the hospitals financed by the rich after the Revolution. The poor exchange their bodies for medical care. Clinical knowledge of diseases occurs by means of the political subjection that opens up the body to the clinical gaze.

---

[15] Michel Foucault, "Nietzsche, Genealogy, History," *Language, Counter-Memory, and Practice*, 148.
[16] *Ibid.*, 26.

Madness is also constituted in the domination of the body. Madness as a mental disease arises from the practice of confining bodies in the eighteenth century. *Madness and Civilization* focuses on the isolation of madness from the generality of unreason by the intervention of the moral law in confinement and through the construction of asylums in which madness became a subjectivity through the experience of moral guilt. The mad are confined as the consequence of a moral perception. Madness, sloth, and poverty intermingle. The body of unreason is distinguished from the body of labor. In confinement, madness is isolated by breaking the classical unity of the soul and the body. The unity of unreason is broken by viewing madness as a state of animality inhabited by the frenzy of an unchained freedom, and, in the therapeutics of madness, by associating madness with delirium and dissociating it from passion, the untrammeled desire of the body. The moralization of madness in the rise of the asylums creates the moral subjectivity of madness against the background of a fractured body. Likewise, reason is separated from unreason by separating the soul from the body. The body is dismembered to produce a soul which has its existence in the movements of a delirious language tortured by the guilt produced by moral punishment. Subjectivity is the object of psychological observation and knowledge. Subjectivity, thereby, comes into existence by the subjection of the body in confinement. It is the internalization of moral subjection in the asylum. In the history of madness, the subjectivity of madness is the result of the subjection of the body. The body in subjection is the site in which emerges the field of objectivity that psychology will claim as its own.

In *Discipline and Punish*, Foucault confronts knowledge (*savoir*) with the epistemological technology that defines its object, the semio-techniques of disciplinary codes. Here, quite explicitly, is the body "totally imprinted by history and the process of history's destruction of the body." The body in *Discipline and Punish* is the fractured body, inscribed with a multiplicity of individuating and objectifying techniques. The initial scene with which *Discipline and Punish* begins is the execution of Damiens. His body is tortured by pincers and quartered. The four horses are unable to separate his limbs from his trunk. He must be hacked apart. This fragmentation is a sign of sovereign, unlimited power. At the end of *Discipline and Punish* the body is subjected to the panoptic gaze and to the regime of isolation. It is thrown back on its own conscience to produce a new morality. Its movements through the day and night of the prison are ordered according to a rigorous schedule. Movements are subjected to the discipline of labor. In brief, the body is now cut into a soul and physical body and dispersed among the fragments of mechanical time. The fractured body inscribed with the history of penal institutions and their discipline is caught up in a continuous movement of desynthesization.

In the distance between these two images of the body Foucault writes the history of punishment and prisons. The distance is traversed by a "political technology of the body." What is Foucault's aim in writing *Discipline and Punish*? One sentence spells it out: "In short, try to study the metamorphosis of punitive methods on the basis of a political technology of the body in which might be read a common history of power relations and object relations."[17] Foucault's problem in *Discipline and Punish* is the rise of the prison to dominate the field of penal punishment and the means used to create the disciplinary codes of the prison, the school, military life, and religious practice. This historical problem requires the exposition of the relations of power and knowledge and the formulation of the concept power-knowledge. In turn, such a theoretical formulation involves the description of the ways that power and knowledge are inscribed upon the body. Inscription, thus, is a political technology of the body in which cognitive relations are the exercise of power and power relations are objectifying.

The fracturing of the body not only corresponds to the fragmentation of the body in disciplinary codes, it also corresponds to the dispersion of power relations. Foucault views power not as a privilege to be defended, but as a contract governing exchange. The model Foucault prefers is that of a "network of relations, constantly in tension" and "a perpetual battle."[18] The rise of the prison as a dominant form of judicial punishment in the eighteenth and nineteenth centuries is not an isolated event. The discipline of the body introduced by the prison gathers together disciplinary codes originating at different points in society. The confrontation of power and knowledge comes to a head in the history of penality because penal practices pervade society. Disciplinary codes are a "microphysics of power," the crucial nature of which is that they are a strategy. Power is not privilege, but strategy. Its dispersion within the social body is direct evidence for the process that associated the accumulation of capital in the West with the accumulation of men.[19] The accumulation of capital is accompanied by strategies for marshalling the productive force of the body, intensifying its productivity by disciplining its movements. The economic use of the body is related to the political use of the body. As labor power disciplined for productivity, the body is also need, calculatedly nurtured in subjection. The body is politicized. "But the body is also directly involved in a political field; power relations have an immediate hold upon it, they invest it, mask it, train it,

---

[17] Foucault, *Discipline and Punish*, 24.   [18] *Ibid.*, 26.   [19] *Ibid.*, 220–221.

torture it, force it to carry out tasks, to perform ceremonies, to emit signs."[20]

This political technology of the body is also a strategy and technique for delimiting the natural movements of the body: "there may be a 'knowledge' of the body that is not exactly the science of its functioning, and a mastery of its forces that is more than the ability to conquer them: this knowledge and this mastery constitute what might be called the political technology of the body."[21] This knowledge surfaces in military manuals, which translate the natural movements of the body into the most precise and efficient drills. It is the knowledge formulated in the Christian schools of La Salle, in which the body is subjected to the regime of pedagogy. It is a knowledge that produces a docile body, taught by turning its own forces against itself. This knowledge is a power. It intensifies the efficiency and productivity of the body.

Discipline and Punish, therefore, is a study of political anatomy. The material support for the relations of power and knowledge in society is the body politic. The political anatomy of society is the political economy of the body. Both images involve a set of correspondences and transferences that define the strategies inscribed upon the body as the social strategies by which power works. The body politic is "a set of material elements and techniques that serve as weapons, relays, communication routes, and supports for the power and knowledge relations that invest human bodies and subjugate them by turning them into objects of knowledge."[22] The fractured and subjected body of penal practices is the body in a political field in which power is exercised in society. Damiens's body was drawn to the four quarters of the earth. The docile body of penal practices and disciplinary codes is pulverized into a multiplicity of details, directions, attitudes, and postures anchored in the body of society. The exercise of the microphysics of power on the docile body is its dispersion, its fragmentation into its internal parts that, left intact, produce a living division within the body.

One of the principal effects of the body's division is the doubling of the imprisoned body into the soul. The soul as it is encountered in the extrajudicial, administrative practices of penality in the eighteenth century and in the practices of the disciplinary codes of the eighteenth and nineteenth centuries is the result of the individuation of punishment. The

[20] *Ibid.,* 25.   [21] *Ibid.,* 26.
[22] *Ibid.,* 28. For the same conception expressed in other terms, see: Michel Foucault, "Body/Power," *Power/Knowledge,* 55. "I believe the great fantasy is the idea of a social body constituted by the universality of wills. Now the phenomenon of the social body is the effect not of a consensus but of the materiality of power operating on the very bodies of individuals."

individuation of punishment creates an object for the application of power in which consideration must be given to extenuating circumstances, intentions, psychological abnormality, and legal responsibility. In developing the application of punishment, the political technology of power effects an internalization of its own relations within the body of the imprisoned. If the surplus power of the king in the *ancien régime* gave rise to the duplication of his body in the body politic, then Foucault sees the surplus power exercised on the body of the condemned as giving rise to another kind of duplication, the soul. The genealogy of the modern soul has its roots in the microphysics of power.[23] The soul is not the metaphysical double of the body. Power turns the body against itself, divides it from itself into the imprisoned body and the soul in the throes of remorse.

Thus, where power and knowledge meet in the fragmenting of the body, the soul arises as the object of knowledge and as the subject of individuation. "It would be wrong," Foucault writes in *Discipline and Punish*,

to say that the soul is an illusion, or an ideological effect. On the contrary, it exists, it has a reality, it is produced permanently around, on, within the body by the functioning of a power that is exercised on those punished – and, in a more general way, on those one supervises, trains, and corrects, over madmen, children at home and at school, the colonized, over those who are stuck at a machine and supervised for the rest of their lives.[24]

This psychological complex of power and knowledge is not simply the field of the concepts of psyche, personality, subjectivity, and consciousness. It is also the reference for the construction of the psychological sciences. They, and their field of objectivity, the soul, are the result of a "new political anatomy of the body."[25]

A political anatomy of the body is also a new political economy of desire. It is the former in *The Birth of the Clinic, Madness and Civilization,* and *Discipline and Punish*; the latter in *The History of Sexuality*. The body of desire in *The History of Sexuality* is the domain of a knowledge (*savoir*) that constitutes itself in the myth of repression in modern societies. In confronting the body of desire as the secret forbidden by the prohibition upon sexuality,[26] the will to know (*volonté de savoir*) is transformed into the discourse on sexuality for whom repression is merely an index of its proliferation throughout society. Shame was the limit transgressed in the desire to know (*libido sciendi*) when, in the nineteenth century, doctors dared to examine the visible body by touch. Likewise, repression is the myth transgressed by the will to know taking form in the discourse on

---

[23] Foucault, *Discipline and Punish*, 29.   [24] *Ibid.*   [25] *Ibid.*, 193.
[26] Foucault, *History of Sexuality*, 49.

sexuality. The desire to know is a form of knowledge in which to know life is also to control it; in which to know desire is also to shape it politically from within. Discourse on sexuality is a form of power-knowledge.

The emergence of the discourse of sexuality entails the appearance of a "new distribution of pleasures, types of discourses, truths, and kinds of powers."[27] This is the affective mechanism of sexuality (*dispositif de sexualité*), which, beginning with the eighteenth century, involves four strategies centered on four privileged objects: the hysterical woman, the masturbating child, the Malthusian couple, the adult pervert. To these objects four strategies: hystericalization of the body of the woman, the pedagogization of the sex of the child, the socialization of the procreative activities, and the psychiatrization of perverse pleasures.[28]

What is involved in these strategies? Nothing less than the production of the affective mechanism of sexuality itself, and the sexed body. Sexuality is not a repressed, hidden instinct, difficult to conceptualize. The discourse of sexuality produces the truth of the sexual body in such a manner that the desires of the flesh come to know themselves and are known as objects of knowledge (*savoir*). The affective mechanism of sexuality is the "great surface network in which the stimulation of bodies, the intensification of pleasures, the incitement to discourse, the formation of special knowledges, the strengthening of controls and resistances, are linked to one another in accordance with a few major strategies of knowledge and power."[29] The history of this sexuality is the history of the discourse in which the strategies of knowledge and power come to the surface.

What is at work in this shameless discourse that constantly reveals its own secrets? Above all, the masking of power in the myth of repression. Repression is represented as the imposition of an interdiction coming from the outside, an imposition of power external to the discourse of sexuality. Its model is the power of right (*pouvoir de droit*), liberation from

---

[27] *Ibid.*, 123.   [28] *Ibid.*, 104–105.

[29] *Ibid.*, 105–106. In "Confession of the Flesh" (in *Power/Knowledge*, 194–195) Foucault amplifies this definition: "What I'm trying to pick out with this term is, firstly, a thoroughly heterogeneous ensemble consisting of discourses, institutions, architectural forms, regulatory decisions, laws, administrative measures, scientific statements, philosophical, moral and philanthropic propositions – in short, the said as much as the unsaid. Such are the elements of the apparatus. The apparatus itself is the system of relationships that can be established between these elements. Secondly, what I am trying to identify in this apparatus is precisely the nature of the connection that can exist between these heterogeneous elements. Thus, a particular discourse can figure at one time as the programme of an institution, and at another it can function as a means of justifying or masking a practice which itself remains silent, or as a secondary re-interpretation of this practice, opening out for it a new field of rationality." "Apparatus of sexuality" here refers to what we have translated as "affective mechanism of sexuality."

which is the assertion of a corresponding right, the right of sexuality to be free. The liberation of sexuality is based on freeing sexuality from a *"juridico-discursive"* power in which, on one side, there is the legislating power and, on the other, the obedient subject.[30] It is, in fact, a game of the licit and the illicit, of transgression and punishment. The model of juridico-discursive power conceals a power that operates through the discourse of sexuality not in terms of law, but normalization; not in terms of right, but technique; not in terms of punishment, but control.[31] This power is the object of an analytic of power, rather than a theory of power. "The definition of the specific domain which relations of power form and the determination of the instruments which make it possible to analyse it."[32] In formulating the method appropriate to a history of sexuality, *The History of Sexuality* presents, at the same time, a critique of power as normalization, technique, and social control.

The sexual body is revealed as an effect of power and knowledge. *The History of Sexuality* analyzes the sexualization of the body as the production of a specific type of desire. The discourse of sexuality is a definite desire to know. The sexual body, therefore, is a specific form of desire in which subjectivity is produced. *Madness and Civilization* and *Discipline and Punish* deal with the constitution of subjectivity in the confined and incarcerated body. *The History of Sexuality* plunges deeper into that morass by concentrating on the constitution of subjectivity in the self-consciousness of desire. If Hegel, in the *Phenomenology of Spirit*, saw the formation of a dialectic in the birth of self-consciousness's desire for the other, then Foucault sees the analytic of power subjected to political critique.

The sexualization of the body is the effect of power in the discourse of sexuality. In particular, it is the discourse in which the rising bourgeois class creates for itself a distinctive relationship to sexuality. For the symbolic significance of blood, the bourgeoisie substitutes an analytic of sexuality. Where the traditional aristocracy relied on parentage, the bourgeoisie employed heredity, eugenics, and degeneration. Sex for the bourgeoisie is the autosexualization of its body in which it affirms itself by raising the political price of its body.[33] What differentiated the bourgeoisie from other classes was not the quality of its sexuality, but the intensity of its repression.[34] At the moment when programs were being launched to repress incest in the rural population, psychoanalysis was aiding the bourgeoisie to discover incest in the midst of family relationships

---

[30] Foucault, *History of Sexuality*, 82. Compare the discussions of power and power and sovereignty and right in the West in "Two Lectures" (in *Power/Knowledge*, 95–96) and in "Power and Strategies" (in *Power/Knowledge*).
[31] Foucault, *History of Sexuality*, 89–90.   [32] *Ibid.*, 82 (translation altered).
[33] *Ibid.*, 123.   [34] *Ibid.*, 128 (translation altered).

and to liberate their incestuous desires. The price of repression is high, but affordable. The discourse of sexuality pays the price by proliferating a multitude of ways in which sexuality is tied to the value of life. The increase in the number of writings on health and long life attest to this coupling of the vigor of the body with political and economic hegemony. Here, for Foucault, is the social significance of repression.

The discourse of sexuality is not, therefore, a power exercised over other classes. It is a strategy in which the bourgeoisie develops its own sexuality first of all. The battle against sexual repression in the name of sexual freedom is part of the apparatus of repression. The theory of repression is part and parcel of the affective mechanism of sexuality. Repression is for the bourgeoisie a sign of the difference of its sexuality and sexualized body. The myth of repression is tied to the diffusion of the discourse of sexuality throughout the whole social body. In becoming generalized, in sexualizing the bodies of other classes, the myth of repression sets apart the bodies of the bourgeoisie. They are more repressed. The sexuality of the bourgeoisie is under a more intense interdict than is the sexuality of others. "Henceforth," Foucault writes, "social differentiation will be affirmed not by the 'sexual' quality of the body, but by the intensity of its repression."[35]

The analytic gaze of clinical medicine was made possible by the installation of death into the living, viable body; the power-knowledge of the discourse of sexuality is a prolongation of the monarchical power over life and death. For the monarch, the power over life is the power over death: "the right to put to death and let live."[36] This is juridico-discursive power. But, since the Classical Age and the *ancien régime*, the power to allow someone to live has taken the form of controlling life. In the Modern Age the power to put to death has been transformed into the power to make live, "a power that exerts a positive influence on life, that endeavors to administer, optimize, and multiply it, subjecting it to precise controls and comprehensive regulations."[37] This is bio-power, a politics in which the body is subject to the control of discipline and, as the subject of biological processes, to population controls.

In disciplinary controls, the body is viewed as a machine. In population controls, the body is the "mechanism of life" that can be channeled, increased, extended, and decreased. The body is the object of a political anatomy and of a bio-politics of population.[38] These are the two poles for the development of the power of life from which emerge the sexed body and the discourse of sexuality. In bio-power, the body, as the seat of biological processes, enters into history and knowledge as a specific

[35] *Ibid.*, 129.   [36] *Ibid.*, 136.   [37] *Ibid.*, 137.   [38] *Ibid.*, 139.

domain. The important phenomenon taking place in social history with the beginning of capitalism was not the ascetic morality that disparaged the body, but the entrance into power-knowledge of biological processes as the object of political techniques.[39] The knowledge of the body is gained through a pulverization of the body, a dispersion of the body into a multiplicity of political strategies and techniques.

Sexuality is the truth of desire. In the politics of life the truth of man is in question. The anthropological view of man is equally a descendant of madness,[40] of the discourse of sexuality, and of the politics of life. Man comes to occupy a biological space in which desire is turned into self-knowledge and humanity is in question. In contrast to Aristotelian man, a living being with the capacity for political existence, modern man, for Foucault, is "an animal whose politics places his existence as a living being in question."[41] This biological space is where the truth of man appears, not only because history is surrounded by biological events, but because biological life has taken a place in history. Biological life is the interior truth of humanity. Here *The History of Sexuality* joins *Madness and Civilization* and *The Order of Things*. In contrast to the Classical Age, in which man was viewed in relationship to truth, the Modern Age views humanity as truth taking shape within itself. Hence, the madman, finitude, and biological life are the figures which characterize modernity. But *The History of Sexuality* adds an important qualification. Biological life is where humanity is turned back upon itself. Where it becomes true, on the basis of a history infused with the techniques of knowledge and power. The truth of humanity and the possibility of an anthropological view of man as a living being is born in the development of a bio-power and bio-politics.

The analyses of the discourse of sexuality in *The History of Sexuality* depend, therefore, on an analysis of power and knowledge: a knowledge of life and a power over life at the limits of death. The sexed body, sex, is born in the politics of the discipline of the body and the control of populations.[42] Sexuality is the meaning inscribed on the body by the politics of life. In the case of psychonanalysis, the discourse of sexuality is a dematerialization of the body. It is an effacement of the body in a politics of desire dominated by the figures of law, the prohibition of incest, the Father-Sovereign. But the politics of life does not destroy the body. Rather *The History of Sexuality* takes the body's effacement as its object. "In any

---

[39] *Ibid.*, 141.
[40] Foucault, *Folie et Déraison: Histoire de la Folie à L'âge Classique*, 2nd ed. (Paris: Gallimard, 1972 (1962)), 535–547.
[41] Foucault, *History of Sexuality, Vol. 1*, 143.   [42] *Ibid.*, 145.

case," Foucault writes of this book, "the goal of the present study is to show how the affective mechanisms of power are articulated directly upon the body – upon bodies, functions, physiological processes, sensations, and pleasures."[43] The body is not merely the field in which the game of power is played out. The desire for sex is the effect of the discourse of sexuality, a sexuality affected by the power over life.

Sex is not an autonomous function of the body corrupted by power. Sex is a knowledge of sexuality that uses the findings of the biological sciences to normalize sexual behavior. In normalizing the sexual behavior of the body, in creating a norm against which the body will measure itself, sex interjects within the body the residue of power. Sexual instinct, thereby, becomes a power opposed to power; hence a force that must be forbidden and repressed. This sex is not an autonomous biological force, an instinct inherent in the body, a dynamism of pure nature. Sex is a theory.[44] It is a speculative and ideal construction, the result of a discourse of sexuality embedded in the strategies and techniques of power. Sex is not the body in its most intimate and secret parts, but a discursive body, a fractured and divided body, a body whose inner articulation of desire is a political pulverization.

The history of the material body proposed in the first volume of *The History of Sexuality* would expose the façade of an autonomous, unified, and integral sex for what it is: the result of a history in which the body is fractured by power. As instinct and function, as the generation of goals and meanings, sexuality is first of all conceived on the model of perversion, fetishism. Fetishism serves as the basis for the analysis of other deviations and for the way in which the sexual instinct is related to its object. Sexuality is under the reign of the norm and the power of normalization. In addition, in the affective mechanism of sexuality, sex appears against the background cast by the four great figures of sexuality: hysteria, onanism, fetishism, and coitus interruptus. In its knowledge of its sexuality, the body is divided against itself. It is dispersed among a range of phenomena objectified in the discourse of sexuality. Thus, within the strategies of the affective mechanism of sexuality, sex appears as a series of divisions "of whole and part, principle and lack, absence and presence,

---

[43] *Ibid.*, 151–152. *Dispositif* generally refers to the internal workings of a machine, such as a drive gear. Consequently, we have translated *dispositif de sexualité* as "affective mechanisms of sexuality." In addition to being more literal than "deployment of sexuality" in the standard English translation, affective mechanism also conveys the possible allusion on Foucault's part to the theory of desiring machines in Deleuze and Guattari's *Anti-Oedipus* (Gilles Deleuze and Félix Guattari, *Anti-Oedipus: Capitalism and Schizophrenia* [New York: Viking, 1977]). The translation has been so altered.
[44] Foucault, *History of Sexuality, Vol. 1*, 154–155.

excess and deficiency, by the function of instinct, finality, and meaning, of reality and pleasure."[45]

From *Madness and Civilization* to *The History of Sexuality* the body is cut to pieces and scattered over the field created by the strategies of political technology. The divided and fractured body is marked by the historical events of discourse, of power-knowledge, of politics, and of class struggle. Foucault's history, thereby, is material, not incarnational. The figure of Damiens at the beginning of *Discipline and Punish*, his flesh ripped by pincers and finally hacked apart, is, in a sense, an *Urleib*, a proto-Body, but not as the primeval source of all the meanings lived in the conscious experience of the social body. Damiens's body is the *Urleib* of politics in which anthropological and psychological man appeared. The soul and the consciousness of modern man are the dematerialization of the bodies of the madman, the sick, the imprisoned, and the repressed. But, even more, this body is also used like so many cobblestones to erect a barricade against death.

Power does not deal with death by repressing the consciousness of death, but by constructing a dialogue with death in which life is the object of power and knowledge. The two, power and death, belong together for Foucault, just as writing and death belong together for Blanchot, and death and sensuality for Bataille. The space in which consciousness and language can turn back over themselves and against death is a doubled space thrown up against death: the constant play of setting up limits and transgressing them, the play of mirrors at the heart of consciousness in which consciousness finds security in seeing itself seeing itself to infinity. Power-knowledge is the objectification of the body within the limits established by strategies. Is it not a technology whose inner passion is to indefinitely stave off the fatal sentence of death?

Death has a place in Foucault's writings because his historical analyses are political. Foucault's history charts the divisions, caesuras, reversals, and changes that are the specific configurations of power and knowledge. Politics involves a dialogue with death because death divides and fractures the body. Politics is not a tender caress that plays over the surface of the body. It disciplines and punishes the body, breaks it down into its parts in order to turn its natural forces into the instruments of its bondage. Politics installs death within the very core of the body's visibility, so that the truth of its visible surface is the black night of the corpse. Politics maintains power over life by transforming death into its private secret, suicide, and it infuses the body with a sexuality worth the price of death.

[45] *Ibid.*, 154.

The power and knowledge that politics uses are the horrifying images of death in history. And it is the transgression of the limits within which the circularity of language and consciousness makes possible, in history, a critical discourse by which the strategies and objectifications of power-knowledge can be analyzed.

Death is not an experience. It is an absence, a void. There is no reflection that can indirectly or directly discover signs of its plenitude, of its full presence. Without that discovery, death can never be an object of thought. To be face to face with death is not to be confronted with another visage. Death is the exterior space, the dissimulating time, in which subjectivity and the self cannot rejoin themselves in self-consciousness and self-knowledge. Death is not their object. Subjectivity and the self are not mirrored in death. Death is the disruption of the circularity of the self and subjectivity in the yawning of an unclosable rupture. To be face to face with death is for subjectivity to be dispersed into an indefinite space. Death is the absence of totality and plenitude. It is the sign of the failure of subjectivity to justify self-presence as the ground of being.

Power and knowledge are established in a space in which there is no balance of forces. There is no equilibrium in the relations of power and knowledge. The space in which death figures is an asymmetrical space in which the eruption of violence in social relations is the very measure of the imbalance death introduces. Truth cannot be the measured equilibrium of the forces at play between subjectivity and the world. The will to truth cannot be the intention to express that equilibrium. Installed in an asymmetrical space in which experience is made possible by what cannot be experienced, the will to truth must be violence. Knowledge must be power. Power must be objectivity. The scales of truth are only balanced by an act of violence in which the asymmetry of the space of power and knowledge is contorted into the image of a writhing serenity.

Death is the final fracturing of the body, the transgression of the living, visible body in which the body becomes an object of knowledge and the space for the maneuvers of power. *The Birth of the Clinic* describes this transgression. Life is objectified in terms of death and degeneration. And, in *Madness and Civilization*, death is also the power that madness yields. At the end of the fifteenth century, madness replaces the theme of death. *Praise of Folly* replaces Marchant's *Danse Macabre*. Death is not expunged from the world, but installed in the image of madness as, in the nineteenth century, it is in the living body. Death is no longer the limit of existence, but the object of mockery and derision. The substitution of madness for death gives death a tamed form, one in which the futility of existence is made concrete in the everyday experience of the world. "Death's annihilation is no longer anything because it was already everything, because life itself was only futility, vain words, a squabble of cap and bells. The head that will become a skull is already empty. Madness is the *déjà-là* of death."[46] This substitution is not a replacement, but a displacement of the same anxiety. The nothingness of existence, the futility of life, is no longer an external threat, but an interior doubt. The domination of the mad in the positivist asylum plays on the erosion of existence prefigured in madness and taking form in subjective guilt. In its ultimate antecedents psychological subjectivity derives from the twisted form – the "torsion within the same anxiety" – in which madness displaced death. The displacement of death into the figure of madness mirrors the contortion of the body in which the body becomes soul.

At every point where power is applied, there is an image of death. The confinement of the mad replaces the exclusion of the leper in *Madness and Civilization*. The plague is the image around which disciplinary power is organized in *Discipline and Punish*. In the application and development of power and knowledge the fear of death is mundanized and interiorized. The effectiveness of the strategies at work in power is not due to the fact that they exorcise death and allay anguish over the futility of life. Rather, these strategies work by their ability to mobilize that fear of death by objectifying death. The effectiveness of power is knowledge. And, the effectiveness of knowledge is the power to delimit objects by drawing around them the lines of nothingness. Power-knowledge makes objects visible by sketching their nothingness.

It is thus not toward nature that Foucault's conception of politics turns, but toward history. The space of the body is not only the space of historical events, but of historical events as the object of politics. Foucault's works must be read politically. Their truth is not their historical accuracy, but their confrontation of contemporary reality with its past. Out of that confrontation comes a new future. "What I am trying to do is provoke an interface between our reality and the knowledge of our past history. If I succeed, this will have real effects in our present history. My hope is my books become true after they have been written – not before."[47]

---

46 Foucault, *Madness and Civilization: A History of Insanity in the Age of Reason*, trans. and ed. Richard Howard (New York: Random House, 1965 [1961]), 24.

47 Foucault, "Interview with Millicent Dillon," *Three Penny Review* 1 (1) (1980): 5. Along the same lines, Foucault says in "The History of Sexuality: An Interview" (in *Power/Knowledge*, 193): "As to the problem of fiction, it seems to me to be a very important one; I am well aware that I have never written anything but fictions. I do not mean to say, however, that truth is therefore absent. It seems to me that the possibility exists for fiction to function in truth, for a fictional discourse to induce effects of truth, and for bringing it about that a true discourse engenders or 'manufactures' something that does not as yet exist, that is, 'fictions' it. One 'fictions' history on the basis of a political reality that makes it true."

Foucault's writings, then, are themselves political interventions. They strive to pry apart power-knowledge, to unmask the violence that has wed this couple.

Madness and Civilization, The Birth of the Clinic, The Order of Things, Discipline and Punish, and *The History of Sexuality* are then political works in two senses: they analyze the political complex of power-knowledge, and they are political interventions against power. The first, as we have seen, is the critical work of the historian. The second, a more direct political confrontation, involves the political work, and responsibility, of the intellectual.

11

Fernand Braudel and Immanuel Wallerstein and why globalization is a social geography of inequalities

As well he should be, Immanuel Wallerstein (1930–) is scornful of the term "globalization," as it has come to be used early in the 2000s. He and the French historian Fernand Braudel (1902–85) have for years, since at least 1949 when Braudel's first great book appeared, treated the world as a global geography of time – hence, of culture. Their ideas are not the same. But they converge on one point.

Braudel, beginning with his 1947 Sorbonne thesis, *La Méditerranée et le monde méditerranéen à l'époque de Philippe II*, was (among much else) the first to take seriously and to demonstrate the difference between worlds, as spheres of cultural organization, and global realities, as hard geographies with their own times thus independent of shorter-run cultural times. Wallerstein, beginning with the first volume of *The Modern World-System* in 1974, demonstrated that when social science gives up the idealized national society as its unit of analysis, then it is forced, against all of its liberal impulses, to take seriously the histories of the hard realities of global differences. If Braudel disabused history of its silly infatuation with the grand moments of political culture, Wallerstein disabused social science of its motivated ideology of the world as one, of which modernization theory is the principal offender. Together with the historians and social scientists in France, America, and the world that each in his own time influenced, Braudel and Wallerstein have, in effect, done for social science what, years before, Einstein did in 1905 for physics and Picasso in 1907 for culture, while Durkheim looked on thinking about collective representations.

Social things imagined are cultural geographies of social spaces – spaces that are uncertain, constantly shifting, continually at odds with each other. What the event history of classical positivism tried to do was to regularize history as the story of great men and the events they pretended to have caused. What all sociologies beholden to convictions like those held by Durkheim in Bordeaux tried to do was to broadcast the societal community of the nation-state unto the universal screen of global differences. Braudel and Wallerstein initiated and represent the resistance to social science as the ideology of one world – a world that can only be when the differences outside the scope of enlightenment are accepted for what they are. In the case of sociology among the social sciences one must use the word resistance, rather than revolution, because, unlike Durkheim himself, professional sociology has tenaciously held tight to its foundational attitudes against all the evidence of global realities that, instead of a societal community (even one or ones in tension and conflict), there are irreducible differences.

The relations between Wallerstein and Braudel are, therefore, of unique importance in understanding the history and future prospects of social science, including the sociologies of culture. In *Uncertainties of Knowledge* Wallerstein has said of the influences on his thinking:

I acknowledge a continuing intellectual debt to Marx, Freud, Schumpeter, and Karl Polanyi. Among persons, I have personally known and read very extensively, the three that have had the most impact in modifying my line of argument (as opposed to deepening a parallel line of argument) have been Frantz Fanon, Fernand Braudel, and Ilya Prigogine. And of course their influence occurred in that chronological order. Fanon represented for me the sharp culmination of the insistence by the persons left out of the modern world-system that they have a voice, a vision, and a claim not merely to justice but to intellectual valuation. Braudel made me conscious, as no one else did, of the central importance of a social construction of time and space, its impact on our analyses. And Prigogine forced me to face all the implications of a world in which certainties did not exist but knowledge did.

What strikes about the description of the three influences is the role of Braudel between the other two.

Fanon, on the side, not only called attention to the intellectual value of the colonized but, by being the Negro intellectual he signified the end of the language of the colonizer, which after all became the language of development theory. If the Negro can be an intellectual, then even the cleverest of the logics modern culture used to disguise its racism collapse. And, important to add, Fanon's international status as an intellectual was certified by his visible relations with Jean-Paul Sartre, of whom none was at the time more the embodiment of *the* intellectual. Thus, the more upsetting passages in *Wretched of the Earth* (and the ones white liberals skip over) are those in which Fanon says of the Negro intellectual that, in the post-colonial situation, he can only deal with Negritude by being the dirty nigger the white culture fears most.

The native intellectual decides to make an inventory of the bad habits drawn from the colonial world, and hastens to remind everyone of the good old customs of the people, that people which he has decided contains all truth and goodness. The scandalized attitude with which the settlers who live in the colonial territory greet this new departure only serves to strengthen the native's decision. When the colonialists who had tasted the sweets of their victory over these assimilated people, realize that these men whom they considered as saved souls are beginning to fall back into the ways of niggers, the whole system totters. . . . Each native who goes back over the line is a radical condemnation of the methods and of the regime; and the native intellectual finds in the scandal he gives rise to a justification and an encouragement to persevere in the path he has chosen. (Fanon, *Wretched of the Earth*, 221–222)

At the other side, the influence of the Ilya Prigigone (1917–2003), the Nobel Prize winning chemist, would seem odd, were it not for the fact that Prigigone's enduring achievement, known today as complexity or chaos theory, is the establishment of the principle that in all things, social as well as natural, non-equilibrium is more normal that equilibrium. In his own words:

Dynamics and thermodynamics become two complementary descriptions of nature, bound by a new theory of non-unitary transformation. . . . As we started from specific problems, such as the thermodynamic signification of non-equilibrium stationary states, or of transport phenomena in dense systems, we have been faced, almost against our will, with problems of great generality and complexity, which call for reconsideration of the relation of physico-chemical structures to biological ones, while they express the limits of Hamiltonian description in physics. . . . Indeed, all these problems have a common element: time. . . . Almost by instinct, I turned myself later towards problems of increasing complexity, perhaps in the belief that I could find there a junction in physical science on the one hand, and in biology and human science on the other. . . . In addition, the research conducted with my friend R. Herman on the theory of car traffic gave me confirmation of the supposition that even human behavior, with all its complexity, would eventually be susceptible of a mathematical formulation. In this way the dichotomy of the "two cultures" could and should be removed. There would correspond to the breakthrough of biologists and anthropologists towards the molecular description or the "elementary structures", if we are to use the formulation by Lévi-Strauss, a complementary move by the physico-chemist towards complexity. Time and complexity are concepts that present intrinsic mutual relations. (Ilya Prigigone, *Autobiography for the Nobel Prize*, 1977)

That time is complex, as opposed to linear, was known since 1905. What remained was to advance the notion that complexity, rather than being a short-run obstacle to knowledge, is an entity in and of itself – on a par with and mixed up in time. Or, as Wallerstein has described Prigigone's contribution:

Prigogone's position is the call for an "unexcluded middle" (determined order and inexplicable chaos) and is, in this regard, absolutely parallel to that of Braudel, who also rejects the two extremes presented as the exclusive antinomies of particularism and eternal universals, insists on orders (structural time) that inevitably undo themselves and come to an end. (Wallerstein, *The Uncertainties of Knowledge* (2004), 103)

Or, one might also say that Fanon was the particular whose determinate Negritude called into question of social universals of modern culture, and that Prigigone did the same with respect to physico-chemical universals, then Braudel fixed the terms and conditions of the particular and the universal in the sphere of social things. Wallerstein, granting that the three pursued independent lines of inquiry, fashioned world-systems analysis as (his word) a resistance to the orthodoxy whereby the world is viewed as one. Such a resistance requires a method that allows the particular to stand on its own terms. This cannot be done from within the centering confinements of essentializing cultures of the world as one – common humanity, family of man, and all that malarkey. To cede the particular its due is to concede that the universal is a metaphor of uncertain value. It has its value, but cannot be established as the exhaustive truth it seeks to be. Hence, against all odds, the parallel between Wallerstein and Derrida, behind the both of whom one can find Braudel lurking in the shadows – that structures are fine only if they are liberated from the constraining effects of an organizing center. The structurality of structures is that structuring is the uncertain play of particulars.

Thus the irony of Wallerstein's scheme portraying the global whole as a system structured around a series of hegemonic core states. The apparent certitude of this condition is qualified by the uncertainties of which it warns – that the periphery, having no final stake in the universal condition of man, will sooner or latter attack, one way or another. In the long run, Molotov cocktails trump smart bombs, which has proven to be the case, even when the cocktails take the form of crude oil pricing so pungent that not even the corporate greed of the core can refine away the putrid stink of the system.

Hence, also, Braudel's singular importance, as in effect the shifter between Fanon and Prigigone, was to name and describe the times of the global order, of which the most upsetting to tradition is the time of the long-duration – that is, the history of physical geography against which social history and the more immediate events of social life are set, fixed, and determined. *La longue durée* is the slowest of historical times and the one that stood behind Braudel's key idea, basic to Wallerstein, that social structures, like the Mediterranean world in the sixteenth century, are world-economies; or in the language of the 2000s, global structures. The time of natural history is necessarily global in that the particulars of local or regional places are not so much linked as micro to the macro of the global whole as dispersed upon the global surfaces – just as, beginning with the long sixteenth century, the economic trade system centered in the Mediterranean world was, by its nature, a system of global ambition.

Long-enduring time is slow. It is the time of faults, shifts, cleavages, crevasses, floods, ice, sand, wind, and all the other raw elements and effects of climate, biology, and the material spaces that mark the earth's surface before and during the time of human being. Social time is the somewhat faster time of social geography that develops in the conjuncture between the slow movement of physical geography and the more fragile, hence speedier, movement of social things. This is the time of what, since Braudel, has come to be recognized as the social history of ordinary life out from which is built the stable institutional structures that outlive the common and immediate even as they remain finite in their relations to the global surface.

A very old bell struck the hour in the small Lorraine village where I grew up as a child: the village pond drove an old mill wheel; a stone path, as old as the world, plunged down like a torrent in front of my house; the house itself had been rebuilt in 1806, the year of Jena, and flax used to retted in the stream at the bottom of the meadows. I only have to think of these things and this book opens out for me afresh. Every reader can do the same. (Braudel, *Capitalism and Material Life, 1400–1800*, 441)

True it is that every reader, every person, can if she would look out the door at stone paths, even if covered over, that are "as old as the world." She would look from a house built at some or another time, distant or near, but still not anywhere so distant as the earth and rock upon which it stands.

Then, tucked innocently in Braudel's recollection, there is the joke – the passing reference to Jena, the decisive battle in 1806 in which Napoleon crushed the Prussian army of Frederick William III. The joke – "the old house was rebuilt in 1806, the year of Jena" – made on the retrospect of time. The old house of childhood Braudel recalls was marked in memory for its year of reconstruction in 1806 which, by the way, was during one of the most important military events of modern European history on a field that, like the house's stone path, is as old as the world. The method puts the fast time of military battles, diplomatic decisions, nation-building, economic markets, and all the other episodes to which traditional positivist history is drawn into uncertain relation with the slower time of social history in which houses and mills are built, used, then rebuilt or abandoned, which in turn occur ever so slowly against the backdrop of streams and paths cut out of the ages of geographical time which are hardly measurable at all from any point with the passings of local events at Jena or wherever.

Then, of course, there is Braudel himself, recalling the scene of childhood later in life. At the time of the recollection, he would have twenty years to live – a lifetime for many, but by the measure of the time of the childhood house rebuilt in 1806 alongside a stone path as old as the world, the time then remaining to him, like the time remaining to any of us, would be but an instant – an imponderable instant. This precisely is the time of social science. Social science might be said to be the time of a present ever fading into the times it looks upon – times that cannot be seen as such because they move, like the stars and rocks, at different speeds against the paths and battlefields that themselves no longer appear for what they were at their crucial moments in some grand or minor social history. There are times as rock certain as anything can be, but when viewed (if that is the word) as social things they are dispersed and deferred like the *global* things that since forever were behind the phantasmagorias of enlightenment – always necessarily moving at different speeds, establishing the inherent inequalities of social things.

The system of future worlds: can the modern outlive the capitalist world-system? (2003*)

The most curious thing about postmodernism – a subject of endless discussion and reckless confusion – is that, though it is treated by many as if it were a theoretical thing, the postmodern question is interesting only to the extent that it invites *empirical* answers, not *theoretical* ones.[1] The logic here is so plain that one wonders how the whole discussion got turned in the wrong direction: If a *post-* can be meaningfully prefixed to *modern* or *modernity* (or its cultural forms, *modernism*), then it must be that the prefix enters public discussion because someone somewhere recognizes, at the least, that something important may have changed with respect to the historical forms identifed as modern. There cannot be a *post-* anything unless the thing itself, real by some or another accord, is thought to have changed. One needs to believe that it has – or, if one believes such he need not believe that the thing is unalterably or definitively changed. All that is necessary – and it really is necessary – for proper use of the prefix *post-* with respect to any certifiably historical thing is that thing be different either in fact or in form or in the illusions it creates to what all along people thought it had been.

This, it seems to me is the only serious attitude one can honestly adopt when considering the question of the postmodern – a term that, by the way, has been used and abused for a long while, since at least Daniel Bell in the 1950s, for all manner of political and ideological purposes. Thus, it is surprising that the one school of thought that has done the most both to describe the political and economic history of the modern world is not more often looked upon, either by its adherents or its opponents, as a resource with respect to the postmodern question. All the more since, as

* Reprinted with permission from *New Theoretical Directions for the Twenty-first Century of World-Systems Analysis*, edited by Wilma Dunaway (Westport, CT: Greenwood Publishing, 2003). The paper was originally presented in April 2001 at the 25th Annual International Congress of the World-Systems Analysis Section at Virginia Tech University. The essay has been cut to eliminate a number of references that applied to members of the World-Systems Analysis group.
[1] Charles Lemert, *Postmodernism Is Not What You Think* (Oxford: Basil Blackwell, 1997).

in the following I attempt to demonstrate, those writers associated with the description of the modern world system have also been chief among its critiques, thus prophets of its decline. Plus which, even more, those French social thinkers who are most often thought of as postmodern theorists are in fact theorists because they have a definite empirical view of the way the world has changed (or ought to change) – though without having evidence, much less thinking of themselves, or their theories, as postmodern. Most notable, though by no means alone on the former horn of the dilemma is Immanuel Wallerstein. Most striking for his historical work among those on the latter horn is Michel Foucault. Taking them each for what they are and have been, without reducing them each to the other either by intent or analogy, it is of even greater interest in that in important ways both are indebted, though differently, to the same French social historian.

Foucault was, in fact, less a theorist than, above all else, a historian. He was heir to the influences of his youth in Paris, which (among much else) accounts for his having opposed the neoclassical, positivist methods of event history. In this he was, more or less, a proponent of the kind of history that displaced the famous into their relations with the ordinary, and the ordinary into the normal life relations with the natural envelope around the tissue-thin layer of human endeavor – with, that is, nature, climate, physical geography, and the like. When put this way, it is apparent that Foucault's approach was close kin to the method of the *Annales* historians, of Braudel most notably.[2] Or, more cautiously, it is fair to say that Braudel's *La Méditerranée et le monde méditerranéen à l'époque de Philippe II* (originally published in 1949)[3] was as much the locus classicus of the French Revolution in social thought as was Heidegger's *Sein und Zeit* (originally published in 1927).[4]

Much the same could be said of others of Foucault's literary (as opposed to biographical) generation in France, particularly Barthes, Lacan, Bourdieu, Derrida, Deleuze, and Baudrillard. Though the precise filaments connecting this group made passingly famous by the special issue of *Théorie d'ensemble* of 1968 are devilishly difficult to trace, the astonishing rupture they fashioned may be said to be traceably formed by the shifts of the immediately previous generation of literary figures, of

---

[2] Though there are surely other, and better, works on the subject of Foucault's relations to Braudel, the one with which I am most familiar is: Charles Lemert and Garth Gillan, *Michel Foucault: Social Theory and Transgression* (New York: Columbia University Press, 1982).

[3] Fernand Braudel, *The Mediterranean and the Mediterranean World in the Age of Philip II* (New York: HarperCollins, 1972).

[4] Martin Heidegger, *Being and Time*, trans. J. Macquerrie and E. Robinson (New York: Harper, 1962).

which Braudel was a moving force.[5] If Foucault's can be called the generation of the 1960s, then Braudel's might be the generation of the 1940s, or more exactly that fraction of the generation that lived through the Resistance on its own terms by resisting the subjectivist appeal of the existential hero in favor of a more deliberate, if occasionally objectivist, structuralism. The debt of the former to the latter came down in various ways. At times the gift was drawn on oppositional accounts, as in Derrida's famous critique of Lévi-Strauss which led to the structuralism/post-structuralism dispute, just as Lévi-Strauss's critique of Sartre helped define the subjectivist/objectivism dilemma. In other instances, the patrimony was handed down more directly but with a dramatic flourish of application, as in Emmanuel Lévinas's reconsideration of Heidegger or in Althusser's of Canguilheim and Bachelard and in Hyppolite's of Hegel. In still other instances, the reach of the younger generation was very much over the immediate elders of the *champs*, as in Lacan's return to Freud by means of a largely idiosyncratic semiotic, or Bourdieu's leapfrogging of Raymond Aron in the shaping of his creative mélange of Weber, Durkheim, and Marx, or Barthes's very early rethinking of classical semiotics and Saussure.[6] There were many means for the establishment in the 1960s of a new generation of French social thought. Most borrowed heavily, but none more lavishly than Foucault's assortment of takings from Nietzsche, Bataille, Hyppolite, Canguilheim, Dumézil, Freud, Blanchot, and others.[7] But where Foucault or anyone of this emergent generation was a historian, he and they were of the *Annales* tradition, if not exactly of the school.

Quite apart from the obvious and explicit debt world-system analysis and the yet-to-be-properly-named period of French social theory owed to Braudel, both also have in common a debt to what may be called the cultural conjuncture of the world revolution of 1968. The popular name for the political and cultural effects of that conjuncture is, of course, *decentering*. Though susceptible to misuse, decentering is, at the very least, vastly better than *deconstruction* (which term is hopelessly beyond salvation) and, at the most, is a passable way to cover the complicated structural shift in culture and world politics associated with the 1960s.

The decentering of social thought from its classical metaphysical and cryptometaphysical reliance on an organizing principle was always

[5] The reference is to a special 1968 edition of the journal *Tel Quel* in which many of the soon-to-be leaders of the new wave of social theory published manifestos of one or another kind.

[6] For these theoretical derivations and critiques, see: Charles Lemert, ed., *French Sociology* (New York: Columbia University Press, 1981).

[7] Lemert and Garth Gillan, *Michel Foucault*.

well-understood from within the tradition of the then new French social
thought to be the result not so much of a change of the collective mind as
of an overwhelming of the modernist *mentalité* by the shifts in geopolitical
history that allow, even invite, Wallerstein to use the locution "world revolution of 1968." This is not the place to go into the history and the details,
but the point itself can be made in a propositional inventory, stated (not
entirely facetiously) as a series of series – as, in Deleuze and Guattari's
alternative to the genealogical metaphor, a plateau upon plateaus arising
not from meanings but from forces beyond but appropriate to the refusal
to set cultural and material things into analytically autonomous states of
being.[8] Hence:

- *Insofar* as decentering entails critiques of the Subject, of Being, of
  Event History, of the Unconscious–Conscious dichotomy, of the Voice
  as full of meaning, of science as truth, of the objectivist-subjectivist
  dichotomy, *inter alia*;
- *then* also decentering entails critiques of the Nation-State as the unit of
  analysis.
- *If this, then,* decentering is a sufficient if not necessary name for the
  work of Foucault, Deleuze, Derrida, Lacan, Barthes, Derrida, Bourdieu, *inter alia*;
- *then also*: Wallerstein.

Put this way, we can appreciate, at one and the same time, the two sides of
the inconvenience of a slogan like "postmodernism" to the more serious
and prior events that were part of, without fully exhausting, the global
conjuncture of structural shifts in 1968 to which the term *decentering*
refers ever more aptly.[9]

It would be outright foolishness to suggest that the names in my series
refer to thinkers who are in accord about the essentials of social thought.
Indeed, the preoccupations that form the series of methodological turns
are wildly out of kilter with each other. But it would not be quite so silly to
say that the preoccupations that form the previous series of methodological turns are wildly out of kilter with each other. In fact, even so crude a
formulation as this one suggests the single most important provocation of
the cultural conjuncture. It remains less a new theory of the world as such
than it was a complication of the methodological default whereby, for the
duration of modernist culture, it was assumed that method is merely a
matter of technique because truth was simply a matter of discovery.[10]

[8] Gilles Deleuze and Félix Guattari, *A Thousand Plateaus: Capitalism and Schizo-Phrenia*,
trans. Brian Massumi (Minneapolis: University of Minnesota Press, 1987).
[9] Lemert, *Postmodernism Is Not What You Think*.
[10] In short, truth is simply a dream of reason. Or to put it another way, words are words,
not realities.

If you doubt that this series of thinkers (several of whom might even recoil at the thought of it) could form a tangent, if not a parallel, to the series of methodological ideas (to, that is, a cultural conjuncture), consider one of the key passages in *The Modern World-System I*. It was only in the concluding epilogue that Wallerstein abandoned his strict objection to theory as a thing sufficient unto itself.[11] Yet in that one place, he states with definitive clarity the underlying and enduring principles of the analytic method he was just then inventing. The first of those principles is his most basic critique of the modern capitalist political economy: that its economic gains are advanced against the *externalization* of the costs of doing business in a global marketplace. These costs, he explains, are borne by the private sector at the insistence of the nation-state through taxation directly and through elevated (often regulated) prices indirectly. Hence, the central idea that the world-system is global in nature while being centered on one of a series of core states. Or more *abstractly*: capitalist economics requires a pseudodemocratic polity. Or more *methodologically*: the global unit of analysis reveals the trickery of the nation-state's false status as the unit of political participation. Or more *traditionally* (after Marx): what presents itself as human nature (the democratic state) is revealed for what it is (the avaricious greed of capitalism). Though indebted especially in its early formulation to Marx, these first principles of the new analytic method were no less indebted to the French conjuncture, and nowhere more so than in the key passage on culture that follows the discussion of externalization of costs and the perverse centrality of the nation-state in the capitalist world-system:

While, in an empire, the political structure tends to link culture with occupation, in a world-economy the political structure tends to link culture with spatial location. The reason is that in a world-economy the first point of political pressure available to groups is the local (national) state structure. Cultural homogenization tends to serve the interest of key groups and the pressures build up to create cultural-national identities.[12]

Then, immediately after, follows the single most succinct statement of the famous core/periphery/semiperiphery scheme.

The title of the epilogue, "Theoretical Reprise," is itself a bit surprising for an author who in subsequent years would insist that world-system analysis is not a theory. Quite apart from the fact that the underlying scheme for the analysis of the capitalist world-system is *taken* as a theory,

---

[11] Immanuel Wallerstein, *The Modern World-System 1: Capitalist Agriculture and the Origins of the European World-Economy in the Sixteenth Century* (New York: Academic Press, 1974), 347–354.

[12] *Ibid.*, 349.

Wallerstein's insistence arises, one supposes, less because of a reluctance to suffer association with what was going on in Paris at the time, than from the experience of brutal confusions of then reigning traditions of *sociological theory* in American sociology in general, and Columbia University in particular. In retrospect, one of the surprises of sociology in the last quarter-century of the previous millennium is that it came down, as I said earlier, so oddly on the Nixonian side of the barriers – professing liberal principles while calling the campus cops. Wallerstein himself was famously on the student side of the trouble during April and May of 1968 in Morningside Heights. When Wallerstein insists that he does not consider world-system analysis a theory, he is situating his work against the then, and sadly still, prevailing mechanisms of official sociology whereby the tidy little goal of "explaining the world" by reference to causal logics of a very linear sort turned out to be little more than a cosy portico that kept academic sociology out of the controversies of the day – embroiled, instead, in local technical discussions that led nowhere.

It should not, therefore, shock anyone that many of the experiments in sociological theorizing that marked the years in and around 1968 (experiments that replayed older philosophical principles from Husserl to Weber as phenomenological and/or critical sociologies) either fell by the wayside or otherwise into a rut. Of all the experiments of that era, only two have endured as ways of rethinking the modern world by calling into question that world's most fundamental organizing principle – the subtle but ubiquitous myth that the world is a centered reality.

If it is true that Derrida's notorious 1966 lecture at Johns Hopkins was the first fully articulated call for the decentering of modern culture, then it could just as well be said that Wallerstein's *Modern World-System I* was the first fully articulated critique of the modern world as an economic machine. And, if true, then it is not too far wrong to say that the tradition in Paris to which Derrida belongs transposed Nietzsche's critique of European manners into a critique of the global aspirations of European culture. And, *mutatis mutandis*, Wallerstein transposed Marx's critique of capitalist exploitation as rooted in a European mode of production into the critique of capitalism as a mode of externalization of the costs of production onto a global periphery. Marx aimed to destroy the ideas of the nineteenth-century political economists by shifting the analysis from their emphasis on the visible marketplace to his focus on the hidden-from-view shop floor of production. In this, Marx kept the fourfold analytic terms of nineteenth-century political economy: production, distribution, exchange, and consumption. But in so doing Marx ignored, as did they, and as do their heirs in the World Bank today, the insidious fact that ownership of the means of production lies not in the *camera obscura* of

European liberal democracies, but in the ever more hidden realities of sixteenth-century Europe's reliance on its own world trade triangle in which trading in slaves from the periphery was at one and the same time the pure, original form for exploiting *both* the resource means *and* labor power of the global marketplace.

Thus it happened that, among other extratheoretical contributions, the analysis of the world-system covered the two flanks exposed by the then-prevailing critical theories of the academic left. On the French hand, as powerful as those new theories were, they were, with the exception of Foucault's, not empirical – at least not in ways that would permit a direct influence on social science. On the Marxian hand, the Marxism of the day (just then coming into its own in the United States) was deeply wedded to its own modernist principles of the universal class, the classless revolution, the binary class contradiction, the mono-causal mode of production, and the like. As a result, those French theories had less impact on empirical social science than they might have while Marxism made deep inroads at the cost of maintaining its own resistance to decentering.[13] While it could not be said (or at least I would not say it) that world-system analysis escaped the normal limitations of the day, it did in fact introduce a powerful critique of the modernist social sciences of the Center that prevails, even today, in the academy and in policy-making. Of course, I am referring here to the conundrum of the time – that just as the United States was the political Center, so too was American sociology close to the cultural Center in the academy. To be an American sociologist was not necessarily to be American. In any case, the generation of sociologists in France (then taking up the space created but soon to be vacated by Aron) made youthful travels to the United States and often to Columbia University. One curious result was that, with the possible exceptions of Bourdieu and Alain Touraine and a few others, most of these French sociologists kept their distance from the new theoretical movements in Paris.[14] More interesting still is that, in the United States, Wallerstein stood clearly as the only existing bridge between American sociology and French social thought.

---

[13] I can offer two instances of this trend. First, several prominent Marxists from the old days currently chair sociology departments that enforce rigid entrepreneurial standards for promotion and hiring. The second example is the journal of Alvin Gouldner, perhaps the discipline's last truly critical Marxist. From time to time, even that publication is preoccupied with the goal of becoming the profession's most prestigious journal.

[14] Raymond Boudon, and many in his circle, spent a year or more at Columbia. Michel Crozier's work over the years has been decidedly affected by American sociology's tradition of industrial and organizational studies. Even Bourdieu had visited the United States, perhaps at the insistence of his predecessor and one-time mentor, Raymond Aron. One of the more interesting organizational conduits for French–American exchange is the Société Tocqueville. For some of the details, see: Lemert, ed., *French Sociology*, ch. 1.

In the retrospect of the events of the new millennium, this turns out to be a strikingly important fact of sociological life. In the years since 1968, American sociology has, for the most part, held rigidly to its duplicitous Nixon-like strategy of liberal rhetoric and revisionist practices. What there was of consistently critical and persuasive empirical sociology was largely the work of the world-system tradition and its affines, including writers like Charles Tilly and Theda Skocpol, among others associated with the study of social movements, revolution, and state formation. Though there were exceptions (such as cultural studies, feminist, and ethnic studies), none was as consistently *both* an empirical study and a critical theory of the half-millennium of the capitalist world-system. Even though cultural and feminist studies, as they evolved in the late 1970s, were both critical and empirical, neither was consistently global and structural in its approach to modernity.[15]

Thus, while the importance of world-system analysis was slowly and necessarily recognized in the academic social sciences, its extramural significance was perhaps even greater, though generally repressed for cause. The cause, of course, was the suffocating dominance of modernization theory over the foreign policies of the core states and their semiperipheral allies. Modernization theory is the preposterously influential idea that the world of nations might be arrayed along an imputed historical axis of economic development understood to be that form of capital productivity that takes off only when there is a sufficient level of capitalist culture in the "undeveloped" states.[16] Modernization theory has been, over a good bit of the last century, the most important ideology behind the West's geopolitical strategy. It has also been, not coincidentally, a leading ideology of the modern world as *centered*. What else is the modernization dogma if not a recasting of the global economy according to an unstated moral standard whereby so-called underdeveloped nations are judged by the extent to which they approximate the cultural and economic conditions of the Center? For the last three decades, world-system analysis has generated the most important empirical works that have informed the opposition to the foreign policy establishment, including the International Monetary Fund and the World Bank. No doubt that is why in those circles the work is so systematically ignored even when it is well understood.

Still, the suggestion of these affinities leaves open at least two questions. For one, how can any analytic method that relies so heavily on the

---

[15] Which is not to say that there were no works of this sort, but that many of them came late in the game, notably Stuart Hall: Stuart Hall, ed., *Modernity: An Introduction to Modern Societies* (Oxford: Basil Blackwell, 1996).

[16] For example: W. W. Rostow, *Stages of Economic Growth* (Cambridge: Cambridge University Press, 1971).

principle of the organizing core serve as kin of some kind to the explicitly decentering philosophies of the French tradition, much less as a critique of modernization theory? And, for the second: Is not the world-system scheme itself a variant of the same functionalist principles that led to modernization theory in the 1950s? Of course, this second complaint is easily answered by the record – by the fact that the work, whatever one thinks of the scheme, has been that critique both by its content and its influence.

The former question is somewhat more complicated, if only because Wallerstein himself has not entered into the theoretical controversy – at least not directly. What is at issue here is the question of the limits of critical tools when the object of criticism has itself taught, shaped, and determined the critic. Or to borrow the famous line from Audre Lorde: "Can one dismantle the master's house with the master's tools?"[17] Can one, that is, critique the modern world-system with the very analytic tools that the system has itself invented and diffused? Here I think world-system analysis is a bit vulnerable. Its deep references to units of analysis, the analytic ideal itself, the world as a system, and to the development/underdevelopment nomenclature are beholden (even when they are used with irony) to the tradition's respect for social science which itself is very much a modernist principle. Of course, I admit that when the question is asked this way, it is asked very much as a theorist would.

Accordingly, the answer to this complaint could be much the same as that to the other – namely, the proof is in the pudding. To offer just one example, it was exceedingly important to raise the ante on sociology's *unit of analysis* from the nation-state to the global whole. And tactically in the 1970s and 1980s, it was prudent to use the rhetoric of science (whether seriously or ironically). Then one could hardly train students for jobs in the social sciences from within any other (if you'll pardon the expression) discursive practice. In the era of sociology when liberal or left values were little more than rhetoric, world-system analysis deployed radical values in decidedly concrete and hard-to-dismiss ways. By describing the world-system for what it was, capitalism was revealed for what it truly is. World-system analysis, whatever one thinks of its science rhetoric, told the truth that few others on the left had barely begun to describe. Modern capitalism is not at all a *progressive* order of good and better-off peoples who suffer mild, but sincere, liberal regret that the poor on their periphery fail consistently to heed the missionary message of the spirit of capitalism. Behind all of its liberal pretenses, capitalism is, in fact, a system of global exploitation that advances the better-off with no more

---

[17] Audre Lorde, *Sister Outsider* (Trumansburg, NY: Crossing Press, 1984).

than financial interests in the people and resources of the periphery it must maintain. Even when put this crudely, the critique stings. One can hardly imagine that a field agent of the World Bank does not understand somewhere in his heart of hearts that the extreme suffering in Somalia or Mozambique is a result, instead of a cause, of the core's monetary policy. Liberals are a bit callous, to be sure; but they are not stupid.

One might suggest, even, that though world-system analysis is very serious business, the deployment of "analysis" as the key word to distinguish the work from "theory" is probably more ironic than most outsiders (and many insiders) suppose. To produce the analysis that results in a critique of the modernist culture is both heroic and a kind of turning of the master's tool against his house. In this sense, world-system analysis may well be an exception to Audre Lorde's rule. But if it is, this is apparent nowhere more powerfully than in its ability to anticipate, see, and interpret the events of 1989–91 with absolute clarity. While American political heirs of Nixon in the Reagan–Bush regime of 1980–92 were proclaiming the end of the evil empire and the emergence of a new world order, Wallerstein was among the first to see *The End of the World as We Know It*.[18] Today there are numerous books with similar titles. Still no one saw this End sooner than did Wallerstein (unless it was the French theorists who as early as the 1960s stipulated it as a condition of their enterprise). To predict an ending is one thing, but to be able to see when it occurs is quite another.

But of what did this cognition consist? Simply: in the ability to recognize that the capitalist world-system elaborates and advances a theory-of-itself. This, of course, is the immediate and necessary entailment of the original theory of culture found at the end of Wallerstein's *Modern World-System I*.[19] If this world-system is distinguished from empires by the linking of culture to nationalized territories, then it follows that such a link is forged only as a theory of nationalizing cultures presented as though they were the universal truth itself. Wallerstein offers four distinguishing features of modernity's theory-of-itself. None is surprising, but all are subjected to their proper criticism: (1) the free market, (2) state sovereignty, (3) equal citizenship rights, and (4) value-neutral science.[20] In an essay such as this one, it may even seem a bit absurd to enunciate the list. Yet it is important to remind readers that discussions like this one do not occur in the Oval Office or in the lesser roundtables

---

[18] Immanuel Wallerstein, *The End of the World as We Know It: Social Science for the Twenty-First Century* (Minneapolis: University of Minnesota Press, 1999).
[19] Wallerstein, *The Modern World-System 1*.
[20] I take liberties with Wallerstein's points, which are presented in Wallerstein, *The End of the World as We Know It*, ch. 2.

of public opinion where, for the most part, these principles are taken literally as the truth behind the embodiment of the core state that sponsors the roundtables.

Hence, the criticisms of the capitalist world-system's fourfold theory of itself, though in the light of day so obviously to the point, are treated by the general public as if they were, if not quite treasonous, at least unpatriotic. This is to be understood because what Wallerstein does is to peel back the capitalist system's veil of righteousness to expose the nakedness of its cultural myth: (1) that the free market requires state power to enforce or create the actually existing monopolies necessary for profit; (2) that state sovereignty depends always and necessarily on an interstate system; (3) that equality of citizenship rights is an illusion of which the reality is in constant flux in order to disguise the essentially binary and unequal distribution of rights; (4) that value-neutral science is, no less than the others, a myth that serves, among other things, to buttress the appearance of universality attributed to what is in fact a historically local theory of the culture of modernity.

Such a culture is, in and of itself, little more than the modern world-system's theory of itself. In point of fact, the social scientific concept *culture* came into its own in the nineteenth century, just as the world-system was solidifying its late modern form as a system of industrialized states in ever more urgent need of peripheral resources. At the least it is accurate to say that the industrial and post-industrial period of the modern world-system – from say Hobsbawm's age of capital[21] through the outer limits of George Bush the elder's new world order; from, that is, 1848–1991 – was a phase in which the revealing strains of what Wallerstein calls capitalism's dirty secrets[22] became more and more acute. Thus, as the secrets were told, the core of the world-system was forced to exert more and more control over its periphery precisely when control was more difficult to assert.[23] If the capitalist world-system depends on the *externalization* and *democratization* of its costs of production in order to assure profit, then it follows that as (first) the urban populations within the core states are becoming politically more heterogeneous and that as (second) the decolonization of the periphery renews post-colonial resistance to the colonizing culture, then global politics will invite resistance

---

21 E. J. Hobsbawm, *The Age of Capital, 1848–1875* (New York: Mentor Books, 1979).
22 Wallerstein, *The End of the World as We Know It.*
23 This seems an appropriate moment to express my appreciation for several conversations with Immanuel Wallerstein and for his work as a whole, from which I have borrowed many ideas. I plead guilty to having read him for so long that I have embraced him as the Newton to my physics, or at least to what I may know about global political economy.

to the political, as well as cultural, demands of the core, that is, the system itself.

Consider, for just one current example, the now likely prospect that the externalization of the environmental costs of industrial production will achieve a cross-over point at which private capitalism's unwillingness to pay for the clean-up will produce a state of capital entropy, if not atrophy. If, for example, each day Hong Kong alone belches 26,000 tons of carbon dioxide into the global atmosphere, at no important cost to private enterprises responsible for the belching, does not the system come eventually to a point where the declining natural resources and the atmospheric poisons meet the limit of the nation-state's ability to insure capitalism's need to put off payment of its real costs? When that happens, will not the system itself fail or at least cease to grow? It may be that through the long duration of the capitalist world-system, the Kondratieff cycles signal the rise and fall of profits and corporate wealth. But still it must be asked whether or not it is possible that, if we are indeed facing the end of the world as we know it, whether that end does not mean necessarily the end of prospects for cyclical fluctuations? This consideration would necessary mean the end of the world-system, not just as a culture of itself or as a political masquerade for economic secrets, but as the end of the system itself, including the economic possibilities for capitalist profit.

I call upon the ghost of maximum entropy because it seems to me entirely possible that the events of 1989–91 (not to mention 2001) have, in their growing urgency, posed the nasty prospect that social science will return to its foundational ideal. This would amount, in effect, to a return of Nixon's ghost, thus confirming the suggestion that Nixon was in fact, if not the father, at least the godfather of the Bush regimes. Braudel's most enduring contribution may well have been the idea that social history takes place within the limits and upon the surface of the earth's natural surfaces. If so, then, under present conditions, the very ideal of social science as a science of the human may well come to the end of its line just at the moment when (and because of) the human itself is at risk of being swallowed up by what it has wrought in Nature. This possibility is encouraged by the fact that we speak today less of a *world* (which, etymologically, is an ancient term for describing the imagined community of *this*-worldly as opposed to *other*-worldly life) than a globe. Global things are first and foremost physical ones – that is, the globe is the sphere (quite literally) upon which social things seek temporarily to colonize locales for their own purposes, until such time as the land runs fallow or the waters dry or, in our day, the air putrid.

Hence, to conclude, it is necessary to consider the prospect that there will be no system to future worlds. In the state of maximum economic entropy all profits are in the short run, as the limits to growth become the defining feature of the global landscape. This, then, invites the further consideration that the ironic use of scientific figures of speech in the tradition of world-system analysis may itself be open to inspection. Put otherwise, there is in effect a fifth myth at the foundation of modernity's theory-of-itself, namely: that the world is itself intelligible. Perhaps, in a sense, one could say that the fourth myth of a value-neutral science is but a desideratum of the principle of the intelligibility of the world. Science, whether social or otherwise, is that aspect of the culture of the modern world-system that asserts, with impunity and without commentary, the underlying supposition that the system requires in order to operate as it means to. To describe, or to imply, that the modern world is systemic in nature is the first requirement of the assertion of the naturalness of the colonial system that issued from the explorations and settlements early in the long sixteenth century only to be transposed into an almost pure culture of economic reality in the globalizing arm waving at the end of the short twentieth century. What else is the information age but a high cultural expression for the reality that there would not be a global network of information transfers were it not for the nation-state's interest in protecting and building the information highways for good business?

At the beginning of *Seeing Like a State*, James Scott offers what to me is a far more persuasive account for the foundational culture of capitalism than Benedict Anderson's *Imagined Communities*.[24] According to Scott, it was not newspapers, but bills of lading that gave rise to the modern state. Without the standardization of weights and measures, trade between locales and, eventually, within the global system of national communities would never have been possible. To the extent that Marx is right to say that production is more profound than exchange, the fact is that the political economists of the early nineteenth century helped invent modernity's theory-of-itself by pointing to this fundamental fact. There can be no capital production, whether in a national or global system, without markets; and no markets without exchange; and no exchange without a standard and universal system of measures. The modern world-system was, if I may borrow loosely from Jim Scott, first of all mathematical, before it could be a global economy sufficient unto a theory-of-itself. Just

---

[24] James Scott, *Seeing Like a State* (New Haven: Yale University Press, 1996). Benedict Anderson, *Imagined Communities: Reflections on the Origin and Spread of Nationalism* (London: Verso, 1983).

as the early explorers invented and imposed the coordinates of longitude as a condition for exploration, so too the early colonizers required and imposed weights and measures as the coordinates for global markets, beginning with the slave markets in Bristol and Charleston.

Science, including social science, was one of the beneficiaries of capitalism's functional need for the rational means for standard measures. Thus it is that the capitalist world-system is itself a product of the analytic needed to cut the world into parts.[25] Just as longitude – as opposed to latitude – is a completely arbitrary system of analytic cuts, so too are prices and market values little more than the social measures of currently marketable fads. If these, then too: social science is the short-run work necessary unto an account of the arbitrarily cut-upon world. In short, if somewhat shorthandedly, social science requires variables, which require concepts, which require the analytical reorganization of real things into socially arbitrary ones like *developed/underdeveloped*. Such categorical distinctions as these, without which one could not possibly think scientifically, are in fact much like the weights and measures to which Scott refers.[26] They are the condition and the consequence for a world trade triangle and for a world-system in which some people are cut off from others in order to be pressed into service for the mining and harvesting of physical and natural resources which are themselves analytically cut off from the sphere of the human societies that require nature, as much for sheer survival as for profit-making.

Though much has been said in the name of social science to advance the *analysis* of the *world-system*, the underlying fact may be that, all seriousness aside, the terms are ironic. Were they held in utter literalness, then it would have been impossible to expose so sharply the myths of the modern system's theory-of-itself, much less the substantial facts of its own global exploitations done in the name of liberal good will. Since in fact the undressing has been done for all to see, then at least one must consider this bold body of social science as itself, certainly not a trick or a joke, but still as an irony of ironies. Of all the social ideas, including the many theories and methods, none has so well described the end of the capitalist world-system, and the reasons for its ending. If so, then does not this urgently important accomplishment also entail the prospect that future worlds, such as they may be, will lack all the system qualities that the mathematized modern system founded itself upon?

---

[25] I develop this in detail in: Charles Lemert, *Dark Thoughts: Race and the Eclipse of Society* (New York: Routledge, 2002), esp. chs. 1 and 2.
[26] Scott, *Seeing Like a State.*

Whether world-system analysis itself will outlast the capitalist world-system remains to be seen. If it does, it will survive as that same irony that world-system analysis has so cunningly created. It will persist as a dialectical discourse through which one can examine the system of analytic worlds by applying from within an analytic tool that is held loosely in the hand in order to preserve sufficient energy, after the pounding, to pick up the pieces of global things that they might be put back together, however unsystematically.

Postscript:
What culture is not

Culture, like money, is time. Like money, culture is always a structured system of values meant for exchange between and among social others. Values are meanings. Meanings, when signified, are signified over time, however fractional. The illusion of speech is that the face-to-face is an effective co-presence through which time does not pass. But writing trumps speech, as Derrida and Barthes realized (and Saussure did not), because the written letter (even today) broadcasts its meaningful signs over the space of deferral. As the gift must be repaid in time, after a while, as Mauss and Bourdieu taught, so too are meanings in discourse limited by the destructive urge to give back in the instant. Co-presence violates the fundamental law of social time that nothing is immediate with anything else.

Every thing, little and big, moves in its own time – as Einstein and Picasso, like Braudel and Wallerstein, understood (and Durkheim in 1907 was trying to figure out). True, some things, even social ones, exist at the same time, but the sense in which they are thrown together in Being, as Heidegger and Levinas and Derrida understood, is at best metaphorical. Metaphors are necessary to meaning, but they can be dangerous, as in the case of the metaphoric power of Derrida's Center, Foucault's Subject, and Wallersetin's Core – which were ripe for the calling out they got, at long last.

Culture, itself, is indeed a welter of signs awaiting their call into the present from which they, in the time of their social contract, are for the most part excluded. Only one sign at a time. The traffic STOP sign cannot mean GO; but it *must* mean Not-GO, which is to signify that there is a GO in the offing, as Prigigone would say (referring to Lévi-Strauss but in ways that would have pleased Saussure). The structural value of the sign resides in the determinacy created by the absence of a GO in the STOP. In social time STOP and GO may be said, metaphorically, to be simultaneous. But simultaneity is itself meaningful only in the instant where it is at best a figure of speech, which is not a slur. Figures of speech like metaphors help the beings to organize themselves against the absences and presences that would unsettle daily life were it not for the discursive ability of ordinary people to to-and-fro the uncertainties. A STOP is a GO waiting to happen – but necessarily assigned to an absent place, which is, in fact, a space in time, which is itself, as we now know, uncertain.

What is culture? Whatever it is, if anything in and other than itself, it is first and foremost a name for the time of human meaning. Culture is the absent repository of all that could be but is not and cannot be without disrupting the illusion that daily life is forward progress of some unexplained kind. What actually passes through the quotidian are times which are measured by all manner of arbitrary means that are taken, if taken at all, as the terms of the social contract. The lived time of the present is actually lived against the times of culture, moving out of synch at their different rates of speed. Were those living it to pay attention, they would go nuts. Fortunately for them, they don't or can't, which amounts to the same thing. Still, one wonders how many innocent victims would have been spared had the powers ever once understood that the times are not theirs alone.

Were culture a certain social thing, susceptible to definition, then it literally would not *be*; hence the frustration of sciences that would define it. Far better simply to laugh at its impossible varieties. Culture is, at the least, the knowable (perhaps better to say, workable) uncertainty that is the source of any and all social meanings. One of the reasons *meaning* is hardly ever defined, or defined well (not even by Dilthey, much less Weber or Alexander, or even the existentialists who gave it *cachet*), is that meaning is a surd – a thing that is its own *reductio ad absurdum,* both true and false at the same time, thus neither at once, because there can be no once and for all.

Culture – if it is a system of meanings (provided of course one can use the word *system* or even one like *structure* in relation to surds like *meaning*) – is, from the point of view of the time of its articulation, nothing at all. Meaning thrives in the performance itself, which is a practice that – like the exchange of commodities, of signs, and of gifts (which, come to think of it, are much the same sort of social thing) – relies on a comparison to that which it is not.

Culture, it could be said, is the Not-there by which meaning overcomes its absurdity to serve the moment surrounded by the absences upon which it relies in order to to-and-fro with the irregularities of events that seem so certain when in fact they are lodged in a beyond that can only be collectively represented by Death itself.

– Charles Lemert,
August 21, 2004, two days before the birthday of his dead son.
Written in New Haven facing East Rock;
which faces West Rock painted by Fredrick Edwin Church in 1849;
who must have found meaning in the landscape of rocks fallen
since the Ice Age if not the beginning of the world.
But this one can only suppose, which is not nothing.

Index

Index

Printed in Great Britain
by Amazon